KEELE
UNIVERSITY LIBRARY

Please return by the last date or time shown

Building Paris provides an overview of the various architectural bodies that collectively gave shape to the French capital during a period of explosive growth from 1830 to 1870. In his analysis of the transformation of Paris during this period, David Van Zanten demonstrates how a succession of monarchs used urban projects as representations of their authority. This study also chronicles the dissolution of the traditional absolutist political structures before the emergence of national consciousness and amid the splintering of centralized state authority into an array of distinct and competing architectural services. *Building Paris* explores, moveover, how private architectural enterprise, which grew vastly in this period, was accommodated by government institutions, and how it evolved to achieve dominance in the building profession by the end of the century.

Building Paris

Building Paris

Architectural Institutions and the Transformation of the French Capital, 1830–1870

David Van Zanten

Northwestern University

CAMBRIDGE
UNIVERSITY PRESS

Published by the Press Syndicate of the University of Cambridge
The Pitt Building, Trumpington Street, Cambridge CB2 1RP
40 West 20th Street, New York, NY 10011-4211, USA
10 Stamford Road, Oakleigh, Melbourne 3166, Australia

First published 1994

Printed in the United States of America

Library of Congress Cataloging-in-Publication Data
Van Zanten, David, 1943–
    Building Paris : architectural institutions and the transformation of the French
capital, 1830–1870 / David Van Zanten
        p.   cm.
    Includes bibliographical references (p.   ) and index.
    1. Neoclassicism (Architecture)—France—Paris.   2. Architects and patrons –
France – Paris – History – 19th century.   3. City planning – France – Paris – His-
tory – 19th century.   4. Architecture and state – France – Paris.   5. Paris (France)
– Buildings, stuctures, etc.
    I. Title
    NA1050.V358   1994
    720' .944'36109034 – dc20   93-34299
                                                              CIP

A catalog record for this book is available from the British Library

ISBN 0-521-39421-X hardback

For Martha, Clara, and Nicholas,
For my mother
And in memory of my father

CONTENTS

ILLUSTRATIONS

Illustrations

ACKNOWLEDGMENTS

The research for this volume began in 1987 immediately after the publication of my last book, *Designing Paris,* with a summer in Paris supported by a grant from the American Philosophical Society. That was followed, in 1989–1990, by a year's leave supported by the National Endowment for the Humanities and further contributions from the Graham Foundation for Advanced Studies in the Fine Arts and from Northwestern University. I am very grateful to all these agencies and institutions for their generous support.

The matter *Building Paris* addresses – the institutional control of the monumental form of Paris – was explored in a session at the College Art Association in Boston in February 1987, where Michael Driskel, Christopher Mead, Charles Millard, Jane Roos, and Pierre Vaisse presented papers, and Marco Diani, Albert Boime, and Neil Levine served as respondents. It was sketched in an article in the *Art Journal* of spring 1989. Parts appeared in the catalog *Visconti, 1796–1853* of 1991.

I owe the warmest thanks to many friends and fellow researchers: Marthe Bernus, Christian and Marina Devillers, Karen Bowie, and Catherine Weese; Count M. Hervé du Périer, Jean-Marie Pérouse de Montclos, André Maman, Françoise and Philippe Hamon; Françoise and Philippe Boudon, Charles MacCallum, François Loyer, Pierre Vaisse, Emmanuel Jacquin, Daniela Gallo, Pierre Guinard, Werner Szambien, Pierre Pinon, Pierre de Peretti, Gérard Rousset-Charny, Marie-Laure Leconte, Jean-Michel Leniaud, and Thomas von Joest; as well as Bruno Foucart of the Institut d'Art et Archéologie and Annie Jacques, bibliothécaire of the Ecole des Beaux-Arts, Claudine de Vaulchier at the Académie d'Architecture, and Nicole Felkay at the Archives Nationales. I have discussed this project with researchers here in the United States, Katherine Taylor, Barry Bergdoll, Sylvia Lavin, Jane Roos, Patricia Mainardi, Gabriel Weisberg, Anthony Vidler, Jacques de Caso, Nancy Davenport, and Paul Tucker. Conversations with my colleagues in Chicago and at Northwestern, Garry Wills, Marco Diani, Russell Maylone, David Jordan, and Sarah Maza, have been very helpful, especially a seminar Hollis Clayson and I taught with the participation of Karl Werckmeister in the spring of 1989. I have also learned a great deal from my own students, those of long standing like Christopher Mead (whose work has become a book, *Charles Garnier's Paris Opera*), Todd Porterfield, and Sharon Irish, or those recently finishing their dissertations on this subject, like Kevin Murphy on French restoration policy or Julia Sagraves on Empire culture, or parallel developments, Steven Moyano's study of Schinkel and the Prussian bureaucracy and Ellen Christensen's of British imperial capitals.

I also owe deepest thanks to my wife, Martha, for reading the manuscript and for all her reassurance – as well as to my children Clara and Nicholas for refreshing interludes and moral support.

Evanston, Illinois
March 1994

ABBREVIATIONS

AN	Archives Nationales, Paris
AS	Archives du Département de la Seine et de Paris
Ill	*L'Illustration*
JD	*Journal des débats*
MU	*Moniteur universel*
RGA	*Revue générale de l'architecture et des travaux publics*

Building Paris

INTRODUCTION

This book examines mid-nineteenth-century French architecture from the perspective of its architectural institutions. What made the evolution of architecture in Paris so distinctive was the dominant role played by the government's architectural services. Contemporaneous Anglo-American architecture produced cities like London and Manchester, New York and Chicago – collections of variously shaped and scaled business blocks – through the agency of architects working as free agents out of their own professional offices, mixing private and government commissions. French architecture made Paris – specifically the Second Empire Paris that has never been fundamentally altered since the dismissal of the prefect Haussmann in 1870: a city in which private and institutional architecture was strictly disciplined to serve as the background to a display of monuments standing as the representation of the government.

The authors of the Parisian monuments worked on retainer to the state in offices provided and staffed by the state. The designers of the private buildings that constituted the mass and flesh of the city were carefully controlled by other architect-agents of the state, the commissaires voyers, so that their work set off the public monuments. An unusually broad span of buildings fell under direct government control: besides political monuments and social institutions, theaters because of censorship, churches in the Gallican tradition, historic monuments, and even thermal baths. Their architects were the leaders of the profession – Percier and Fontaine; Duban, Labrouste, Duc, and Vaudoyer; Baltard, Viollet-le-Duc, and Charles Garnier. These men devoted the majority of their time to government work and received most of their income from it. Their success was measured in terms of their contribution to the monumental form of Paris. This had been the French tradition since at least the reign of Louis XIV. The Ecole des Beaux-Arts – by the end of the century the leading architecture school in the world – was intended to train architects for French government service. The Académie had been founded to formulate state architectural policy. The government services and the French architectural profession were essentially congruent until 1870.

French state architecture, however, is not so simple to define as this might imply. It was not a single, unified entity in the nineteenth century. In 1791 the old Bâtiments du Roi was disestablished and a series of services grew up in its place, fragmented into an array of local cultures quite consciously distinct. The foreground architecture of representational monuments manifesting the authority of the state fragmented into two services: the Bâtiments Civils, administering the principal parliamentary monuments like the Chambre des Députés or the Arc de Triomphe, and the Palais Royaux (or Impériaux, depending on the regime), maintaining the stock of palaces that manifested the authority of the sovereign. Closely connected to the Bâtiments Civils were several less formally constituted administrations, the Inspection Générale des Prisons and the Assistance Publique, in charge of a growing array of utilitarian social establishments, carried out in the traditional severe style of background buildings. Distinct from these was the burgeoning Travaux d'Architecture of the city of Paris, which felt itself relatively free of the burden of representation (and thus not dramatically affected by the Revolution of 1789) and increasingly sought to be more experimental and efficient, drawing on innovations made in private construction. This service was expanding, relatively progressive, and more and more independent, but the parallel service of the Edifices Diocésains was increasingly weaker in its purpose so that religious architecture became a sort of void into which other services expanded, especially the newly created Commission des Monuments Historiques (1831) animated by Eugène-Emmanuel Viollet-le-Duc, transforming places of worship into documents of the history of architecture. It was opposed in Paris by Travaux d'Architecture led by Victor Baltard and Théodore Ballu, which treated parish churches as markers in the new Haussmannian cityscape. The very fragmentation of the old Bâtiments du Roi with the accompanying discontinuities of architectural conception and the parallel play of opposing forces could give purchase to concerted individual efforts to shape the face of Paris and thus to affect the course of building. We shall see how this functioned in the case of Viollet-le-Duc as well as for Fontaine, Duban, and Baltard, among others.

As the government services expanded and differentiated themselves, another, tangential force increasingly made itself felt – private construction: houses, apartment buildings, hotels, clubs, department stores, banks, railroad stations. Technological innovation was much quicker here, growth faster. The French architectural practitioners had always reserved some independence from total submersion in state service. Only in certain cases did architects give up all right to private practice and become state *fonction-naires* like the inspecteurs généraux of the Bâtiments Civils or the Second Empire architectes d'arrondissements and commissaires voyers in Paris. As private construction expanded rapidly under Haussmann what had been the cadre of the government services was lured into it. After 1870 this accelerated, and by 1900 state and private practice seem to have stood on an equal footing. The Art Nouveau was the first style to originate in the private rather than the state context. Private construction, however, responded to very different demands and worked by very different standards than those traditionally controlling state building so that gradually the culture of government architecture attrophied and dissolved.

✻   ✻   ✻

The definition and play of these competing forces founded in the distinctive structure of mid-nineteenth-century French architectural institutions is the subject of this volume. However, for all of the complexity of the situation among the architects themselves, we should not forget that this was also the broader moment of the emergence of professionalism as a force in Western society, especially in the case of architecture, which physically set the lines of the new capitalist world and required of that world huge investments to carry out its projects. No art is less isolated than architecture. Behind every design strategy are the questions of why the community would spend all the time and effort required to carry these things out, why it would wish to reshape its environment in this manner, and why it has created for its distinctive needs a class of experts that we designate – too glibly perhaps – with an ancient Greco-Roman word, *architect*.

Such a profession embedded in a specific society is shaped by compromises between its internal principles and what that society supports. There is the local culture of the profession shaped both by traditions of form and by closed vocabularies preserving the "intellectual capital" of the practitioners, but this profession survives and thrives only by serving – on its own terms – certain of the community's needs. In the case of nineteenth-century European architecture this area of compromise was especially complex because of the span of highly inflected traditional branches – the Italian, French, and English in particular – that were now broken in upon by new and relatively consistent practices determined by the economic and technological revolutions. What in Italy had been the shaping of space and in France the laying out of gardens and cities as the representation of central authority became increasingly after 1800 (especially in Britain) the provision of large amounts of cheap but efficient covered square footage. Furthermore, as Harold Perkin has insisted, the professionals – the architects –

have not been passive in this. They are fundamentally planners, minds synthesizing the evidence so concretely manifested in the face of Europe's cities, and attempting to map its advantageous exploitation.

In 1987 I published *Designing Paris* offering an interpretation of the design principles guiding the work of the four leading architects of the Monarchy of July: Duban, Labrouste, Duc, and Vaudoyer. Taken in terms of form, their work appears quite disparate – Labrouste's Bibliothèque Sainte-Geneviève, for example, compared to Vaudoyer's Marseilles Cathedral – and also not clearly distinct from the broader French monumental tradition. In that book I tried to prove that behind the shapes, mouldings, and stylistic motifs lay a consistency of rationalist historicist principles that made these four artists' work a common enterprise – and a rich and impressive one.

One thing, however, seemed unsatisfying to me in *Designing Paris:* I was still treating the principles, if no longer the forms, in isolation, as contributions to an abstract continuum of architectural conceptualization. It was obvious that, on the contrary, these architects were thoroughly enmeshed in a demanding and distinctive professional situation controlled by the state architectural administration and focused on the task of shaping Paris. It was also obvious that in this sense these four must be seen as competitors of a larger group of designers working in this context – Fontaine, Baltard, Viollet-le-Duc, Garnier. If in *Designing Paris* I treated form as the manifestation of design principles, in the present work it is my ambition to treat design principles as professional strategies and, as such, things much more complex, shifting, and elaborately negotiated.

In Chapter 2 I sketch in greater detail the system of distinct services that was embraced by French state architecture. Chapters 3 and 4 explore its central tradition in city-making, the foreground building representative of authority in the Absolutist tradition – broad and roomy, scenographic, using the conventions of axes and Greco-Roman forms once constituent of the king's style – and background construction – self-effacing in form but tightly packed in space and function. Chapters 5 and 6 move on to explore two aspects in greater detail: the place of the individual architects in the system and how they might take advantage of it; the nature of the great rebuilding of Paris under Haussmann and how his municipal architecture negotiated a place in Paris's traditional urban order. Finally in Chapter 7 I delineate one of the most dramatic struggles in this story, the weakening of the sense of the ecclesiastical in church architecture and that genre's appropriation as the documentation of the history of architecture (by the service of the Monuments Historiques) or as street furniture (by the Service des Travaux of the city of Paris). Chapter 1 – to come last to the first – sets the stage for all this by depicting the transformation around 1860 of one piece of the city, the quartier de l'Opéra, to introduce the formal relation of foreground architecture to background, of state regulation to city and both to looser private construction, and of the designers' intentions to the uses and experiences of the resulting construction. This whole narrative is necessarily the story of the architecture of authority and it must be remembered – in spite of the exclusive emphasis architecture has received in the French tradition – that there were other architectures embedded in it and other observers than the politicians, functionaries, and state architects who initially shaped it.

THE QUARTIER DE L'OPERA

The Opéra, the most remarked building of mid-nineteenth-century Paris, works as the centerpiece of an entire quarter built together with it (Figure 1). This quarter measured about 500 yards on a side reaching north from the boulevard des Capucines and was cleared following a plan worked out in 1857–1860 (Figure 9). It was built up rapidly in 1860–1870. The Opéra itself was erected and decorated in 1862–1875 after a competition in the winter of 1860–1861, won by the brilliant young designer Charles Garnier (1825–1898).[1]

Garnier's Opéra is striking for how effectively it appropriates the surrounding urban spaces and masses into its own monumental ensemble. Its composition ripples away from the richly decorated central dome. The facade supports that dome as a platform and enframes it with two end pavilions topped by winged sculptural groups. The side wings repeat its shape in their smaller domes leading the eye back around the ensemble. The massive fly tower enframes the central motif and carries up its axis in the terminal group of Apollo holding aloft his lyre.

The force of this composition and the relief of these masses seem to require response beyond the street line that immediately defines it, and that response appears satisfactorily given in the three shaped plazas opened around the Opéra, the square place de l'Opéra in front and the triangular places Garnier and Rouché extending back on each side, deep and narrow urban spaces within a wall of uniform street line, cornice line, and pilastered decoration. Garnier himself later complained the spaces around his building were too tight, but it is that very compression which makes the house masses opposite read as part of a larger architectural whole and creates of that whole not merely an opera house, but an urban quarter of symphonically coordinated architecture.[2]

Figure 1. Opéra, Paris (Charles Garnier, architect, 1861–1875) from across the place de l'Opéra, the Grand Hôtel de la Paix on the left (Alfred Armand, architect, 1861–1862).

Working within the dense and ancient texture of Paris, French nineteenth-century architects could be very precise in shaping spaces and creating tableaux characterizing their buildings. The work of Félix Duban (1797–1870) at the Ecole des Beaux-Arts in 1832–1840 was praised as exemplary (Figure 2): Two courtyards in sequence opened from the rue Bonaparte toward the main building, the first telescoping slightly inward to enframe a vista of its central facade through the openwork screen formed by an early Renaissance fragment, the facade from Gaillon, the second widening out to embrace it in quarter circles hidden beyond.[3] The axis continues through the central door in the facade, across a courtyard, and ends in the

Figure 2. Ecole des Beaux-Arts (Félix Duban, architect, 1832–1840).

Figure 3. Collège de France, from the rue Saint-Jacques (Paul-Marie Letarouilly, architect, 1832–1838).

ceremonial Salle des Prix at the heart of the structure. This effect was approximated in similar situations by Jules de Joly (1788–1865) at the Chamber of Deputies as it addresses the place Bourbon (1828–1836) or by Paul-Marie Letarouilly (1795–1855) in the Collège de France (1832–1838) and seems to have its immediate origin a generation earlier in the work of Charles Percier (1764–1838) (Figure 3). It was a fundamental principle of Beaux-Arts architectural composition and one which Garnier's Opéra was thought to impressively exemplify and extend to the scale of a whole city quarter.[4]

✳   ✳   ✳

Encountering the quartier de l'Opéra from the quarters around about 1870 one entered a surprising new architectural world centering on and characterized by that arresting crownlike dome. The continuous limestone cliff out of which the place de l'Opéra and the streets extending from it seem cut is composed of a new, denser unit of urban construction, the "*immeuble haussmannien*," the Haussmannian apartment house.[5] The impressionist Gustave Caillebotte lived in the quarter and depicted his surroundings in a series of paintings of 1878–1881 from a peculiarly high vantage point, as if the architecture were excavated downward rather than built up (Figure 4).[6] Photographs of the quarter when it was just completed show how distinct was its urban texture in contrast to the surrounding areas: taller, broader in its units, these unified into whole *îlots* defining wide, even streets with what still were very light colored limestone walls (Figure 99).[7] These houses were no longer shallow front blocks with courts and gardens behind. Now the whole house lot is covered, the dense construction relieved only by narrow light courts (Figures 64 and 65). These *immeubles* are built right up to the Haussmannian zoning envelope, their cornices and mansards sliced off uniformly along its invisible line. Today, a century and a quarter later, the rest of the city has been rebuilt up to that limit so the contrast is lost. In early views like Monet's *Boulevard des Capucines* (Figure 5) or Caillebotte's *Balcony* (1880)[8] the massive blocks of the quartier de l'Opéra rise up above the lower, heterogeneous, narrow houses of old Paris and seem a thing apart, somewhat like Radio City seventy years later rising among the brownstones of New York.

The Opéra and its surroundings seem of a piece and once were very distinct from what lay around them. The ensemble has now been taken for granted for a century as the quintessence of the monumental, orderly Paris, which that new human type appearing just at this moment, the tourist, discovered and uncritically admired. But how did the quartier de

Figure 4. Gustave Caillebotte, *Un Balcon*, 1880.

l'Opéra come into being? It appears to be a work of state art, but only the Opéra itself (finished late, in 1875) is so, the rest of the quarter being private construction. It appears to be the work of one artist, the celebrated Garnier (whose name is perpetuated in that of the square at the west), yet the history of the project shows a number of architects contributed and that the objective was continuity, not innovation, at least in general external appearance. It appears to be something that should be admired head on, axially, in the conventionally monumental way, yet it was a piece of the city rich in new and surprising architectural experiences, as Caillebotte's paintings show. It is the centerpiece of nineteenth-century Paris and the passage that we might take most quickly for granted, yet it is, in fact, deceptive and complex.

Figure 5. Claude Monet,
Boulevard des Capucines, 1873.

II

The famous ring of Paris Right Bank boulevards (decreed in 1670) had become the city's promenade and shopping and theater district by the mid-nineteenth century (Figure 6).[9] The most fashionable and active portion was the straight section from the Madeleine to the rue de Richelieu embracing successively the boulevards de la Madeleine, des Capucines, and des Italiens. The Napoleonic rue de la Paix cuts tangentially down to the place Vendôme at the midpoint. In the early nineteenth century new housing quarters had grown up beyond the boulevards, "la Nouvelle Athènes," the place Saint-Georges, the rue Poissonnière.[10] As a result the Right Bank railroad stations established during the Monarchy of July had to be erected almost a mile beyond the old boulevards: the Gare Saint-Lazare (1837; 1840–1843), the Gare de l'Est (1844–1849), the Gare du Nord (1845–1846), and the Gare

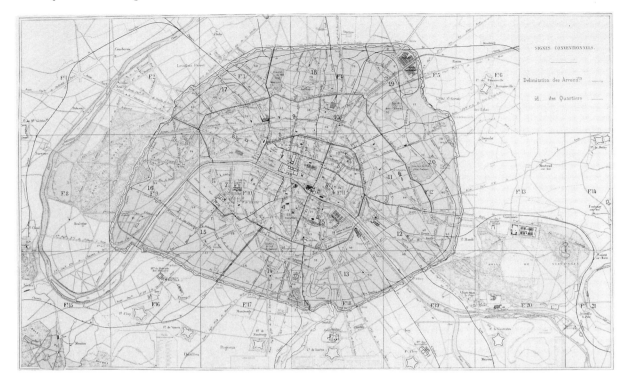

Figure 6. Plan of Paris, 1868.

de Lyon (1847–1852).[11] (Plans to push the Gare Saint-Lazare to the place de la Madeleine were blocked.) As rail traffic rapidly increased, links to the annular boulevard were obviously needed and were very early projected, in the rue du Havre (1843), the rue (later boulevard) de Lyon (1847), and the boulevard de Strasbourg (1852), each named after the principal destination of the line at its termination.[12]

This system of links was expanded in Napoleon III's new boulevards (Figure 6). The east-west rue de Rivoli and the north-south "boulevard du Centre" constituting the so-called First Network of Second Empire avenues were spokes leading straight into the city center, but the Second Network commenced in 1858 was a system of tangents to the boulevard ring spreading from a series of new squares to the stations and beyond, into the outer arrondissements annexed January 1, 1860. The place du Prince Eugène (now de la République) at the northwest corner of the boulevards projected the boulevard Magenta to the gares de l'Est and Nord (as well as the rue de Turbigo into the Halles Centrales); the place de l'Etoile sent boulevards to the Gare Saint-Lazare as well as into the Bois de Boulogne and to the Pont d'Alma; and finally a square proposed to open at the crossing point of the rue de la Paix and the boulevard des Capucines cast out the rue de Rouen leading to the Gare Saint-Lazare and the extension of the rue Lafayette linking to the Gare du Nord (this last, in 1860, in the process of reconstruction). These *places* promised to be important nodes in the city's traffic pattern and were to be treated monumentally, like the new place du Châtelet laid out earlier in 1854 at the crossing point of the First Network *percements*.

Among the many changes in the city structure occasioned by the First and Second networks was the topography of the city's theaters. They had formerly been concentrated in two tight knots, the higher class around the old Opéra in the region of the rue de Richelieu, the lower class on the "boulevard du Crime" where the place du Prince Eugène now was opened. Haussmann proposed a general relocation of the theaters to the new boulevards and *places:* Five were to be erected along the boulevard de Sébastopol – two at the Châtelet, two on the Ile de la Cité (which never materialized), the Théâtre de la Gaité on the south side of the place des Arts et Métiers. The democratic Orphaeum for workers' choral societies was planned to dominate the place du Prince Eugène and the new Opéra the boulevard des Capucines, with the Théâtre du Vaudeville nearby.[13]

The Opéra, for all its apparent monumental pristineness, clearly functioned by the time of its competiton in late 1860 as merely one factor in a complex evolution of urban topography. That would only get more so. Once the site was set and well before the monument itself was open in 1875 (or even under construction in 1863) an extraordinary neighborhood of commerce and pleasure had been engendered around it. In terms of external architecture, however, that neighborhood seemed unexceptional – a backdrop of identical facades along rigid street lines and built to a facade pattern set in the drawings attached to the decree of September 29, 1860 (Figures 7 and 8), defining spaces to set off the projected Opéra as well as to permit a very dense flow of traffic. But tucked in behind these anonymous facades, like mouse nests in palace woodwork, were many of the most remarkable new private establishments of Second Empire Paris.

*   *   *

The north side of the boulevard des Capucines had lagged behind the commercial development of the street in the mid-nineteenth century because it opened onto a depressed strip of roadway, the rue Basse du Rempart, never raised and integrated into the larger space (Figures 7, 9, and 10).[14] Land prices were low and developers had had an eye on it. Already in 1853 the Pereire brothers had purchased the Hôtel Osmond on the rue Basse du

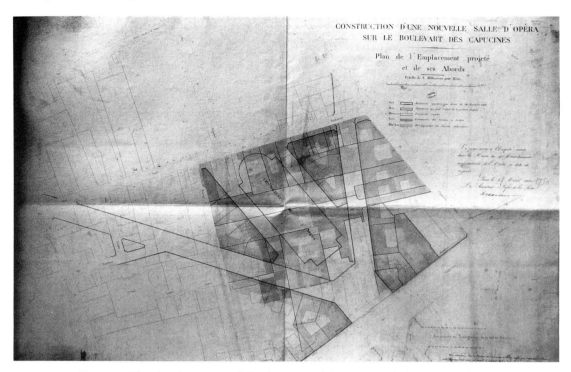

Figure 7. Plan for the projected development of the quartier de l'Opéra made public April 1860.

Rempart (nos. 6–10, boulevard des Capucines) through their Compagnie des Immeubles et de l'Hôtel de la Rue de Rivoli (controlled, in turn, by their Crédit Mobilier).[15] In 1859 they transformed this company into the Compagnie Immobilière de Paris and with an eleven million franc loan from the state mortgage bank, the Crédit Foncier, began buying most of the land in the southern part of what would be the Opéra quarter and to build. In the last days of July 1859 (Isaac Pereire wrote in the company's annual report of April 1860) demolition and construction were begun on the four apartment houses in the area east of the projected place de l'Opéra, today 8 and 10, boulevard des Capucines and 2 and 4, rue Halévy. He notes that this did not constitute all of the company's land holdings but that they were waiting for the Opéra's site to be finalized, which (as we noted) came only with the decree of September 29, 1860.

The Compagnie had been buying land to the west of the projected square (rue Basse du Rempart, nos. 28, 30, 34, 42, 46), by early 1861 possessing most of the stretch mirroring their holdings to the east, up to and past the

Figure 8. Model facade projected for the quartier de l'Opéra made public April 1860.

projected rue Mogador (renamed rue Scribe) to the rue Caumartin. By agreement with the city of Paris of April 1861 this area was regularized in a land trade.[16] Beginning in July 1859, even before the street lines had been set, they projected coordinated development here according to a strategy Emile Pereire explained to their shareholders in his annual report of April 30, 1861.

The predecessor company, the Compagnie des Immeubles et de l'Hôtel de

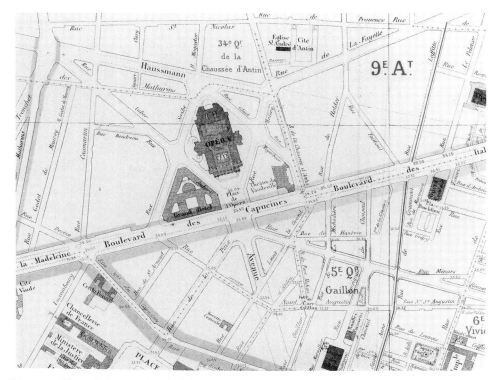

Figure 9. Plan of the quartier de l'Opéra, 1868.
Figure 10. Plan of the future quartier de l'Opéra from Théodore Jacoubet's *Atlas de Paris* (1834–1841) with P.-F.-L. Fontaine's sketch of the rue de Rouen, c. 1852.

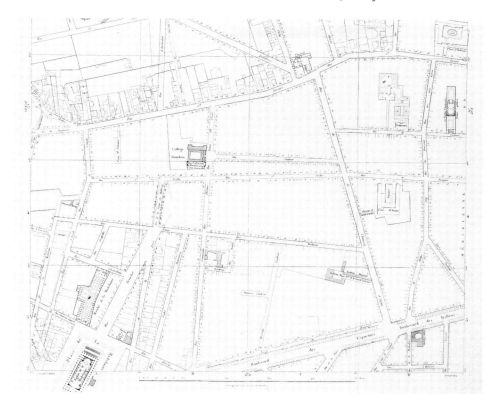

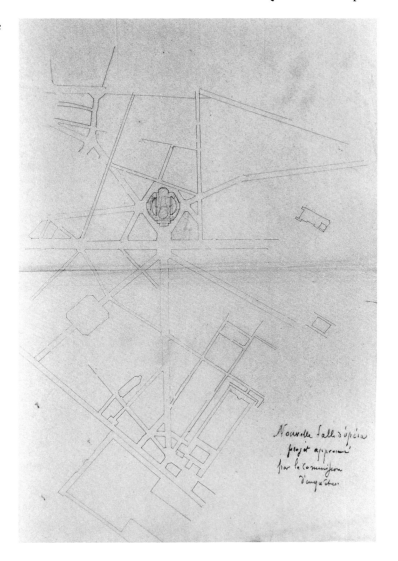

Figure 11. Sketch plan of the quartier de l'Opéra and the avenue de l'Opéra, 1860.

la rue de Rivoli (created in 1853 when the rue de Rivoli development was faltering) had devoted its largest parcel to the Grand Hôtel du Louvre, a huge structure on the luxurious "American" model unprecedented in Paris.[17] This expediency, the Pereires' previous reports indicated, could be pictured as a tremendous success, and they now proposed to extend and perfect it in the heart of the quartier de l'Opéra.

The center of Paris, or, more accurately, of Parisian society, today is the boulevard des Capucines at its meeting with the rue de la Paix and the rue de la Chaussée d'Antin. The projected *percements,* which will bring together here broad thorough-fares extending to the extreme points of the capital, will definitively fix this [circumstance] and produce a movement [here] of population only a feeble idea of which is given us by what we have before our eyes.[18]

A great hotel at this spot would respond to this evolution and increase the value of the surrounding real estate.

The shops that we have and shall have in the future to rent on the boulevard des Capucines, the rues de Rouen, Mogador, and Lafayette *prolongée* [rue Halévy] will gain in value from our having established here a larger mass of rich travelers. . . .

In addition, on the boulevard the second floors will rent at a high rate because they are appropriate for business enterprises. It is otherwise for the upper stories. Their special location generally elevates their rent too high for private apartments. Only devoting them to furnished apartments gives them a practical function. Therefore the establishment [here] of the Grand Hôtel de la Paix might result in higher than ordinary rents for these upper stories; it is logical, in fact, that, when one rents an apartment for a shorter period, one might be paid more than when one occupies it permanently. . . .

The lots on the boulevard des Capucines and the rue Mogador (left side) will be devoted to clubs, furnished apartments, and rental houses.[19]

Soon afterward 1, rue Scribe was rented to the Jockey Club for its magnificent rooms (erected by the Compagnie Immobilière and their architect Henri Dubois). In the annual report of April 28, 1862, Emile Pereire noted, "This rental will add a mass of rich clients in this quarter and will provide sustenance for a large number of luxury industries."[20] He added that the other spaces were renting well because they "adapt themselves, both by their situation in the center of Paris and by their generous proportions, to industry and commerce."[21] Several banks had already let space.

The Pereires' architect, Alfred Armand (1805–1888), known for his railroad work (especially the Gare Saint-Lazare), assembled a design staff led by A.-N. Crépinet (1827–1892), who had been *en loge* in the Grand Prix competition in 1848, *inspecteur* at the New Louvre (1852–1859),[22] one of the five finalists in the competition for the new Opéra, and later architect of the Invalides.[23] Work was pushed as rapidly as possible. Paneling and furniture were fabricated off site while the masonry shell was erected. Electric lights were used to permit work at night. The building was complete in fourteen months. (Later, in 1876–1878, the Crédit Lyonnais building nearby – Figures 23 and 24 – was completed in eighteen months within a huge glazed scaffolding covering the whole site that permitted uninterrupted work in any weather and at all hours inside.[24])

Pivoting this project on the Grand Hôtel de la Paix was a brilliant way of taking advantage of the intersection of streets leading to three railroad stations (significantly those serving England and Germany) and of increasing and concentrating a clientele for the luxury trade, given further cachet by the contemplated arrival of the Opéra. The translation of the Jockey Club from its old rooms on the boulevard des Italiens from the rue Gramont was the capstone.

III

Perhaps when seen in the context of these real estate developments, the Opéra itself – begun after the Grand Hôtel de la Paix opened in 1862 and finally opened in 1875 – might seem less the central fact of the *quartier* than an excuse. The Pereires' had begun their purchases in 1853 and their demolitions in 1859 while it was not until April 15, 1860, that an official plan for the redevelopment of the quarter was posted for a legal inquiry into the shape of the Opéra mass and, indeed, even into whether it would be erected at the spot. Until the resulting decree of September 29, 1860, it was still a possibility that it might have been at its old site on the rue Lepelletier or one of several other sites nearby. Contemporaries joked about this, *l'Illustration* in 1866 calling it the "théâtre de la Café de la Paix," as if it were an annex to the Grand Hôtel, and not the opposite.[25] Architecturally, however, the Opéra today appears to command the quarter, and the time has come to tell the history of the development from the monumental standpoint.

In the seventeenth, eighteenth, and early nineteenth centuries carefully shaped and proportioned spaces had been cut out of the thick medieval texture of Paris: the place des Vosges, the place Vendôme, the Odéon quarter, or the courtyards of the Ecole des Beaux-Arts.[26] As we have noted, these were defined works of spatial art, and architects designed them. All of them, however, occupied a single large original lot that they opened or subdivided: There were no problems of through traffic or multiple ownership, and consistent facade designs could be enforced in the deeds of sale. This was not the case of the quartier de l'Opéra at the height of the Second Empire, for all its eventual orderliness and effect. Here a large number of separate lots had to be acquired and a network of important city thoroughfares accommodated. There were multiple designers and authorities cooperating and complex restraints – making the harmony of the end result all the more impressive.

The first problem was expropriation. It has often been noted that Haussmann's transformation of Paris would have been impossible without two recent laws: that of May 3, 1841, establishing clear procedures for the expropriation of private property for cause of *utilité publique,* and that of March 26, 1852, permitting the expropriation of whole lots, not just their affected portions, if it appeared that the *salubrité* (healthfulness, ventilation) of the remaining portion would be inadequate in reconstruction.[27] These laws facilitated an earlier law of September 16, 1807, requiring every city and commune to draw up a regularized street plan to be put into effect as the conurbation was rebuilt and extended.[28] The 1841 legislation simplified the cutting of new streets and that of 1852 (as interpreted by Haussmann after his assumption of office on June 29, 1853) permitted the clearing of buildings on either side to such a depth that new rows of "healthful" (and thus more generously dimensioned but denser) houses could be erected defining them. Thus arose the constructions marking the first *percements* like the rue de Rivoli and the boulevard de Strasbourg as a double spine of tall new houses running through the hodgepodge of medieval Paris (Figure 117). With the help of the Pereires, in the case of the quartier de l'Opéra, this could be used to create a whole new quarter, initially some 500 yards on a side and later expanded still further by the boulevard Haussmann and the avenue de l'Opéra.

The procedure for expropriation established in the 1841 law was as follows: First, a plan was drawn by a committee of the responsible agents (engineers of the Ponts et Chaussées, architects, or commissaires voyers, depending on the locality[29]). Second, this plan with all the affected properties marked was made public at the local *mairie* for a period of eight days and published in the local newspaper after which a committee of inquiry was convened (*commission d'enquête*) by the *sous-préfet*. That committee was to have four members from the Conseil Général of the department or arrondissement named by the prefect or mayor and, as one additional member, an engineer or the commissaire voyer concerned. Third, after receiving petitions from the public for another eight days, the committee was to present an analysis and recommendations to the prefect. Fourth, after this report had been available for public examination for another eight days, the prefect framed the expropriations by an *arrêté* and set their date. Fifth, the project was examined and approved by the Conseil des Bâtiments Civils and the Conseil d'Etat. If there were important modifications, the project was sent back for the process to be repeated for the whole or a part of it. Sixth, the project was sanctioned by an imperial (or royal) decree.

Simple as this sounds, in the case of the quartier de l'Opéra the process proceeded slowly and with many slight variations and modifications. The effective initial decree of *utilité publique* was that of November 14, 1858, opening the rues de Rouen and Halévy and the place de l'Opéra.[30] On March 16, 1860, the architect of the Opéra (then located on the rue Lepelletier), Charles Rohault de Fleury (1801–1875), submitted to the ministre d'état, Achille Fould, three possible site plans projecting the building as either a narrow rectangle or as a polygon occupying all the space between the rues de Rouen and Lafayette. The rectangular project was selected by Haussmann and displayed for the public inquiry of April 15–May 15, 1860 (Figures 7 and 8). It shows the rues de Rouen and de Lafayette, each 15 meters broad, brought to the boulevard des Capucines at equal angles to open a square 40 meters on a side. The Opéra itself extends back between them, a narrow block with 10-meter streets along each side. Dotted lines suggest the eventual extension of the plaza across the boulevard, the mirroring of the angling rue de la Paix by what would become the rue du 4 Septembre, and the cutting of the avenue de l'Opéra at right angles to the boulevard between. The street pattern north of the boulevard appeared in Haussmann's plan for the Second Network (dated 1854 and based on Napoleon III's original plan, Figure 100[31]) and is sketched by Fontaine in his copy of Jacoubet's plan (Figure 10), necessarily before his death on October 10, 1853. This was the armature of Rohault de Fleury's project of 1857, although there he had already indicated its inadequacy by widening the theater into a pentagonal mass along the rues de Rouen and de Lafayette to fit more embracingly into the quarter.

The *enquête* was carried out by a commission that produced a report broaching practical and monumental issues. The commission was an impressive one, presided over by G.-L.-A.-V.-A.-C.-St.-Q. Chaix d'Est-Ange, a lawyer (and later senator) much involved in urban affairs, and included Auguste-Nicolas Caristie (1783–1862) of the Conseil des Bâtiments Civils, the composer Scribe, the theater manager and journalist Véron as well as Louis Cornudet, Guillaume Denière, and the engraver Louis-Désiré Varin. They reviewed the various possible sites and confirmed that the Opéra should indeed be moved to this one on the boulevard des Capucines. They proposed that the site be expanded laterally into an hexagon to include courtyards along the side behind the facades on the rues de Rouen and de Lafayette, one for the emperor's entrance, the other for subscribers. The *place* in front and the avenues leading into it they discussed monumentally. (Drawings that accompanied the report appear to be lost but a sketch by Rohault de Fleury survives; Figure 11.[32])

The street projected in front of the Opéra across the boulevard should have a calculated width [with] all proportions graduated. . . .

The most unsatisfactory effect would be produced if the building were erected without a clear understanding that a broad street should be opened directly in front of it across the boulevard. Because, however much of a *chef d'oeuvre* the Opéra might be, if one arrives before it only *obliquely* up the rue de la Paix, there will be a *universal disenchantment* and there will be raised against the administration a chorus of *just* and *severe* reproaches when it is seen how the rue de la Paix terminates against the construction on the boulevard without any connection and in complete disharmony with the structure's facade.

The Commission also thinks that in order to make the square in front of the Opéra appear more satisfactory, it would be appropriate to round off the houses at the corners with the boulevard des Capucines by a break in the facade line and to thus erase the angles where the square opens to the boulevard. (the commission's emphasis)[33]

Uniform facades on the model displayed at the *enquête* were to be stipulated for the quarter: "But the monumental aspect that must mark the Opéra does not permit the surrounding lots to be built up according to the caprice of the landowners."[34] These should extend around the Opéra itself, up the rue de Rouen and along the boulevard to the passage Sendrié.

Christopher Mead has shown that the official *enquête,* for all its appearance of considering alternative sites and in its assiduity in suggesting the expansion of the building site, was actually approving the project that Rohault de Fleury and Haussmann had been refining for some years.[35] Drawings exist for the polygonal complex on the boulevard des Capucines from July 29, 1857, modified in a report of July 28, 1858, and updated in a project of February 23, 1859.[36] There is no evidence that alternative sites were considered after 1858 (that is, after the decree that the rue de Rouen was of *utilité publique*). The goal of the *enquête* seems to have been to disarm public opinion.

Tellingly, in his report of 1858 Rohault de Fleury emphasizes that this project is a matter of rebuilding a city quarter, not just a single building.[37]

To build a permanent Opéra; to open a broad thoroughfare between the most busy point on the boulevards and the Chemin de Fer de l'Ouest while transforming one of the most wealthy quarters of Paris, that is what is proposed in the project we have drawn up.

The Opéra should be in a wealthy quarter. If one moves it [from the rue Lepelletier], one must follow the movement Paris has made westward away from the center so that one will find a site sufficient for the immense constructions today necessary for the functioning of this great national institution. The building, however, should not be isolated in a vacant space; it should rather be a center of social and commercial activity.

We thus have not hesitated to surround the Opéra with private houses enlivened at the ground floor by shopping and by the lights that this consequently scatters along the public thoroughfare, [and] so contributes to the evening by putting, in a sense, the stores out in the street.[38]

On May 8, 1858, the opposition politician Emile Ollivier noted in his diary a pointed joke of Leclerc d'Osmonville: "Making allusion to the private adventures of the prefect with a dancer and referring to the Opéra which one disapproves, 'It is annoying that the prefect of the Seine brings in the Opéra where it is inappropriate.'"[39]

The Conseil des Bâtiments Civils analyzed the project at its meeting of June 27 and 30, 1860, Duban reporting.[40] Although accepting the basic site and street skeleton, they proposed restudying the details: widening the rues de Rouen and Lafayette; widening the *place* both north and south of the boulevard; expanding and perfecting the Opéra site. This revision was quickly accomplished by Rohault de Fleury, and the project was approved by the Conseil Municipal de la Ville de Paris on August 4, 1860, submitted for the emperor's approval on June 28, approved by the Conseil d'Etat on September 12, and formally decreed on September 29. That last document included a model facade design. The plan was now what we see published in the program of the Opéra competition announced in the *Moniteur universel,* December 31, 1860 (Figure 12). The site of the Opéra has been expanded to

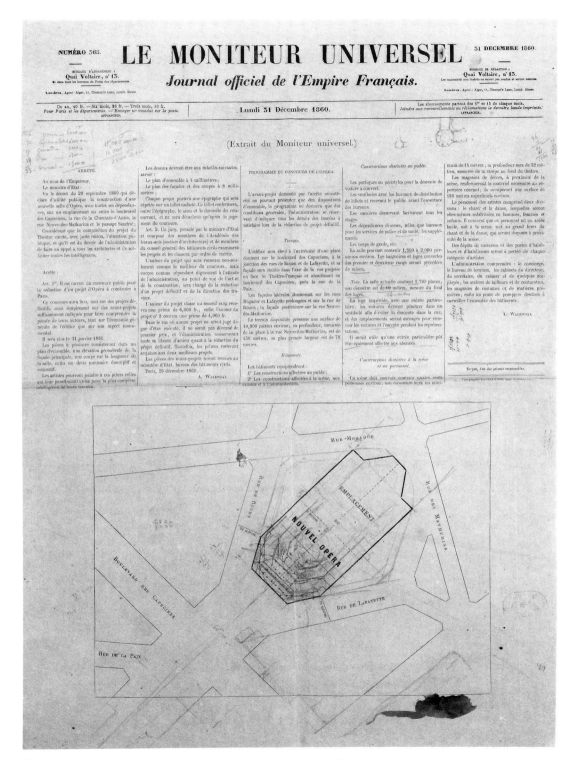

Figure 12. Announcement of the Opéra competition. Broadside, with P.-F.-Louis Fontaine's sketches of a solution, c. December 1860.

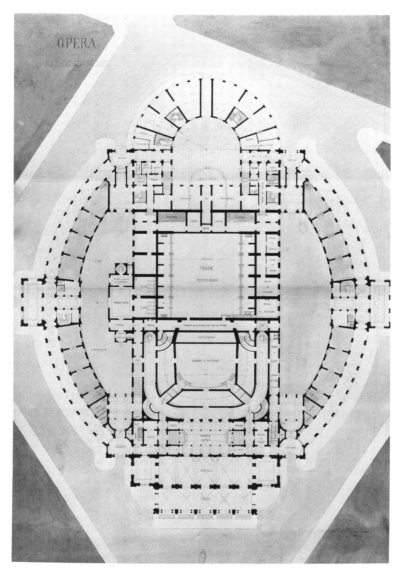

Figure 13. Project for the Opéra, 1860, by Charles Rohault de Fleury. Plan.

become a hexagon defined by two *étoiles* at each side, one formed by the intersection of the rue de Rouen (now 22 meters wide) and the rue Mogador (20 meters wide), the other by the intersection of the rue Lafayette by a 20-meter wide street mirroring the rue Mogador. The *place* on the boulevard was now 60 meters wide and – not included in the text of the decree – it appears in the drawing extended across the boulevard to the opening of the rue de la Paix. (Subsequently the streets would be renamed respectively the rue de Rouen, rue Auber; the rue Mogador, rue Scribe; the rue Lafayette, rue Halévy; and the unnamed street the rue Gluck.)

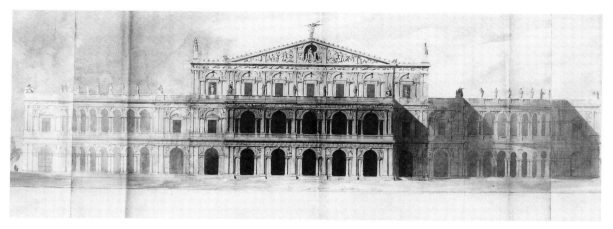

Figure 14. Project for the Opéra, 1860, by Charles Rohault de Fleury.

The shape of the quarter, at least along the north side of the boulevard, was now set and the Pereires pushed construction of the Grand Hôtel, begun in April-May 1860, and finished fourteen months later.[41] (Some modifications of the quarter's plan were submitted to an *enquête* in August 1861, and decreed July 16, 1862.[42]) Meanwhile Rohault de Fleury prepared a definitive project for the Opéra itself, dated November 1860, and sent it to the ministre d'état on December 12 (Figures 13 and 14).[43]

Only now comes a surprising twist in the story: the removal of the project from Rohault de Fleury's hands and the announcement of an open architectural competition. This coincided with the replacement of Achille Fould as ministre d'état responsible for the Opéra by Count Walewski on November 23, 1860.

The Opéra competition plan of Figure 12 belonged to Fontaine's nephew, Pierre-François-Louis Fontaine, and he sketched architectural suggestions of a project on it. He was particularly concerned with shaping the space around the site, suggesting broadening the boulevard des Capucines but narrowing the place de l'Opéra and rounding the facade of the theater. Students at the Ecole des Beaux-Arts often delineated the urban texture around their projects to create more resonant spatial compositions.[44] But, in fact, the plan of the quartier de l'Opéra was now fixed between the boulevard and the rue Neuve des Mathurins and – by December 1860 – being rapidly built up. (Fontaine never submitted his project.) Garnier's solution (Figure 1) was to draw the wings into the composition with domes, echoing his central crown over the auditorium, to rest that on a Corinthian colonnade continuing that of the facades around the place, and to set the scenographic composition against the blank peaked mass of the fly tower at the back. Rohault de Fleury's original project had been much more modest (Figures 13 and 14).[45] It pushed a low underscaled loggia of seven bays out to the place de l'Opéra, richly but diminutively articulated on the model of Sansovino's library in Venice. In its consequent use of the Palladian motif it is reminiscent of Debret's old Opéra on the rue Lepelletier. This projecting frontispiece was the only articulate passage in the composition: Behind it was a taller, broader mass enclosing the lobbies and stairways only lightly ornamented, beyond that the disappointingly modest pent-roofed masses of the auditorium and the fly tower. The facades fronting the diagonal streets are not shown. The side facades of the Opéra proper fronting on courtyards behind these are purely utilitarian.

When Garnier's building was completed in 1875 and the avenue de l'Opéra opened in 1878 the effect was at least as impressive as what the commission had hoped. Seen mounting the avenue, the colonnade, crown, and fly tower fit into the tableau enframed by the domes of the Dépôts et des Comptes Courants and the Splendide Hôtel. Upon entering the *place,* two more domes, part of the Opéra itself and more splendid than the first pair, lead the eye around the theater's mass to the right and left into the places Garnier and Rouché where the carriage entrances opened. Inside a series of magnificent spaces opened in the style set by the Pereires' Grand Hôtel and the Jockey Club fifteen years before (Figure 28).

It is not entirely true to say that Garnier respected the space as it was given in the decree of September 29, 1860. The projection of the boulevard Haussmann behind the Opéra by decree of December 27, 1865, permitted him to define a monumental courtyard in the rear. In front, the avenue de l'Opéra, the extension of the place de l'Opéra and the place du Théâtre Français at its two ends, was set by decree of August 24, 1864. Construction here was begun at the two ends in 1868 when the Société des Dépôts et des Comptes Courants (by Henri Blondel, 1832–1897) was built carrying the place de l'Opéra across the boulevard (Figure 16), their two domes perhaps the eventual transformation of the suggestion of the commission of 1860. In 1867–1869 Auguste-Joseph Magne (1816–1885) erected the Théâtre du Vaudeville where the Pereire property on the boulevard met the rue de la Chaussée d'Antin (Figure 18). The middle section of the avenue de l'Opéra was cut in 1876–1878.

✳   ✳   ✳

The important point in the history of the shaping of the quartier de l'Opéra is that it was not conceived fully formed and imposed on the site, but instead that it evolved, inflected by both practical and monumental concerns, reflecting in sequence the hands of Rohault de Fleury, Garnier, Crépinet, and Blondel – with Caristie, Duban, Armand, and the Pereires in the background. The point is made again in the case of the model facade design imposed by the decree of September 29. A drawing of five typical bays was displayed at the *enquête* of April 15–May 15, 1860 (Figure 8). The sheet itself is unsigned and for generations its authorship has been a mystery, although Rohault de Fleury – still architect of the Opéra at that time – is the logical candidate and Haussmann suggests Rohault's authorship in his *Mémoires*.[46] Christopher Mead, however, cites a letter from Rohault of April 1860, criticizing the model as if not his own.[47] Since the Pereires were already building to this model in early 1860 one even might attribute it to their architects Armand and Crépinet.[48]

One might, however, question whether the point is to seek a single author, especially since *alignements* were the work of a committee. The sheet from the *enquête* shows little below the third floor and above that displays only a file of fluted pilasters below a full entablature and balcony. In execution, the architects building around the Opéra took considerable liberties with this (Figures 15, 16, 17, and 18): The two lower stories might be open in glass panes as in Armand's Grand Hôtel, or closed and arcaded, even heavily rusticated, as in Blondel's Dépôt; the main order might enframe simple windows like those in the drawing or at the Grand Hôtel, or baroque pedimented ones like those on the Jockey Club or the Dépôt; the order might become three-quarter columns as over the entrance of the Grand Hôtel and the curve of the Jockey Club, or even freestanding as in Magne's Théâtre du Vaudeville; corners might be managed with doublings of the pilasters or with rotundas, and so on. The pattern set in the *enquête* drawing is so simple that what really matters is what Armand, Blondel, and Magne did with it.

More importantly, the device of an order of colossal fluted pilasters was appearing all over Haussmann's Paris in 1860 and was not at all new or unique in the quartier de l'Opéra. The motif had already been set in Gabriel Davioud's designs for the place Saint-Michel of 1858 and had been sketched in Hittorff's facades around the place de l'Etoile of 1854 as well as proposed by Duban for the place du Louvre in 1853.[49] It was to appear again in Ballu's square de la Trinité (Figure 132) and in the place du Prince Eugène (Figure 130). Henri Blondel made it a kind of signature of his work at the Cercle Agricole (Figure 93), the Belle Jardinière, and in the Bourse de Commerce quarter (Figures 94 and 95). This model differs from the plain Italianate one of Percier and Fonatine's rue de Rivoli (Figure 61) of 1804, extended by decree of 1852 and repeated in the place du Louvre (1853, Figure 117). The first Haussmannian constructions were quite modestly articulated, for example, those erected in 1854 to fill the parcel of the abandoned Ministère des Affaires Etrangères on the boulevards (Figure 19).

The giant order has a series of impressive eighteenth-century precedents: Victor Louis's facade of the Théâtre Français (Figure 80, which would be expanded by Davioud to the whole place du Théâtre Français and eventu-

Figure 15. Grand Hôtel de la Paix (Alfred Armand, architect, 1861–1862).

ally linked to the quartier de l'Opéra by the avenue de l'Opéra), by Jules-Hardouin Mansart in the place des Victoires and the place Vendôme (all with unfluted pilasters), and Louis's house facades defining the garden of the Palais Royale (with fluted pilasters brought to the ground, Figure 20), and – most important – Gabriel's facades on the place de la Concorde. Like Garnier's Opéra, the order suggests in its modest way the baroque world before the revolution, but it is so generic that the model itself seems less a piece of architecture than a general solution.[50]

Figure 16. Société des Dépôts et des Comptes Courants (Henri Blondel, architect,

Figure 17. Jockey Club (Alfred Armand, architect, 1861–1862; Henri Dubois assisting).

IV

Glancing at the *quartier* in old photographs (Figure 1), the immediate impression is that there is no individual aesthetic of private building at all. The building envelope and the facade articulation have been set by the state authorities in anonymous committee to oblige private interests to create a modest backdrop for a public monument, the Opéra. Yet we know the Opéra was only shaped after the quarter itself. It was not the Opéra that visitors experienced most intensely in the quarter – all the more so because

Figure 18. Théâtre du Vaudeville (Auguste-Joseph Magne, architect, 1868).

Figure 19. Facades on the boulevard des Capucines on the former site of the Ministère des Affaires Etrangères, built 1854–1855.

its doors were not open until January 1875, and then only twice a week – and most of the seats were already designated for state dignitaries.[51] Visitors were there for the hotels, the clubs, the department stores, and all the other components of that extraordinary cluster of luxury businesses. On the street floor of the Grand Hôtel, in 1874 Baedeker recommended l'Escalier de Cristal for glassware, Martinet for engravings, and Violet (in the round corner at the boulevard and the rue Scribe) for perfumes. Facing the place de

Figure 20. Facades on the garden of the Palais Royal (Victor Louis, architect, 1781).

l'Opéra, of course, was the Café de la Paix. Excellent boots were to be had along the west side of the rue Scribe and luggage at 1 and 3, place de l'Opéra, the latter establishment occupying the street floor of the Splendide Hôtel. Perfumes (both chez Angel and Rimmel) were sold in the *îlot* north of the Dépôts et des Comptes Courants as well as gloves (Rist), lace accessories (Boissier), and photographs (Braun). Most extraordinary of all, however, were the establishments of the *îlot* facing that across the boulevard des

Capucines and between the place de l'Opéra and the rue de la Chaussée d'Antin, where the Pereire development had begun. At 6, boulevard des Capucines was the celebrated linen store "La Maison du Blanc" as well as Klein's leather goods; at 8, Cavaly silks and Dusatory the tailors while at the end of the rue de la Chaussée d'Antin, across from the Théâtre du Vaudeville, were the jewelers Philippi (no. 4), the shirtmakers Demare and the mourning clothiers "Au Cyprès" (no. 5), the silk store "Ville de Lyon" (no. 6), and laces "A la Glaneuse" (no. 7). From 1860 Nadar occupied the fourth floor at 35, boulevard des Capucines, across from the Jockey Club; Bisson frères, daguerrotypists, were on the floor below. The first group exhibition of the Impressionists was held in Nadar's studio in 1874. When the avenue de l'Opéra opened a few years later an even greater concentration of luxury merchants gathered in the quarter (Figure 21).

All this, however, was on the street level. Above gathered banks, insurance companies, and clubs. In 1867 the Crédit Lyonnais established its fledgling Paris branch in one of the Pereire buildings, 6, boulevard des Capucines, above the "Maison du Blanc."

Figure 21. Avenue de l'Opéra looking north from the place du Théâtre Français (Gabriel Davioud providing model facade design, 1864–1868).

Figure 22. Société Générale (Achille Hermant, architect, 1908–1912) behind Second Empire facades, 1865–1871.

The quarter evolved with time. By the turn of the century Tiffany was at 1, place de l'Opéra, the American Express Company ensconced on the place Garnier, and the Société Générale Transatlantique at 6, rue Auber facing it. In 1908–1912 Achille Hermant erected the great headquarters of the Société Générale behind the Second Empire facades of the *îlot* demarcated by the rues Halévy and Gluck and the boulevard Haussmann (Figure 22).[52] In 1876–1878 the Crédit Lyonnais had erected its "palace" a block up the boulevard at the corner of the rue de Choiseul (Figure 23 and 24; Bouwens van der Boyen, architect). In 1881–1882 Au Printemps erected its celebrated store to the west of the immediate quarter, where the rue de Rouen crosses the boulevard Haussmann (Figure 25; Paul Sédille, architect).

The point of this ennumeration is that regulated as the facades and envelopes were in the quartier de l'Opéra, what came within was very pretentious indeed and housed in interior spaces of great expansiveness and elegance. These interiors could be very grand. In the case of Armand's Grand Hôtel one entered by carriage unassumingly enough through a triple portal on the boulevard des Capucines facade to discover one's self in a breathtak-

Figure 23. Crédit Lyonnais (Bouwens van der Boyen, architect, 1876–1878, 1881–1883).

ing broad *cour d'honneur* conveniently roofed against inclement weather in iron and glass at the fourth floor (Figures 26 and 27). A broad staircase and terrace at the far side permitted a dignified entry through an arcade the whole width of the space to a rococo salon with stairways and elevators at its ends. Across this, matching the facade arcade, was a second row of arches admitting the visitor into an amazing semicircular dining room, mirrors below and windows (filled with etched glass) above opening the superimposed arcades of its curving wall (Figure 28). A private salon, as large as the entrance salon below it, the Salon du Zodiac, looked down into the dining room across the second story, connected at one point by a circular staircase. On December 10, 1896, an elaborate dinner was arranged in this space to honor Sarah Bernhardt. After five hundred guests had sat down to table in the semicircular room, the actress made her entry descending the spiral staircase from the Salon du Zodiac and proceeding to a purple throne at the apex of the apsidal wall. Lights twinkled, unseen voices intoned a "Hymne à Sarah Bernhardt," and a massive repast was consumed before

Figure 24. Crédit Lyonnais (Bouwens van der Boyen, architect, 1876–1878, 1881–1883).
Cross section of main banking room.

Figure 25. Department store Au Printemps (Paul Sédille, architect, 1881–1882).

the whole party moved on to the Théâtre de la Renaissance up the boulevards for a performance and another ceremony of adoration.[53]

Henri Blondel's Dépôts et des Comptes Courants (Figure 16) was more staid in its decoration but as powerful in its spaces. A porte cochère penetrated below the rotunda on the place de l'Opéra past a formal entrance to a triangular glass-roofed court. Opening into this were the public offices of the bank with, on the floor above, the bank's administration. More modestly, in the cases of the Splendide Hôtel and the Théâtre du Vaudeville (Figure 18), one entered circular vestibules on the boulevard or *place,* then mounted ceremonial stairways to round salons on the second floor before (in the case of the Vaudeville) entering the large and richly decorated space of the theater itself (Figure 29).

The Jockey Club was the most fabled interior experience, perhaps because it was the most difficult to gain admittance to (Figure 17). This was felt to be the Second Empire club par excellence, the richest and most dissipated, near the Opéra among whose *corps de ballet* the members (like Haussmann himself) had mistresses. The principal rooms stretched across the piano nobile, or principal floor, behind the giant order externally, in two enfilades departing from an oval salon at the corner, one suite of two chambers down the boulevard des Capucines (the billiard room and the library),

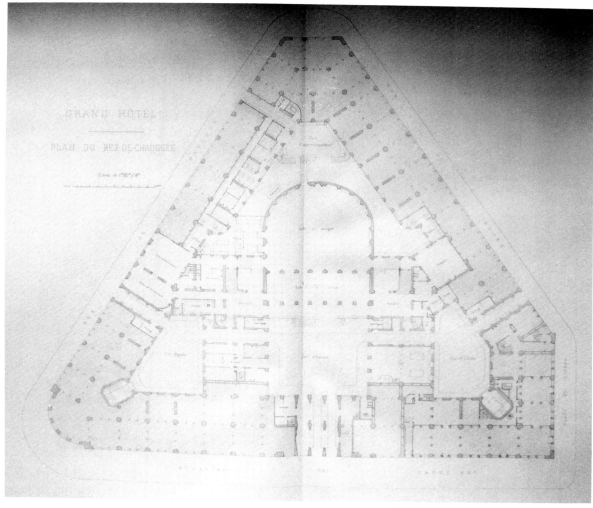

Figure 26. Grand Hôtel de la Paix (Alfred Armand, architect, 1861–1862). Plan.

Figure 27. Grand Hôtel de la Paix. Cross section.

Figure 28. Grand Hôtel de la Paix. Dining room.

the other of four up the rue Scribe devoted to gaming. Laterally, it occupied a span of twenty-two windows. One mounted a circular staircase from a carriage entrance at 1, rue Scribe and emerged into the central salon, called the Camp de Chalons after the cavalry camp. The ex-architect (and onetime member of Garnier's Opéra staff), Charles Yriarte, summarized the effect: "This adoption of a truly amazing luxury that recalls the splendors of Versailles is of an effect all the more powerful in that it contrasts to the simple comfort of all the other rooms."[54]

Jean Bouvier published in his study of the first years of the Crédit Lyonnais several interesting letters from the internal correspondence of the directors apropos of their "palace" erected from the designs of Bouwens van der Boyen in 1876–1878 a few hundred yards eastward up the boulevard (Figures 23 and 24).[55] The administrator Henri Bouthier writes to his colleague, Adrian Mazerat, September 6, 1876, that they want "to have an immense *boutique* on the most frequented sidewalk. . . . With our facade we will have the largest advertisement possible; 200,000 people will pass before it every day and we will be able to say in all languages that we offer them all

Figure 29. Théâtre du Vaudeville (Auguste-Joseph Magne, architect, 1868). Upper vestibule.

our services."[56] They proclaimed this with a beautifully finished facade and – significantly – with an immense interior hall, dramatically glass-roofed, beyond which a circular staircase led to the directors' offices. The bank saw to it that the building received appreciative coverage from the *Journal des débats*,[57] *l'Illustration*,[58] and *Le Figaro* after its opening on March 23, 1878.

The directors were very pleased with the result and projected an extension almost at once. Bouthier again writes Mazerat on October 29, 1879:

In eighteen months the number of our employees will have risen from 250 to 1,000. . . . M. Germain [president of the bank] thinks we should consider the convenience for us of housing in the Crédit Lyonnais a certain number of the business that are linked to it: the Chemins Autrichiens, with which our relations will become closer; the Nord-Espagne, which we wish to control; the Foncière Lyonnais, the Mône, the Caisse Paternelle, the Gaz de France, Chatillon-Commentry, Decazeville are all businesses that we want near at hand. Perhaps in the future we will have other businesses to shelter here: a gas company, a coal mine, a metallurgical company, a railroad. We must predict such initiatives. We need more sophisticated machinery, a bigger factory.[59]

Hector Horeau (1801–1872) did a number of projects for iron and glass rental structures in this quarter and in 1866 proposed simply roofing the

Figure 30. Hector Horeau, Project to roof the boulevard des Capucines in front of the Grand Hôtel, 1866.

boulevard des Capucines itself along the front of the Grand Hôtel to begin to put the whole Nouveau Paris under an industrial roof (Figure 30).[60]

* * *

It was the nature of these institutions that they were open to a numerous if socially circumscribed public and that a visit to the quarter constituted a promenade through these spaces, randomly as one's taste or curiosity directed, each interior an episode defined by a return to the boulevard or *place.* We must understand it as an ensemble – for guests in the Grand Hôtel or families in the *maisons meublés,* a world.

Figure 9 shows the quarter's building in the year 1868. The most impressive experience was the discovery of the spreading, silent skylit spaces of the largest institutions beyond the packed hubbub of the boulevard: the *cour d'honneur* and the dining room at the Grand Hôtel, the banking court at the Dépôt, the interior spaces of Bouwens's Crédit Lyonnais, Sédille's Au Printemps, and later Hermant's Société Générale. In contradiction to the Beaux-Arts rules that the interior space should push through to express itself on the exterior (like *repoussoir,* Théophile Gautier admonishes), there is no hint of these spaces externally, yet they are broader and more fantastically constructed than the central chambers of the traditional monuments of the city.

At the beginning of this chapter we discussed the precision with which a good Beaux-Arts architect framed his tableaux and drew his visitors through his composition, altering them to what would come next. In these private buildings in the quartier de l'Opéra the essence of the experience lies precisely in the frustration of such expectations. Small doors in anonymous facades become grand axes through spacious sunlit courts; outsides become insides through unexpected glass roofs; insides become outsides in the etched-glass windows circling the Grand Hôtel dining room. It is that peculiar bourgeois play of modesty amid splendor made spatial – the noble (the Opéra) is humbled and the humble (the hotel) is ennobled. This fascinated Baudelaire and, reading him, Walter Benjamin.[61]

A promenade around the quartier de l'Opéra would be punctuated by repeated penetrations into these hidden gardens but also by encounters with another spatial effect, the elevated belvedere. The oval Camp de Chalons at the Jockey Club on the second floor at the corner of the rue Scribe and the boulevard was the most splendid of these. Echoing it at the corner of the boulevard and the rue de la Chaussée d'Antin was the upper salon of the Théâtre du Vaudeville (Figure 29), and on the corresponding floor in the western rotunda of the place de l'Opéra was the Splendide Hôtel's main lobby – looking across to the director's room at the Dépôts et des Comptes Courants. The best suites at the Grand Hôtel faced on the place et de l'Opéra at this level. From these lookouts the visitor could really admire the shapes and masses of the quartier de l'Opéra, enjoy the tumult of the streets at ease, and plan the next foray.

Caillebotte painted such views from the balcony of his apartment behind the Opéra on the boulevard Haussmann in 1880 (Figure 31).[62] If head-on views of the Opéra like that of Adolphe Braun in Figure 1 are the mechanical equivalent of formal portraits, Caillebotte's views are like touristic snapshots: idle, informal views exploring the new spatial experiences of the quarter from elevated safety, including odd views through the railings and suicidal perspectives of the pavement below of a sort that would become a basic motif in twentieth-century skyscraper city views. Henry James uses this motif in his *Ambassadors* (1903) to introduce his elusive hero, Chad, to

Figure 31. Gustave Caillebotte, *Boulevard vu d'en Haut*, 1880.

Struther at his apartment on the boulevard Malesherbes (if we might be permitted to move several hundred yards westward down the boulevard Haussmann).

But his actual business . . . was with a third floor on the Boulevard Malesherbes . . . and the fact of the enjoyment by the third floor windows of a continuous balcony . . . had perhaps something to do with his lingering for five minutes on the opposite side of the street. . . . The chance he had allowed for – the chance of being seen, in time, from the balcony – had become a fact. Two or three of the windows stood open to the violet air; and, before Struther had cut the knot by crossing, a young man had come out and looked about him, had lighted a cigarette and tossed the match over, and then, resting on the rail, had given himself up, while he smoked, to watching the life below.[63]

Beside the elevated salon belvederes and the secret skylit courts of the quarter there was, of course, the mass of tall square shops, tightly packed with tempting goods. Pretty temptations and invitations to fantasy were the ultimate contents of the quarter, the temptations to rest and eat expensively in the hotels, to enjoy the performances at the Opéra and Vaudeville, to purchase items of adornment, apparel, and delectation in the shops.

In fact, it is surprising that, for all the external urbanistic deference to the central monument, the Opéra, internally and in the visitor's experience, the whole quarter's texture was the same. A dinner in the rooms of the Jockey Club or the grand dining room of the Grand Hôtel took place in spaces quite as large and gorgeous as Garnier's foyers and auditorium. It is the nature of this promenade through the consumerist fantasyland that gives us the quality of Second Empire building. Where once the city had been a series of closed cells – walled hotels opening on their gardens, only certain ones open on certain terms to certain people, and shops squeezed against the street – now space was open almost everywhere to a broad class (defined by dress and means, not by individual allegiance) and so become just one big building composed in contrasting parts. Where once there had been private gardens and salons there were now palm courts and hotel lobbies, shops and restaurants, all tinkling and tantalizing. The city's ceremonial axes were clearer than ever, but laid out on a plane tangential to them was a labyrinth of informal touristic paths and vantage points from which to observe the public representations at leisure, like Caillebotte's and James's figures or Baudelaire's *flâneur*.

✳   ✳   ✳

Zola vividly depicts the experience of the Nouveau Paris, starting with a carriage drive in 1861 in *La Curée* (1871–1872, Chapter 5).

The lovers adored the New Paris. They frequently toured the city in a carriage, making a detour to traverse certain boulevards that they loved with a personal tenderness. The houses, tall with sculpted doorways, laden with balconies where there shown, in great letters of gold, names, mottoes, and exhortations, ravished them. While the coupé rolled along they followed with a friendly gaze the gray bands of the sidewalks – broad, interminable, with their benches, their poster-kiosks, their skinny trees. That open canyon which extends to the horizon, repeating itself and opening on the bluish square of the sky, that uninterrupted double row of stores where the employees smile for the customers, these flows of the crowd shuffling and droning, filled them bit by bit with an absolute and complete satisfaction with the life of the street. They loved even the street cleaning jets that passed like a white smoke before their horses, falling as a fine rain beneath the wheels of the coupe as they made brown streaks on the pavement, raising a light wisp of dust. They rolled constantly and it seemed as if the carriage was passing over a carpet, along the straight and endless pavement that had been made specifically for them to avoid the dark back streets. Each boulevard became a corridor of their house.[64]

These evocations of carpetlike asphalt-paved boulevards across the light-tamed city contrast to the jolting, congested environment of the quarters before Haussmann with its theaters and labyrinthine galleries, the old Opéra and the Jockey Club wedged into their midst. (Zola depicted this in the early chapters of *Nana* of 1878–1880.)

One of Zola's novels was entirely devoted to the life and transformations of the quartier de l'Opéra, *Au Bonheur des dames* (1881–1883).[65] The framework is the story of the growth of a department store, originally wedged into the corner of the place Gaillon, but bit by bit expanding to finally reach the boulevard du 4 Septembre when it was cut through (beginning in 1864[66]). Here there appears another important motif in the depiction of the new quarter: the fantasy world of interior space devoted to ritual consumption. The store's interior centered on a three-story glass-roofed nave, "like a railroad station shed," surrounded by superimposed galleries linked by suspended staircases and flying bridges, "the modern realization of a dream palace, a Babel piling up stories, opening out spaces, creating perspectives to other floors and to other rooms, to infinity."[67] The facades of the early sections of the building are likened to barracks, distinguished only by the glittering contents of their show windows. But by the end of the novel Zola permits himself a peculiar flight of fancy (apparently helped by the imaginings of his young architect friend Frantz Jourdain) in describing the new facade inaugurated on the boulevard du 4 Septembre as built in iron and glass and colored materials with statues and ornaments poured across its silhouette. In reality this would have been impossible before the loosening of zoning laws in 1902. But it is fundamental to the novel in expressing the ultimate arrogant feature of the store owner, Mouret, proclaiming the presence of commece on the monumental thoroughfare, and it is important for us in emphasizing that in the tight urban order of the quartier de l'Opéra there lay a tremendous tension – an antihieratic, antilithic, untraditional vision of a new commercial city – implicit in the ferro-vitreous interior spaces, breaking through to view in the utopian projects of Horeau and Jourdain or the depictions of Zola.[68]

✳   ✳   ✳

In the chapters that follow we will reencounter certain points delineated here in the story of the quartier de l'Opéra: the details of the system of government architectural services (Chapter 2), the nature of a system of foreground and background buildings (Chapters 3 and 4), the interplay of personalities within the system and outside it in confrontation with private architecture and everyday life (Chapters 5 and 6). In spite of the unique consistency of classical design in nineteenth-century Paris, in spite of the powerful control of the monumental form of Paris exercised then by the government (especially by Haussmann), we must remember that several different architectures were struggling to emerge in that cityscape: Besides the heavy official stone architecture, another created the private developers in iron, glass, and brilliantly colored tiles, as well as a third architecture made by its observers – one of impressions, pretenses, and perspectives – leveling both the official and the private to episodes in a stroll.

THE GOVERNMENT
ARCHITECTURAL SERVICES

I

The first chapter depicted the power of the mid-nineteenth-century French state architectural apparatus in shaping Paris but indicated as well the peculiar influence of private designers – Armand and Crépinet, Blondel, Bouwens van der Boyen, and Sédille – behind the facades. Beside this tension in architectural practice there is another, within the state administration, among the individual services comprising it, the Bâtiments Civils and the Travaux de Paris, the Palais Royaux (or Impériaux), Edifices Diocésains, and Monuments Historiques – not to mention the corps of the commissaires voyers and the bureau of the Plan de Paris. Never before or since in France during the years 1830 to 1870 was government control of architecture and urbanism so pervasive and powerful; never before or since was the corps of government architects so tightly organized and so dominant within the profession. Yet one does not seem to be able to speak of a simple, consistent bureaucratic mentality informing this architecture. Instead there seems a series of distinct local "cultures" making individual compromises with the burgeoning field of private practice.[1]

French architecture was the state art, a circumscribed and refined arena for the expression of the character and power of the regime and the "policing" of society, parallel to ceremonial etiquette, dress, and furnishings.[2] In the concrete context of Paris, the practice of architecture in the government services was the enterprise of the maintenance and inflection of the array of monuments constituting the capital. This always took thought and cleverness, especially after the Revolution when the definition of authority became fluid.

The state teaching and doctrinal institutions – the Ecole des Beaux-Arts and the Académie des Beaux-Arts – existed to support the formulation of public architecture. Government buildings constituted the programs in the Grand Prix competitions and often referred to current building projects.[3] From 1843 to 1847, for example, these were a "Palais de l'Institut," an "Edifice pour l'Académie de Paris," an "Eglise cathédrale pour un capitale," a "Musée d'histoire naturelle," and a "Palais de la chambre des deputés." (When a "Hôtel pour un riche banquier" was given in 1866 it was regarded as a revolution and not repeated.[4]) The final project to be executed by the Grand Prix winners after their five-year *pension* in Rome was a "Project for a public monument of his own conception and conforming to French habits."[5] In these years these were a "Panthéon" (Morey, 1837), a "Cour de Cassation" (Leveil, 1838), a "Conservatoire de Musique" (Baltard, 1839), a "Mairie" (Clerget, 1840), a "Palais de l'Institut de France" (Boulanger, 1842), and a "Hôtel des Invalides de la Marine" (Guénepin, 1843).[6]

Positions in the Service des Bâtiments Civils were to be given, first and foremost, to Grand Prix winners, entering immediately upon their return from Rome.[7] All the members of the Académie des Beaux-Arts were engaged in the Bâtiments Civils – or, failing that, the very most important posts in parallel services.[8] Their letters of candidacy listed their government posts and only mentioned private works in a body at the end as unworthy of further specification.[9] The same formula was used in official necrologies upon academicians' deaths.

Virtually every architect in the received canon of historically significant designers in nineteenth-century France worked in the corps of the government services: Charles Percier, P.-F.-L. Fontaine, L.-T.-J. Visconti, Hector Lefuel, Félix Duban, Henri Labrouste, Louis Duc, Léon Vaudoyer, Victor Baltard, Théodore Ballu, E.-E. Viollet-le-Duc, Charles Garnier. Even the radical utopian Hector Horeau aspired to an influential state position, and gained it for a moment during the Commune.[10] The politically radical Gabriel Toudouze and the clever decorator Léon Feuchère eventually retired into it.[11] Writers and theorists like César Daly and Charles Chipiez found places in it.[12]

A remarkably broad array of buildings were under direct control of the government: state, departmental, and municipal monuments and institutions, of course – city halls, law courts, palaces, prisons, hospitals, libraries – but theaters too and, due to state control of religion (until 1913), all church buildings, as well as, due to centralized state education, all lycée and college buildings. Even thermal baths were included. As we have seen, tight control was established over city plans and building envelopes, calling forth another whole body of state architectural functionaries, the commissaires voyers.

By decree of October 27, 1808, the state provided offices and staffs for the architects of public monuments. Only in the rare cases like those of Hittorff, Visconti, and Bailly where prominent architects maintained extensive private practices did they even have active offices of their own.[13] Much state work, furthermore, was not design, but rather oversight and inspection, carried out on lengthy tours or in meetings at the ministries and city halls. Elsewhere we have calculated that in 1858 Henri Labrouste spent four afternoons a week in meetings of oversight boards and seven or eight weeks a year on inspection trips – this exclusive of the time spent on design and on supervising government construction.[14] What we judge to be the leaders of the French architectural profession were profoundly committed to the state administration.

The received history of French nineteenth-century building is that of government architecture almost exclusively. It was formulated within it by Julien Guadet (professor of theory at the Ecole des Beaux-Arts, 1894–1908) in his *Eléments et théorie de l'architecture* of 1901–1904, by Georges Gromort (also professor of theory at the Ecole, 1937–1940) in his volume in the *Histoire générale de l'art français de la révolution à nos jours* of 1922, and finally by Louis Hautecoeur (Directeur des Beaux-Arts in the Vichy government and later secrétaire perpétuel of the Académie des Beaux-Arts) in his monumental seven-volume *Histoire de l'architecture classique en France* of 1943 to 1957.[15] The basic documents from which they worked were likewise products of the institution: the necrologies of the leading figures delivered by tradition by their successors in the administrations, the publications of government construction like Biet, Gourlier, Grillon, and Tardieu, *Choix des édifices publics projetés et construits en France depuis le commencement du XIXe siècle* (3 vols., 1825–1850), and Félix Narjoux's *Paris: Monuments éléves par la ville, 1850–1880* (4 vols., 1881–1883). Important buildings were published in special monographs, usually by their architects, like Jules de Joly's *Chambre des députés* (1840), Alphonse de Gisors's *Le palais du Luxembourg* (1847), and Baltard and Callet's *Monographie des halles centrales* (1863). Charles Bauchal, a functionary, published a biographical dictionary that in its nineteenth-century section was, effectively, of government place holders.[16] Special interests wrote their own histories in opposition to this – Anatole de Baudot's *L'Architecture: le passé, le présent, l'avenir* (1914) or Sigfried Giedion's *Bauen in Frankreich* (1928) – but these did not come close to equaling the weight and detail of the official presentation. The relevant chapters of the *Pelican History of Art* (1958) written by the modernist Henry-Russell Hitchcock are dependent on Gromort, Hautecoeur, Gourlier, and Narjoux.

II

The first established and most central of the nineteenth-century French architectural services and the model for the others was that of the Bâtiments Civils.[17] It had been founded in 1791, to replace the disestablished Surintendance des Bâtiments du Roi, and continued down to 1896, periodically reorganized (1794, 1812, 1832, 1838–1841, 1854, 1870).[18] It was a *division,* usually in the Ministry of the Interior (but during the Second Empire attached to the unique and particularly powerful Ministère d'Etat) under the direction of a sequence of surprisingly permanent bureaucrats – Hely d'Oissel and Héricart de Thury during the Restoration, Jean Vatout during the Monarchy of July, F.-H.-C. de B. de Noué during the Second Republic, J.-E.-M. de Cardaillac during the Second Empire, this last working under the surintendant des beaux-arts, Nieuwerkerke, after a reorganization of 1863.[19] The division's offices were in the Hôtel de Conti on the rue de Grenelle before being moved into the north wing of the New Louvre, inaugurated in 1857.

The division embraced two quite distinct agencies: a corps of architects, charged with the erection and maintenance of Parisian buildings pertaining to the central government, and the Conseil des Bâtiments Civils empowered to examine and approve at the behest of the minister all government construction in France, all historic restoration work, and all city street plans. The two agencies were distinct from the Travaux de Paris, created in 1811, until their amalgamation on December 30, 1841, but often their chief, the directeur des travaux and the prêsident of the Conseil des Bâtiments Civils, were the same individual, for example, in the case of Hely d'Oissel from 1820 to 1823. This confusion of the capital's and the nation's architectural services dates from the seventeenth century.

As parallel oversight commissions were created in other branches of the government the span of the Conseil's authority steadily diminished: the Palais Impériaux (or Royaux) in 1804, the Monuments Historiques in 1840, the Edifices Diocésains in 1848 and 1853, the Travaux de Paris in 1860.

The architects of the Service des Bâtiments Civils were responsible for the monumental representation of the state and were seen as the most prestigious and solemn corps of the profession. The array of buildings embraced by the service's competence was clear and consistent: former palaces housing central government functions (the Chamber of Deputies, the Senate, the Cour des Comptes), ministries, monuments (Arc de Triomphe, the Chapelle Expiatoire, colonnes Vendôme and de Juillet), certain central scientific establishments (Bibliothèque Nationale, Observatory, Conservatoire, the structures in the Jardin des Plantes), certain central hospices (Sourds-Muets, Jeunes-Aveugles), specialized central schools (Ecole des Beaux-Arts, Ecole des Arts et Métiers), technical establishments like the Dépôt des Marbres and the Garde-Meuble National, and the central post office – in other words, those structures under the direct supervision of the Ministry of the Interior.[20] In 1881 the total properties concerned numbered ninety-six.[21]

They were an odd lot of establishments – some splendid, some quite humble – but all part of this prestigious service, and we find the leaders of the profession setting down that they were architect of the Observatory or even the Dépôt des Marbres less for the architectural splendor they might have created in those posts than for the trust the appointments implied.

Each property had an *architecte-en-chef* on retainer with a drafting room or *agence,* usually on the premises themselves, with a permanent state-paid staff of *architecte-inspecteurs* and *vérificateurs.* The service was divided into the *service ordinaire* charged with the maintenance of existing buildings and the *service extraordinaire* charged with the erection of new structures or of major extensions. The *agence* was most often a staff of three or four working in a wooden shed on the construction site itself, but in large projects like Visconti and Lefuel's New Louvre or Garnier's Opéra it might be an expansive drafting hall with dozens of architects.[22] At the New Louvre there was, in addition to the *architectes-en-chefs,* one to three *inspecteurs principaux, inspecteurs* of the first, second, third, fourth, and fifth classes, and *agents* of as many grades. Promising architects worked their way up through this hierarchy by successive promotions, Grand Prix winners mixed in with the rest (but evidently were more upwardly mobile).[23] Salaries were fixed ones for all the staff except the *architecte-en-chef,* who usually received a percentage of the construction costs in addition.[24]

As was traditional in every ministry, at the end of December each year this staff waited on the ministre de l'intérieur and from the guest lists surviving from 1844 to 1848 we get an idea of the size of the corps.[25] In 1844 there were 38 *architectes-en-chefs,* 27 *inspecteurs,* and 18 *vérificateurs*; in 1846 36 architects and 22 *inspecteurs*; in 1848 (June 30) 51 architects and 25 *inspecteurs*. In 1846 the architects included 16 Grand Prix winners (roughly 40 percent of the approximately 40 then alive) and 6 winners of the Second Grand Prix or the Prix Départmental. Among the *inspecteurs* 5 had won the Grand Prix, 2 the Second Grand Prix, and 1 had been *en loge*.

By decree of July 22, 1832, *architectes-en-chefs* could be assigned only one major building within the government services, although that was later rescinded and had not been true before 1832. They could usually maintain a private practice on the side. By the same decree *inspecteurs* had to be present on the site all day, but the *architecte-en-chef* only had to visit once a week. While the *architectes-en-chefs* rarely resigned their positions before death, the *inspecteurs* changed positions relatively frequently.

Entry into the service was by nomination by the minister, first as *inspecteur* of various grades, then as *architecte-en-chef.* Aspiring candidates wrote the minister and sent testimonials, often political.[26] Preference was given to Grand Prix winners. If one resigned from one's post in an *agence,* one had to reapply to the minister; there was no tenure in the service.[27] It is evident in the manuscript of Visconti's autobiography and in C.-H.-M de Rémusat's papers in Toulouse that the minister involved himself personally in staffing.[28]

The Conseil des Bâtiments Civils was a quite different agency, much broader in its territory but only having the function of criticism and advice. However, from 1812 absolutely no outside work could be engaged in by its six permanent members, the *inspecteurs généraux* des Bâtiments Civils.[29] They met twice a week, analyzing and approving projects on the basis of reports written by the individual members. They also had the responsibility of examining periodically active construction sites in Paris and in the provinces, divided into *inspections*.

The promising Empire designer A.-J.-B.-G. de Gisors (1762–1835), inspecteur général from 1812 to his death in 1835, left a manuscript in the Institut library in which he speaks sadly of having to give up active practice, but writes that the loss was compensated for by the fact that he was effectively redesigning a large number of government structures all over France by his intervention.[30] This he documents dramatically in two folio volumes of drawings showing designs submitted to him in his capacity before and after his intervention, proving his impact. These include a small number of designs executed directly by the Conseil, especially the plan of the new town, Napoléonville (Pontivy). De Gisors evidently intended this collection of documents to be published as an approximation of the *oeuvre* that he otherwise might have produced.

The service des Bâtiments Civils celebrated itself in a monumental publication of the public buildings of France published in fascicles comprising three folio volumes between 1825 and 1850, *Choix des édifices* (cited earlier). In 1848 it published its own administrative history in Gourlier's *Notice historique sur le service des travaux des bâtiments civils* updated in later editions of Charles Questel's editorship in 1886 and 1895.

✻   ✻   ✻

Within the Bâtiments Civils certain building types might be specially treated, notably prisons during the reforming years of the early nineteenth century.[31] One of the great accomplishments of the Empire was penal reform embodied in the Code Napoléon. This, which furthered humane incarceration instead of corporal punishment, necessitated prison construction by localities and called forth central intervention in funding and in specifying the architectural layout. This emanated from the administration and from reformers close to it and grew by degrees into a national program of prison construction. In 1810 eleven million francs was authorized for the construction of large *maisons centrales,* disbursed in annual amounts ranging from 5,000,000 to 900,000 francs. Legislation of 1840 and 1843 established the cellular type nationally as a result of Abel Blouet's trip to study American prisons in 1836 (with the jurist F.-A. Demetz) and his lengthy report (1837) advocating the individual cellular regime.[32] Blouet (1795–1853) himself had been named inspecteur général des prisons in 1838 with an ex-officio seat on the Conseil des Bâtiments Civils. In 1841 Blouet together with Harou-Romain and Hector Horeau put together a book of model prison plans to accompany a ministerial *instruction* to the prefects.[33] In 1843 he showed a model prison design at the Salon and desseminated it in a pamphlet (Figure 68).[34] In 1843–1850 that model materialized in Paris as the model prison of the Nouvelle Force (or the "Mazas") by his friend Emile Gilbert (1793–1874). Contemporaneously in 1839 Blouet designed the juvenile prison farm at Mettray for a private philanthropic society led by Demetz.[35]

In 1848 the Inspection Générale was temporarily discontinued. When reestablished in 1849 Charles Gourlier was in charge. In 1853 Persigny, minister of the interior, legislated a more practical but less philosophically nuanced regime of prison design.[36]

Both Blouet and Gilbert were Grand Prix winners, Blouet the professor of theory at the Ecole des Beaux-Arts, architect of the Arc de Triomphe before his appointment to the prison administration, and designer of a project to establish the Chamber of Deputies in the Tuileries after the abolition of his post in 1848. For all their engagement in these institutional activities, they had qualified themselves in the most traditional way and were respected for that. (We return to this subject in Chapter 4.)

✻　　✻　　✻

For all the relative systematization of the Bâtiments Civils, it was never a completely closed, focused administration. That of the Ponts et Chaussées, in contrast, was so after reorganizations of 1716 and 1738.[37] Training at the Ecole des Ponts et Chaussées (established in 1747) ended with a diploma (not established at the Ecole des Beaux-Arts until 1867) and led directly to posts in the central or departmental administrations reserved for graduates. No outside employment was allowed and retirement pensions were provided. This service was continually cited by *fonctionnaires* as a model for architects. In 1819 the engineer Alexander de Laborde proposed that all government building and town planning be placed under a single directeur général des Bâtiments Civils and that the Ecole d'Architecture be reorganized as an Ecole des Bâtiments Civils to provide a cadre of designers who would, in turn, enter government service by examination.[38] De Laborde repeated his proposals in 1830. Haussmann would seem to have spoken for many administrators when he wrote of architects in his *Memoires:* "Architecture for all of them is a profession; for many, no doubt, an art; but for none is this public responsibility what it should be in the eyes of those really worthy of it: a sort of priesthood."[39]

The architects resisted complete integration into the administration. Except for a few positions, they maintained the right to private practice (even if that was officially deemed unworthy). Prosper Mérimée explained the problem in a letter of February 24, 1853, discussing the possibility of establishing a corps of inspectors of diocesan building.

One cannot make architects into functionaries. There is no seniority among artists and rank is only achieved by public success. Regardless of the title the government might give an architect he will never exercise moral authority over his colleagues if respected works have not placed him in high public esteem. If the *inspecteurs* are to have the authority they must exercise, they must be chosen from among the architects who have acquired reputations. But it is almost impossible to acquire such before the age of forty or forty-five (because before that age one does not have important work to design). Now, what artist with a reputation, forty or forty-five years old, would renounce a brilliant career, glory, perhaps even a fortune, for the precarious position of *inspecteur*? Where might one find an artist who might renounce great works, a private clientele, for a mediocrely paying job that he could occupy for only a few years? A public functionary knows that after thirty years of solid service he will be able to retire. But what retirement is possible for men who become *inspecteurs* at forty-five years of age? From another perspective, what fruitful services might the government expect from *inspecteurs* who have grown old in their position, enfeebled by years, and whose lack of practice has put them long ago outside the continuous progress of their art?

One must never forget what happened in the Conseil des Bâtiments Civils. When it was founded the institution admirably represented the elite of the architects. Distanced from practice, its members promptly lost their authority. Today, the timidity of their decisions lets one divine that even they themselves sense their position behind and outside the evolution of art.[40]

III

As the century progressed several other services emerged parallel to the Bâtiments Civils while municipal and departmental architecture – especially in the department of the Seine – was reorganized on its model.

Until 1792 the sovereign was the personal representation of the state and his palaces were the most important monuments in the charge of the appropriately named Bâtiments du Roi. With the dissolution of royal authority the Bourbon palaces became the seats of various branches of the new evolving government. The Palais Bourbon and the Luxembourg became the Chamber of Deputies and the Senate; the Palais Royal, the Tribunat; the Tuileries, the Assemblée, then the new Emperor Napoleon's palace. In 1804

Napoleon, now emperor, established a Liste Civile – an annual appropriation from the Chamber of twenty-five million francs for the sovereign's personal use balanced by the incorporation of his imperial property into the central government's possessions – supporting the Maison de l'Empereur, within which was established a new architectural service, initially under the intendant des bâtiments, Fleurieu.[41] This service occupied the Hôtel d'Angivillier, the old headquarters of the Bâtiments du Roi. Napoleon's trusted Fontaine (1762–1853) virtually led it from 1804 as architect of the Louvre and the Tuileries (then as premier architecte de l'empereur in 1813) down to his resignation on September 20, 1848, living in the Hôtel d'Angivillier (although he was never intendent). In 1870 the service was amalgamated into the Bâtiments Civils et Palais Nationaux, as it had been temporarily from 1848 to 1852. It was reorganized with each change of regime (1814, 1825, 1832, 1848, 1852, and 1871) but remained administratively static in between times.[42] (It should be noted that beside the Maison du Roi there also existed the private estate of the king with yet another, smaller architectural service in charge, for example, of the Bourbon Chapelle Expiatoire or the Orleans funerary chapel at Dreux.)

The basic organization of the Palais Impériaux (or, during the Restoration and Monarchy of July, Royaux) is familiar from the Bâtiments Civils: There was an *architecte-en-chef* on retainer for each palace (or for several palaces, if small like Meudon), an *agence* with a variable staff of *inspecteurs* at each, and a council of architects (including senior figures from outside the service) to review designs. The architects were allotted apartments in the palaces. The *Almanach Impérial* of 1813 lists ten *architectes-en-chefs* in this service (Fontaine in charge of the Louvre and Tuileries) working under the intendant des bâtiments, Baron Costaz, and a Comité Consultatif des Bâtiments de la Couronne consisting of Gondouin, Molinos, and Rondelet.[43] In 1847 only six *architectes-en-chefs* appear, all having multiple designations, Fontaine handling the Palais Royal and the Elysée as well as the Louvre and Tuileries. The Second Empire reorganized the service by decree of April 16, 1852 and increased the staff.[44] In a document dated June 16, 1853 – a few months after the proclamation of the Empire – we see the following appointments and salaries:

Tuileries: Visconti, architecte: 6,000 francs per annum

Leforest, inspecteur 2: 3,500 francs
Lacost, inspecteur 4: 2,500 francs

Louvre: Duban, architecte: 6,000 francs

Debresfenne, inspecteur 3: 3,000 francs

Louet, inspecteur 4: 2,500 francs
Lambert, inspecteur 5: 2,000 francs

Elysée: Eugène Lacroix, architecte: 6,000 francs

Laisné, inspecteur 3: 3,000 francs
Dainville, inspecteur 5: 2,000 francs
Lisch, agent 1: 1,800 francs
Couvrechef, agent 1: 1,800 francs
Bouchain, agent 2: 1,500 francs

Palais Royal: Chabrol, architecte: 6,000 francs

Rousseau, inspecteur 3: 3,000 francs
Osselin, inspecteur 4: 2,500 francs
Solomon, inspecteur 4: 2,500 francs

Versailles: Questel, architecte: 6,000 francs

Chanlay, inspecteur 3: 3,000 francs
Petit, inspecteur 4: 3,000 francs
Favier, inspecteur 4: 2,400 francs
Melle, inspecteur 5: 2,000 francs
Lue, agent 2: 1,500 francs

Eaux de Versailles: Legny, architecte: 6,000 francs

Bajas, inspecteur 3: 3,000 francs
Dubun, inspecteur 4: 2,500 francs
Trochu, inspecteur 5: 2,000 francs
Gavin, agent 2: 1,500 francs

Eaux de Marly: Dufrayer, inspecteur 2: 3,500 francs

Saint-Cloud: Clerget, architecte: 6,000 francs

Blanchard, inspecteur 4: 2,500 francs
Dubuisson, inspecteur 5: 2,000 francs
Marquet, inspecteur 5: 2,000 francs

Meudon and Sèvres: Landin, architecte: 6,000 francs

Anez, inspecteur 4: 2,500 francs
Delapierre, inspecteur 5: 1,500 francs

Menuci, agent 2: 1,500 francs
Mesnager, agent 2: 1,500 francs

Fontainebleau: Lefuel, architecte: 6,000 *francs*

Tétaz, inspecteur 3: 3,000 francs
Cazeneuve, agent 2: 1,500 francs

Compiègne: Bourgeois, architecte: 4,000 *francs*

Saltet, inspecteur 4: 2,400 francs

Rambouillet: Paccard, architecte: 5,000 *francs*[45]

These were solid salaries, equivalent in the case of the *architectes-en-chefs* to that of an inspecteur général of the Bâtiments Civils – that is, enough to be a professional man's basic source of income. (The architects did not, however, earn a percentage of the construction costs after 1810.[46])

Many of the *architectes-en chefs* worked most of their careers in the service and had minimal private practices: Lepère, Famin, Nepveu, Dufour, and of course Fontaine in the Napoleonic organization; Lefuel, Clerget, Landin, Paccard, and Bourgeois in the Second Empire. Berthault in the first period and Questel in the second were exceptions.[47] Few of these architects, however, were academically distinguished – only the four architects of the Tuileries, Fontaine, Duban, Visconti, and Lefuel (all First or Second Grand Prix winners and members of the Académie) plus Famin, Grand Prix of 1801, at Rambouillet.[48] During the July Monarchy Fontaine was working on a folio-illustrated publication of the royal palaces (with texts by Jean Vatout) copies of which were to be placed in each royal residence, an equivalent, in its way, of the Conseil des Bâtiments Civils's *Choix des édifices*.[49] In addition Fontaine published his *Résidences de souverains* in 1833 and earlier had provided Czar Alexander with a series of illustrated letter-reports on the transformation of Paris during the years 1809 to 1815 (published as a book in 1892).[50]

✣   ✣   ✣

If the royal palaces were the essential representations of the king, the great capital, Paris, at least from the time of Henri IV, had been treated as the broader manifestation of his power.[51] In fact, the directeur des travaux de Paris tended to be named premier architecte du roi. By the time of the establishment of the Empire (1804) there was an inspecteur général des Bâtiments Civils et des Travaux Publics du Département de la Seine, Auguste Molinos (1743–1831), with an array of parallel agencies under him: voirie,

travaux hydrauliques, carrières, tribunaux et prisons, hospices.[52] Two architects were attached to the Administration des Hospices (Clavareau and
Viel), three to the Tribunaux et Prisons (Giraud, Lefebvre, and Beaumont)
while three more functioned in Voirie as "architectes surveillants des bâtiments en construction" (Legrand, Norry, and Renaud). A Conseil des
Travaux-Publics appears in the *Almanach Impérial,* Molinos in charge, Viel
and Beaumont architect-members, Becquey-de-Beaupré and Lamande, engi-
neer-members, Couvreau, inspecteur-controleur. By 1809 the Direction des
Travaux d'Architecture (Molinos, inspecteur général) was divided into three
sections by building type, the first (in charge of the Hôtel de Ville and monumental construction) headed by Molinos himself, the second (churches) by
A.-T. Brongniart (with Hippolyte Godde as inspecteur), the third (schools
and barracks) by C.-E. Beaumont (with Couad as inspecteur). Prisons and
hospices were a separate administration. In 1811 Napoleon further centralized Paris construction in the hands of the engineer Louis Bruyère
(1758–1831), directeur des Travaux de Paris, in charge of both state and
municipal construction until his retirement in 1820 (and contested in his
authority by Fontaine, in 1813 named premier architecte de l'empereur with
ill-defined authority).[53] The post continued in a weakened form under the
direction of two other engineers, A.-P.-F. Hely d'Oissel and A.-M. Héricart
de Thury (the latter promoted from the municipal service), until 1830. Subsequently municipal building became a bureau in the office of the prefect of
the Seine, the Travaux d'Architecture.

The Travaux d'Architecture was reorganized by legislation of 1840,
1854, 1860, and 1871.[54] Like the Bâtiments Civils, there was a distinction
between the *service ordinaire* and the *service extraordinaire,* a system of
agences and *architectes-en-chefs* on retainer, and a central oversight council.
It was unique, however, in the specialized division of responsibilities. By
1831 the *service ordinaire* was divided into five sections by building type:
the first (supervised by Hippolyte Godde after Molinos's retirement in
1830) in charge of the Hôtel de Ville, churches, fêtes publiques, *places,* and
promenades – that is, ceremonial structures; the second (A.-M.-F. Jay), customs houses, abbatoirs, storehouses; the third (Antoine-Marie Peyre), law
courts, barracks, schools; the fourth (J.-F.-J. Ménager), prisons and the
morgue; the fifth (Louis-Pierre Baltard), markets and mairies of the
arrondissements.[55] In 1854 these sections were rearranged to form six;[56] in
1860 rearranged again to form four. These architects were closely identified
with city construction and functioned as a board of experts in various
departments of municipal building. By the reorganization of 1860 they were
formally so constituted. (There was also a more technically competent Conseil des Travaux Publics with authority to review and approve both engineering and architectural projects. In 1830 its members were two architects,

L.-P. Baltard and Molinos, and three engineers, François-Jonas Eustache, Héricart de Thury, and Vallot.)[57] Within the four sections of the 1860 organization were twelve (in 1865 enlarged to twenty) architectes d'arrondissement in charge of each of the twenty districts of the reorganized and extended city. They received 5,000 to 7,000 francs per annum but could execute no outside work.[58]

In 1837 the position of a single professional director was created, inspecteur général des Travaux Ordinaires d'Architecture or directeur général des Beaux-Arts, occupied by L.-P. Baltard (1764–1846) until his death.[59] The position was then discontinued until the reorganization of 1860, but with Baltard's son, Victor (1805–1874), steadily emerging through the posts of inspecteur des Beaux-Arts (1842), then as *architecte-en-chef* of the prestigious first section (1848), finally in 1860 as directeur du Service d'Architecture at a salary of 12,000 to 15,000 francs per annum.[60] In the reorganization of 1871 Adolphe Alphand (1817–1891), Haussmann's deputy, once directeur of the Service des Promenades et Plantations and an engineer, was named directeur des Travaux de Paris – Bruyère's old post now resuscitated with the omission of the emperor – a position in which he dominated Paris municipal construction and engineering until his death in 1891.[61]

As Fontaine dominated the Palais Royaux during the first half of the century, Bruyère, the Baltards, and Alphand did the Travaux d'Architecture of Paris from 1811 to 1891. The bureaucrats in charge in between times, one Planson from 1830 to 1838, replaced by one Darié, were minor figures compared to the professionals functioning as administrators. This was not remarkable for the engineers, but for the architects, the Baltards, it was extraordinary. Effectively they answered directly to the prefect, although Haussmann was to remember Baltard severely in his *Mémoires*.

By law of January 10, 1849, the administration of Paris hospitals was centralized and tightened.[62] In place of the Conseil Général des Hôpitaux et Hospices de Paris a single man was named directeur général, Henri Davenne, formerly in charge of the bureau of Voirie – city planning – in the Ministry of the Interior. Instead of hospital plans being reviewed by a number of committees, among them the Conseil Général des Hospices and the Commission d'Architecture of the city, there was now an *architecte-en-chef,* Théodore Labrouste (1799–1885), with authority over the whole system. This was like Blouet's Inspection Générale des Prisons, organized twelve years before, but its authority extended only to Paris. Labrouste himself designed the most important hospitals, the Maison Dubois in Saint-Denis and the Hospice des Incurables in Ivry. Gilbert (architect of the model prison, the Mazas) was brought in to design the new Hôtel Dieu on the Ile de la Cité (1865–1877).

The Paris architectural service was tightly run under a series of architecturally minded prefects, especially Rambuteau and Haussmann, and it created a very impressive, compact urban artifact. It was as important as the Bâtiments Civils and more visible, publishing its accomplishments in Félix Pigeory's *Monuments de Paris* (1847), Adolphe Alphand's *Promenades de Paris* (1867–1873), and finally Félix Narjoux's monumental *Paris: monuments élevés par la ville, 1850–1880* (4 vols., 1881–1883). (Narjoux was also architect of Haussmann's retirement villa at Montboron, near Nice.) Both Rambuteau and Haussmann flattered themselves in their memoirs that they gave Paris a distinctive and exemplary architecture. Contemporaries agreed – especially in the remarkable case of Haussmann – but disagreed about just how. Pigeory at the end of his *Monuments de Paris* delineates a distinction:

The Imperial School still marches at the head of the artistic generations, stamping its character on completed or restored monuments. Freer in its preferences, not having traditions to maintain and rights to satisfy like royalty or the state, the city of Paris acts with the freedom of its judgments and taste.[63]

He continues:

Finally, private citizens, even more independent than the Conseil Municipal, show themselves less and less constrained by the academic rules. Hence the differences so easy to demonstrate between the works issuing from royal fiat, from the vote of the town counsellors, and from private wealth.[64]

What Pigeory hints at, the conseiller municipal Horace Say made clear in his *Etudes sur l'administration de la ville de Paris* of the year before.[65] He cites Hugo and Michelet to attack the neoclassicism of the Ecole des Beaux-Arts and the Conseil des Bâtiments Civils as fatuous and oppressive. His ideal is the neogothic parish church of Sainte-Clothilde, begun by the city amid great controversy in 1839–1846. But it is less the building's style than its experimental structure that Say praises. He hopes extensive use will be made of iron. He ends, "How much grander results would have been obtained if architecture only knew how to be of its place and of its time!"[66] Haussmann depicts himself during the Second Empire pushing the architects out of their old habits, forcing Victor Baltard to lighten the Halles Centrales – "du fer, du fer, rien que du fer!" – and insisting on the disarming, coquettish massing and decoration of the place du Louvre and the Tribunal de Commerce (Figures 115, 116, and 122).[67]

✳   ✳   ✳

Outside Paris there were official architects or architectural services for each department, arrondissement, and commune.[68] Organization and nomination were in the hands of the prefects and the mayors but designs had to be approved by the Conseil des Bâtiments Civils if the cost exceeded certain limits – 1,000 francs by decree of 1805; 20,000 francs by ordonnances royales of 1821 and 1822; 30,000 francs in communes and 50,000 francs in departments by law of 1837. By decentralization laws of March 25, 1852, and April 13, 1861, control was loosened.[69] From 1861 communal projects only needed central government approval if they were specially funded and then it was the financing, not the design, that was reviewed.[70]

Depending on the department or the town, the architectural service might approach the size of that of Paris or just consist of one man on retainer. The latter case was the most common, perpetuating the eighteenth-century situation of the local generalist architect-builder designing churches, hospitals, and law courts indiscriminantly as well as maintaining a varied private practice – often charging minimal fees multiplied by the volume of work. For example, Antoine Brossard (1800–c. 1880) in La Rochelle occupied the posts of *architecte de la ville* (1825, in succession to his father), *architecte-en-chef* of the department (1850–1873), and *architecte diocésain* (1854–1873), all the while carrying on a private practice in large private residences.[71] Among his projects were a seminary, a public market, a library, an insane asylum, a museum of natural history, and a lycée. Joseph-Théodore Oudet (1798–1865) in Bar-le-Duc, we are told by Gabet, erected or transformed as architect of the department of the Meuse more than sixty government structures by 1831 (his thirty-third year) including six churches, seven presbyteries, seven mairies, six fountains, two cemeteries, eight public washhouses, a seminary, a military hospital, seven bridges of one arch and four of multiple arches.[72] On the other hand, the architectural services in the largest cities like Lyons, Marseilles, and Bordeaux were divided into subdepartments and provided with consultative councils as in Paris.

✶   ✶   ✶

There was a fundamental tendency during the nineteenth century to define the architecture of some type of institution and create a special service to perfect its built form. The administration of prisons and of Paris hospitals set the pattern. Hippolyte Fortoul attempted to centralize lycée construction during his tenure as ministre de l'Instruction Publique et des Cultes and in response to the education law of March 15, 1850, in 1853 creating a commission "to consider if the buildings satisfy their function, to suggest any improvements and to prepare on the basis of these considerations a general project for a model lycée."[73] Viollet-le-Duc and Léon Vaudoyer were members. Final implementation, however, waited until the ministry of Jules Ferry and his law of August 18, 1880, that gave the minister the authority to approve building plans, in which he was advised by a commission.[74] Public libraries were another category suggesting central architectural authority but although administered by a single bureau in the Ministère de l'Instruction Publique, they seem to have been included within the broader, more heterogeneous jurisdiction of the Bâtiments Civils.[75] Nonetheless the principal libraries of Paris – the Bibliothèque Nationale, the Bibliothèque Sainte-Genevieve, and the Arsenal – were built or transformed by the Labrouste brothers, Henri the first two, Théodore the last.

IV

As telling, perhaps, as the evolution of these services paralleling the Bâtiments Civils was the emergence of two services branching from within it as specialties requiring specific training and administration, the service of the Monuments Historiques, founded in 1833, and that of the Edifices Diocésains, centralized in 1848. Both bring to the fore the issue of specific procedures and mentality developed within a narrow competence.

The facts of the history of the Monuments Historiques have often been set down.[76]. Soon after the Revolution of July 1830, the minister of the interior, the historian François Guizot, appointed (October 23) a young literatus and contributor to the *Globe*, Ludovic Vitet, to the newly created post of inspecteur général des Monuments Historiques.[77] Vitet departed on a tour of monuments in his native Normandy and presented a report proposing funding and central direction of preservation work. Predictable developments followed. Funding followed and rose from 59,104 francs in 1831 to 104,281 francs in 1833 to 200,000 francs in 1838. A circular was sent to the prefects (November 16, 1832); twenty churches were designated "monuments historiques" and the concern of the inspecteur général (November 7, 1833). On March 27, 1834, Prosper Mérimée, another literatus from the *Globe,* was named to replace Vitet who left to pursue a political career. On August 29, 1837, an oversight committee was created with a membership of architects (Caristie and Duban) and antiquaries (Baron Taylor, Auguste Leprevost, Charles Lenormant, and the Count de Montesquiou) together with Mérimée and Vitet. Initially this Commission des Monuments Historiques was presided over by Jean Vatout, president of the Conseil des Bâtiments Civils, but when in 1840 the Bâtiments Civils was transferred to the Ministère des Travaux Publics, complete freedom was gained and Vitet named president. The Commission built up a network of correspondents to report from all over France. A group of young architects were engaged for its first projects, especially Viollet-le-Duc (1814–1879), named to restore the abbey church at Vézelay in December 1839, and Jean-Baptiste Lassus (1807–1857), who in partnership were named to restore Notre-Dame in 1844. Viollet-le-Duc became the close friend and collaborator of Mérimée, in 1846–1847 even serving as chef de bureau of the Monuments Historiques (but not being named to the commission itself until 1860). As the services restoration projects expanded in numbers Viollet-le-Duc published articles on its basic materials and techniques, first in the *Annales archéologiques* (1844 ff.) then as his *Dictionnaire raisonné de l'architecture française du XIe au XVIe siècles* (1854–1869). With amazing consistency this administration continued to grow and define itself through the Second Empire and into the Third Republic under the successive direction of Emile Boeswillwald, Anatole de Baudot, and Paul Léon.

What is significant here is the very fact that this story is so well known. This is one case of the management of a government's architectural service being pictured as a distinct and advanced movement in construction and theory. In what perspective, then, does it place the other services?

To explore this, we must examine what makes this service appear cohesive. It had a clearly defined objective, the preservation of the monuments of French architectural culture; it had enlightened and well-connected leadership in Vitet, Mérimée, and Viollet-le-Duc; it had a body of practical principles worked out by its professional staff, especially Lassus and Viollet-le-Duc; and finally it created a specially trained cadre of architects and *inspecteurs*.

Its objectives had been defined by a broad popular movement before its founding in 1830. Beginning with the efforts of the Abbé Grégoire and Albert Lenoir to save the medieval monuments of France during the Revolution, it continued to spread in the writings of Victor Hugo and Jules Michelet and solidified in the Société des Antiquaires de Normandie founded in 1824 and Arcisse de Caumont's Société Française d'Archéologie of 1834 publishing the *Bulletin monumental* starting in that year. In 1830 Guizot had already created the Comité des Arts et Monuments in his ministry with a system of correspondents and a *Bulletin* (1843 ff.) to communicate information and principles of restoration in the broader field of art objects.[78] The Commission des Monuments Historiques was an inevitable extension of this, paralleling the Ecclesiological movement in Britain and the campaign to complete Cologne Cathedral in Germany.[79] In this sense the Monuments Historiques is like the Inspection Générale des Prisons (1838) and the Assistance Publique (1849): a preexisting social movement ultimately integrated into the government structure of responsibility.

Clarity of purpose produced firmness of leadership (both bureaucratic and professional) in each of these three cases, Desmetz and Blouet in prison reform; Davanne and Théodore Labrouste in the Assistance Publique; Vitet, Mérimée, and Viollet-le-Duc in the Monuments Historiques. In other branches of the government's architectural services the leaders were less committed functionaries like Jean Vatout of the Bâtiments Civils (otherwise bibiothécaire du Duc d'Orléans, then du Roi, 1822–1848, and a courtier).

The three successive architectes de l'empereur, Fontaine, Visconti, and Lefuel, defined their function no further than to oblige the sovereign – "J'ai cherché toute ma vie à obliger: ça a été ma seule jouissance" (Visconti).[80] The only large service where one might speak of a force of leadership is the Travaux de Paris under Bruyère, the Baltards, and Alphand.

Rambuteau, Say, and Haussmann felt their administration distinct from that of the state in its restoration policy, but were vague in defining principles to guide it.[81] In the cases of prisons, hospitals, and historic monuments, however, a large body of general theory was developed and specifications for application published, most impressively, for example, in Viollet-le-Duc's *Dictionnaire raisonné*. Here the Bâtiments Civils should have led. The architectural section of the Académie des Beaux-Arts existed to formulate an official doctrine and was not behind at least in the publications of its successive *secrétaires perpetuels* Quatremère de Quincy, D.-D. Raoul-Rochette, and Ernest Beulé. The Ecole des Beaux-Arts existed to teach that doctrine and was the only school providing architects for all the government services yet it failed. If Mérimée and Viollet-le-Duc were to create a cadre of architects working according to special (and different) principles, they would have to retrain them, as they did, or transform the Ecole, as they tried to do in 1863, or create a new school, as Viollet-le-Duc attempted with the Ecole Centrale d'Architecture founded in 1865.

The key to creating purpose and cohesiveness in the Service des Monuments Historiques was building up a cadre of architects. Only in 1887 was a special training course established at the Musée des Monuments Français.[82] Before that, Vitet, Mérimée, and Viollet-le-Duc could only strive to put architects sympathetic to medieval architecture and structural rationalism – Verdier, Millet, Abadie, Boeswillwald, de Baudot – in as many posts as possible and keep them fully occupied so the service might constitute a profession.[83] This was not easy, as makes clear the many conflicts with local interests or with established architects like Debret at Saint-Denis.

✻   ✻   ✻

It is interesting in this light to examine one last service carefully organized in 1848–1852, that of the Edifices Diocésains.[84] This was carried to fruition by the architecturally enlightened ministre de l'instruction publique et des cultes, Hippolyte Fortoul, whose objective again was cohesion. He had been a journalist and critic in the 1830s, then professor of literature at Toulouse (1839–1846) and dean at Aix (1846–1849), then deputy, and finally with the coup d'état of 1851, minister in the cabinet of Napoleon III.[85] During the 1830s he had been very close to the romantic rationalist architects of the circle of Henri Labrouste, especially Léonce Reynaud (1803–1880) and Léon Vaudoyer (1803–1872), with whom he collaborated on the Saint

Simonian *Encyclopédie nouvelle* (1834–1841) under the editorship of Reynaud's brother, Jean. Fortoul made himself this group of architects' spokesman, especially in his didactic *De l'Art en Allemagne* (1842). Upon assuming the direction of church construction with his ministry of December 1851 to July 7, 1856, he had a theory and a group of friends to help him realize it. However, he also inherited an existing structure and staff, and his ideas were not necessarily formulated for this specific task.

Previous to 1848 each bishop appointed his diocesan architect in charge of the cathedral, the seminary, and the episcopal palace, usually a local man, often one of feeble powers. By decree of March 7, 1848, the Commission de Répartition des Fonds et des Subventions pour les Travaux des Edifices Diocésains was created and by degrees the nomination of diocesan architects was placed in the minister's hands.[86] Fortoul, by decrees of May 7 and May 20, 1853, strengthened this and created a central oversight board, the Comité des Inspecteurs Généraux des Edifices Diocésains, the three architect members of which were to visit each diocese once every year.[87] Diocesan building was withdrawn from the competence of the Bâtiments Civils.

What is significant here is that, like Vitet and Mérimée, Fortoul freed his service from the control of the Bâtiments Civils by creating his own review council. Two of his inspecteurs généraux were his old collaborators from the 1830s, Reynaud and Vaudoyer. The third, however, was Viollet-le-Duc, whose knowledge of restoration made him unavoidable and who had been part of the Commission de Répartition (along with Fortoul and Vaudoyer) created in 1848. Personally Fortoul rejected medievalism and tried to limit Viollet-le-Duc's impact.[88] But in order to really balance Viollet-le-Duc's influence, Fortoul, Reynaud, and Vaudoyer had to offer an effective alternative and they could not. In 1850 and 1856 Reynaud published the two volumes of his compendious *Traité d'architecture*, which though awarded the Prix Bordin by the Académie was devastatingly criticized by Viollet-le-Duc.[89] In 1852–1856 Vaudoyer (with Fortoul's active participation) designed for Marseilles the one cathedral erected in France de novo in the nineteenth century, which again was submitted to telling criticism by Viollet-le-Duc and thoroughly redesigned in consequence.[90] In the end, as Jean-Michel Leniaud observes, the Edifices Diocésains became an even more effective instrument than the Monuments Historiques for the exercise of Viollet-le-Duc's ideas.

Just any theory was not sufficient to give purpose to an architectural service. The idea formulated by Fortoul, Reynaud, and Vaudoyer during the 1830s was that the Greco-Roman vocabulary was not fixed and eternal (as Quatremère de Quincy had insisted) but rather that classicism evolved from epoch to epoch, from Egyptian to Greek to Roman to medieval to Renaissance, never losing the traces of its earlier states.[91] They particularly insisted that the gothic was a local aberration in a continuous tradition of round-arched building stretching from the Roman culture through the Byzantine and Romanesque to that of the early Renaissance and quintessentially manifested in the Duomo in Florence. It was this round-arched style, inflected by both the gothic and the Greco-Roman, that should be the basis of nineteenth-century architecture and the model of Vaudoyer's Marseilles Cathedral.

Fortoul's formulation derived from a taste and from a need – undiminished comfort in the classical vocabulary and the need for an elastic transformation to meet modern expectations – but it lacked concreteness. There was no clear principle. Against Viollet-le-Duc's Cuvieresque derivation of form from structure Fortoul could only offer a mysterious evolution of shape in response to a hypothetical evolution of the mind. It was not clear how to apply this and no encyclopedia was provided like Quatremère's *Dictionnaire d'architecture* or Viollet-le-Duc's *Dictionnaire raisonné*.[92]

Fortoul did have one very powerful weapon even if he could not dominate Viollet-le-Duc with Reynaud's *Traité* or Vaudoyer's initial Marseilles design: the nomination of the *architectes diocésains* (especially the nominations to important building projects) and the allocation of funds. As posts came open, he appointed Vaudoyer *architecte diocésain* of Marseilles (July 27, 1855),[93] Labrouste of Rennes (May 12, 1854), Revoil of Montpellier, Nîmes, and Fréjus (1852), Alphonse Durand of Langres (May 25, 1852), Adolphe Lance of Sens (October 26, 1854), Jules André of Ajaccio (January 12, 1856), but also Viollet-le-Duc *architecte diocésain* of Amiens (January 30, 1854) and Carcassonne (August 26, 1856), Danjoy of Coutances (February 9, 1854), Boeswillwald of Orléans (April 12, 1855), and Verdier of Beauvais (February 9, 1854). These last three all were from the service des Monuments Historiques.

More important than the post, of course, was the opportunity to build.[94] Vaudoyer got Marseilles Cathedral; Labrouste the new seminary at Rennes; Revoil the new nave for Montpellier Cathedral. But the Monuments Historiques group were given just as much: the new nave of Moulins Cathedral by Lassus and Millet; the new seminary at Coutances by Danjoy; the restoration of Langres Cathedral by Durand, that of Troyes by Millet, and that of Périgueux by Abadie, as well as Viollet-le-Duc's completion of the restoration of Notre-Dame, facade and towers at Clermont-Ferrand, and restoration of Amiens. Fortoul's impact on the service des Edifices Diocésains was superficial. The purpose and expertise of the Monuments Historiques group permitted them to dominate the administration once it was centralized.

V

There is one last part of the array of the government's architectural services that we must note and do so with care, since it is the least studied and the most subtly effective: the agencies in charge of drawing and enforcing city plans and zoning, functioning in the municipal administrations and dependent on the bureau of Voire in the Ministry of the Interior.

The capital, Paris, of course, was the first and the most important theater of this operation. To simplify greatly, the function was divided between (1) the office of the Plan de Paris projecting the monumental and practical form of the city, (2) the service of the commissaires voyers – applying the *plan d'ensemble* in the individual quarters, enforcing height and sanitary regulations in new construction, disciplining building mass – and (3) the architectural service of the Préfecture de Police charged with the surveillance of existing construction and of street discipline.[95] The distinction between the competences of the commissaires voyers and the architects of the Préfecture of Police derived from that between *grande* and *petite voirie* – between the surveillance of national routes and of local city streets – which, because all the streets of the capital were designated *routes nationales,*[96] resulted in Paris in this distinction between the surveillance of new construction affecting street volume and that of local building condition. Each of these services expanded dramatically during the nineteenth century and evolved in its function as governmental control over city form became tighter. All were staffed almost exclusively by trained architects, cooperating with the municipal service of the Ponts et Chaussées and the Géomètre.

✳   ✳   ✳

The immediate founding legislation for the unification of Parisian city form by the establishment of the Plan de Paris was the "Déclaration du Roi sur les alignements et ouvertures dans la ville de Paris" registered at Parlement on September 7, 1784. Citing the practical and healthful advantages of Paris being *aligné* (that is, with a consistent minimum street-width line being established for all streets and with parallel sides) and the failure of earlier legislation to affect this, the Déclaration specified that a map be drawn of Paris at the expense of the landowners with the existing streets widened to at least 30 feet (9.72 meters), that all new construction or new streets be approved by *lettres patantes,* and that building height correspond to street width.[97] Punishments for infractions were set.

Now began the saga of the plan of Edme Verniquet (1727–1804), carefully recounted by Jeanne Pronteau.[98] The execution of the plan demanded in the Déclaration fell on four commissaires généraux de la Voirie. Of these, one, Verniquet, became completely obsessed in producing the most accurate map of the age. In 1785 he had himself named solely in charge of the project, given a state appropriation of 600,000 francs and a staff and space in the Couvent des Cordeliers. He was to produce a plan of Paris at the scales of 1/144 (with *alignements* indicated), 1/577, 1/577 (this second of the boulevards with trees and defining buildings indicated), and 1/1737 of the entire city and suburbs. He worked until 1795 to produce a huge drawn plan, 5.34 by 4.37 meters (13 by 17 feet), *entoilé* and mounted on an oak stretcher as well as an engraved reproduction of it (made in 1793–1799) in forty folio sheets. This was a good deal less than the array of plans specified in his contract of 1785 but nonetheless an object of remarkable accuracy and physical impressiveness.

This plan, however, was only a start: the *alignements*, which were to be worked out and imposed on future city building, had not been set, although Verniquet intended the printed map to serve as the basis of this work.[99] While he had been at work, the *alignements* had been addressed elsewhere. With the nationalization of church property by the revolutionary decrees of December 23, 1789, and after, large areas of Parisian real estate were appropriated by the state and divided and sold. In 1791 a committee of "artists" – Allais, de Wailly, Percier, Petit Radel, Gilbert, Muty (all architects) – was empaneled to produce a street map of the city showing new streets in the requisitioned areas coordinated with general ameliorations, the so-called Plan des Artistes (unfortunately destroyed in the Hôtel de Ville fire of 1871).[100] That attempt also proved in vain as the sale and subdivision of property had proceeded piecemeal, although certain height restrictions were imposed on new construction in the areas by clauses in the deeds.[101] Coordination of the *alignements* was put in the hands of the state, rather than the city, by laws of 13 Gérminal and 25 Nivôse, An 5, specifically in those of the fledgling Conseil des Bâtiments Civils. By law of September 16, 1807, this was further regularized and the inspecteur général de Gisors placed personally in authority.

Now commenced a second huge project: the actual establishment of the *alignements*, street by street. The Déclaration of 1784 had made this seem simple but, considering the impact on personal property and the size and heterogeneity of Paris, it proved vastly complex. The future street lines were projected one by one, evidently by three-man committees consisting of a representative of the state, the department, and the private owners. They were approved by the Conseil des Bâtiments Civils, then the city committee on *alignements*, then the Conseil Municipal, reviewed and approved by the Conseil d'Etat, and finally signed into law by the minister of the interior. The bureau of Voirie in the Ministry administered this and the city plans of all French towns, headed from 1844 to 1848 by Henri-Jean-Baptiste Davenne (who had first entered the service in 1814).

Verniquet's map was the foundation of this work. In March 1795, it had been moved from the Cordeliers to the Bibliothèque Nationale (much to Verniquet's distress) when the convent had been appropriated for the Ecole de Santé. Now, in 1808, it was moved to the Conseil des Bâtiments Civils's space in the Hôtel de Conti.[102] On January 1, 1823, the Conseil des Bâtiments Civils relinquished responsibility for the *alignements* to the city which, by *arrêtés* of June 14, 1823, and September 28, 1826, named *inspecteurs généraux* to continue the work.[103] Verniquet's plan now evidently moved to the Hôtel de Ville, where it was seen in 1851, but burned in 1871.[104]

The work of drawing the *alignements* continued until in his statistical report of 1823 the prefect of the Seine, Chabrol, could state that 1,024 streets had been *alignée* and that only 220 remained. At this time Théodore Jacoubet began publication of a plan of Paris in forty folio sheets showing the *alignements* in red ink.[105] Pronteau observes that certain sheets must date from the Restoration while certain others from after 1840, and four were (sheets 3–6) registered at the Dépôt Légal on August 31, 1833.

Jacoubet's atlas permits a glimpse of what sort of city form all this work had produced (see Figures 10 and 71). Essentially, it preserved the existing street pattern – widened to ease congestion – rather than projecting new through streets or monumental spaces. Exceptions were a few spaces that had been created by special legislation: the perimeter of the Palais de Justice on the Ile de la Cité, the place de la Madeleine, the place du Panthéon, the boulevard Malesherbes.[106] The one real system of urban planning is the redesigning of the streets around the gates in the Mur d'Octoi, which are corrected to be semicircular with regular *étoiles* of streets radiating from them. This represented a monumental transformation of the city's edge, but on open ground – and it was not carried out.

Louis Lazare writes of the Monarchy of July as a time of drift in the planning of Paris, attributing this to the pursuit of local interests by the elected Conseil Municipal established in 1834.[107] Haussmann in his *Mémoires* wrote with indignation of the somnolent state of the office of the Plan de Paris when he arrived at the Hôtel de Ville in June 1853.[108] There had been pressure for the creation of a coordinated plan of Paris by Jacoubet himself, the brothers Lazare, the city councillor J.-S. Lanquetin, and others.[109] In 1839 a committee had begun deliberations on the question under the chairmanship of Lanquetin.[110] There was great resistance to such a plan articulated in the late 1840s by Horace Say and by the prefect Rambuteau himself.[111]

It was thus left for Napoleon III and Haussmann to take matters dramatically in hand. As we noted in Chapter 1, Haussmann and his secretary, Merruau, record that upon his assuming office (June 29, 1853) the emperor handed the prefect a plan of Paris with a network of new streets marked in blue, red, yellow, and green, following their degree of urgency.[112] This is supposed to have been displayed on the wall in Haussmann's office (and thus, again, to have been destroyed in the 1871 fire).[113] That sketch, however, had to be projected in detail, approved by all the overlapping authorities, and finally carried into execution with special funding. Like Louis XVI in 1783, Haussmann's first step was to commission a new triangulation and mapping of Paris, carried out by Eugène Deschamps, architect (student of Henri Labrouste), in charge of the bureau of the Plan de Paris. Next specific street lines had to be set and approval gained, now simplified by the removal of the Conseil des Bâtiments Civils from the process and the transformation of the Conseil Municipal from an elective to an appointive body.

The first post-1848 *percements* – the extension of the rue de Rivoli, the boulevard de Strasbourg, the rebuilding of the Halles Centrales, the neatening of the Champs-Elysées – were authorized and paid for piecemeal. Upon taking office Haussmann evidently set to work formulating a comprehensive plan – what he came to call the Second Network – and a funding arrangement between the state and the city of Paris. This was approved in 1858 setting the new streets and providing a state contribution of fifty million francs.[114]

By this point Napoleon III's colored sketch plan had been transformed into a huge detailed sheet that Haussmann kept mounted on a folding screen in his office.[115] This map, like Verniquet's plan, Plan des Artistes, and Napoleon III's sketch, was burned in 1871. It presumably was a copy of a map of Paris in twelve folio sheets printed with various dates between 1864 and 1868, cited as the "Deschamps" plan. This was published by the city at half scale as a book in 1868 (*Atlas des 20 arrondissements de Paris*) and reproduced at small scale as the first plate of Alphand's 1867 *Promenades de Paris*.[116] The new *percements* are indicated in yellow, new state construction in pink, and projected future *percements* in outline.

*   *   *

If the bureau of the Plan de Paris maintained the diagram of the gestalt of the city, that of Voirie with its corps of commissaires voyers provided the individual *alignements* that constituted it and oversaw its execution in three dimensions.[117] As was the case with the bureau of the Plan de Paris, the records of the bureau of Voirie were mostly destroyed in the Hôtel de Ville fire of 1871 and its intervention must be reconstructed with some difficulty.[118]

Nineteenth-century regulations summarized the commissaire (or architectes) voyers's responsibilities as ensuring the "salubrité, sûreté, et l'embellissement de la ville" (1826)[119] – that is, to see that the houses were open and healthy, the streets negotiable, and the monumental urban ensemble harmonious. The last point the voyer de Royau restates in his handbook of 1879: "To create as far as is possible by the regularity of lines, a means of embellishment favorable to the progress of the arts."[120]

The service evolved greatly during the century. Before 1826 there were three architectes inspecteurs généraux of Voirie with under them four commissaires voyers aided by four gardes de la grande voirie. These agents earned 6,000, 4,000, and 2,000 francs per annum respectively and could engage in other work as long as any private work was outside their jurisdiction. (Before the Revolution one purchased this office, Verniquet paying 100,000 francs.) Their task was to establish the facade line – the *alignement* – at the commencement of new construction and to verify the height upon the completion of the facade. The annual appropriation for the service in 1818 was 36,000 francs.[121]

The Conseil des Bâtiments Civils withdrew from the administration of the Plan de Paris on January 1, 1823. The effort to finish the *plan d'ensemble* decreed in 1783 and to establish new wider *alignements* for every street led to a reorganization decreed September 28, 1826.[122] There now were to be three commissaires voyers divisionnaires, eight commissaires voyers d'arrondissements overseeing sections of the twelve old arrondissements, and eight sous-inspecteurs voyers. The new commissaires voyers were to work out the *alignements,* street by street, widening them so as to least intrude on existing construction and to obtain "regularity" – that is, parallel street facades. There were also two inspecteurs généraux to oversee the campaign, Chatillon and Lahure, for the two banks of the Seine. The total appropriation for the service rose to 95,000 francs in 1829.

L.-T.-J. Visconti (1791–1853) was one of the new commissaires voyers appointed in 1826. There are a scattering of documents relating to his function among his papers.[123] In 1841 we know he received 4,000 francs annual salary from the post. He felt it time consuming. He also claimed to have done the *alignements* of the rues du Croissant, Saint-Joseph, des Jeuneurs, and J.-J. Rousseau forming a quarter along the rue Montmartre near the Bourse (1826–1828) as well as the *alignement* of the rues des Petits Champs and du Colisée.[124] The other commissaires voyers at this time included the leading architects P.-L. Van Cleemputte, Rohault de Fleury, and A.-F.-M. Guénepin, the successful private architects Paul Lelong, F.-E. Callet, and P.-F. Levicomte, and a number of other men who (though almost all trained at the Ecole des Beaux-Arts) seem to have been of humbler accomplishment.

With the Revolution of 1830 the service was expanded once again, now to twelve commissaires voyers aided by twelve *inspecteurs* – one of each to every arrondissement. Duties were defined more strictly. A *règlement* of June 1, 1842, specified weekly inspection tours of the whole arrondissement, required the prefect's permission for absences from the city, and specified penalties for derelictions.[125] An *arrêté* of June 1, 1845, imposed residence in the voyer's jurisdiction (causing Visconti to resign his post).

This coincided with a major building boom when investors erected large numbers of broad apartment buildings on the scale that was, in the 1850s, to become the Haussmannian *immeuble*.[126] The cityscape began to change from one of winding streets hemmed in by narrow rowhouses to one of broader, parallel-sided canyons defined by broad blocks of apartment houses precisely filling the recently established building envelope – an *architecture règlementaire*, shaped by municipal ordinance. As François Loyer observes, the commissaire voyer emerged during the 1840s as the molder of urban form as a result.[127] It is unclear, however, just how far the voyer's power extended at this period. The facade and cornice lines were set in the *alignements* and the height-street width legislation as were the beveled corners – the *pans coupés* – and laws against projections into the street were applied to keep facade decoration very shallow. For example, a prefectoral *arrêté* of March 31, 1843, set the projection beyond the plane of the *alignement* at 10 centimeters for pilasters (decorating houses facing streets of 12 meters or more) and restricted balconies to a projection of 80 centimeters (on houses facing streets of 10 meters or more, the balconies no lower than 6 meters above the street).[128] However, Henri Davenne (as we have seen, chef de Bureau de la Voirie in the Ministry of the Interior) writes in his *Législation et principes de la voirie* of 1848 that the imposition of "une ordonnance uniforme et symétrique" could only be affected by the initial contract of sale of the land.[129] Otherwise he cites a case decided by the Cour de Cassation in 1840: "A mayor may not impose by *arrêté* a specific sort of architecture for the construction of houses that is not dictated by the necessity to guarantee the safety of the public way."[130] Thus during the Monarchy of July specific *servitudes* set by the city upon the sale of its own property to individuals were the only way to control more than the abstract envelope of private construction. A number of such *servitudes* had been promulgated before the Restoration – from the place des Vosges (1605) to the rue de Rivoli (1802) – and the device was to be used extensively by Haussmann – especially along the Champs-Elysées and in the quartier de l'Opéra – but the only *servitude* decreed between 1815 and 1852 was that determining construction around the place du Panthéon of July 2, 1844.[131]

Haussmann expanded the Service de Voirie and tightened things up. By *arrêtés* of December 31, 1859, and January 20, 1868, he forbade outside commitments on the part of the voyers and set higher salaries.[132] With the expansion of the city's limits and its reorganization into twenty arrondissements in 1860, he reorganized the staff into five architectes voyers divisionnaires each responsible for four arrondissements and twenty commissaires voyers d'arrondissements with twenty adjoints. Drawings of plans and elevations had to be submitted to the city for approval by law of March 26, 1852.[133] The annual appropriation for the service now rose to 220,000 francs.[134]

The *alignements* setting the widening of the existing streets had by now all been set, but a new task appeared in the Haussmannian *percements* the condemnations for which the voyers oversaw. (This was sufficiently complex that when the avenue de l'Opéra was created in the 1870s three voyers were assigned to the task.[135]) Interestingly, Haussmann specifically instructed the voyers by a circular of September 21, 1855, to intervene in the broad lines of facade design to make whole *îlots* unitary compositions:

Messieurs, until recently the Parisian administration of Voirie has left house builders the liberty to design to their own taste, within the legal height limits, the lines of balconies, cornices, and entablatures.

There has resulted from this a grave lack of harmony among contiguous constructions. Most private architects, without concerning themselves, in fact, with the principal lines of neighboring houses, often have created (by the right of *mitroyenneté*) breaks and dislocations of the dominant lines which produce the most disgraceful effects and which depreciate, from the standpoint of good taste, every house in the group of which they form a part.

The general orderly form of the city suffers from this deficiency and it is the duty of the building authorities to remedy it.

It is in order to achieve this objective that I prescribe in the sale contracts of city land the insertion of a clause that obliges the purchasers to give the same major facade lines to each block so that the continuous balconies, the cornices, and the roofs might be as *far as possible* on the same planes.

This arrangement is so essential for architectural effect that I hope to extend it to every house reconstruction made, whether for a new *percement* or for a simple rebuilding. The authority of the administration is incontestable in the former as in the latter case because by the terms of the regulations every builder must submit to the administration a dimensioned plan and section of his building and follow its prescriptions. It results from this legal obligation that the action of the Voirie may impose the harmony that I have in mind in the principal lines of the architecture of houses. (Haussmann's emphasis)[136]

Here is the heart of the matter for us: We know that through *servitudes* established on the sale of city property that Haussmann controlled the details of certain monumental ensembles like the quartier de l'Opéra. We know that the *alignements* established a certain kind of regularity – especially that of parallel street walls – and that beveled corners and consistent height limits carried this to the whole building masses. This circular raises the final but more nebulous question of to what degree the voyers could even control the decorative composition of whole *îlot* facades. It is frustrating that we do not have the office papers of a commissaire voyer or Haussmann's day-to-day notes that might document the intervention this circular suggests.

In 1869, as a young American woman, Frances Willard boarded in Paris in one of the architect Théodore Belle's new *immeubles* defining the rue des Feuillantines (now Claude Bernard) with the family of the commissaire voyer Perrot (Figures 66 and 67). She confided to her diary what she thought of his function.

Antoinette [Mrs. Perrot] told us about Monsieur Perrot – that he was the architect of the thirteenth arrondissement of Paris (Gobelins), that no one could make the least alteration in his house – to put in a window or a pane of glass, without his permission. We told her how in "free America" every man chose the materials and the style that suited him and that no one dare molest. She thought it, evidently, a liberty not to be envied, and said that we must have all sorts of odd looking streets as a result. Paris is to be beautiful – that is decreed, and no one is permitted to interfere with his private tastes or ignorances.[137]

✻   ✻   ✻

The architectural service of the Prefecture of Police made an interesting contrast to the service of Voirie in the Prefecture of the Seine. This other service was in charge of building safety, health, and neatness[138] – the things we assume the responsibility of the municipal building department. Its concern was not new construction but existing conditions. The staff had to be architects. There was a chief of the service and agents of the first and second classes, five of each in the 1860s. They could be architects of some competence – like J.-M.-V. Viel, architect of the Palais de l'Industrie of 1855, or Malary, architect of the Abbatoirs du Roule – but never men of the first rank, like the voyers Visconti, Rohault de Fleury, and Van Cleemputte. The voyers were a great deal more than mere building inspectors, and their function in the shaping of the city was characteristic and fundamental in the conception of the profession's contribution to the community.

THE FOREGROUND: THE FUNDAMENTALS OF REPRESENTATIONAL BUILDING

I

The essence of the representation of the state in architecture in France lies in the word *palais*. It derives from the Latin "palatium," which by the height of the ancient Roman Empire designated the whole palace quarter, the Palatine Hill. Amaury Duval, in his text for Louis-Pierre Baltard's *Paris et ses Monumens* (1803), points out that while in Italy the derivative "palazzo" might designate any splendid house, in French the parallel derivative "palais" retained its exclusively royal meaning and denoted either the sovereign's formal residence, as in the Palais des Tuileries, or the seat of some agency (especially of justice) acting in his name (and thus *censé sa demeure* the *Encyclopédie* notes), as in the Palais de Justice on the Ile de la Cité or the academies in the Palais du Louvre, and later the Chamber of Deputies in the Palais Bourbon, or the Senate in the Palais du Luxembourg (these last two formerly palaces of regents).[1] Basically it is, as Blondel states in his *Cours* (1771), "the residence of the monarch at the capital of his domain."[2] "In sum," concludes the *Encyclopédie* (1765), "no [private] person of whatever rank may put the title *palais* on the door of his house, but instead only *hôtel*."[3]

The word *palais* evoked the central authority. This was an absolute distinction, not one of grade: No common building could physically touch the palace. It was the nature of such a building to dominate architecturally and urbanistically. Quatremère de Quincy wrote in the third volume of his dictionary *Architecture* (1825), "A palace is thus an edifice which should elevate itself above ordinary houses and distinguish itself above them by the several means that architecture can employ to give every [construction] the

Figure 32. J.-N.-L. Durand, Palace, *Précis des leçons d'architecture données à l'Ecole Poly-technique,* 1802–1805, plate 3.

degree of richness and splendor that is appropriate."[4] Blondel specified these in his *Cours.*

The third plate (and the first plan type) in Durand's *Précis des leçons* (1802–1805) shows a palace in extensive grounds, with government ministries satellite to it amid a sunburst of *allées* (Figure 32), reshaping a project of 1785 by his master, Boullée, intended for Saint-Germain-en-Laye.[5] In 1810 Percier and Fontaine planned and began construction of such a palace for Napoleon on the Colline de Chaillot with state and municipal institutions spread out in front of it down the Champs de Mars constituting what they termed "une ville nouvelle" (Figure 33),[6] an administrative city repeating the models of Richelieu and Versailles in the seventeenth century.[7]

As the center of authority – the king – was himself the state, so the palace was the capital city. Norbert Elias in his *Höfische Gesellschaft* characterizes court society as a series of concentric repetitions of the structure of the household of the patriarch-king, the palace itself the tightest and most central, the nation the broadest, and the capital city intermediary.[8] Jean Bodin, writing in 1576 to sketch what would become absolutism, starts with the model of the family as the microcosm of the state.[9]

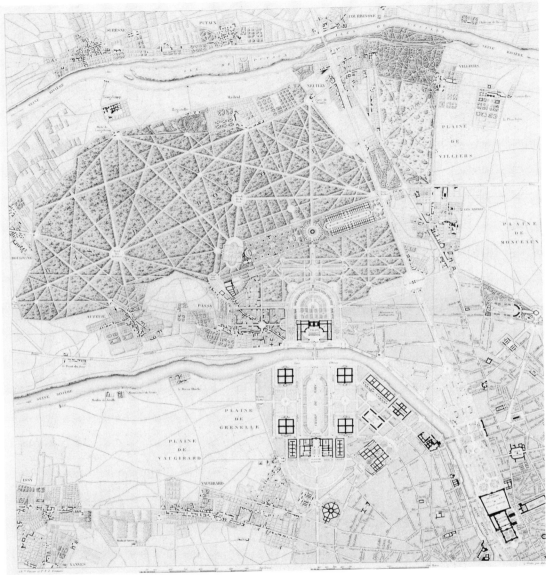

Figure 33. Charles Percier and P.-F.-L. Fontaine, project for the Palais du Roi de Rome on the Colline de Chaillot with government institutions on axis down the Champs de Mars, 1810.

II

On July 17, 18, and 20, 1848, the Conseil des Bâtiments Civils analyzed and approved in general plan (but not in detail) what was to become the definitive project by Visconti (working with his student assistant Emile Trélat, 1821–1907) for the union of the Louvre and the Tuileries to pro-

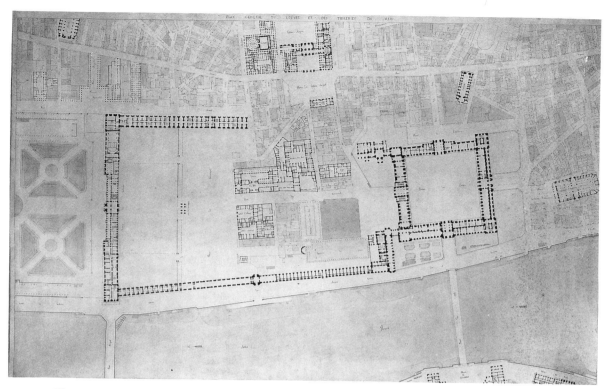

Figure 34. Percier and Fontaine, plan of the Tuileries and the Louvre in 1830.

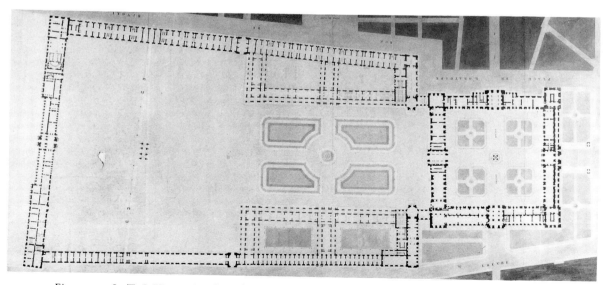

Figure 35. L.-T.-J. Visconti and Emile Trélat, project for the union of the Tuileries and the Louvre, 1848.

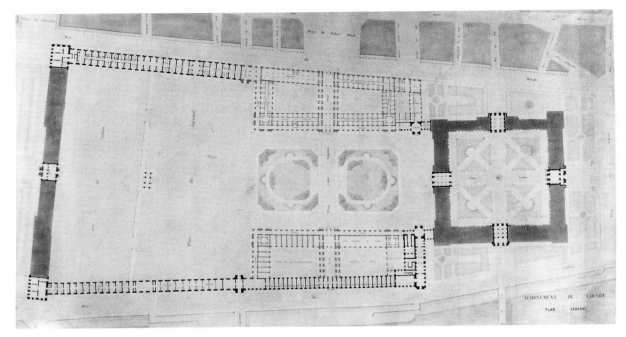

Figure 36. Visconti and Trélat, project for the union of the Tuileries and the Louvre, 1852.

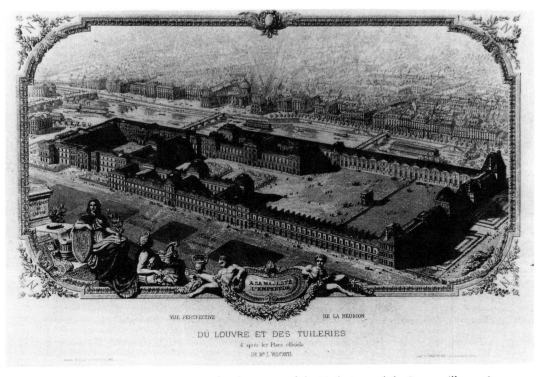

Figure 37. Visconti, project for the union of the Tuileries and the Louvre illustrating *Description du modèle,* 1853.

duce the most impressive palatial complex in Europe (Figures 34–45).[10] It was a huge project to cost thirty-one million francs – more than any single Parisian building before (with the exception of the unexecuted Palais du Roi de Rome). Combined with the extension of the rue de Rivoli to the place du Louvre, the erection of the Halles Centrales decreed in 1845 and the *percement* of the boulevard du Centre (later renamed Sébastopol), decreed September 28, 1854, this would fix the proposed "Grande Croisée" opening the heart of Paris as had been proposed in 1839. Visconti's project was to join the two palaces, suggestively close together (Figure 34), to produce a gigantic representation of the state at the city's core, fulfilling propositions of the great urbanists Henri IV, Louis XIV, and Napoleon I. In inaugurating construction in 1852 the minister of the Interior, Casabianca, emphasized that it symbolized Napoleon III's commitment to the city of Paris, in contrast to Louis-Philippe's expensive restoration of suburban Versailles.[11]

The great project had been decreed by the provisional government on March 24, 1848, as the "Palais du Peuple" to give employment to building workers and to house the Bibliothèque Nationale, the annual Salon, and the Exposition des Produits de l'Industrie. Visconti's scheme – in a slightly modified form of February 1849 – was approved by the Assemblée Nationale on October 4, 1849. Nothing was accomplished, however, until the coup d'état of December 2, 1851, after which the prince-president, Louis Bonaparte, announced his removal from the Elysée to the Tuileries (January 2, 1852) and decreed the completion of Visconti's project in five years (March 12, 1852).

The project was hurriedly analyzed again by the Conseil des Bâtiments Civils February 26–March 1, 1852 (Figure 36). Externally it had not changed from the 1848 composition. Internally, however, it was totally different, now containing the Salle des Etats for the head of state's annual convocation of the legislature, two ministries, a barracks, immense stables, a telegraph and printing office as well as museum spaces.

There had been many official and unofficial designs for this union of the Louvre and Tuileries, including one by Duban, architect of the Louvre, in competition with that of Visconti.[12] Most were quite complex, filling the space with shaped building volumes or interlocking courtyards on the model already set in Perrault's proposals of the 1670s (Figure 40). Napoleon and Fontaine, however, had early set the model for a broad open space, a gallery along the extended rue de Rivoli mirroring Henri IV's Galerie du Bord de l'Eau, with two blocks at the east end, telescoping the internal gap down from the broad Tuileries front to the narrower Louvre facade (Figures 41 and 42). A narrow gallery runs north-south through the

Figure 38. Courtyard of the New Louvre looking west toward the Tuileries, the Arc de Triomphe silhouetted on the horizon, c. 1860 (Visconti, succeeded by Hector Lefuel, architects, 1852–1857).

central space to conceal the slight misalignment of the two palaces and to define two courtyards facing each. Publishing a modified version of his project in 1833, Fontaine explained that the detailing of the Louvre and the Tuileries would be repeated in the contiguous courtyards. Of the west courtyard Fontaine wrote, "The exterior decoration . . . will repeat that of the museum wing and of the new wing [on the rue de Rivoli] almost complete in front." Of the east: "The plan and the decoration are established by the earlier constructions and by the form of the entrance pavilion of the museum [the Pavillon de l'Horloge]."[13]

This was the official, inside project, and Visconti – Percier's student and Fontaine's successor – seems to have respected it while introducing two refinements and perfecting the composition. He eliminated Fontaine's narrow north-south gallery, assuming the sheer immensity of the space opened would make the misalignment inconsequential, and found a large-scale motif common to both palaces – the striking pavilions echoing the Pavillon de l'Horloge in the Louvre and those of the Tuileries – so that in this and in his detailing he could create a synthetic vocabulary rather than merely mirror each palace in a distinct courtyard. Napoleon had wanted the space left

Figure 39. Northern block of the New Louvre (Visconti and Lefuel, 1852–1857).

clear in its full grandeur, and as recently as 1847 Pigeory had written in his *Monuments de Paris*, "This past [embodied in the palaces] has it not a striking analogy with our own epoch? Indeed! You have a magnificent parallelogram, an immense square such as there exists no equal; and you propose to diminish it by half, to change its shape, when nothing makes that necessary!"[14] Visconti claimed, just as Fontaine had, to be faithful to the decoration of the existing monuments, writing in a brochure printed to explain his project, "The character of the new architecture will be borrowed religiously

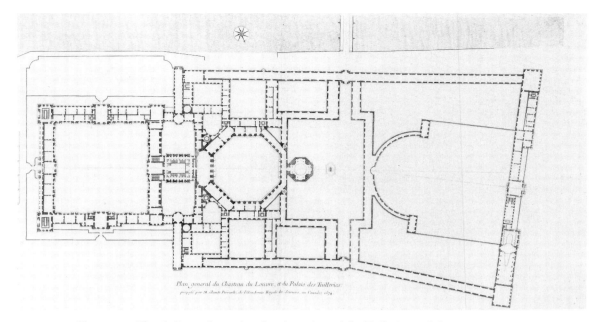

Figure 40. Claude Perrault, project for the union of the Tuileries and the Louvre, 1674. Engraving.

from the Old Louvre; all the details have already been molded and the architect will abnegate all amour propre to conserve in this monument that which was stamped upon it by his predecessors."[15]

Among Visconti's papers is a short essay reviewing the history of the design solutions to the union of the palaces that favors Percier and Fontaine's designs over more complex ones that would place "une ville au milieu du Carrousel" and putting his plan in this tradition.[16] In 1853 he wrote to a cousin in Rome, "My task is henceforth entirely set out[:] to complete the Louvre is to harmonize with what has already been built[.] [I] do not have great feats of imagination to accomplish[; I] only need good sense in order to choose well."[17]

Aside from cutting the Gordian Knot of harmonizing the two existing monuments, Visconti's opening of the single telescoping central courtyard had tremendous scenographic impact. The Tuileries when seen from the archway of the Pavillon de l'Horloge of the Louvre is precisely framed by the corner pavilions of the narrrower, eastern courtyard, then again by the north and south galleries of the broader, western space (Figure 38). Conversely, the Louvre when seen from the Tuileries is enframed by the eastern court and its lone pavilion strengthened by repetition on the two sides. In a word Visconti has extended the great west axis from the Arc de Triomphe to the central pavilion of the Tuileries now eastward, across the once-built-

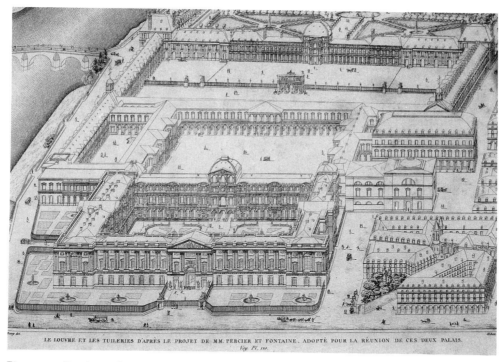

Figure 41. Percier and Fontaine, project for the union of the Tuileries and the Louvre, 1809.

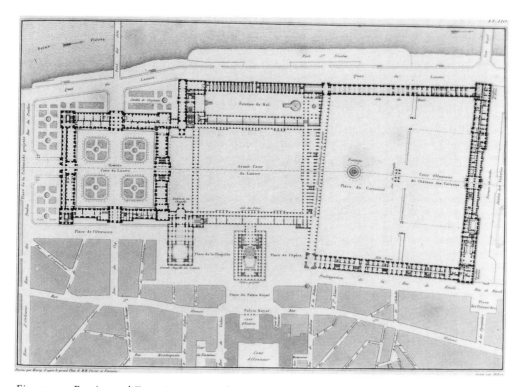

Figure 42. Percier and Fontaine, project for the union of the Tuileries and the Louvre, 1809.

83

up space between the palaces, to the Louvre, making a scenographic whole of the complex through enframing and the repetition of the pavilion motif.

Visconti thus did nothing and yet a great deal: nothing because he accepts as his "religious" duty to negate his artistic presence before the existing monuments; a great deal because in repeating, enframing, and focusing their architecture he recreates it, like a musician making variations on a theme.

An intelligent observer (and friend of Visconti),[18] Ludovic Vitet, produced a series of criticisms of the New Louvre and his analysis brings forward this fundamental quality in the work. In 1849, reading in the Chamber the report of the parliamentary committee examining the first project, Vitet insisted that the site be cleared but that no new construction be undertaken.

It is necessary, in our opinion, that a monument express something. For the Louvre to be completed it must have a serious and concrete function. There is no question of building a palace today; what would be better, what would be more frank, is thus to leave the Louvre [in its] interrupted [state]: that state will constitute historic witness that would have value and which, in my opinion, I prefer to a useless and artificial completeness. Leave the Louvre unfinished; stop work where it is. . . .[19]

The committee wanted to leave it as a monument to a dead past and pointed out that clearing would employ almost as many men as continuing construction. The Assembly, however, voted construction, 310 to 239, although it was not begun before the fall of the Republic.

In 1852, reviewing Visconti's now sanctioned plan in the *Revue contemporaine,* Vitet expressed a preference that the new construction be restricted to galleries along the north and south limits of the site and that their decoration harmonize with the modest Renaissance parts of the monument rather than with the monumental additions of Perrault.[20] In 1866 he published a lengthy review of the almost completed transformation in the *Revue des deux mondes.* There he praises Visconti for making his new construction relatively unobtrusive and excoriates his successor, Hector Lefuel (1810–1880), for elaborating the decoration and adding high mansards when he took over as architect in 1854.

One loses with him [Visconti] not only his talent, his taste, his experience, his respectful veneration of this noble monument, his scrupulous efforts above all to accommodate; one loses something more unusual, an authority sufficient to oppose the fantasies and caprices that besiege all architects. . . .[21]

Vitet's desire was to preserve the original monument as far as possible and in the end Visconti's more modest project seemed preferable to Lefuel's.

The fundamentally self-effacing, scenographic function of Visconti's

Figure 43. New Louvre, Pavillon de la Bibliothèque facing the place du Palais Royal (Visconti and Lefuel, architects, 1852–1857).

exterior may explain how he could use the scheme for the Republican "Palais du Peuple" of 1848 for what was to become the central imperial monument of the Second Empire: It was fundamentally an extension of the urban order, designed from the outside in. Inside, however, Visconti in 1852 created a second more specifically characterized spatial order laid out at right angles to the traditional west axis that controls the exterior. The extension of the rue de Rivoli created the place du Palais Royal in front of that monument's *cour d'honneur,* in place of the *château d'eau,* and beside the Grand Hôtel du Louvre. The axis of this space Visconti carried into the New Louvre at the strongly articulated Pavillon de la Bibliothèque (Figure 43), down the length of an arcaded passage through the northern block's double mass and out into what became the Cour Napoléon III under the Pavillon Richelieu, facing the Pavillon Denon (Figure 44). Although when encountered in idle promenade this last pavilion seemed just like the old Pavillon de l'Horloge or the mirroring Pavillon Richelieu, when approached ceremonially down this axis, it showed itself as the main entrance, Napoleon III himself appearing for the only time in the building's initial decoration in this pediment, conjuring peace and prosperity.[22] Beyond its door was the ceremonial carriage entrance and the

Figure 44. New Louvre, Pavillon Denon, pediment (Visconti and Lefuel, architects, 1852–1857; Charles Simart, sculptor).

stair up to the Vestibule Denon – that space extended thunderously up into the mansarded roof – and beyond that the Salle des Etats (Figure 45). This last was the most important public ceremonial space in Second Empire Paris, yet it was not expressed externally at all.

One of the most significant annual political ceremonies was the sovereign's opening of the houses of the legislature in joint session. Napoleon I in 1806 commissioned Bernard Poyet, architect of the Corps Législatif in the Palais Bourbon, to erect a monumental entrance portico reversing the building's axis to face north across the Pont de la Concorde toward the Madeleine (which had been ordered completed as a temple of glory to the French army). Napoleon henceforth opened the sessions of the Senate and Corps Législatif in the hemicycle there, by arriving ceremonially down the axis of the Tuileries gardens, turning south in the place de la Concorde, and proceeding across the bridge to dismount under a canopy on the steps of the new portico.[23] Louis XVIII went to the Palais Bourbon for his oath to uphold the constitution on October 7, 1815, and subsequently opened the session there until infirmity in 1820 forced him to call the legislators to the Grande Salle of the Louvre. Louis-Philippe also opened the session at the Palais Bourbon, arriving from the Tuileries by the Pont de la Concorde, but riding in a carriage around into the newly completed courtyard on the south. Napoleon III, however, insisted that the legislators come to him for their annual instruction, held first in the Salle des Maréchaux in the Tui-

Figure 45. New Louvre, Salle des Etats, 1859 (Charles Mueller, painter).

leries, then in this new Salle des Etats dominating the south wing of the New Louvre. At the end of the Second Empire he built another, larger Salle des Etats in the rebuilt Galerie du Bord de l'Eau.[24] The New Louvre was the ultimate seat of authority in the new Second Empire Paris.

❊   ❊   ❊

All of the significant representational projects from the Revolution of 1830 to the initiation of the New Louvre had been alterations and extensions of existing monuments executed with loudly proclaimed historical conscious-ness and respect. Late in 1834 Adolphe Thiers, then minister of the interior, asked Alphonse de Gisors to present a project for the extension of Salomon de Brosse's Luxembourg to expand the deliberative chamber and to provide more ceremonial and bureaucratic space.[25] This was executed at a cost of three million francs in 1836–1841 by reproducing de Brosse's facade with new stone set 30 meters southward into the garden and demanding two additional corner pavilions. Although the original facade survives built over inside the new structure, it was carefully reproduced in the new construc-

Figure 46. Luxembourg Palace, garden (south) facade (Salomon de Brosse, architect, 1615–1620).

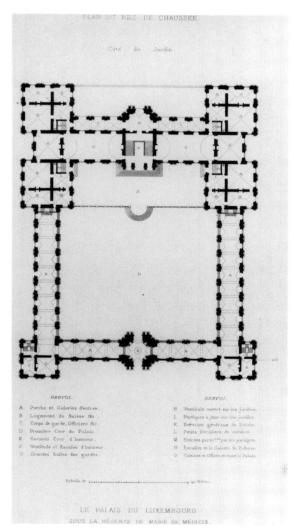

Figure 47. Luxembourg Palace, plan (Salomon de Brosse, architect, 1615–1620).

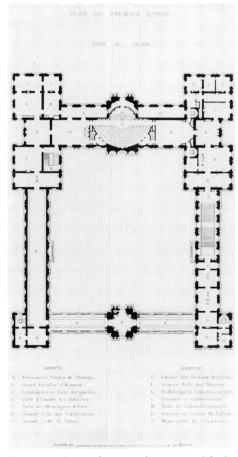

Figure 48. Luxembourg Palace as modified 1795–1804. Plan.

Figure 49. Luxembourg Palace as extended 1836–1841, garden (south) facade (Alphonse de Gisors, architect).

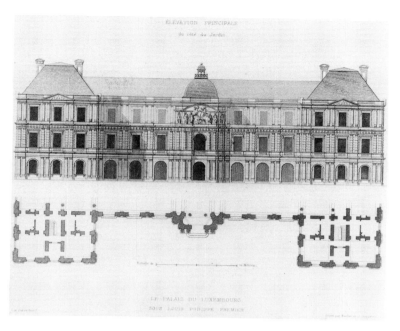

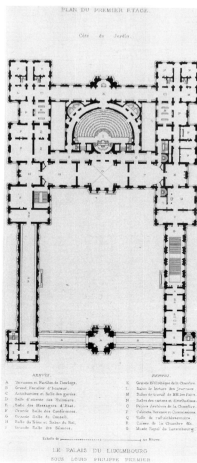

Figure 50. Luxembourg Palace as extended 1836–1841. Plan (Alphonse de Gisors, architect).

tion, which otherwise has no overt nineteenth-century signature (Figures 46 and 50). Publishing a history of the building and his extension in 1847 de Gisors seems oblivious of the scale of his alterations and presents the structure as a living historic monument of which he was merely the guardian. He ends: "Most of these events are already far in our past, but the palace of Marie, as grand and as magnificent as ever, is here to perpetuate their memory."[26] Interestingly, another architect, Jean-Louis Provost, initially asked in 1835 to carry out these alterations, had refused the commission rather than alter such an important monument.[27]

The Hôtel de Ville was expanded in the manner of the Luxembourg, only

Figure 51. Hôtel de Ville as extended, 1837–1841 (Hippolyte Godde and J.-B.-C. Lesueur, architects). Destroyed 1871.

(Opposite above) Figure 52. Axial staircase erected in the courtyard of Godde and Lesueur's Hôtel de Ville, 1855 (Victor Baltard, architect, assisted by Max Vauthier; A.-J.-B. Lechesne, sculptor). Destroyed 1871.
(Opposite below) Figure 53. Axial staircase in the courtyard of Godde and Lesueur's Hôtel de Ville, 1855 (Victor Baltard, architect, assisted by Max Vauthier, A.-J.-B. Lechesne, sculptor). Destroyed 1871.

103

104

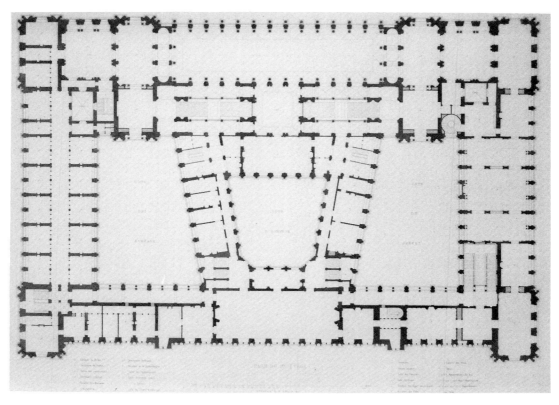

Figure 54. Hôtel de Ville as extended, 1837–1841. Plan of second floor.

on an even larger scale (costing twelve million francs initially with additional millions for decoration).[28] Three wings were erected by Hippolyte Godde (1781–1869) and J.-B.-C. Lesueur (1792–1883) in 1837–1841 beside and behind the seventeenth-century building (Figures 51–53). The new parts religiously repeated the older construction's *ordonnance*. The structure was published in two folio volumes in 1846–1864 by Victor Calliat whose text, like de Gisors', recounts the whole history of the monument and emphasizes the faithfulness of the new construction to the old. "The lines of the architecture of the new block reflect in perfect symmetry those of the old constructions; even the details of these last have been reproduced in some of the new parts. . . ."[29] Pigeory remarked, "Old buildings are not to be transplanted any more than old trees and, in the interest of art, it is advantageous that the Hôtel de Ville might be finished while remaining on the site that it has traditionally occupied."[30]

The contemporaneous plans for the extension of the Palais de Justice were more complex, embracing the eighteenth-century Cour de Mai, the

Renaissance Salle des Pas Perdus (again by de Brosse), and the medieval Conciergerie and Sainte-Chapelle.[31] The architect, Jean-Nicolas Huyot (1780–1840), in his first project of 1835, applied gothic ornament to the buildings to be erected around the Sainte-Chapelle, regularized the Conciergerie with a new tower at the west, and drew the complex together into a monumental composition at the new west facade in the pavilioned baroque style of the Cour de Mai (Figures 55 and 56).[32] Contemporary journals did not see this as pastiche but rather as supreme architectural diplomacy.[33] The *Journal des débats* intoned, "The knowledge and skill of the architect have achieved a whole from so many different parts. His elastic and fertile talent is adapted to all these variations, to the satisfaction of all these proprieties, to all the needs of the magistrature which has been judiciously consulted on every point."[34] The Conseil des Bâtiments Civils, however, was more difficult to convince, ruling out the gothic decoration and questioning the prominence of the pavilion.[35]

The most calculated example of respectful alteration in the representational cityscape of mid-century Paris was Visconti's own Tomb of Napoleon of 1841–1864 under Jules Hardouin Mansart's Dôme des Invalides.[36] Duban was initially named architect, but Visconti won the commission when a competition was instituted (or at least gave the jurors what they told him they wanted) by lowering the sarcophagus into a circular crypt opened in the floor so as not to disrupt the Louis XIV surroundings. (Political observers understood this to be Louis-Philippe's way of subtly diminishing the triumphant quality of the monument.[37])

In the introduction to his *Monuments de Paris* of 1847 Félix Pigeory evokes the new monumental order of the city sketched by Napoleon, denounces the Restoration for abandoning the project to instead concentrate on religious and expiatory fragments, and then proclaims the Monarchy of July's faithfulness to the monumental tradition:

Content to build calvaries and expiatory chapels, [the Restoration] left incomplete all the monuments begun under the Empire, and it could not have been otherwise, because, rejecting any sympathy with the deeds accomplished during that period, . . . the statesmen of that time could not consent to contribute to the apotheosis of the sovereign that they called a fallen usurper by completing or terminating the monuments of his reign.

The Revolution of July, in suppressing a dynasty, established a principle. It reconstructed the broken chain of social conquests realized since the beginning of the century; and by the very fact that it adopted all the examples, all the glories of the past, without repudiating a single one of the traditions sanctioned by the national will, it undertook to give just satisfaction to all. From that moment, no equivocation, no uncertainty. The rehabilitation of the memory of Napoleon was soon followed by that of the great feats of arms which illuminated the Republic and the Empire.

Figure 55. Jean-Nicolas Huyot, project for the extension of the Palais de Justice, 1835–1838.

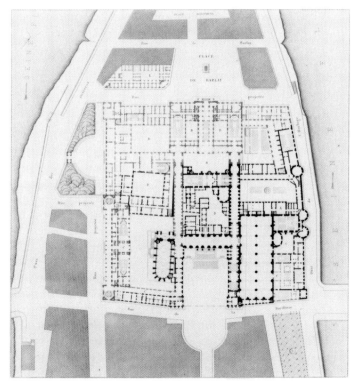

Figure 56. Jean-Nicolas Huyot, project for the extension of the
Palais de Justice, 1835–1838. Plan.

A new era opened for architecture and it was given back the place it had lost. . . .
As in all popular movements, that of July began, by destruction, its task, which was
to repair and complete what of beauty and utility others had established.[38]

*   *   *

In early 1833, a comprehensive 100 million franc appropriation bill
intended to revive the postrevolutionary economy provided special credits
for roads, canals, coastal improvements, and the representational buildings
of Paris was presented to the Chamber of Deputies by Adolphe Thiers, ministre de commerce et des travaux publics.[39] Thiers had distinguished himself
during the Restoration with a popular and powerful *Histoire de la Révolution* (as well as a *Salon,* in 1822) and he would become premier, lead the
Orleanist opposition during the Second Empire, and finally become the Versailles premier in 1871.[40]

The 1833 bill made possible the completion or transformation of the
half-finished Napoleonic monuments of the capital – the Arc de Triomphe, the Madeleine, the Panthéon, the Chamber of Deputies, Saint-Denis,
the Monument de la Bastille, the Rive Gauche ministry building called the
"Palais d'Orsay" – as well as the completion (or, in some cases, initiation)
of instructional structures – the Musée de l'Histoire Naturelle, the Ecole
des Beaux-Arts, the Collège de France, the Institut, the Archives
Nationales, the Institut des Sourds-Muets. (One unexecuted part of the
bill was 18 million francs for the completion of the Louvre with the Bibliothèque Nationale in Fontaine's transverse gallery proposed dividing the
eastern and western courtyards.) A number of these buildings involved
major decorative programs, which Thiers also saw funded and, in large
part, administered.

This incident is interesting in permitting us a glimpse of the government
making a large coordinated representational statement on the face of Paris,
in part to restart the economy, in part to assert the new authority. Thiers
was an intelligent and bold politician wanting to make a mark; one would
expect his choice of artists to be striking and the results remarkable. Yet, in
fact, while he did make a few bold appointments – Rude at the Arc de Triomphe (along with Etex and Cortot), Duc at the Bastille, Duban at the
Ecole des Beaux-Arts, and Letarouilly at the Collège de France – he by and
large kept the architects already in place and selected artists eclectically,
from the whole span of schools and degrees of talent.[41] His most striking
accomplishment was ephemeral: appointing Duban to design the decorations for the celebration of the Revolution of July in 1833 and giving him
580,000 francs to execute the elaborate "Moorish" fantasies.[42] In the end
the power of Thiers's gesture lay in his merely making it, in committing the

government to the program that in 1847 Pigeory would proudly proclaim in his *Monuments de Paris,* the commemoration of the Revolution and Napoleon and the service of the people of Paris. His accomplishment was to write that history in stone, one with the inflections and eclecticism characteristic of his principles and of the Monarchy of July.[43]

✳   ✳   ✳

The method of accomplishing this inflection and expansion of the monumental order of Paris I have called "scenographic" in the case of Visconti's central monument. That is, the designer enframes, repeats, and clarifies the architectural themes discovered in his site. Duban – the man initially named architect of both the Tomb of Napoleon and the Louvre project – presented this solution in his completion of the Ecole des Beaux-Arts (Figure 2; 1832–1840), as we noted in Chapter 1. The tableau was precisely calculated to work when seen on axis from the gate on the rue Bonaparte, as Visconti's New Louvre was from the Pavillon de l'Horloge.

Jacoubet's 1830s *Atlas* shows a series of such shaped, telescoping spaces recently cut into the medieval texture of Paris, like Jules de Joly's constructions in the Palais Bourbon or Letarouilly's exquisite courtyard extension of the Collège de France (Figure 3). Huyot proposed to evolve it into what might have been the most powerful scenographic composition in Paris in his western extension of the Palais de Justice into the seventeenth-century place Dauphine. Looking eastward from the statue of Henri IV on the island's tip the place Dauphine would have opened out from the narrow west aperture, then closed again to enframe Huyot's tall, powerful pavilion (Figures 55 and 56). One might also look westward from that pavilion; a writer for the *Journal des débats* evokes this tableau: "From this entrance, which will be marked by all appropriate grandeur, the glance, crossing the place Dauphine, will espy the statue on the Pont Neuf, the Louvre, and the Tuileries."[44]

Such scenographic schemes only work when seen from certain points along a central axis: the gate on the rue Bonaparte at the Ecole; the pavilion threshold at the projected Palais de Justice. This is an essentially ceremonial method of composition. In the case of Visconti's New Louvre the composition flashes into focus at the central portal of the Pavillon de l'Horloge and the Tuileries (Figure 38). As we saw at the beginning of this section, the axis thus defined was already the ceremonial spine of royal Paris. Napoleon had concretized it with the Arc de Triomphe, silhouetted on the hilltop to the west. Louis-Philippe, for all of his lack of progress in uniting the palaces, had articulated the axis further with an equestrian statue of the Duc d'Orléans in the center of the Louvre courtyard and a projected triumphal arch marking where it passed from the Tuileries gardens into the place de la

Concorde. (The arch, significantly, was not to be a new construction like the Arc du Carrousel, but an ancient Roman one transported in pieces from Djemila in Algeria.) Fontaine, however, had already erected a temporary arch on this site in 1810 for Napoleon's marriage to Marie-Louise.[45] The axis would then have passed through the thin Obelisk de Luxor (erected in 1836) to mount the Champs-Elysées and end in the Arc de Triomphe (completed likewise in 1836). The Napoleonic cross axis pivoted on the obelisk and joined the Madeleine (dedicated in 1840) with the Chamber of Deputies (rebuilt 1828–1832). Thiers had completed this part of the composition with his bill of 1833.

Equally important were the prefect Rambuteau's efforts to continue the axis eastward, up to the Hôtel de Ville (and even beyond). A "rue Louis-Philippe" was to isolate the Louvre and link it to the Hôtel de Ville with the Tour Saint-Jacques (purchased by the city in 1836) as an ornament. The rebuilt Hôtel de Ville would terminate the great cermonial way in a spreading *place* and an extensive suite of ceremonial chambers, more majestic than that of the Tuileries and ultimately equaled only by the Salle des Etats in the New Louvre. It was in the Hôtel de Ville that the leading citizens of Paris received their sovereign, celebrated events of his succession, and honored state visitors.[46]

To justify the expansion of the Hôtel de Ville Rambuteau cited, among other things, the expense of temporary pavilions that had been erected in the place de Grève.[47] Indeed, the expanded building was essentially a huge reception suite (Figure 54). To fulfill this function an enfilade of five salons was erected across the piano nobile behind the old structure and beyond it at both ends, the 160-foot long Galerie des Fêtes in the center with the Salon Louis-Philippe (later de la Paix) opening to the north and the Salon Napoléon to the south. Joining this enfilade to the old building was an elaborate double staircase leading into two other salons. The Galerie de Fêtes opened at its cross axis into the Salle du Conseil Municipal, looking out in the courtyard of the old structure. A new wing of offices filled out the block at the north; the prefect's apartments balanced that at the south, facing the quai across a private garden.

Guests were to arrive by carriage through the new north and south courtyards (the "Cour des Bureaux" and the "Cour du Préfet"), alight in the cavernous space under the salons at the back, and mount the stairs. In 1855 an important change was made when Baltard covered the old central courtyard with an iron and glass roof and erected beneath it an elaborately carved ceremonial staircase mounting directly to the Salle du Conseil Municipal, now functioning as an introductory salon on the cross axis of the Galerie des Fêtes (Figures 52 and 53).[48] Queen Victoria, visiting the Hôtel de Ville on August 23, 1855, was one of the first to use this approach.[49] This brought things back decisively to the single, central west cut axis, extended toward the Louvre from the place de Grève by the avenue Victoria cut through to the Châtelet in 1855.

Bit by bit, until 1855 and the completion of Baltard's staircase in the Hôtel de Ville, the great west axis was extended, focused, and refined. All of this and more had been envisioned by the seminal Fontaine. He ends his discussion of the Louvre in his 1833 *Résidences de souverains* by walking the reader down the completed axis from east to west across Paris.

When all of these projects will have been realized, what will be the impressions of a visitor who, entering Paris for the first time down the long avenue de Vincennes, after having remarked the tall columns of the Barrière du Trône, espies at the end of a broad street the fountain of the Bastille and the great canal of which it appears the source? What sensation will he experience when after having crossed squares embellished with useful monuments, after having seen the bridges and the new quais along the course of the Seine, he arrives down a broad and splendid avenue before the colonnade of the Louvre? When he then traverses the great courtyard of this palace and the even larger *avant-cour*, the vestibule and the portico of the place du Carrousel, passing under the Arc du Carrousel, after passing the fountains marking the two axes, when entering the *cour d'honneur* of the Tuileries Palace and from there the garden, moving still in the same direction across the Place Louis XV [place de la Concorde] and up the Champs-Elysées to the Barrière de Chaillot [place de l'Etoile], he stops beneath the immense Arc de Triomphe built to the glory of the French armies, on the summit of the Montagne des Champs-Elysées, what will be his thought about such a number of marvels? What will he think of this combination of prodigious accomplishments that this short traversal of the city has offered him the astonishing spectacle? Surely, even in spite of the most hostile predispositions, he could not prevent himself from confessing that no where else in the world there exists a more admirable place; he would congratulate the French on having been governed successively since Henri IV by sovereigns who, despite reverses and disasters, have known how to make them enjoy the benefits of brilliant civilization, and who, through a sincere love of their country, by the advantages of wise economizing, have found means to make good the misfortunes with which fate has so many times encumbered them.[50]

Fontaine was envisioning in monumental terms an axis the Revolution had traced in a brilliantly hopeful gesture when the first Constitution of 1791 was proclaimed from a hot air balloon following this route in the air. "Standing upright, bareheaded, holding the constitution in my hand, I passed straight over the Champs-Elysées, the Tuileries, the Louvre, the rue du Faubourg Saint-Antoine," wrote the anonymous aeronaut.[51]

III

The ceremonial axes and the representational monuments orienting them came alive in the processions and ceremonies still at the center of French political display. These, however, changed tellingly in their nature and in their relationship to the cityscape as the century progressed and the city was transformed.

✳   ✳   ✳

On May 3, 1814, Louis XVI's brother, Louis XVIII, entered Paris to restore the Bourbon monarchy.[52] The ceremony had been carefully if swiftly planned by F.-J. Bélanger, reappointed to his prerevolutionary post, architecte des fêtes et cérémonies. As a condition for this, on May 2, preparing for his entry at Saint-Ouen outside the *barrières* on the route de Saint-Denis, the Bourbon pretender issued a declaration accepting the constitution promulgated by the Napoleonic Senate (which, in the Roman tradition, had been given the power to name the sovereign) on April 6, four days after it had declared the emperor *déchu*. Louis XVIII rode in procession to the seventeenth-century arch at the Porte Saint-Denis where he was received by the Napoleonic prefect of the Seine, Chabrol, the mayors of the twelve arrondissements, and the Conseil Municipal. Chabrol made a short discourse citing the reerection of the statue of Henri IV on the Pont Neuf, destroyed by Napoleon and recreated using the metal from the Napoleon statue on the Colonne Vendôme. Louis then descended the rue Saint-Denis to the Halles where two orchestras played at the Marché des Innocents and he received the *Dames de la Halle* (the corporation of the merchants of the Halles). From there his procession proceeded to Notre-Dame where Louis was received by the chapter, Abbé de la Myre greeting him, "The God of Saint-Louis has established your throne, will reestablish his altars. *Dieu et Roi*, that is our motto. . . ."[53] Led to the sanctuary under a canopy held by four canons, the king knelt and prayed in silence for more than a quarter hour. We read, "All the bodies of the State and the high nobility of the kingdom were present."[54] A *Te Deum* followed, then twice "Domine, salvem fac Regem nostrum Ludovicum," finally tumultuous cries of "Vive le Roi!" The king then proceeded down the Ile de la Cité to the Pont Neuf, and the reerected statue of Henri IV, then crossed to take possession again of the Tuileries for the Bourbon line.

*　　*　　*

Sixteen years later the junior branch of the Bourbon line replaced the senior with a series of actions using the city very differently.[55] At 2 P.M., July 31, 1830, Louis-Philippe d'Orléans, Charles X's cousin and son of a regicide, was proclaimed lieutenant-general of the kingdom at the central window of the Hôtel de Ville.[56] The event had been very quickly arranged. The king's suspension of the Constitution had caused the people of Paris to erect barricades and, on July 30, had forced Charles X to flee Saint-Cloud. Lafayette had gathered a provisional government at the Hôtel de Ville, where revolutionary governments were to proclaim themselves again in 1848, 1870, and 1871. On condition that he accept the modified and strengthened Constitution, they offered Louis-Philippe their nomination as head of state (lieutenant-general until Charles X should abdicate) on August 6 so that Louis-Philippe could be proclaimed king by the Senate. In the interim, on Wednesday, August 4, Louis-Philippe accompanied by his sons presented himself to his subjects to be. He met his sons, officers in the army hurrying to Paris, at the place du Trône and reviewed troops gone over to the new government. (In 1662 Louis XIV had entered Paris in particular splendor from this point and had subsequently begun construction of a triumphal arch there.[57]) From there they proceeded through the eastern suburbs to the boulevards at the faubourg Saint-Antoine, past the half-dismantled barricades. A band of the Garde Nationale led the way, followed by the principals, then a mass of Parisians. A black and white banner led the way inscribed, "La charte: vaincre ou mourir" – "The Constitution: victory or death." We read, "No troops formed a cordon, not even the Garde Nationale; thus the people pressed forward desiring, not [only] to see, but to touch the prince. There was nothing but handshaking all along the route. The horses could barely move. Workers took them by the bridle and the two princes had both their hands entwined with those of the people, who came on in a prodigious crowd."[58] This ad hoc procession proceeded around the boulevards and down the rue de la Paix into the place Vendôme dominated by the Colonne de la Grande Armée with its scroll of military accomplishments, topped now only with a fleur de lys. "M. the Duc d'Orléans bowed several times before the column . . . and the acclamations redoubled."[59] The cavalcade moved on to the Palais Royal, the Orleans city residence. The liberal *Journal des débats* ends its description of these events insisting that their democratic point was successful:

A remarkable thing: during the long procession and amid extraordinary enthusiasm, the only cries heard were 'Vive la charte', Vive le duc d'Orleans." The word republic was not once pronounced, even in the [working class] suburbs; and by a miraculous instinct for legal form, the people, who mostly forbore to cry "Vive Louis Philippe VII!," seemed to wish not to precipitate the decision of the Chambers, to whom alone belongs the right to place on another head – on condition of the maintenance and extension of our liberties – the crown that the senior branch of the Bourbons has permitted to fall to earth and which the people will never consent to offer.[60]

On August 9 Louis-Philippe read Charles X's letter of abdication to the Chamber of Deputies and accepted their appointment as king with an oath to uphold the modified Constitution.[61]

✳   ✳   ✳

There were two axes of ceremonial approach to Paris, the old medieval one from the north and the Royal Abbey of Saint-Denis followed by Louis XVIII, and the newer one from the east, in the steps of Louis XIV, on the one hand, and of the Revolution, around the boulevards, on the other. It was just at this time, however, that a third axis began to assert itself, that from the west, marked out when Chalgrin convinced Napoleon to shift the Arc de Triomphe from the place de la Bastille to the porte de Neuilly.[62]

On May 30, 1837, the Duc d'Orléans, Louis-Philippe's eldest son and heir apparent, married Helena of Mecklenberg in civil and religious ceremonies at Fontainebleau.[63] The expanded royal family then set out on a progress – enthusiastically celebrated along its route, we are told – up the west bank of the Seine to Longjumeau above Paris, then (on Sunday, June 4) around the city to the Orleans villa at Neuilly. Reorganized, the king and his sons, accompanying a carriage with the queen and the new princess, rode to the Arc de Triomphe that had just been completed after thirty years of sporadic construction.[64] The prefect and the Conseil Municipal received them there amid a circle of the Garde Nationale. Louis-Philippe declared, "The City of Paris knows my affection for her! I am pleased and proud to present to her my adopted daughter. May Parisians hold her in affection!"[65] The procession thence proceeded down the axis of the Champs-Elysées, through the Tuileries gardens to the central pavilion of the palace, the Pavillon de l'Horloge. The principals then turned to face the newly erected obelisk of the place de la Concorde to review a two-hour military parade. Retreating into the Tuileries, the princess was called to the window of the Pavillon de l'Horloge by the crowd. Louis-Philippe shouted in response, "I thank you with all my heart, my friends! I am deeply touched by your reception. . . ."[66] On June 15 a grand fete was offered at the Hôtel de Ville.

Six years later, on July 24, 1842, the Duc d'Orléans returned down the same route, dead from a riding accident on the way to Neuilly. His body was carried in military procession past the Tuileries to Notre-Dame where the funeral service was held August 3. A triumphal arch was projected to preserve his memory at the center of the east side of the Place de la concorde where the axis of the Champs-Elysées becomes that of the Tuileries gardens.

✳   ✳   ✳

Louis Bonaparte played out his political theater in this setting, using the popular boulevards and the ceremonial west axis as his needs demanded.

On Thursday, December 2, 1852, Louis Bonaparte, nephew of Napoleon, entered Paris for the first time as Napoleon III.[67] This was the anniversary of Austerlitz, of Napoleon's *sacre*, and of Louis Bonaparte's coup d'état the year before.

The evening before the entire Senate and the Corps Législatif had traveled to the palace at Saint-Cloud – "en costume," "escortés par des détachements de cavalerie" – to present the prince-president with the positive results of the plebiscite on whether the Empire should be reestablished, validated by the Corps Législatif earlier that evening. Louis Bonaparte received their report declaring, "The new reign that you inaugurate today . . . you have just declared to be the lawful result of the wishes of a whole population who consolidate in tranquility what they initiated amid agitation."[68]

At 10:00 A.M., December 2, the prefect of the Seine, Jean-Jacques Berger, after a 101-gun salute, read the proclamation of the Empire from a pavilion erected in front of the Hôtel de Ville, decorated with the tricolor and the emblem N III.[69] At noon the new emperor left Saint-Cloud with a large military escort, dressed in the uniform of général-en-chef of the army and wearing the *grand cordon* of the Légion d'Honneur. He traversed the Bois de Boulogne to the Arc de Triomphe. The prefects of the Seine and of the police as well as the commander of the Paris garrison met him there. After a greeting, the emperor descended the Champs-Elysées between a double row of troops, circled the place de la Concorde to inspect the display, then rode up the axis of the Tuileries gardens to dismount and enter the central Pavillon de l'Horloge to a 101-gun salute from the Invalides, Montmartre, and the Place du Trône. He then acknowledged the acclamation of the troops in the gardens and in the courtyard from the east and west windows. After this he sat down to a state banquet while Persigny, minister of the interior, read the proclamation of the Empire to the troops in the place de la Concorde.

There was no church service. The next day, December 3, Napoleon III visited the military and indigent patients at the Val de Grâce and the Hôtel Dieu.[70]

However, somewhat as in the case of Louis-Philippe, this formal ceremony was secondary to a previous, more spontaneous one in the boulevards. In September and October of that year, after his coup d'état of December 2, 1851, but while still prince-president, Louis Bonaparte had made a theatrical tour through the southern part of France. His visits to Marseilles and Bordeaux had been particularly triumphant (the latter stage managed by the prefect Georges Haussmann who won Louis's firm admiration).[71] He returned to Paris on October 13. He arrived by train from Orléans at the Gare d'Orléans (erected 1840–1843) on the quai d'Austerlitz where – inside the decorated train shed – he was received by the Senate, the Corps Législatif, and the Conseil d'Etat as well as by the commanders of the army, navy, police, prefects and members of the Institut, and Légion d'Honneur.[72] Prince Jérôme Bonaparte, his uncle who had stood in Louis's stead during the trip, led the reception. A canon salute and vocal cantatas marked the prince-president's emergence from his car and he warmly embraced the leading men receiving him.

The railroad changed the topography of a Parisian *entrée*, but only slightly. Louis Bonaparte now mounted on horseback and rode out of the station yard with an escort of dignitaries and officers to the place Valhumbert facing it at the bottom of the Jardin des Plantes. Here he was greeted by the city and the prefect Berger delivered a short discourse. Meanwhile a large procession was forming with squadrons of cavalry, mounted artillery, and police. Other troops lined the boulevards, and temporary arches were found to have been erected straddling the thoroughfare bearing explanatory inscriptions like this:

LES ARTISTES D'HIPPODROME ET DES ARÈNES À NAPOLÉON III – 1852 – LA DIRECTION DES THÉÂTRES RÉUNIS, LE CIRQUE, LES FOLIES, LES FUNAMBULES, LES LAZARI, LA GAITÉ, LES DÉLASSEMENTS, LES CONCERTS.

The parade proceeded across the Seine and down the canal Saint-Martin to the place de la Bastille, then around the boulevards past the theaters to the place de la Concorde and finally down the axis of the Tuileries gardens into the royal residence. A final arch at the Tuileries grill facing the place de la Concorde gave an official summary of Louis Bonaparte's pretenses:

A NAPOLÉON III
EMPEREUR
ET SAUVEUR DE LA CIVILIZATION MODERNE
PROTECTEUR DES ARTS ET DES SCIENCES
DE L'AGRICULTEUR, DE L'INDUSTRIE ET DU COMMERCE,
LES OUVRIERS RECONNAISSANTS.

CONSTITUTION DE L'AN VIII
CONSTITUTION DE L'AN 1852
CONVERSION DES RENTES
CRÉDIT FONCIER

TRAVAUX D'UTILITÉ
CHEMINS DE FER
ACHÈVEMENT DU LOUVRE
RUE DE RIVOLI

L'Illustration noted of the mysterious authorship of this demonstration, "*Le Patrie* has announced that this fine triumph was owed to the efforts of the Ministre d'Etat; but the *Moniteur*, correcting this bit of news, declared that all the demonstrations by the citizens of Paris were spontaneous and that the government had done nothing to inspire them."[73]

✼   ✼   ✼

The review of these events highlights the ceremonial topography of Paris. It emerges as a complex and shifting one: Different events touch on different places and monuments; different regimes mount similar ceremonies differently; points of entry evolve with the transportation system; monuments are rebuilt or constructed and participate in new ways. Yet a basic structure emerges: the north, east, and west axes; the Tuileries, the Hôtel de Ville, Saint-Denis, Notre-Dame; les Halles, the boulevards; the Madeleine, the Chamber of Deputies. These were the chords from which successive ceremonial melodies were composed.

One last ceremony comes beyond the period defined in this book, but powerfully summarizes the symbolization of places we have seen emerging. On May 22, 1885, Victor Hugo died, eighty-three years old, the great writer of the Restoration and the Monarchy of July, as well as the adamant exile of the Second Empire. A state funeral was proclaimed for June 1 and Charles Garnier named to design it.[74] The lying in state was to be under the Arc de Triomphe. Garnier proposed to close three sides of the Arch and to erect a huge catafalque in the archway open eastward down the Champs-Elysées. Masts with the banner of Paris and Hugo's escutcheon were to ring the place de l'Etoile. A huge black velum was to be draped asymmetrically across the mass of the Arch. After a memorial service (that was civil at Hugo's specification) the body was to be carried in a *corbillard des pauvres* (again at Hugo's wish) down the Champs-Elysées to the playing of Saint-Saens's "Hymne à Victor Hugo" by military bands. From the place de la Concorde it was to proceed around the boulevards to the place de la République (created during the Second Empire and to be the site of the democratic choral Orphaeum) to pause for funeral anthems sung by the combined choruses of the Opéra, the Conservatoires, and the Opéra Comique. It would then move on through the poor eastern quarters to Père-Lachaise.

This, in fact, was not the ceremony carried out. The Conseil Municipal declared that Hugo should join the heroes of French civilization in the Panthéon, transformed once again into a national shrine. The route of the procession was changed from popular to official – down the Champs-Elysées between lines of troops, across the Pont de la Concorde and down the newly opened boulevard Saint-Germain to the Haussmannian boulevard Saint-Michel and up, via the rue Soufflot, to the Panthéon. Demonstration by socialist groups at the Arc de Triomphe were firmly repressed.

IV

Citing the ceremonies that animated the monumental topography of nineteenth-century Paris and then depicting the city's representational architecture as a permanent scenographic setting for them brings us to a last fundamental part of the system: decoration – carved symbolic facade ornamentation and monumental interior paintings, usually ceilings. It could, as in the pediment of the Pavillon Denon, communicate specific significance in the more anonymous urban structure. It might be replaced to respond to political nuances. The city of Paris planned an equestrian statue of Louis XV by Bouchardon in the center of the place de la Concorde upon its creation in 1750; the Revolution toppled it (April 11, 1792) and set up a statue of Liberty on the old plinth with, nearby, the guillotine (May 10, 1793–June 11, 1794). The Restoration proclaimed the Madeleine overlooking it an expiatory chapel and projected a statue of Louis XVI as martyr by Cortot for the *place*. Louis-Philippe, after considering erecting a monument to the victims of the Revolution of July, finally set up a strangely mute ancient Egyptian obelisk in its center.[75]

Symbolic decoration was the architectural adjunct that most immediately made a representational building just that: This represented, literally, what the building "represented" institutionally. In this aspect the habitation, the business building, the social service structure was immediately distinguishable.

Blondel in his *Cours d'architecture* (Vol. 2, 1771) follows his discussion of palaces with that of "Monuments élevés pour la magnificence." (Erected by the king for his magnificence, it is assumed.) "Independently of edifices erected as the habitation of crowned heads, there are monuments which express more specifically the glory and magnificence of monarchs, as well as the splendor of the cities where the monuments are located."[76] These were, first and foremost, triumphal gates and arches – "des monuments qui tiennent le premier rang dans les différents productions de l'architecture"; "monuments that hold first place among the different productions of architecture" – and, secondly, *places royales* – spaces decorated with monumental orders around equestrian statues of the sovereign. Henri IV built the places des Vosges and Dauphine, centering on equestrian statues of Louis XIII and himself, and projected the place de France as a northeastern gateway.[77] Louis XIV built the place des Victoires and projected the place Vendôme, both enframing statues of himself (standing and on horseback, respectively), erected the triumphal portes Saint-Denis and Saint-Martin as well as projecting Perrault's huge triumphal arch at the place du Trône after his entry in 1662.[78] The city of Paris erected the place de la Concorde around Bouchardon's statue of Louis XV.

The Revolution emptied these spaces of their royal emblems. Napoleon re-established and developed the old structure, but now communicating the double symbolism of the army and himself in the Arc du Carrousel (1806–1809), the Colonne de la Grande Armée (Vendôme, 1806–1810) topped with his own figure in antique dress by Chaudet (replacing the

Charlemagne originally planned), the Madeleine transformed into a Temple à la Gloire (begun 1806), and the Arc de Triomphe (begun 1806).[79] The cross axis commenced in the Madeleine was ended in Poyet's portico on the Chamber of Deputies (1806–1811) with a pediment carved by Chaudet to show the emperor's military prowess and political dominance – "His Majesty the Emperor returning from the battlefield of Austerlitz, received by the president of the deputies and followed by the flags which he will present to the Corps Législatif, coming to open the session of 1805."[80]

The Restoration melted down Chaudet's Napoleon on the Colonne Vendôme to remake the destroyed equestrian statue of Henri IV on the Pont Neuf (replacing the former with a simple fleur de lys).[81] Louis XIV was returned to the center of the place des Victoires, now equestrian (by Bosio, 1822); Louis XVI projected in the place de la Concorde. The regime stopped construction on the Arc de Triomphe (before recommencing it in 1823, now dedicated to "la Victoire et la Paix,"[82] to commemorate the Duc d'Angoulême's short campaign in Spain), and plastered over Chaudet's pediment on the Chamber of Deputies with A.-E. Fragonard's "La Charte accompagnée de la France et de la Justice, protègeant les Sciences, les Arts et l'"Industrie" – "The Constitution accompanied by France and Justice protecting the Sciences, Arts and Industries." The Pantheon became again a church and Gérard painted four monumental pendentives of saints and the dome representing Louis XVIII and the Duchesse d'Angoulème.[83]

During the enthusiastic first months of the Monarchy of July, the regime linked itself to the Revolution, the people, and a humanized Napoleon (as Michael Marrinan has explored[84]). The Arc de Triomphe was completed with four huge reliefs of citizen soldiers against each pier (including Rude's *La Marseillaise*) in lieu of columns. The Colonne de Juillet was erected visible over the housetops and visually extending the west axis to the east boulevards with the names of all those killed for the new monarchy inscribed around its shaft. Three great lunettes were commissioned for the interior of the Chamber of Deputies depicting Louis-Philippe's oath to support the constitution with, flanking it, two scenes from revolutionary parliamentary history symbolizing resistance to despotism and to sedition – Mirabeau's answer to Deux-Brézé in 1789 and Boisy d'Anglas's confrontation of the crowd in the Chamber in 1793.[85] The Panthéon was made again a monument to French heroes and the pediment was recut by David d'Angers to represent "Les grands hommes qui se sont illustrés par la science, par les lettres, et par les armes" – "Great men who have distinguished themselves in science, letters and war."[86] Napoleon was replaced atop the Colonne Vendôme, now in the form imagined by Seurre, a soldier in a campaign cloak, the historical Napoleon leading his troops. As the regime continued, the revolutionary and Napoleonic themes became an embarrassment (as Marrinan has observed). In 1840 Napoleon's tomb was erected off the city's axis, under the dome of the Invalides, after much sharp discussion of more central sites.[87] The axis itself was coopted for the regime by the projected Arc de Djemila and the equestrian statue of the Duc d'Orléans.[88]

Louis-Philippe used the monumental city as a canvas on which to depict the nature of his new and strangely undefined (or, perhaps better, multiply-defined) regime, especially in the great campaign to complete the monuments of Paris formulated by Adolphe Thiers in 1833.[89] Napoleon had imprinted his authority on the west axis and the *places royales* wholesale; the Restoration had erased it, again wholesale. Louis-Philippe and Thiers, in contrast, were much more discriminating, finishing revolutionary, Bourbon, and Napoleonic monuments neatly but evenhandedly – the Panthéon and the place de la Bastille; the Arc de Triomphe and the Madeleine; Saint-Denis, Notre-Dame, and Versailles – but with imprecise symbolic keying, like the obelisk used to fill the place de la Concorde, the generalized dedication of the Arc de Triomphe or the use of the Madeleine as an ordinary parish church. Cortot cut a new pediment for the Chamber of Deputies: "France entre la Liberté et l'Ordre public avec les génies du commerce, de l'agriculture, de la paix, de la guerre, et de l'éloquence" – "France between Liberty and Public Order with the geniuses of Commerce, Agriculture, Peace, War and Eloquence."

Napoleon III[90] completed the west axis with the union of the Louvre and Tuileries, the extension of the rue de Rivoli and the decoration of the Hôtel de Ville, but also transformed this into one axis of a rough *étoile* with the cutting of the north-south boulevards and the diagonals of the rue de Turbigo (culminating in the place du Prince Eugène (now de la République) with its projected Orphaeum) and the responding avenue Napoléon leading to the Opéra. The symbolic representation of the west axis remained dynastic and authoritarian, pivoting on the themes of peace, prosperity, and imperial omnipotence – manifesting the catch phrase "l'Empire c'est la paix." Seurre's humane Napoleon on the Colonne Vendôme became Dumont's "Napoléon-César," once again in antique dress, holding a victory. (This was the incarnation toppled by the Commune, then reerected at Courbet's expense in 1875, and which one sees today.) Delacroix and Ingres were commissioned to paint the ceilings of the two salons terminating the enfilade of the Hôtel de Ville, the "Salon de la Paix" and the "Salon de l'Empereur" (respectively). The former showed "La Terre" saved from War and Famine by Peace; the latter the Apotheosis of Napoleon I, the emperor shown drawn up to heaven in a chariot accompanied by victories and *renommés*.[91] Between these salons stretched the huge Galerie des Fêtes with fifty-six allegorical pendentives of productive activities painted in 1852–1853 by Lehmann.[92] But no crowning was erected on the Arc de Triomphe (although artists were quick to suggest such)[4] nor was a central group set up in the Cour Napoléon of the New Louvre. The Colonne de Juillet – commemorating the Revolution of 1830 specifically, but also revolution in general – was left untouched.

Elsewhere in the city Napeolon III transformed the Panthéon back into a church (the apse to be painted by Amaury-Duval to show "Christ dans son manteau celeste flanqué des patrons de l'Eglise, Saint Pierre, Saint Paul, Sainte Geneviève et Saint Germain l'Auxerrois") and erected the magnificent Salle du Trône at the Luxembourg with its hemicycles painted by Lehmann of 1852–1854 to represent his authority over that body.[94]

*   *   *

In terms of the amount of sculptural decoration externally and of painted decoration inside, the New Louvre was the most heavily ornamented building erected in France since Versailles. But the principal external ornament – the range of free-standing statues of the great men of France around the Cour Napoléon – had been projected during the Second Republic and was of imprecise significance.[95]

There were three major pediments around the Cour Napoléon III, those of the pavillons Richelieu, Denon, and on the back of the Pavillon de l'Horloge of the old Louvre. These are repetitions and inflections of the three major pediments of the outer facades of the old Louvre as recut under Fontaine's direction for Napoleon I. The pediment above Perrault's great colonnade was executed first, in 1808, by Lamot, showing "Minerve, entourée des muses et de la Victoire, couronne le buste de Napoléon" – "Minerva, surrounded by the muses of victory, crowns the bust of Napoleon";[96] that on axis westward on the back facade of the Pavillon de l'Horloge carved by Bayre to depict "le buste de Napoléon Ier couronné par les deux figures de l'Histoire et des Beaux-Arts" – "the bust of Napoleon I crowned by the figures of History and the Fine Arts."[97] (The Restoration had replaced Napoleon's head on the old Louvre with that of Louis XIV, which Napoleon III respected, so that when Napoleon reappeared, it was as part of an historical continuum.) The northern pediment on the old Louvre was balanced in the southern pavilion of the Cour Napoléon III, Ramey's 1811 "Génie de la France, sous les traits de Napoléon, évoque Minerve, Mercure, la Paix et Législation pour qu'elles succèdent à Mars et à l'appareil guerrier que la Victoire a rendu inutile" – "The Genius of France, with the features of Napoleon, evokes Minerva, Mercury, Peace and Law to succeed Mars with his martial equipment which Victory has rendered unnecessary" against Simart's Pavillon Denon pediment of "Napoléon III entouré de la Paix et des arts." The southern pediment of the old Louvre depicted "Minerve aux Sciences et les Arts" while Duret's Pavillon Richelieu pediments represents "France protègeant les Sciences et les Arts."

The great symbolic space of the Second Empire was the Salle des Etats. Unfortunately its checkered decorative history has not been comprehensively studied (Figure 45).[98] The main space was painted in 1857–1859 by Charles-Louis Mueller (1815–1892), author of a huge Napoleonic canvas shown at the Exposition Universelle of 1855, "Vive L'Empereur!" At the Salle des Etats Mueller painted a vast lunette behind the imperial dais with an equestrian Charlemagne. Above, across the vaulted ceiling, he depicted France flanked by Wisdom, Justice, Force, Abundance, and Liberality floating in the skylike center field, with grouped around the edge religion, agriculture, peace, the sciences, and the arts.[99] This was destroyed in 1885 when the space was incorporated into the museum. The tall vestibule in the Pavillon Denon might have been more interesting had Couture executed the series he projected in 1856 (evidently to a program of his own conception). There were to be on the four walls, "The Baptism of the Prince Imperial," "The Empire Relying on the Church and the Army to Suppress Anarchy," "The Enrollment of the Volunteers," and "The Return of the Troops from the Crimea." (The first use of the *salle* was for a dinner of the officers of the Crimean army.) Mueller in the end painted the vestibule as well in four great lunettes characterizing now four great royal builders, shown amid their ministers, architects, and artists: Saint Louis enframed by the Sainte-Chapelle; François Ier before the chateau of Chambord; Louis XIV in front of the Dôme des Invalides; and Napoleon I enframed by the Arc du Carrousel.

✳   ✳   ✳

In the context of this chapter, there are two things of importance about this decorative keying monumental of the urban form: first, that it tended to be compressed at the beginnings of the successive regimes, as if the initial challenge for each was to master the city symbolically; second, that it existed in complex reciprocal relationship with the architectural setting, as if building and decorative tableau might be two ends of a continuous scale. The first, in fact, leads to the second because after a few prominent pediments had been recarved and several ceilings repainted, the regime's representational nature settled down to manifest itself more permanently in whole buildings, like the Tomb of Napoleon, the Opéra, or the Palais de Justice. The themes changed too, from the statement of principle to (as Marrinan observes) the assertion of dynastic continuity. Each regime came to terms with the self-imposing pattern of monumental Paris, first stamping itself quickly on the symbolic pressure points – the Colonne Vendôme, the Panthéon, the Tuileries – then slowly but surely turning to the bigger task of maintaining its continuity.

V

One of the most interesting and peculiar aspects of the evolution of architectural decoration in nineteenth-century Paris is the steady erosion of political specificity – from the categorical decoration campaigns of Napoleon and the Restoration to Louis-Philippe's eclectic combination of traditions and finally to Napoleon III's insertion of himself in a continuous tradition – Saint Louis, François Ier, Louis XIV, Napoleon – at the Louvre. As Visconti observed, the problem in designing the New Louvre was fundamentally a historical one. Jules de Joly, architect of the Chamber of Deputies, explained this most vividly in his introduction to his publication of that monument of 1840:

Monuments – human creations embellishing the work of God – are of two sorts. Some are conceived and executed according to a single plan where the genius of the artist may spread itself out without impediment and make a complete whole. Here, if all the parts do not present relation and harmony between themselves it is the fault of the author alone. Other [monuments] are the result of successive campaigns, undertaken at different times, often on modified plans. Here the talent of the architect who adds the finishing touches can only hope for the credit of having taken the greatest possible advantage of the work of his predecessors. He is necessarily subservient to the demands of the plan, to the weakness in the construction, to the conventions of another time, to the provisions for another function. He must accept constructions and projects utterly opposed, perhaps, to what he would have conceived and he must make them contribute to the completed edifice as if he were a poet from whom one commissions a tragedy on the condition that he include acts already sketched and scenes previously written. Can one deny that in this case his task might be painful, more difficult than if he was to conceive and execute the monument in its ensemble and in its details?[100]

The necessity of compromising with existing construction was balanced by a second necessary compromise for the representational architect, that with the sovereign himself. He was no ordinary client. Des Essarts puts it succinctly in his *Dictionnaire universel de la police* (1786): "Sa majesté ordonne Elle-même de tous ce qui regarde les maisons royales . . ." – "His Majesty himself determines everything that relates to royal residences. . . ."[101] This makes comprehensible Vanvitelli's peculiar introduction to his publication of his projected palace at Caserta (1756) where he depicts the king's thoughts and gestures but says nothing about his own contribution: The king's architect was but the executant of the king's personal ideas.[102] In this the palace itself was an entity like the most important state ceremonies, the personal conception of the sovereign himself. Fontaine's diary functions as a record of Napoleon's wishes and orders as much as an introspective commentary on the architect's part. Receiving a visit from the Prussian crown prince (the future Friedrich Wilhelm IV) in August 1815, Fontaine depicts architecture to the young man as the royal art, "celui dont l'exercice plus particulièrement convenir aux souverains . . ." – "that [art] the practice of which is especially appropriate for sovereigns. . . ."[103]

We should note, however, Des Essarts modifies his initial declaration in the next clause: "He leaves the responsibility for the other edifices that he controls to different administrations that are knowledgeable about the repairs necessary to keep them in good condition."[104] That is to say, the sovereign concerns himself personally only with the palace while the rest of government construction is the charge of the appointed bureaucracy. And this introduces a further complication: that the taste of the sovereign qua king was not just a personal one, but "kingly" – that which tradition and court functionaries (and court artists) had established as worthy of the ruler.[105] This "goût du Roi" came with that state and did not die with one specific monarch any more than did his authority. ("Le Roi est mort. Vive le Roi!") A person assuming authority at a mature age, like the regent in 1715, might have developed a personal style in his private artistic arrangements in Paris, but – once king and when such at Versailles – would accept the ceremonial and the trappings that a whole great machine existed to maintain.

This is not the sort of architecture that modern historians are accustomed to deal with or nineteenth-century architects were really satisfied with doing, as the disgruntled undertones in de Joly's remarks imply. They all would have preferred the clean, free conception of new buildings projected on open sites, working as untrammelled specialists, demonstrating intellectual and imaginative virtù. This was possible in school projects and liberally taken advantage of. Nonetheless, the biggest and most important jobs in nineteenth-century France were the representational ones – the Luxembourg, the Chamber of Deputies, the Hôtel de Ville, and especially the New Louvre – and these were essentially problems in continuity and diplomacy.

Continuity, however, is perhaps too mild a word for the massive momentum embodied in the construction of the representational infrastructure of Paris. The money and the staff required merely to maintain this array of monuments was great, that required to bring them to some sort of completion under Louis-Philippe was greater, while that required to extend the system to control the whole city under Napoleon III and Haussmann was, of course, without parallel in the nineteenth century.

The Arc de Triomphe was begun in 1809 with a projected cost of 7 million francs and was finished in 1836 having cost 9.8 million.[106] The Madeleine, begun as a church in 1764, was redesigned as a "Temple à la Gloire" not to cost more than 3 million francs in 1806 and was finished in 1842 having cost 14.7 million. The Bourse was projected to cost 3.2 million francs when begun in 1808 and had swallowed up 8.1 million francs by the time of its completion in 1827. The Hôtel de Ville extension begun in 1836 cost 12 million francs, exclusive of decoration and alteration that extended into the Second Empire. The Opéra was projected 25 million francs during five years of construction and, in fact, cost 35 million over thirteen years. (In illuminating contrast, Henri Labrouste's Bibliothèque Sainte-Geneviève was projected to cost a very modest 1,775,000 francs and came in on budget.)

The decorative elements of a structure like the Madeleine were extraordinarily expensive. In that instance we find thirty-two Corinthian capitals, twenty pilaster capitals, and interior decorative cutting budgeted at 748,252.19 francs – almost half the total cost of the Bibliothèque Sainte-Geneviève. Again, in Thiers's bill of 1833 fluting the Madeleine's columns is set at 150,570.06 francs.[107]

In the case of immemorial buildings like the Louvre, the Palais Royal, the Panthéon, or Versailles one cannot speak of totals, only of campaigns and of annual upkeep. Under Napoleon I the Louvre swallowed up a million francs a year from 1805 to 1810, a half million from 1811–1813, then a hundred thousand to a quarter million francs annually during the Restoration.[108] The New Louvre was erected for 25 million francs from 1852 to 1857, but that was only the shell – millions more were spent for interiors and extensions until 1870, and millions more after that for reconstruction. In the annual budgets buildings like the Louvre were permanent line items, as were their architects' retainers, the support of their *agences*, and the costs of oversight bodies like the Conseil des Bâtiments Civils. And these all grew. In 1829, for example, the Conseil des Bâtiments Civils was budgeted at 44,000 francs, in 1854, 52,000 francs; in 1860 at 55,000 francs.[109] The budget of the city of Paris in 1828 records in 1828 salaries totaling 23,000 francs, plus 20,000 francs for the directeur des travaux and 305,840 francs for construction in the *service ordinaire* and 48,000 francs for "fêtes et cérémonies publiques." In 1835 these allocations were 30,550 francs in salaries and 1.4 million francs in construction with 230,000 francs for "fêtes publiques." In 1860 these had grown to 255,000 francs in salaries, 4,272,000 francs in construction and 400,000 francs for "fêtes publiques." Again, the budget for the Service des Palais Impériaux in 1853 attributed 281,840 francs for architects' retainers, 1 million francs for *entretien*, and 1.8 million francs for "grands travaux," especially at the Elysée.[110] (The New Louvre was specially funded.)

*   *   *

Representational architects like Fontaine and Visconti, Huyot, de Joly, de Gisors, Baltard Godde, and Lesueur obligingly carried on a history of which they were an institutional part. Brilliance for them – whether they wished it or not – lay in adjustment and practical compromise, rather than abstract conception: in interweaving scenographic axes and orchestrating along them elegant but conventional (and repetitive) declarations of authority in columns, sculptural figures, and fields of allegorical painting.

They regarded the traditional classicism of the seventeenth and eighteenth centuries as their guide. Fontaine, in his one lengthy published text, that of his *Résidences de souverains* (1833), presents the history of French architecture as commencing with François Ier's Chambord, achieving scale (at the expense of vulgar ostentation) with Louis XIV, and emerging as a great manifestation of culture in Soufflot's Sainte-Geneviève, Gondoin's Ecole de Médecine, and Victor Louis's Bordeaux Opéra, before falling into chaos with the Revolution from which it has yet to emerge.[111] Huyot's lectures as professor of the history of architecture at the Ecole des Beaux-Arts (1818–1840) propounded a similar point of view.[112] Jacques Lacornée particularly acted on this precedent in his completion of the "Palais d'Orsay" and in his baroque design for the Ministère des Affaires Etrangères (1854–1856), especially in the decoration of the latter's suite of reception rooms.[113] Visconti repeats it in the letter to his cousin of 1852 cited at the beginning of this chapter.

I have also examined the French monuments erected under Louis XIV because I have to tell you, dear cousin, that that period was admirable for France. It produced monuments like Versailles, St. Cloud, most of the Louvre, the Monnaie [sic], the Tuileries, the Invalides, the Panthéon [sic] and what have you, monuments which would be envied by Italy. . . . The capital of the world has only this epoch that possesses *grand cachet* . (Visconti's emphasis)[114]

In 1861 Haussmann cited de Tourny's eighteenth-century transformation of Bordeaux as his model.[115]

The academic classicism of the seventeenth, eighteenth, and nineteenth centuries, of course, evolved. Some very fine minds have devoted themselves to its formulation and reformulation; some very careful scholars have traced it, starting with Louis Hautecoeur in his seven volumes.[116] The question we need to examine here is less how the tradition changed in time than how it took form to begin with, and help in this comes principally from social history, especially the work a generation ago of Norbert Elias and Richard Allewyn and today of Louis Marin or Jean-Marie Apostolides.[117] Elias and Allewyn studied the "classical" age in France less in terms of an abstract mentality than as a reflection of a system of political centralization and personal constraint perfected at Louis XIV's Versailles and spreading thence over all western Europe.[118] This construction is helpful here because it eluci-dates the acts of axiality and constraint that we have found fundamental to Parisian state architecture. These were not artistic gestures on the part of free artists made for their own elegance, but were the "representation" of the absolute sovereign and as such were to come forth from him and con-stantly lead back to him as all-animating, sunlike, and so the only subject, both as motif and as architect. Jean Chapelain (the leader of Colbert's Petit Conseil) is quoted to have said that artists are but docile instruments of the king, "qui résonnent quand le Roi les touche" – "which sound when touched by the King."[119]

François Blondel in inaugurating the Académie d'Architecture on Decem-ber 31, 1672, sketched architecture's place in the king's scheme. The foun-dation of power he depicts as the town with its perfection of industry, trade, and overseas commerce. Thence flows the economic resources for great and efficient armies that, prevailing in battle, create an empire. Finally, as the tribute of subject peoples flows into the king's treasury, triumphs, fetes, buildings, and decoration are indulged in as a celebration and representa-tion of power.

If architecture is so involved in the work, the risk, and the victory, it is no less involved in the magnificence of the Triumph. It first of all erects memorials on the field of battle which it embroiders with the detritus of the enemy. It assembles the remains of the citizens who died for their homeland. . . .
Then architecture prepares for the return of the victor. . . .
For it is now that architecture spreads out what it possesses of the most grand and the most magnificent, once fate and victory have put in the hands of the victor the riches of subject nations. It is then that it holds back nothing in order to orna-ment the State with splendid buildings, temples, basilicas, theaters, circuses, porti-cos, baths, and all the other masterpieces that give pleasure to the citizens and inspire the admiration of strangers."[120]

Blondel himself was the mathematics tutor of the dauphin, a member of the Académie des Sciences, a fortification engineer, and only lastly an architect.

Colbert is celebrated for having organized the arts and architecture – as well as the economy and the army – to represent the power of the king. He took office as surintendant des bâtiments, arts, tapisseries, et manufactures de France in 1664.[121] His tool was a system of royal academies, groups of artists, or *savants* on retainer, presided over by the surintendant acting as surrogate for the king. These included the Académie des Inscriptions (1663, 1669), Académie de Peinture et de Sculpture (1648, reorganized 1663), Académie de France à Rome (1666), Académie des Sciences (1666), Académie d'Architecture (1671), Académie d'Opéra (1671, become the Académie de Musique, 1672), and the abortive Académie des Spectacles

(1674). The earliest, the Académie des Inscriptions, was clear in its function: to compose the inscriptions on royal monuments and the iconography of medals struck to commemorate the reign.

Beginning in 1667 Colbert gathered an informal committee of architects to advise him on state building. In 1671 he formalized this as the Académie Royale d'Architecture with twenty-four members in two classes to analyze state designs (and sometimes to produce them, the Académie working as a body), to discuss the theory of architecture and to prepare students to enter state service. Charles Perrault was Colbert's *premier commis* in the Surintendance des Bâtiments; his brother, Claude, the designer of the eastern facade of the Louvre (chosen over Bernini); both Perraults members of the Académie and Claude the author of a book of doctrine, *Abrégé des dix livres de Vitruve*, 1674.

The ubiquitous Charles Perrault, in his manuscript "Mémoire de ma vie" (published posthumously by Pierre Patte in 1759), describes Colbert's campaign to fix the representation of the king, centering on his celebration in fetes and monuments, then the perpetuation of these in engravings and medals, and finally their written description in books, usually from the hand of the historiograph du roi, André Félibien. With Colbert's death in 1683 and his replacement by the general Louvois (surintendant des bâtiments, 1685–1691) and eventually by the architect Jules Hardouin Mansart (surintendant, 1699–1708) the system was formalized into a tentacular and smoothly running machine of representation, André Lenôtre and Sébastien Vauban joining the Perraults in the secondary posts.[122]

What is important here is not only the domination of this machinery by the necessity to represent the king but also that what we today would call architecture constitutes only a small part of a much larger, double continuum: the first, that sketched by Blondel, from town and economic planning to military maneuvers and fortifications to celebrations and monuments; the second that embodied in the engravings and medals as well as Félibien's texts, a series of elaborately symbolic productions acted out within an architectural frame. Both Blondel and Félibien tellingly assert that Vitruvius's descriptions of the rules of solid, static architecture are quite inadequate for the framing of their art and must be supplemented by the study of the festivals and symbols sketched in the mysterious Venetian Renaissance illustrated treatise, the *Hypnerotomachia Poliphili* (1499). This is a love fantasy in which the hero, one Poliphilius, finds himself traveling through a wild world of ancient Roman ruins, heavily symbolic in their shape and decoration, to find his loved one and to enjoy elaborate triumphs in splendid architectural settings – before waking up to find it all a dream. It had already been translated into French in 1546. It is cited by François Blondel

(1685) and Félibien (1699) and its decor was reconstructed in the gardens at Versailles by J. H. Mansart.[123] Félibien explained,

because, however useful is the idea that Vitruvius gave of ancient architecture, Poliphilius seems to depict it with more majesty and splendor: He made it be perceived as the one science that controls all the arts and embraces in itself the most sublime conceptions. He relates to this science not only the Orders and the construction of all kinds of buildings, but he has also perfect comprehension of what must decorate and accompany such great works.[124]

As the balance to Vitruvius, providing a sketch of the symbolic-ceremonial content of classical building to reanimate its architectural skeleton, the *Hypnerotomachia* remained a fundamental text for Quatremère de Quincy, J.-G. Legrand, Huyot, A.-L.-T. Vaudoyer, and even Hippolyte Fortoul.[125]

Apostolides observes that opera was the great state art form created at the beginning of Louis XIV's reign, and the fairy tale (perfected by Charles Perrault, among others) was the characteristic production of the end.

The life filling Louis XIV's paradigmatic architecture survives only in Silvestre's engravings and Félibien's descriptions. (Blondel's and Perrault's architectural treatises are fragments of the whole their authors, in other places, evoke – Vitruvius as against the *Hypnerotomachia Poliphili*.) What the nineteenth century inherited was the stone architectural skeleton of that wonderful symbolic organism, the Vitruvian shadow of lines of columnar orders arranged axially around voids.

✳   ✳   ✳

There is one note that des Essarts adds (writing in the 1780s) that is missing from Elias's analysis: We saw at the beginning of this section that he recognized the bureaucracy as a thing in itself, acting for the sovereign where he could not. As such it was the embryo of a specialty, a profession. Architecture, like other professions in the nineteenth century, would increasingly assert its independence and present its service as a communal function, not just a reflection of the state.[126] It thus became a living intellectual subject, not just ritual, and pushed outward to make alliances with history and science. Yet simultaneously a conflict arose between the ideal of community service cherished within the new profession and the necessity of satisfying the new power in society, the middle class, for whom architecture was important as real estate and as the creation of the places of exchange, as we discuss in the next chapter.

The great fact of nineteenth-century architecture was the slow disengagement of the profession from the representation of the state and this had repercussions on design. The last great effort to project absolute uniformity was Napoleon I's Paris projects. After 1814 representational design eroded to a continuation of momentum slightly deflected by the acknowledgment of local history, justified in part by nostalgia for the seventeenth- and eighteenth-century authoritarian tradition. The new terrain for the extension of civilization was technological, in the perfection of social institutions, or bourgeois in stores and rental blocks. The language of the representational architects became anecdotal and self-effacing, as with Visconti at the New Louvre – deceptively so since the mere act of completing the monumental axes of Paris was itself as great a display of central power as any number of new colonnades or pediments might once have been. Under Napoleon III and Haussmann the representational vocabulary returned to its essence, axiality, and proportion.

VI

We began this chapter with the central representational monument of Paris, the Louvre, and we end it now with the one major extension postdating Visconti's scheme, his successor Hector Lefuel's rebuilding in 1864–1869 of the Galerie du Bord de l'Eau around the "Guichets" as a composition of pure axiality (Figures 57–60).[127] These were three monumental archways cut through the southern limb of the New Louvre to permit the passage of traffic from the place du Palais Royal and the bottom of the avenue de l'Opéra to the Left Bank across the Pont du Carrousel.

We have mentioned that it was over this gateway that Napoleon III himself finally appeared in conventional equestrian pose (if only in relief). The "Deschamps" plan of Paris (c. 1865, Figure 57) shows that the passage was to terminate converging *percements* projected on the Left Bank, one leading in from the Invalides (at the place Vauban), the other from the place Saint-Sulpice. A deep square was to be cut behind the Ecole des Beaux-Arts and its axis was carried across the Seine by the rebuilt Pont du Carrousel.

In a preliminary project (Figure 58) Lefuel reproduced the square, columned vocabulary of Visconti's pavilions in the New Louvre, elaborated at the roof line and like Henri IV's contiguous Galerie d'Apollon. Three archways strain to achieve adequate breadth within this scheme by touching the entablature vertically and expanding to the columns horizontally, giving up any individual articulation in the process – they are holes, but big ones. Lefuel then produced a second project (Figures 59 and 60), in what his necrologist Henri Delaborde described as a brilliant imaginative leap, eliminating the columns to value the arch itself, stating the axis and enframing the void.[128] Now it is asserted by deeply relieved voussoirs, unrestrained by orders or entablatures, flying across the space between the two pavilions, descending at two intermediate points onto piers thickened to receive its weight, and seemingly pushed off again by sculptural groups thrusting upward and outward (by Jouffroy depicting, incidentally, "Marine de Guerre" and "Marine Marchande").[129] The rebuilt Seine

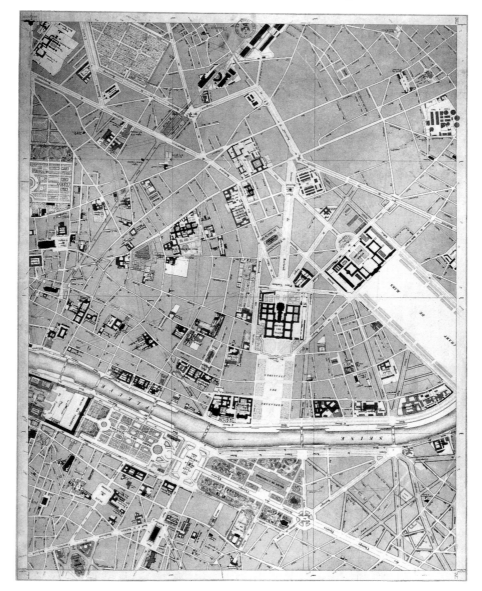

Figure 57. "Plan Deschamps," 1865, faubourgs Saint-Honoré and Saint-Germain with the Tuileries showing avenues projected to Opéra and at Pont du Carrousel.

facade of the Louvre was made symmetrical around this point, creating the largest coordinated monumental passage of Napoleon III's Paris.

In the sixth chapter of *Designing Paris* I document the evolution of French nineteenth-century classicism from the static reproduction of Greek

Figure 58. Hector Lefuel, preliminary project for the "Guichets du Louvre" facing the Pont du Carrousel, 1861.

models to an elastic, empathic abstraction, especially in the colonnaded facade of the Palais de Justice (from the designs of Louis Duc, replacing Huyot upon his death in 1840, and under construction since 1857) facing the "Guichets" up the Seine (Figures 85, 86, and 87). Here the conventional elements of the classical vocabulary are fragmented and blended with the building's surfaces to create thick, seemingly struggling masses supporting broad window arches and stone-arched ceilings. The ultimate formulation of this was the "empathic" theory of Charles Blanc that he summarized in

Figure 59. "Guichets du Louvre" from across the Pont du Carrousel (Hector Lefuel, architect, 1864–1869).

his *Grammaire des arts de dessin* (1861–1864, 1867) and demonstrated with particular effectiveness in his 1868 critique of Duc's facade.[130]

Lefuel took this sympathetic abstraction one step further, freeing the arch and blending its suggested movement with that of the decorative sculpture – below Bayre's equestrian representation of Napoleon III. Henri Delaborde concluded:

The *Guichets* of the Louvre are one of the masterpieces of modern architecture, one of those definitive inventions [trouvailles], one of those absolutely successful undertakings, like those which we admire, in other realms of art and function, the new facade and vestibule of the Palais de Justice, the Halles Centrales, and the grand staircase of the Opéra.[131]

There always had been *guichets* cutting through the basement of the Long Gallery of the Louvre to expedite traffic, but they had formerly been just what their collo-

Figure 60. "Guichets du Louvre" (Hector Lefuel, architect, 1864–1869).

quial name implies – mere holes. Lefuel and Napoleon III have made them broad tunnels. They are the largest openings in the Louvre, New or Old, but where do they go? – right out the other side again; what do they channel? – city traffic: carriages, carts, pedestrians, beggars. This is not like Visconti's north-south axis from the Palais Royal to the Pavillon Denon. The processional path here has become a traffic artery. The architectural celebration of passage has blurred to proclaim mere heft.

THE BACKGROUND:
THE FUNDAMENTALS OF PRIVATE
AND INSTITUTIONAL BUILDING

I

To summarize in reverse the analysis of the last chapter: The ceremonial representation of the state implies a setting speaking in painted and sculpted images; these painted and sculpted images demand an architectural ground and armature to organize them; this ground and armature, the representational foreground building, implies a disciplined – "policed" – background to set it off, one either of nature (as west of the chateau at Versailles) or of city masses (as east of that chateau).

Appropriately in the more prominent case of nineteenth-century Paris the great west axis defined by the urban mass was edged in a disciplined manner by the facades along the rue de Rivoli (Figure 61). During the seventeenth and eighteenth centuries this side of the Tuileries gardens had backed up against the gardens and outbuildings of the hotels and religious houses along the rue Saint-Honoré.[1] In 1802, however, Napoleon ordered Fontaine to organize this area as a backdrop to the Tuileries by erecting a continuous line of structures, correctly subordinate, without any decoration beyond window surrounds and balconies.[2] Des Essarts (1786) cites Lamarre (1705–1738) of the king's perogatives in shaping private building around his palace: "If the king judges it right to build near his residences or châteaux in order to ameliorate the appearance or for public convenience, this must always be in conformity with plans approved by His Majesty and following *alignements* set by the superintendent of buildings."[3] He gives the example of the Collège des Quatre Nations erected to carry the axis of the Louvre southward across the Seine.[4]

Behind the anonymous facades of the rue de Rivoli Napoleon and Fontaine placed the expanded Tuileries stables, the projected post office (eventually completed as the Ministry of Finance), lodgings for palace offi-

Figure 61. Rue de Rivoli looking east from the place de la Concorde with the Tuileries Palace, c. 1860. Ministère des Finances (Bernard and Destailleur, architects successively, 1812–1824) second block in.

cials (Viollet-le-Duc, son of the gouverneur of the Tuileries, was raised at number 16) and a goodly scattering of private houses. The construction was also developed commercially by opening a public thoroughfare along it with a ground floor arcade and shops, on the model of the constructions defining the garden of the Palais Royal erected for the duc d'Orléans "Philippe Egalité" by Victor Louis in 1781–1788, but without their immodest giant order. The rue de Rivoli originally only extended up to the northern corner of the Tuileries. On March 24, 1848, it was ordered extended eastward to the rue de Richelieu, then in 1848–1852, as we have seen, further along the northern facade of the Louvre and the Hôtel de Ville to the rue Saint-Antoine and thus made a street, not an edge.[5]

The modesty of the rue de Rivoli facade is deceptive. It appears to be the neatly sliced-off edge of the chaotic "unrepresentational" texture of everyday Paris, a sort of dam erected against this by the palace architect working here with the cold accuracy of a military engineer. But what it is that has been so sliced off and dammed up is the real Paris of history, people, and commercial activity; what is before the facade line of the rue de Rivoli is the mere symbol of authority – a spreading garden and a palace – that would have been essentially the same whether erected here or elsewhere in the open country, as we see it in Fontaine's plan of 1810 for the Palais du Roi de Rome on the Colline de Chaillot (Figure 33). From the representational standpoint the city itself is the lowest term in a scrupulously observed hierarchy and might be eliminated altogether, replaced by *bosquets* and *parterres*, as for example in Durand's "palais" in his *Précis des Leçons* (1802, Figure 32).

Stating this so categorically, however, makes one wonder whether here, early in the nineteenth century, the city really was so insignificant. Does the architect's job really stop at edging it firmly and neatly, as along the rue de Rivoli?

The French mind in the early nineteenth century recognized the city under very different competing, evolving aspects, which might be defined as the representational, the institutional, and the organic (sedimentary), responding tangentially to the array of services combined in the government architectural administration as we characterized them in Chapter 2.[6] (As is often noted, the general abstract subject of city shaping per se, closing the gap between these conflicting perceptions, was not broached until the end of the century.[7])

From the traditional representational point of view – that perpetuated by Fontaine as premier architecte de l'empereur in the rue de Rivoli – the city did not exist as a subject of composition, as far as it was recognized at all, but rather as something to be policed, disciplined, and set out in neat, anonymous boxes. The entry "Villes" in Diderot's *Encyclopédie* (vol. XVII, 1765) presages this view:

For a *city* to be beautiful, the principal streets must connect with the gates, be perpendicular to each other as far as possible so that the corners of the houses be at right angles, [the streets] be eight toises [52 feet] broad and the minor streets four [26 feet]. It is also necessary that the distance between parallel streets be such as to leave space for two bourgeois houses, of which one would give upon the one street, the other upon that opposite. Each of these houses should be about four or five toises broad by six or seven toises deep [30 by 40 feet], with a courtyard of the same size: which gives a distance from one street to another of thirty-two to thirty-three toises. Along the length of the streets one opens squares the principal among which is that where the main streets begin, and one ornaments these squares by establishing uniformity in the facades of the residences and houses that surround them and by statues and fountains. If in addition the houses are well built and their facades decorated, little [more] is left to be desired.[8]

This might be describing Versailles, laid out in 1678 when Louis XIV created it as his capital, neatly but anonymously spreading out from the *bas cour* of the chateau.[9] Quatremère de Quincy in his entry "Ville" in the third volume (1825) of his dictionary *Architecture* evoked the same ideal historically, setting the gridded Hellenistic city of Rhodes (as known in literary descriptions) as the model: "With Rhodes . . . one never sees a small house next to a large one; . . . all of the habitations are of the same height and show the same architectural arrangement [*ordonnance d'architecture*], so that the whole seems to appear a single edifice."[10]

In contrast, from the institutional, legal perspective, the city was not simply a quantity of matter to be neatly gridded and policed. Here one does not use the word *ville* but instead *commune*. The administrative philosopher C.-P.-Marie Haas defines that succinctly in 1861: ". . . political association with its separate municipal regime and magistrature, a sort of republic within the State but intimately attached to the State by the close ties of centralization, law, public duty, and national interest."[11] The commune was a democratic community standing against the central, representational state, with its own array of institutions and – potentially – its own vocabulary of representation. Any intruding national authority (or international church) had to negotiate a place in the commune.

The medieval and Renaissance free town had a marketplace in its center dominated by the city hall and its bell (later clock) tower containing a series of functions: weigh house, tribunal, ceremonial chamber, municipal office, prison. The parish church balanced it and attached to itself the schools and hospitals that in the nineteenth century were shifted back and forth between religious and municipal responsibility. After the Revolution and centralization, specialization and the increase of scale and amenity transformed this into an array of separate urban elements constituting the organs of the commune. Around 1805 this was given clear urban form by the engineers Chabrol and Pichot in the plan of the new town of Napoléonville (Pontivy) in the Vendée and by Bruyère in that at Comacchio near Ravenna in Italy (Figures 62 and 63).[12] These cities are fields of institutions, the municipal functions fractioned into the city hall, law courts, prison, and theater, facing the church – the schools and hospital nearby – with a new element, the prefecture, asserting the presence of the newly centralized state. As Bernard Lepetit has documented, this pattern now spread across France as a result of the division of the country into newly created departments with developing *chefs-lieux*, each with its array of municipal and departmental institutions.[13] Georges Teyssot proposes that this explosion of institutional architecture transformed the Bâtiments Civils from a fundamentally representational organism into one serving an institutional reformulation of the urban face of France.[14]

Both the representational and the institutional perspectives of the city, regardless of how antithetical they were in detail, were formulated from above, from the viewpoint of authority. There was also a third perspective, that from the inside, of the newly appeared "social scientist," seeking to discover the natural, practical, economic order of the city and to give it more efficient shape.[15] Auguste Comte had created the concept of a science of society and his utopian contemporaries the Saint-Simoniens and the Fourierists pursued it with conviction, if also sometimes in extravagant formulations. The Saint-Simoniens in particular made the capitalist structure of a commercial city a principle of urban form. In the various writings emanating from this group around 1830 the city appears as the quintessential accomplishment of society as a whole – a huge, spontaneous "symbol" of it. The most dramatic of these was Charles Duveyrier's "La Ville nouvelle ou le Paris des Saint-Simoniens" developed from the ideas of "Père" Enfantin.[16] He depicts Paris reshaped as a human body with its urbanistic organs interrelated on that analogy, the whole splendidly built up and ornamented when seen from the surrounding hills, drawing people from all over the world to admire it. Less dramatic but much more realizable was the urban vision of Jean Reynaud published in his entry "Ville" in the Saint-Simonien *Encyclopédie nouvelle* (1841) and revised by his architect brother Léonce Reynaud in his influential *Traité d'architecture* (1850–1856).[17] "Le tracé d'une ville est oeuvre de temps plutôt d'architecte" – "the plan of a city is the work of time rather than of an architect," he starts. He evokes the multiplicity of inflections and irregularities a town's history creates in its form. How, then, to plan a city? he asks. He rejects Vitruvius's idea of a regular geometric form as well as the continuous "American" grid. "Cities thus traced are what one calls *belles villes* as a result of false ideas current about beauty; but how sad they are! How they inspire boredom!"[18] Worse, such is against the organic nature of a town.

One part of the city, advantageously located, will be particularly inhabited by the rich[est] class; another will attract the major part of the commercial activity; in the

Figure 62. Plan for a city projected near Comacchio, Italy (Louis Bruyère, engineer).

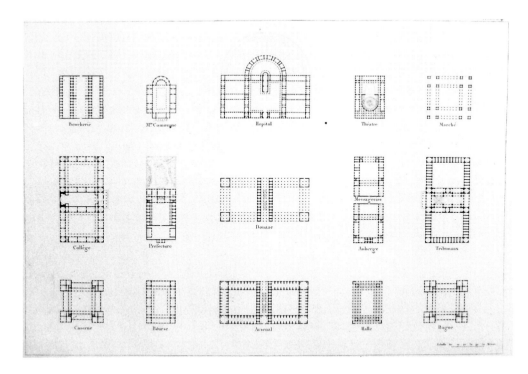

Figure 63. Plans of public buildings designed for the city near Comacchio, Italy (Louis Bruyère, engineer).

first will group themselves the establishments which seek to avoid clamor and find open ground; in the second gather the factories and the crowds of workers they employ; in a word there will coalesce several distinct subdivisions in the interior of the city, each having its special requirements in the nature of the number, breadth and route of the streets.[19]

Rather than having a geometric plan imposed on it a city must be permitted to assume an irregular, natural shape in which each quarter and the arrangement of quarters finds an individual form. The quarters, like the whole, are always a combination of particularities – the houses as different as their inhabitants "puisque ce sont leurs personnes que doivent représenter les maisons" – "because it is themselves that their houses should depict." It is the architect's task to understand all this in his city.

He must envision his city as a vast monument, simultaneously unitary and multiple, responding fully to the needs of a collective life and to those of individual existence, presenting like these the most diverse aspects, combining a judicious measure of order and of freedom, and constituting a sort of sublime concert by the intelligent combination of all these varied and harmonious forms, the faithful expression of diverse tastes, states and requirements, of the ties that bind and the esthetic sentiments that enliven the inhabitants.[20]

He ends strikingly with the declaration that the city he has just evoked – it is Paris (at least the Paris of the time of writing, of 1850). It is the modern architect's task to understand Paris's history, society, and urbanistic organs as he adds judiciously to its fabric. In his projects of the 1840s, 1850s and 1860s Hector Horeau was to people the city with new ferro-vitreous elements at points of economic pressure (Figure 30).

Here the strict though conflicting orders of the representational capital and the institutional *chef-lieu* is replaced in the Saint-Simonien vision by an elastic cityscape where various institutions and orders – public and private – negotiate individual relationships, the incidental specificity of the result expressing the nature of the community. The Saint-Simoniens grasped what, in fact, was really happening – first of all, rapid, shifting change; secondly, the emergence of a new force in urban forming, the "natural" force of what Adam Smith had called capitalism's "invisible hand."[21]

II

The representational buildings were the "foreground" monuments. I began this book with the quartier de l'Opéra with Garnier's powerful monument looming at its heart, but surrounded by a very important complex of "background" buildings – the Grand Hôtel de la Paix, the Jockey Club, the Dépôts et des Comptes Courants, the Splendide Hôtel, the Crédit Lyonnais, the mass of habitations, commercial establishments, and institutions that constituted the texture, the flesh, of the living city itself. We saw in Chapter 2 that it was this constantly self-renewing flesh of the city that the bureau of the Plan de Paris had been organized to control and the corps of the commissaire voyers employed to shape and police. It was also the part of the city most rapidly changing and asserting itself during the nineteenth century until, by the time of the "modernist" revolution in urban conceptualization of the 1920s, this and not the representational monuments had come to constitute the city itself – for example, in Le Corbusier's *Ville Contemporaine* of 1922. In this flesh everything other than representational monuments were embedded. As the century progressed, especially during the hyperactivity of the Second Empire and the 1870s, this "everything else" came to encapsulate some very new and extraordinary items, as is evident in the quartier de l'Opéra – things not yet clearly differentiated and, before the 1920s, always partially concealed. Seeking to shock, Georges d'Avenel starts his treatment of the "Maison parisienne" in his popular *Mécanismes de la vie moderne* (1897) thus:

Paris is old but its houses are young. Half of them are twenty-five years old at best – the life span of a horse – There is not one in fifteen that claims 150 years of existence – the age in forestry when one cuts oaks: – Once lodgings renewed themselves less quickly than the generations passed; in our capital today it is the opposite: the majority of its inhabitants were born before the apartments in which they live.[22]

D'Avenel contrasts the slowness of government construction to the rapidity of private building. It is typical of the former, he says, to expend the first year's appropriation setting up an elaborate scaffolding, next for work to cease until further funds are voted, then for work to start and stop for years (or decades, as we have seen in the cases of the Arc de Triomphe, the Madeleine, the Louvre, and the Panthéon). In contrast, Avenel depicts lighter private construction as shooting up in months, as indeed we know it did. The houses on the site of the vacated Hôtel des Affaires Etrangères on the boulevard des Capucines (Figure 19) were open in January 1855, nine months after the demolitions.[23] We noted in Chapter 1 that the Pereires' Grands Hôtels both took just a year to erect, construction in both cases being pushed at night with the help of electric lights, the interior finishes and furniture being fabricated off site simultaneously with the construction.

François Loyer in his precise and evocative book *Paris dix-neuvième siècle: l'immeuble et la rue* (1987) depicts the evolution of the city texture from the Empire to the Art Nouveau. This texture's constituents, for the first half of the century, were repetitive cells with shops on the ground floor and habitations above. At first these were narrow vertical slabs in the medieval "row house" system where the artisan or merchant lived above his work space, but increasingly during the century there emerged large horizontal blocks of single-floor apartments above complexes of shops built by speculators and rented – *immeubles*.[24] This change, hinted just before the Revolution and made systematic in the building boom of the 1840s, was the product of the economic revolution introducing the wage-rent nexus – the dissolution of private ownership and traditional socially constructed space in the face of the emergence of the efficient quantification of rental cells and its drive for ever greater density.[25] These new speculative blocks grew up to the limits of the regulatory envelope and produced, in the 1850s, what we recognize today as the *immeuble haussmannien.*

The generating force of the *immeuble haussmannien* was rent, and its principle was the ever more dense, concentrated utilization of the parcel occupied. Traditionally, the dwelling had covered the street front of a deep, narrow lot with open space behind. Now, however, the parcels became wider and shallower, their whole surfaces covered with building, the gardens surviving only as courtyards if not mere light wells (Figures 64 and 65). Victor Fournel in his *Paris nouveau, Paris futur* (1865) and d'Avenel later in 1897 describe with some chagrin this new tightly packed condition

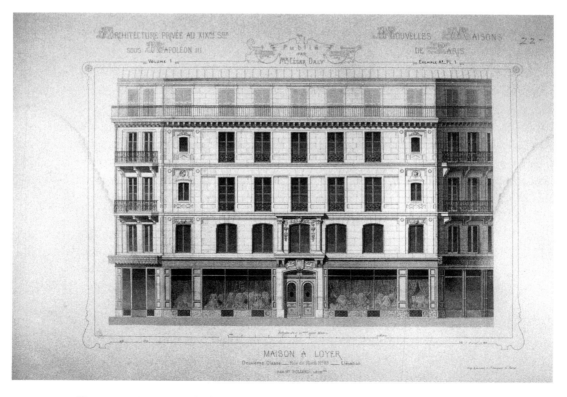

Figure 64. Apartment building, 88, rue de Rivoli, elevation (François Rolland, architect), c. 1853.

of living; Caillebotte, as we saw in Chapter 1, painted it cautiously from his balcony on the boulevard Haussmann. Fournel's volume moves from a depiction of the new Haussmannian Paris to an evocation of a mad, disciplined future when the principles controlling modern construction will have come to term and produced a tightly packed Paris pressed into an *étoile* of boulevards spreading from the Hôtel de Ville, panoptically maintaining perfect discipline both in building mass and in social conduct.

There were concomitant rapid advances in construction techniques, construction methods, and mechanical amenity.[26] The traditional Paris house

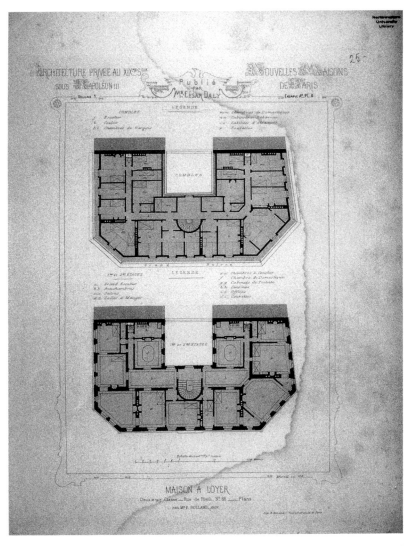

Figure 65. Apartment building, 88, rue de Rivoli, plans of second, third, and fifth floors (François Rolland, architect), c. 1853.

had been of wood with brick or rubble nogging in the street facade, plastered externally. In the 1840s the facades came to be built of limestone – lightly cut – and in the Second Empire cut stone appeared on the front and court facades – thick now, with rubble walls inside. This increase in the use of stone coincided with the introduction of quarrying machines, construction hoists, assembly-line stone finishing, and rail transportation of building stones from long distances. D'Avenel writes, "Napoleon III's Louvre came from the Aisne and Oise departments; the Hôtel de Ville came from Burgundy; it was rebuilt after the Commune with Chatenay and Courson stone (Yonne)."[27] Inside, plumbing, running water, gas, and eventually elevators made life easier.

Parallel to the technical sophistication of the *immeuble* evolved a differentiation and concentration in the contents of the buildings, especially in the central quarters. The great hotel type emerged, first in the Pereires' Grand Hôtel du Louvre (1853–1855), then in the Grand Hôtel de la Paix (1861–1862), both discreetly concealed within the reglementary building envelope behind anonymous facades, but covering whole *îlots* and centering on glass-covered courtyards and palatial public rooms. The Grand Hôtel du Louvre during the 1870s transformed its lower story by degrees into the department store, the Grands Magasins du Louvre, while in 1864–1867 Henri Blondel erected the Belle Jardinière and in 1869 Gustave Eiffel and Louis-Charles Boileau began construction of the Bon Marché, both designed specifically and exclusively as department stores with three floors of open selling space, offices and habitations above, around astonishing skylit interior courtyards.[28] Paul Sédille's Printemps followed in 1881–1882 (Figure 25) and Jourdain's Samaritaine in 1905–1910.[29] Bank buildings emerged as a type with Blondel's Dépôts et des Comptes Courants (1867–1868) and Bouwens van der Boyen's Crédit Lyonnais (1876–1878, 1881–1883; Figures 23 and 24);[30] clubs with Dubois's Jockey Club and Blondel's Cercle Agricole (Figure 93).[31] Seemingly ordinary *immeubles* like those on the rue Scribe became *apartements meublés* or bank offices, while their ground floors and mezzanines became small department stores like the Maison du Blanc at 6, boulevard des Capucines. The *immeuble* increasingly blended with the whole *îlot* and its interior became more densely utilized, public, labryinthine, and efficiently constructed in iron and glass, as we saw in Chapter 1. If outside the late Second Empire Parisian cityscape was Roman in its consistent monumentality, inside the central *îlots* it was more and more Chicago.

These increasingly sophisticated rent machines ballooned to fill and push against the zoning envelope established by the *alignements* and enforced by the commissaires voyers, as we saw in Chapter 2. In this, propelled by the economic boom of the Second Empire, the once abstract lines of the *aligne-ments* on the plans of Paris became concretized as the geometry of Hauss-mann's New Paris, Loyer has observed, and the increasing numbers of com-missaires voyers effectively became its designers – much more than the architects of the individual background buildings, clever as the ornament they provided might have been. The commissiares voyers remodeled the masses of *immeubles haussmanniens* into a pattern of *îlots haussmanniens* producing the new cityscape – for example, that of the quartier de l'Opéra, explored in Chapter 1, or those of the Châtelet, the Gare du Nord, or the rue des Ecoles, which we examine in Chapter 6.

Haussmann's new city texture is usually pictured as one of boulevards framed between the new *immeubles* cut through an older texture of quarters with narrower, less frequented streets and lower, more reassuring old habi-tations. Loyer develops this evocation, but there seems another, contrary vector in the Haussmannian evolution, toward a grid of densely utilized *îlots* characterized by an undifferentiated web of streets wide enough to accommodate the mass of traffic engendered, the old medieval texture com-pletely obliterated. This emerged at the central points where the traffic was already heavy, in the quarters of the Opéra and the Châtelet, but also in some more peripheral areas newly constructed, like that north of the rue des Ecoles or along the rue Claude Bernard (Figures 66 and 67).

Loyer carefully documents the evolution of the exterior treatment of these immeubles comprising the Paris city texture. The first modest develop-ment of Restoration in stuccoed rubble and wood built up the church lands expropriated as *biens nationaux* – the quartier de Bellechasse, for example, or the rue de l'Abbaye – he compares to the charming regularity of contem-porary development. Then he shows how the fully "Rambuteauan" *immeu-ble* of the 1840s grows to fill its regulementary envelope but has no mansard (only a less visible 45-degree sloping roof with dormers), few bal-conies, and a light paneled treatment of its stone facade. Next, in the 1850s appears the *immeuble haussmannien* with its beveled corners and bulging mansards underlining its mass and its increasingly heavily ornamented stone facade centering on triplet windows, half columns supporting balconies, cornices, and richly articulated door surrounds. The culmination is the Gar-nieresque ornamental effusion of the late 1860s. This evolution continued after the collapse of the Second Empire, forcing the relaxation of zoning regulations in 1884 and especially in 1902, permitting higher mansards, bow windows, and breaks in the facade and cornice lines seen along the rue Réaumur. Finally in the design of the Samaritaine department store of 1905 even the traditional stone carapace, which so unified the nineteenth-century Paris cityscape, dissolves, as Zola had predicted in *Au Bonheur des dames,*

Figure 66. Apartment buildings erected on the rue Claude Bernard by the Compagnie Immobilière du Luxembourg (Théodore Belle, architect), c. 1860.

replaced by steel, glass, and enameled panels in floral designs with colored domes illuminated at night with electricity.

III

The city texture of nineteenth-century Paris waxed and pressed against the resistant reglamentory envelope maintained by the commissaires voyers like the Paris crowds depicted by Baudelaire, Le Bon, and Benjamin.[32] It is an

Figure 67. Apartment buildings erected on the rue Claude Bernard by the Compagnie Immobilière du Luxembourg (Théodore Belle, architect), c. 1860.

extraordinary and somewhat frightening sight. Buried in this tide of sternly regulated private development lie an array of heterogeneous social institutions, likewise new with the century and attempting alongside the *immeuble* and the *magasin* to find their urbanistic place: service institutions like hospitals, schools, prisons, libraries, and ministries. Such institutions were an especially acute monumental problem, first, because they were evolving in size and complexity during the century (and indeed by the mid-twentieth century would replace traditional representational structures as the expression of the state); second, because an uniquely close collaboration evolved between their administrators and their architects so that one can speak of an esprit de corps and a local mentality – one that Teyssot would elevate to a fundamental vision of architecture and of the city; third, because service institutions did have a traditional place in the French monumental urban order, a place that became increasingly inappropriate and fragile so that, fourth, a new place in and relationship to the cityscape eventually emerged.

*　　*　　*

One of the most fundamental changes in Western civilization around 1800 was the creation of an array of institutions to heal and control the population – hospitals, prisons, insane asylums – as well as to train the new citizens of the bourgeois state – schools, libraries, museums. A new array of highly specialized buildings appeared in the European city. Michel Foucault has explored this on the broad plane; Anthony Vidler, Bernard Lepetit, and Georges Teyssot on the more concrete.[33] This array of new institutional types was sketched repeatedly around 1800, for example, in the fantasy city of Chaux by Ledoux (1804), in J.-N.-L. Durand's *Recueil* (1801) and the "Partie Graphique" of his *Précis des leçons* (1821), in the new town of Napoléonville (Pontivy, 1805),[34] in Bruyère's projected new city at Comacchio near Ravenna, published in his *Art des constructions* (1823–1828; Figures 62 and 63). The array includes, in the case of Bruyère, a hospital, a stock exchange, a college, a theater, law courts, a prefecture, a city hall, a customs house, a hostel, public baths, an abbatoir, a market, and a barracks. Napoleon himself initiated a massive project to equip Paris with markets, fountains, abbatoirs, boulevards, bridges, schools, prisons, cemeteries, and the Bourse.[35]

Foucault and Vidler have explored how extraordinary were many of these institutions and their workings. One of the primary functions of the Conseil des Bâtiments Civils was to approve the designs of local architects for the institutions that constituted this massive campaign of construction all over France, a task very different from that addressed by the old Surintendance des Bâtiments du Roi, which had been fundamentally representational. Tremendous knowledge was required of the members. As we have seen, bureaucratic specialization evolved with the architectural administration, and within the Bâtiments Civils several subadministrations asserted themselves, especially the Inspection Générale des Prisons (1838) under Blouet and the Assistance Publique (reorganized with the city of Paris in 1849) under Henri Davenne and Théodore Labrouste. Government officials and architects became specialists passionately committed to the perfection of certain institutions and their architectural frame. There was no vagueness of purpose; one does not have to search for the principles of these men as we did in the case of the representational designers. Instead we read of Abel

Blouet, inspecteur général des prisons, for example, that prison reform, "s'était pour ainsi dire incarné en lui" – "was, in a sense, incarnate in him."[36] This intense commitment on the part of the architects was important because the unifying concept of the service institutions came to be that the buildings themselves were the most powerful instruments of control or cure. The hospital became a "machine à guérir."[37] "The plan of an insane asylum," wrote the great psychologist J.-E.-D. Esquirol in his *Etablissements des aliénés en France* (1818), "is not an indifferent thing that might be left to the architects alone; the function of an ordinary hospital is to make easy and economical the treatment given to the resident sick. A mental asylum is an instrument of cure."[38] "To build prisons," pronounced the minister Gasparin, "one must have a system of which the program is the conception and the plan the expression."[39]

We have noted that Blouet's early career positioned him to be an important representational architect. A student of Delespine, he won the Grand Prix in 1821 and produced a splendid fourth-year *envoi* reconstructing the Baths of Caracalla, published by the Académie des Beaux-Arts in 1828.[40] Upon his return in 1827 he opened a successful atelier and was asked to accompany the French military expedition to the Peloponnesus. Consequently in 1831–1838 he published a magnificent study of the southern Greek remains in three volumes.[41] In recognition, although still quite young, he was named to finish the Arc de Triomphe (in succession to Huyot) in 1832–1836. At this point Blouet had acquired the archeological knowledge and the practical experience to be a leading representational designer. But now, in 1836, he accepted the invitation of the jurist Fréderic-Auguste Demetz to accompany him on an inspection trip of U.S. prisons and helped write the compendious report published in 1837 setting out strictures for model prison design on the penitentiary system. In 1838 the post of inspecteur général des prisons with a permanent seat on the Conseil des Bâtiments Civils was created for him. In this capacity he drew up and published several series of model prison designs as we have noted in Chapter 2, especially one for 585 occupants (Figure 68) shown at the Salon of 1843, sent on tour around Europe, published in a pamphlet, and finally actually built in Paris by Blouet's close friend Emile Gilbert as the "Mazas" or the Nouvelle Force, near the Gare de Lyon (1842–1850). In 1839 he had helped organize and had designed the model juvenile prison camp at Mettray near Tours.

The objective of the penitentiary system was suggested in its name, penitence, to oblige prisoners to contemplate their offenses in a regulated regime of solitary confinement.[42] Blouet's perfect prison was an eight-winged panoptic arrangement of individual cells, like his proclaimed model, the Eastern State Penitentiary in Philadelphia.[43] The Pennsylvania prison, however, was all

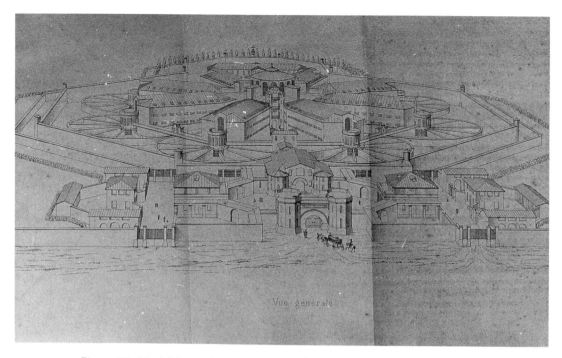

Figure 68. Model Panopticon Penitentiary for 585 criminals (Abel Blouet, architect), 1843.

on one floor with individual exercise yards behind each cell to maintain perfect solitude. Food was passed to the prisoner through a hatch in the door. Blouet altered this: He angled the inner cell walls so the prisoner might look through a small window to see the central guardpost, which was topped by an altar for the daily celebration of the Mass. These cells were piled in three stories with larger separate exercise yards in between the wings to which the prisoners were led each day. These changes, Blouet explained, introduced the therapeutic influence of religion and human contact – the guards having been trained to instruct the prisoners morally during the exercise periods. Thus, Blouet concludes, it is only the inert walls of the building itself that punishes – the human staff are kind and uplifting, "les murs sont terribles; l'homme est bon. . . ."[44] The shapes and spaces of the prison are the most direct manifestations of the penal regime.

Blouet's friend Gilbert built the Mazas on this pattern and also produced a variation on its principles in his earlier construction, the insane asylum at Charenton, begun in 1834 for Esquirol (Figures 69 and 70).[45] Gilbert had won the Grand Prix the year after Blouet, 1822, and upon his return from Rome had worked as Blouet's *inspecteur* at the Arc de Triomphe. Subsequently, he became the institutional architect par excellence, designing the Pré-

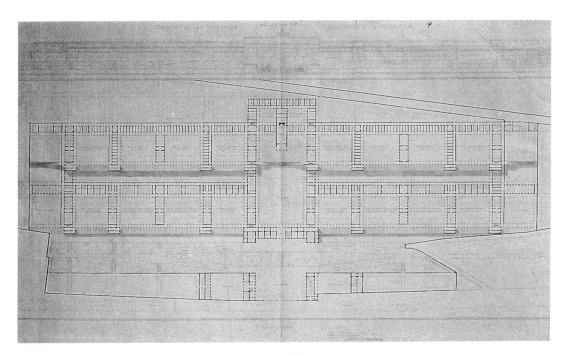

Figure 69. Insane asylum at Charenton. Plan (Emile Gilbert, architect, 1834–1844).

Figure 70. Insane asylum at Charenton. Detail of one of the wards (Emile Gilbert, architect, 1834–1844).

fecture de Police (with Dubois, then his son-in-law A.-N. Diet, 1855–1869), the Hôtel Dieu (1865–1877, succeeded by Diet), and the Morgue (1861–1863) on the Ile de la Cité, in addition to the Mazas and Charenton.[46]

Esquirol's innovation was therapy rather than indiscriminant incarceration.[47] Architecturally, this determined three principles: separation of different classes of dementia; removal of all visible signs of repression; the creation of an entirely rational, subdued visual environment. At Charenton he and Gilbert laid out a series of courtyards in two tall terraces across the hillside above the Marne, each court to accommodate one class of patient, all open to views of the valley over the terrace walls that prevented escape.[48] For the structure of the courtyards Gilbert conceived a simple reconstruction of the primitive Tuscan order that was rational and archeological.[49] Gilbert's admirer L.-C. Cernesson explained in his necrology,

The regularity of lines is thus presented as proper to the regularity of ideas and judgment. The broad, unified surfaces of the walls and the simple disposition of rooves permit the eye to rest upon them with ease and to follow the contours with tranquility. Stones projecting excessively, mouldings too vigorously relieved, sometimes producing more or less bizarre effects of chiaroscuro are carefully avoided in order to offer nothing to worry or arouse overexcited imaginations.[50]

César Daly praised the resulting building not just as an excellent hospital but as a general model of architectural rationalism.[51]

Later Henri Labrouste's brother Théodore achieved a similar position in the administration of the Assistance Publique as *architecte-en-chef* and designer of the Maison Dubois at Saint-Denis and the Hospice des Incurables at Ivry.[52]

❊   ❊   ❊

The most committed architects of these "machines à guérir" accepted that their task was the precise execution of their programs and the restriction of decoration to a minimum or, in the case of Charenton, reformulation by the principles of the system of therapy. Bruno Foucart has called these architects "rationalists," and François Loyer has compared their designs to contemporary factory architecture. There is something distinctly "futuristic" about these buildings, and they have been depicted as artistically advanced, presaging twentieth-century "functionalist" design. However, as we mentioned at the beginning of this chapter, institutional buildings had a place in the monumental order and one must explore whether this "rationalism" was a matter of conventional genre or of fundamental ethos – whether it was the nature of such buildings to be simply made as background structures or whether they were being formulated as the organs of a general, functionalist architecture. Both Blouet and Gilbert were elected to the Académie des Beaux-Arts in 1850 and 1853, respectively; Blouet was named to the pivotal post of professor of theory at the Ecole des Beaux-Arts in 1846, and after the elimination of his *inspection* in 1848, he received the post of architect for the emplacement of the Chamber of Deputies in the Tuileries, a purely representational task, and then architect of the Palace at Fontainebleau.

We have noted that in 1810 Napoleon had begun construction of the huge (and abortive) Palais du Roi de Rome on the slope of the Colline de Chaillot on the axis of the Champs de Mars (Figure 33). A series of institutional buildings were projected to enframe that axis from the Ecole Militaire to the Seine. Percier and Fontaine's palace was the representational culmination of the ensemble with dome and colonnades. The institutional buildings were distinctly more modest, Cellerier's archives simply displaying the arches of its actual construction.[53] Such a contrast between representational "functional" was traditional in palatial ensembles: We see it in the contrast between the palace proper and the outbuildings at Versailles or in chateaux like Richelieu and Vaux-le-Vicomte or (more dramatically) in large foreign complexes like those at Stupinigi and Karlsruhe.

In the last chapter we analyzed the wings of the New Louvre as scenographic, framing "flats" erected to set off the older historic parts of the complex. They contained two ministries, stables, a barracks, printing and telegraph offices. The rue de Rivoli (Figure 61) was even more unmistakably a background mass, setting off the Tuileries and its gardens but containing the massive Ministère des Finances as well as palace stables. Similarly, when the surroundings of the Hôtel de Ville were regularized in the 1850s, a very large proportion of the functional administrative space was accommodated behind the anonymous facades across from the representational monument itself (of which Merruau had noted, "One criticizes the excessive amount of space the city devotes in its palace to ceremonial affairs and the pleasure of privileged society, and to the parsimony with which the administration [itself] is housed."[54]). It was conventional to distinguish between the merely administrative and the representational government functions and to use the former to enframe and give hieratic value to the latter.

✻   ✻   ✻

Regardless of institutional, administrative architecture having a traditional place in the urban order, these architects – Blouet, Gilbert, Théodore Labrouste – were linked to a circle of opponents of traditional academicism advocating a kind of general "structural rationalism," led by Henri Labrouste.[55] Middleton and Watkin quote Gilbert of the Mazas: "The Mazas prison is not only a fine piece of building and an administrative instrument, it is a work of art."[56] This rationalism may have been restricted to a subordinate place in the urban order, but it had the potential to break out of that and to assume the pretenses of a general style of architecture.

Gilbert had begun his career with two years at the Ecole Polytechnique, of which Durand's course formed part of the curriculum, and was henceforth celebrated for his impatience with the superfluous or fantastic in design. Guadet wrote of him at the Mazas, "Gilbert . . . was neither broad nor at all liberal in spirit. Obstinate, opinionated, incapable of grace or elegance, he had a forthrightness that brooked no exceptions, a conscience that refused to bend, a sincerity that he did not know how to disguise."[57] He rarely wrote and was a failure as a teacher, taking over Blouet's atelier for a short time after his friend's death in 1853. But we read in his letters to the architect Antoine Desjardins in Lyons (1861), "I hate this grimacing and mannered architecture generally admired today and which, like all that is bad, tends to develop with an appalling exuberance."[58]

We know much more of Blouet's thinking on the general plane. He conducted an atelier, taught as professor of theory at the Ecole, and published a supplement to Rondelet's *Art de bâtir* in 1847–1848.[59] His atelier method was to avoid intruding on his students' individuality and his Ecole lectures were felt to be indecisively eclectic, but parts of the *Art de bâtir* text are clear and pointed. His basic principle is that architecture is the natural product of program and structure. A new style will result from a new structural principle and only from that. The history of architecture is a slow perfection of the technique of spanning. The late Romans are to be praised for escaping decorative cladding. Gothic is the pinnacle – "In that epoch structure based on reason constituted the building all by itself; and the building was beautiful because the useless had been proscribed."[60] The Renaissance is a retreat. A modern architecture will evolve and impose itself with imaginative labor on the architects' part once a new structural system – probably based on metal – emerges completely.

The simple, eternal and fundamental principle of all good architecture is . . . (1) to conceive what is necessary, nothing more, and to realize it in the simplest possible [manner] which can only be accomplished by subordinating one's projections of what will become reality from the start to the properties of the materials that you have and the means of construction; (2) to employ decoration only to articulate the expression already present in the shape of the construction, to accent the parts in relation to their relative functions, and to thus express the character of the building with greater precision by the aid of treatments that are suggested by the materials to which they are applied, so that – in a word – the structure of the building and its function are simultaneously communicated.[61]

*   *   *

In the cases of Blouet and Gilbert their "rationalism" seems not a function of genre but a general principle. Nonetheless, all of their major buildings were urbanistically subordinate institutional structures (and the two most famous, the Mazas and Charenton, outside the monumental center of the city). We do not know what their "rationalist" architecture would look like when applied to a central representational program, unless we count Blouet's disappointing Chamber of Deputies project.[62] This issue is posed more decisively in the cases of the bibliothèques Sainte-Geneviève and Nationale by the most brilliant of the group, Henri Labrouste (1801–1875).

The three great free-standing public libraries of Paris are the Bibliothèque Sainte-Geneviève, the Bibliothèque Nationale, and the Bibliothèque de l'Arsenal (Figures 71–77).[63] All three were built or rebuilt by the Labrouste brothers, Henri the first two, Théodore the third. A library was a subordinate structure, like the Ministère des Finances on the rue de Rivoli (Figure 61) or Cellerier's archive projected for the Champs de Mars (Figure 33), merely a windowed box. (The bibliothèques de l'Institut and Mazarine and the Bibliothèque Administrative de la Ville de Paris, which were likewise administered as national libraries, all occupied parts of larger buildings.)

The Bibliothèque Sainte-Geneviève (1838–1850, Figures 72–75) was the only one built entirely ex novo, along the north side of the place du Panthéon, containing the books formerly housed on the top floor of the Abbaye Sainte-Geneviève, now made the Lycée Henri IV.[64] The building has a cen-

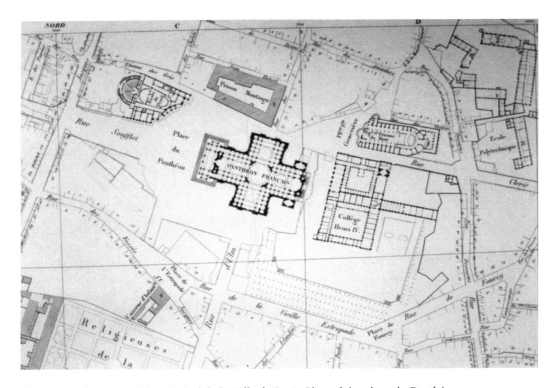

Figure 71. Jacoubet, *Atlas général de la Ville de Paris.* Plan of the place du Panthéon c.

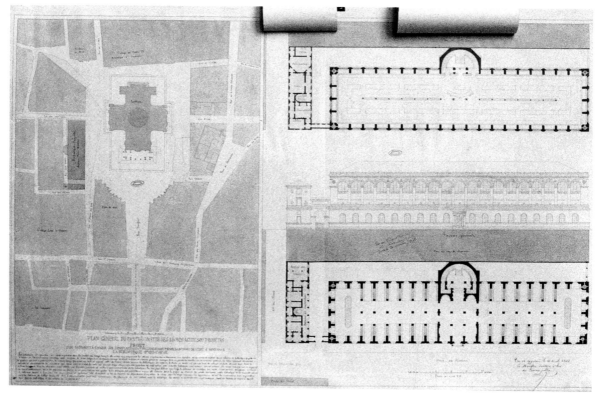

Figure 72. Plan of the place du Panthéon as shaped by the projected construction of the Bibliothèque Sainte-Geneviève, 1839 (Henri Labrouste, architect).

tral place in the history of "rationalist" design with its skeletal stone exterior and exposed iron interior structure as well as in the history of ornamental style with its exquisite neo-Grec detailing.[65] However, it has never been analyzed in terms of its very loaded institutional and urban context. Its site was one of the most stringently controlled in Paris. Its shape and volume were set at the beginning of Labrouste's campaign. Soufflot had intended an architectural facade around his Panthéon defining the *place* and had erected a portion in his Ecole du Droit (1763) forming a half hemicycle in the northwest corner.[66] A *décision ministral* of June 13, 1807, specified the repetition of the Ecole du Droit demi-hemicycle symmetrically at the southwest corner and the setting of northern and southern limits parallel with the Panthéon axis, 34 meters from the transept ends, the existing facade of the Lycée Henri IV left to form the east side.[67] (The city owned the land at the southwest corner and along most of the north side in the form of the Prison Montaigu.) In 1811 Napoleon designated the southwestern corner the site for the Palais du Grand Maître de l'Université. In 1844, after a decade of

Figure 73. Bibliothèque Sainte-Geneviève (Henri Labrouste, architect, 1838–1850).

negotiations, it was redesignated the site for a new *mairie,* actually constructed, first by Guénepin, then Hittorff, in 1849–1855.[68] The relocation of the Bibliothèque Sainte-Geneviève to the north side, on the site of the Prison Montaigu, was broached beginning in 1836. Labrouste was named architect in 1838; construction was funded in 1843 and commenced in 1844. Both the *mairie* and the library were the subject of an agreement between the city and the state of July 2, 1844, trading certain land parcels, specifying the sites, delimiting the *place,* and giving the state the responsibility for leveling and paving (appropriating 280,000 francs for this).[69]

The initial letter of appointment to Labrouste from the directeur des travaux publics of October 29, 1838, defined his task as creating a gas-lit fireproof structure that would, "former la place" – "shape the square."[70] Labrouste duly filled the designated envelope along the *alignement* up to the cornice of Soufflot's Ecole du Droit (Figure 74). Guénepin and Hittorff were equally respectful in their *mairie.* Later, in the 1880s, Labrouste's student L.-

Figure 74. Bibliothèque Sainte-Geneviève (Henri Labrouste, architect, 1838–1850).

E. Lheureux extended the Ecole du Droit down the rue Soufflot by reproducing Soufflot's side facade exactly – before permitting himself a personal statement in the new entrance on the rue Saint-Jacques around the corner and a display of rationalist *virtù* in the library at the back. If we are to analyze Labrouste's accomplishment in the exterior of the library we must acknowledge these *servitudes* and accept that its parallels are with the Ministère des Finances or Cellerier's projected archives. The building's nature

Figure 75. Bibliothèque Sainte-Geneviève, interior of the reading room (Henri Labrouste, architect, 1838–1850).

and site forbade representational elaboration. A flat arcuated facade was the most appropriate.[71] What is extraordinary is what Labrouste manages to do with these tight limits in the scaling, articulation, and ornamentation of a set facade plane to communicate the nature of the institution hidden behind it.

The issue was essentially the same in the rebuilding of the Bibliothèque Nationale and the Arsenal. In the case of the former, Henri Labrouste was even more tightly constrained, here by the existing walls of the Palais Mazarin, which he had to extend, regularize, and work within (Figures 76 and 77).[72] It was a site in the densest part of the Right Bank and it could not be simply cleared and built over (although Mérimée complained that Labrouste wished to do so).[73] Labrouste began in 1854 by restoring the seventeenth-century Hôtel Tubeuf and clearing the garden behind it along the rue Vivienne, which had been arcaded and used as the Bourse. In 1859

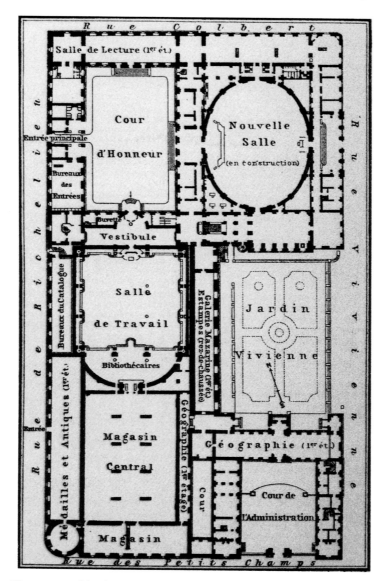

Figure 76. Bibliothèque Nationale. Plan c. 1900 (Henri Labrouste, architect, 1854–1875, succeeded by Jean-Louis Pascal).

he moved the work to the western two-thirds of the site, around Mazarin's "Galerie Mansart," regularizing the perimeter wall down the rue de Richelieu and along the rue des Petits-Champs (adding an understated rotunda to make the turn) and proposing to open an arcade along the newly landscaped place Louvois, thus appropriating it to his building's

Figure 77. Bibliothèque Nationale, interior of the reading room (Henri Labrouste, architect, 1860–1868).

spatial composition.[74] His extension of the building's space to embrace the place Louvois, however, had to balance a dramatic reduction of the old inner courtyards as Labrouste dropped his iron and porcelain reading room into the southern half of the *cour d'honneur* and his iron and glass stack structure into the old back garden and dependencies beyond.[75] The spatial transformation of the building therefore was fundamental, but its exterior manifestation deceptively minimized, Labrouste simply rearranging the elements of the seventeenth-century structure within the existing building lines and masses. The great reading room was not volumetrically expressed on the exterior at all. The building still stood within the shell of the Palais Mazarin, as it had since the seventeenth century, and so was where the visitor expected it to be.

In the case of Théodore Labrouste's transformation of the Bibliothèque de l'Arsenal, its long thin mass was extended about 20 meters at its western end to contain a new entrance stair, the building isolated by the regularization of the defining streets and the creation of a small *place* in front, the decorative vocabulary of the new parts derived impressionistically from that of the old.[76]

Both the bibliothèques Sainte-Geneviève and Nationale are peculiarly decorated internally with large illusionist paintings of treetops and blue sky (Figure 77). These are the equivalent of the symbolically muted external architecture; they contrast with the symbolic decoration used in the major spaces of representational buildings. A symbolic composition of Minerva or of the grove of academe might have been literally appropriate but out of harmony with the architectural genre of Labrouste's buildings. Yet in Labrouste's hands both the architecture and the painting produce a "real allegory" more powerful in its own terms.

*   *   *

The question is: How might one imagine would appear the extension of the institutional "rationalist" system of design to the urban plane? Intuitively we fear the idea of the whole built environment remade on the lines of a huge hospital (or prison). Foucault is explicit when he ends *Surveiller et punir* with a black vision sketched in the Fourierist journal *La Phalange* in 1836.

Moralists, philosophers, legislators, flatterers of Civilization! Here is the plan of your Paris made orderly, here is the perfect plan where everything is classified:
   In the center in a first precinct: hospitals for all ailments, hospices for all misfortunes, lunatic asylums, prisons, penal houses for men, women, children.
   Around this first precinct: barracks and law courts, police stations, guards' houses, scaffolds, houses for the executioner and his assistants.

In the four corners: the Chamber of Deputies, the Senate, the Institute, the Royal Palace.[77]

The rationalized institution is architecturally negative, the bottom of the hierarchy or a sort of hell. Blouet, in order to make his model penitentiary of 1843 identify itself, still felt obliged to give it a gothic (and therefore primitive) appearance with an arched gateway flanked by octagonal towers (Figure 68).

Labrouste would seem to have worked against this. The rationalist skeleton of the Bibliothèque Sainte-Geneviève stands free for appreciation but it is interwoven with two other systems of art not present in the work of Blouet or Gilbert: a scattering externally of hieroglyphs of real life and real function painted or etched on its surface and an illusion internally transforming the space into some imagined exemplar of its function, the garden of the Bibliothèque Sainte-Geneviève vestibule (subsequently expanded into the tent-covered reading room of the Bibliothèque Nationale).[78] A contemporary observer writing in the *Journal des débats* touches on these three aspects as if they were steps in simple architectural exegesis:

Given a lot 84 meters 75 centimeters long and 21 meters wide, an appropriation of 1,500,000 francs, to erect a library the reading room of which will comfortably accommodate beside 95,000 volumes, four hundred readers, with the necessary provision for supervision, book delivery, light, heating, during the daylight and evening hours. That is the program. . . .

For each building, a style, a character, the shapes in harmony with its function. Thus very judiciously has reasoned M. Labrouste. . . .

A moment of reflection explains the exterior. Because, in the end, one builds a library for the books, one must make it for their utilization. Books cannot be placed in front of windows but they do accommodate themselves easily in rows against broad walls. From this the wide space between the windows of the ground floor and the forty openings which light the interior. What has one put on this surface? The names of philosophers, poets, historians, and scholars of all centuries. Inside their works, outside their names, as one puts the title of a good book on its spine. Who would doubt that the architect wishes to place his temple of the muses amid *allées* of trees, near tranquil shadowed places, far from the noise of the public thoroughfare? That was his objective, but the intractable public right of way would not grant him an extra foot. These sheltering [trees] are there, at least in paint, in the vestibule. . . .[79]

A contemporary of Labrouste's, Nicolas Harou-Romain, offered a telling critique of Blouet's institutional rationalism in his model prison of 1840 (Figure 78).[80] In the pages of the Fourierist Daly's *Revue générale de l'architecture* he criticized Blouet's inconveniencing the jailor's apartments with a symbolic arch and turrets at the entrance so that he obliges, "these honest employees live in holes and this in order to give the facades what it is common to call character."[81] What Harou-Romain would prefer is a hivelike cylinder of five tiers of cells transparent (to use his own word) to a central surveillance tower, under a huge iron hemispheric roof, transporting the prisoners from penal boxes "au milieu d'un océan d'air comme les cultivateurs dans les champs" – "in the midst of an ocean of air like farmers in the fields."[82] (Among Labrouste's papers in the Bibliothèque Nationale is a sketch of this project).[83]

The implication is that the rationalized industrial architectural object might produce an experience more powerful than that any utilization of traditional forms might evoke – one liberating and beneficial because taking purchase from the laws of reason and nature. What both Labrouste and Harou-Romain did was to admit light and air through the filigree of an architectural skeleton disencumbered of the clutter of traditional images. This is the theme of the Fourierests and Saint-Simoniens, the idea that we cannot even imagine the wonder of the new world that will result if we rationalize society to achieve harmony (their catchword) with ourselves and with nature.[84] Utopian writers, as we saw at the beginning of this chapter, without budgets to keep within or constructions to keep upright, conceived whole cities in this spirit. Labrouste and Harou-Romain can only give us libraries and prisons – if wondrous ones.

Nonetheless the evidence in Labrouste's and Harou-Romain's magnificently functional structures is inadequate because these genres had always been treated functionally and were externally mute in the traditional order. Furthermore, because of some sort of unadmitted tracking in the government services, they – like Blouet, Gilbert, and Théodore Labrouste – were only given institutional buildings to design. What they would have done had they had the opportunity to execute a representational building – whether a "carceral" conception in the spirit of the *Phalange* article and Fournel's "Paris futur" or some harbinger of a glorious new system in the spirit of Duveyrier and Horeau – we lack the evidence to decide.

One might imagine three possibilities. First, that Labrouste did wish to reduce the city to an array of institutions serving the needs of the general population, but there is no evidence that this son of a high fonctionnaire in the Ministry of Finance was a utopian, in spite of his friendship with César Daly and Hector Horeau. Second, that he believed structure itself could be made expressive so that, working metaphorically, it could express the dignity or gravity (or lack of such) in a building. This was Charles Blanc's formulation, which he shared with (and attributed to) Labrouste's friends Vaudoyer and Duc. Third, that he hoped he might make his designs speak through scattered facts and allusions – the names inscribed on the Bibliothèque Sainte-Geneviève's facade; the naked iron construction within – to

VUE, DE DEDANS UNE CELLULE, SUR LA TOUR DU CENTRE.

Figure 78. Model penitentiary. View from a cell toward the watchtower and altar (Nicolas Harou-Romain, architect, 1840).

produce something lacking conventional unity, something not metaphorical at all, but instead actual, like a story.

Selecting from among these extrapolations would have been important in my last book, *Designing Paris*, but, in fact, it is not so here. What is important now is the professional framework within which Labrouste worked that permitted him to develop his "rationalist" ideas by giving him repeated opportunities to design institutional buildings, and simultaneously kept him from starting an architectural revolution by preventing him from designing anything else.

THE ARCHITECTS

The conventional history of nineteenth-century French architecture between 1830 and 1870 focuses on personalities – imagined embodying styles – divided into three generations. First come the neoclassicists dominated by Percier (rather than his practical partner, Fontaine); then the "romantic" rationalist historicists Duban, Labrouste, Duc, and Vaudoyer; finally the "battle of the styles" embodied in the great antagonists Charles Garnier and Viollet-le-Duc.[1]

In this history we have constructed a different positioning of the personalities has been emerging. We have tried to flatten out again the topography of historical personalities and position them in the institutional structure so the original center points might be seen. The resulting array of central personalities would appear thus:

CONSEIL DES BATIMENTS CIVILS
Président honoraire – Fontaine, 1848–1853
Vice-présidents
   Rohault de Fleury (Hubert), 1838–1847
   Caristie, 1847–1862
   Duban, 1862–1870[2]
   Lefuel, 1870–1881

   Inspecteur Général des Prisons: Blouet, 1837–1848
   Inspecteur Général des Monuments Historiques: Mérimée, 1837–1864[3]

PALAIS ROYAUX
Architect of the Louvre
   Fontaine, 1804–1848, "Premier Architecte de l'Empereur," 1813–1814
   Duban, 1848–1854

Visconti, 1852–1853 (Nouveau Louvre), "Architecte de l'Empereur," 1853

Lefuel, 1854–1881 (Louvre and Tuileries), "Architecte de l'Empereur," 1857–1870

VILLE DE PARIS

Directeur des Travaux d'Architecture: Victor Baltard, 1860–1871

Inspecteur Général des Travaux de la Ville de Paris: Ballu, 1871–1876

Chief of the *Première Section* (religious buildings)
    Molinos, 1817–1831
    Godde, 1831–1848
    Victor Baltard, 1848–1860
    Ballu, 1860–1871 (now designated *quatrième section*)

Architecte-en-chef du Service des Promenades et Plantations: Davioud, 1856–1871

Conseillers municipals
    Caristie, 1859–1860
    Duban, 1864–1870
    Gilbert, 1869–1870
    Viollet-le-Duc, 1874–1879

EDIFICES DIOCESAINS

Inspecteurs Généraux
    Viollet-le-Duc, 1853–1874 (declined title of "Architecte de l'Empereur"?)
    Reynaud, 1853–1858
    Léon Vaudoyer, 1853–1871
    Labrouste, 1858–1875

MONUMENTS HISTORIQUES

Architects on the Commission des Monuments Historiques
    Caristie, 1837–1862
    Duban, 1837–1870
    Labrouste, 1848–1875
    Léon Vaudoyer, 1848–1872
    Questel, 1848–1888
    Viollet-le-Duc, 1860–1879
    Boeswillwald, 1860–1896

This list parallels that of the architects of the principal monuments of Paris and of France:
    Palais du Louvre: Fontaine, Duban, Visconti, Lefuel
    Hôtel de Ville: Molinos, Godde (with Lesueur), Baltard, Ballu (working with Desperthes for the reconstruction)

Cathedral of Notre-Dame: Godde, (Arveuf), Lassus and Viollet-le-Duc
Palais de Justice: Huyot, Duc
Opéra: Charles Rohault de Fleury, Garnier
Halles Centrales: Baltard (with Callet, 1851–1854)
Marseilles Cathedral: Léon Vaudoyer
Lille Cathedral: Lassus

Again these same names dominate the list of the professors and masters of the leading ateliers at Ecole des Beaux-Arts:

ECOLE DES BEAUX-ARTS (1818–1870)
Professors of Theory[4]
   Louis-Pierre Baltard, 1818–1846
   Blouet, 1846–1853
   Lesueur, 1853–1863

Professor of the History of Art and Esthetics
   Viollet-le-Duc, 1863–1864
   Taine, 1864–1874

Masters of the most successful ateliers
   Percier (14 Grand Prix winners, 20 placing, 1800–1823)
   A.-L.-T. Vaudoyer (9 Grand Prix winners, 13 placing, 1806–1830)
   Huyot (9 Grand Prix winners, 13 placing, 1820–1844)
   Lebas (19 Grand Prix winners, 39 placing, 1821–1871)
   Questel (3 Grand Prix winners, 14 placing, 1858–1876)[5]

Synthesizing these lists would suggest that these four personalities stand out as uniquely central in the mid-nineteenth century:
   Fontaine
   Duban
   Baltard
   Viollet-le-Duc

(I must, however, acknowledge the flux of reputation and influence during this relatively long period and note that Fontaine steadily declined after the Empire while Garnier, Lefuel, and Ballu emerged during the Second Empire to become the dominant personalities during the Third Republic.) Another twelve individuals seem of great importance although perhaps not quite as central:
   Caristie
   Hubert and Charles Rohault de Fleury
   Huyot
   Visconti
   Lefuel
   Duc

Labrouste
Gilbert
Davioud
Ballu
Garnier

(One might dispute whether this second list should not be extended to include several narrower specialists like de Gisors and Lebas in the Bâtiments Civils; Molinos, Godde, and Hittorff in the Travaux de Paris; Léon Vaudoyer in the Edifices Diocésains; or Boeswillwald and de Baudot in the Monuments Historiques.)

I distinguish the four most prominent because each was not only the dominant personality in one of the most important services (as well as architect of its chief monuments) – Fontaine of the Palais Royaux, Duban of the Bâtiments Civils, Baltard of the Travaux de Paris, Viollet-le-Duc of the Monuments Historiques – but they were also called to important places in other services – Fontaine as premier architecte de l'empereur in 1813–1814 and later as the président honoraire of the Bâtiments Civils (1848); Duban as a founding member of the Monuments Historiques (1837), architect of the Louvre (1848), and conseiller municipal (1864); Viollet-le-Duc as inspecteur général des Edifices Diocésains (1853) and reformer of the Ecole des Beaux-Arts (1863). Two were among the most prolific public architects of the century, Viollet-le-Duc and Baltard. Two – Fontaine and Viollet-le-Duc – were the leading architectural authors of their generations, both founding schools of publication. Two had ambitions to reorganize the French architectural profession as a whole, Fontaine under Napoleon I and Viollet-le-Duc under Napoleon III.

If we can pretend to level the received topography of nineteenth-century French architecture flat again these four individuals represent particular points to which our attention, I think, would be especially drawn.[6]

*   *   *

All four came from very different backgrounds, but each first gained an important place in one or another government service, then from there emerged as a leader of their art in the general context. Fontaine, the son of a builder in Pontoise near Paris, moved from the first consul's personal architect at Malmaison (1799) to the architect of the Louvre in the Palais Impériaux (1804) to premier architecte de l'empereur (1813) in competition with Bruyère for the direction of all construction in Paris. After retreating to the palatial service during the Restoration and the Monarchy of July, he reemerged (ceremonially at least) as président honoraire of the Conseil des Bâtiments Civils in 1848.

Duban, the son of an ironmonger (but also young brother-in-law of architect academician François Debret), established himself as the eldest of the "romantic" rationalist architects, under Thiers's patronage rebuilding the Ecole des Beaux-Arts (1832–1840) with the assistance of Henri Labrouste. He then was named to a series of important design and advisory posts: member of the Commission des Monuments Historiques (1837) and architect in that service for the restoration of the Sainte-Chapelle (1837) and the chateau at Blois (1843); architect manqué of the Tomb of Napoleon (1840); architect of the Orléans chateau at Chantilly (1845); architect of the Louvre (1848). During the Second Empire he was named inspecteur général des Bâtiments Civils (January 1, 1854) and then vice president of that body replacing Caristie (December 10, 1862), writing a large number of important analyses, and finally adviser to Haussmann and conseiller municipal in 1864, again replacing Caristie.

Victor Baltard was son of the prominent architect Louis-Pierre Baltard (1764–1846) with links to the city administrative service through him and his protector, Edouard Gatteaux, conseiller municipal 1834–1843. His brother-in-law, Paul-Eugène Lequeux, and his cousin, A.-M.-F. Jay, were also in the city service, the first as architect of the arrondissement of Saint-Denis, the latter as chief of the Seconde Section. Victor himself, as we have noted, rose from inspecteur des Beaux-Arts in 1839 to architect of the Première Section (1848) and finally to the specially created post of directeur des Travaux d'Architecture de la Ville de Paris in the reorganization of 1860.

Viollet-le-Duc makes an illuminating parallel and contrast. Like Baltard, he started on the inside track: He was son of the *gouverneur* of the Tuileries (and thus an acquaintance of the palace's architect, Fontaine) as well as nephew of the *Journal des débats's* art critic E.-J. Delécluze. (Viollet-le-Duc's brother Adolphe replaced Delécluze in that post.) He was a brilliant draftsman, trained in the atelier of the academician Leclère, but he refused to formally enter the Ecole des Beaux-Arts, later explaining,

I resolved not to enter the Ecole des Beaux-Arts because I fear so much being carried away by the current into which it draws one. If I have talent, I will succeed anyway, if I have none, the Ecole will not give me any, far from it, because one emerges as a casting. M. Huyot has his mold, M. Percier has his mold, M. Lebas has his mold, so that once finished, I would be classed either among the Huyots, or among the Perciers, or among the Lebas.[7]

This, of course, distinguishes Viollet-le-Duc from Fontaine (Second Grand Prix, 1786), Duban (Grand Prix, 1823), and Baltard (Grand Prix, 1833). Nevertheless he visited Italy on his own in 1836–1837.[8] And it did not deny him government employment: In 1834 he was appointed *suppléant* in the course of *composition d'ornement* at the Ecole Gratuite de Dessin and in 1842 professor there. In 1838 he was named auditeur in the

Conseil des Bâtiments Civils, aiding Leclère, and in 1839 he received his first appointment in the fledgling service of the Monuments Historiques: to restore the cathedral at Narbonne. The rest is well known, how he became Mérimée's right-hand man and most frequently employed restorer, how in 1843–1844 he won the appointment as restorer of Notre-Dame (as Lassus's junior partner), and how in 1848 he became a member of the Commission de Répartition des Fonds et des Subventions pour les Travaux des Edifices Diocésains leading to his appointment as inspecteur général des Edifices Diocésains in the reorganization of 1853. Mérimée provided *entrée* to the imperial household through his friendship with Eugénie de Montijo, who became Empress Eugénie in January 1853. In 1854 Viollet-le-Duc evidently declined the title of architecte de l'empereur vacated by Visconti. He refused to seek election to the Académie. After the Second Empire in 1874 he entered the Conseil Municipal by popular election (rather than by appointment as in the cases of Caristie, Duban, and Gilbert).

What was distinct about Viollet-le-Duc was his refusal to be shaped for government work by the Ecole and the Académie and his persistent efforts to reform them and thus all French architecture. His years of apprenticeship in the Monuments Historiques (1839–1848) might seem conventional enough. He focused on the immediate problem of restoration at the same time that Blouet was focusing on incarceration in his capacity as inspecteur général des prisons and Baltard was working on church decoration as inspecteur des beaux-arts of the city. Like them he formulated and published general principles, in Viollet-le-Duc's case in Didron's *Annales archéologiques* (1844–1849). There in a series of articles of 1844–1846, "De la construction des édifices religieux en France depuis le commencement de christianisme jusqu'au XVIe siècle," he elucidated the principles of medieval construction – a seemingly parochial and innocent subject except he demonstrated that gothic churches were neither fantastic nor merely symbolic in their architecture but instead brilliant pieces of rational construction. In another article of 1846 in response to the controversy over the city's proposal to build the parish church of Sainte-Clothilde in the gothic style, Viollet-le-Duc synthesized his earlier conclusions into a delineation of the humanity and rationality of medieval design formulated as a counterideal to conventional classical design.[9] At the same time he gained recognition as the most skillful restorer of his profession, not only winning the Conseil des Bâtiments Civils's appointment as Lassus's junior partner for the work at Notre-Dame but also being appointed by that body to replace Debret at Saint-Denis in 1846.[10]

With the political upheavals of 1848–1852 – the revolution of February 1848; the election of Louis Bonaparte president in December; the coup d'état of December 1851; the proclamation of the Empire of December

1852 – Viollet-le-Duc found himself in a central position and he took advantage of it, entering the Comité de Répartition in charge of church decoration, repair, and building – sharing authority with Mérimée, Fortoul, Labrouste, Duban, and Vaudoyer.[11] Eugénie de Montijo's becoming empress (in a service at Notre-Dame gorgeously decorated by Viollet-le-Duc) led on, among other things, to the commission to rebuild Pierrefonds as an imperial retreat (1857) and, in November 1863, the reorganization of the Ecole des Beaux-Arts (formulated with the imperial confidant Nieuwerkerke, directeur des Beaux-Arts) and his own appointment there as professor of aesthetics and history. In 1848 he was thirty-four.

Now Viollet-le-Duc began to publish widely on the general reform of architecture. His first lengthy essay published outside the pages of the appropriately titled *Annales archéologiques* was "Un mot sur l'architecture en 1852" in César Daly's *Revue générale de l'architecture,* the leading general professional journal.[12] It constitutes a program of action that he describes as "depuis longtemps née chez nous" – "occurring to us long ago" and put forward now "parce que nous croyons le moment venu de prendre promptement un parti. . . ." – "because we judge the moment to have come to promptly make a stand. . . ." (col. 379). This was the moment when the Bâtiments Civils, the Monuments Historiques, and the Beaux-Arts in general were amalgamated and attached to the new Ministère d'Etat. Viollet-le-Duc had written in a personal letter of January 15, 1852, about this new organization and the possibility it might reanimate building: "This measure is important to the highest degree to the laboring part of the population. I, who know that world, I can tell you how the hope of such an impetus has reanimated many discouraged spirits."[13]

Viollet-le-Duc's program of 1852 was peculiar: It was to free architecture from state control by putting it in the hands of the artists themselves, constituted as an independent "chamber" like the notaries. State architecture, he asserted, produced only formulas. "One still can . . . produce colossal works like the great Roman buildings, like Versailles . . . but if one forgets *dimension*, what remains of these creations? Formulas, nothing more" (Viollet-le-Duc's emphasis).[14]

Provincial state architecture was but degraded copies of these formulas. The architects became the mindless tools in a huge mechanism, or rather, an array of narrowly specialized tools and the administration splintered into specialities. But to Viollet-le-Duc, the architect's usefulness lay in the very generality of his expertise, in his traditional position as planner and director.

The architect was . . . the most vital and palpable expression of the needs of his time; architecture is the book in which one reads the tastes and tendencies, the passions of a society. The architect . . . subsumed . . . in himself alone all the arts, profiting from all the elements that create themselves around him: even if he does not sculpt or paint with his own hands, he is the mind of the sculptor and painter.[15]

To recapture this condition architecture must free itself from state control and seek to remake itself on the basis of practical experience and beholden only to itself. "What must always be sought is truth [and] simplicity in the means of execution; what must be encouraged is conscientiousness and practical study; . . . What must be achieved in the end, if we wish to survive, is the moral association of architects, [that] is a sort of jury or *chamber* composed of men steeped in practice, respected and knowledgeable" (Viollet-le-Duc's emphasis).[16]

There was a fundamental contradiction in Viollet-le-Duc's enterprise: He sought artistic freedom but by imposition, by controlling education and restoration, using the centralized administration to dismantle itself. This was the recurrent nineteenth-century utopian fallacy, the belief that a perfect democratic system could be conceived whole and realized complete. Viollet-le-Duc despised contemporary private architectural practice as chaotic and dominated by economic interest. We read elsewhere in "Un mot sur l'architecture," "The stock market speculators, the successful merchants, are no longer of Jacques Coeur's race; the palaces they erect – brilliant but fragile like their fortunes – are built to the lowest bid by contractors for whom, as for their clients, *art* is the least concern" (Viollet-le-Duc's emphasis).[17]

He could not accept the private sector, as then organized, as a proper counterbalance to the state service. He believed that both of these architectures were unnatural and that a real sense of rightness had retreated to the crafts. "The arts, in abandoning the summits where they can no longer survive, have scattered themselves in the dust of the valleys; for in France they are alive, they circulate in the blood of the nation; they are the emanation of the people, they return to them."[18]

From this point in 1852 began a campaign that consumed the dozen best years of Viollet-le-Duc's extraordinary career. "Un mot sur l'architecture" was followed by a mass of articles in the leading architectural and art journals – *Revue générale de l'architecture, Encyclopédie d'architecture, L'Artiste, Gazette des beaux-arts*. Slowly his focus moved from a general confrontation with the government domination of the profession to education in particular, especially in his series of essays, "Il y a quelque chose à faire" in the *Gazette des beaux-arts* in 1862. In 1863 several friends together with his son founded the *Gazette des architectes et du bâtiment* (1863–1871) as a channel for their views. Finally and most dramatically Viollet-le-Duc engineered the reorganization of the Ecole des Beaux-Arts and the Grand Prix de Rome of November 1863.[19]

With perverse poetic justice the response to the imposition of liberalization was a spontaneous revolt on the part of the students seeking to defend the institution's autonomy. After his lectures were systematically interrupted Viollet-le-Duc resigned his post as Professor of the History of Art and Aesthetics on March 26, 1864. He fired a parting shot with his pamphlet *L'Intervention de l'Etat dans l'enseignement des beaux-arts* and retreated to an even more vigorous campaign of critical writing – now in newspapers like *Le XIXe siècle* and *Le Bien public* as well as in a vastly popular series of didactic books for young people published by Hetzel, *Histoire d'une maison* (1873), *Histoire d'un forteresse* (1874), *Histoire d'un Hôtel de Ville et d'une cathédrale* (1878), *Histoire d'un dessinateur: comment on apprend à dessiner* (1879). In a pamphlet of 1869 (republished as the fourteenth chapter of his second volume of *Entretiens sur l'architecture* of 1872), he returned to the themes of 1852 in an exposé of the collusion of the Académie and the architectural services, sketching again his countermodel for open competition in the profession.[20] On a more practical level he helped Emile Trélat found a private architectural school, the Ecole Spéciale d'Architecture (1864), although he eventually became disillusioned with the latter. He also pushed forward the publication of three collections of designs for smaller provincial buildings, largely in the rationalist neomedieval manner: Anatole de Baudot's *Eglises de bourgs et villages* (1867), Félix Narjoux's *Architecture communale* (1870–1880), and his own *Habitations modernes* (1875). Viollet-le-Duc maintained a basic belief that architecture was a rational enterprise and therefore potentially scientific, free, and democratic, open to any sincere practitioner. The proof of this, he held, lay in the medieval monuments of France produced before political centralization of the Renaissance, as he perceived them after he discovered their inner principle during his restoration work of the 1840s. This was a shining insight for him, a perspective in direct contradiction to the conventional idea of gothic then established in France. These monuments to him were proclamations of a revolutionary social ideal. He states in "Un mot sur l'architecture en 1852,"

For Louis XIV as for the democrats of 1793, archeology seemed like a sort of revolution, a kind of opposition to the established order. Archeology leads to independence in the arts; there is no art without independence. . . .

How does archeology favor independence in the arts? . . . Because it leads to the gathering of facts independently of passing enthusiasms. Because it makes clear that all ages that have produced original works – [ones] logical and beautiful at the same time – are those whose art has developed under the powerful and fructifying influence of artists left to themselves, and not at all at the direction of a sovereign, a minister, or an academy. . . .

Who would not prefer the century of Saint-Louis when one saw built structures so easy to identify by their great unity yet so various in their layout and details, so full of poetry, like the cathedrals of Rheims, of Laon . . . monuments sprung from the same trunk, members of the same family, but in which the genius of each architect is freely developed, where each sculptor produces a distinctive masterpiece, issuing without constraint from his skillful hands.[21]

Even if forced back from the transformation of the Ecole des Beaux-Arts, Viollet-le-Duc nonetheless believed (as we explore further in Chapter 7) that he possessed a powerful instrument in his control of church restoration and construction and in his reputation as a historian to affect public conceptions. He hoped that, at least in the provinces, a vital sense of good construction might be reawakened. He ended his introduction, dated 1869, to Narjoux's *Architecture communale* imagining,

[T]he time when villagers will see strangers stop before their little constructions, examine them curiously, sometimes even draw them, [the villagers] will understand that ridiculous imitations of the great monuments of the rich cities are laughable and not their business, and that, for them, an honest simplicity is one of the qualities of which the charm never fades because it is the real mark of taste.[22]

*   *   *

The government architectural services could function to expand the influence of certain directing personalities if these took advantage of the situation as did Viollet-le-Duc. What did Fontaine, Duban, and Baltard have to put against this? In Fontaine, Viollet-le-Duc faced the past, the sovereign himself as his will moved the hand of his architect, or at least that myth rapidly fading as this sovereignty was passed from Napoleon I to Louis XVIII and Charles X, to Louis-Philippe, and finally to Napoleon III. In Duban and Baltard Viollet-le-Duc faced the present in those two powerful creations of the mid-century administration, the artist (Duban) and the technocrat (Baltard), now free of the sovereign's direct command and representing the new sciences of culture and technique. In this context Viollet-le-Duc's position was that of another characteristically nineteenth-century creation, the radical, the individual who – understanding the natural principles of his art and society – attempts to transform them by carefully applied pressure at key points.

Fontaine held what down through the reign of Napoleon I had been the most important architectural appointment in France. He performed his duties with unique assiduity and wisdom from 1804 to 1848, winning the respect and friendship of the four successive monarchs. Yet, paradoxically, his tenure measured the office's decline. He enjoyed the closest personal relations with both Napoleon I and Louis-Philippe, but while his *Journal* shows that during the Empire his opinion was asked of all the works in Paris, it also shows, during the Monarchy of July, sharp hostility toward Thiers, especially while he was framing his "Loi des Cent Millions" in 1833.[23] Although the project was to complete the Napoleonic monuments of Paris, Fontaine was consulted only about the Louvre, and then belatedly. Also telling is the coldness Fontaine delineates between Thiers and the king, whom he shows defending his right to determine details of his palace reconstruction behind the shield of the Civil List and embattled even there. After his resignation from his Louvre post in 1848 and his appointment as président honoraire of the Conseil des Bâtiments Civils, Fontaine's diary becomes a record of ineffectual fulmination against an administration that seems to give him little notice.

In place of the authority of the king's first architect, however, there emerges during the years 1830–1870 that of the Conseil des Bâtiments Civils. Duban would seem to have understood his opportunity – or perhaps better, his duty – in terms of carrying on traditional authority.

The Revolution had, of course, created the Conseil to replace the Surintendance des Bâtiments du Roi, and when a semblance of that former administration was recreated around Fontaine under Napoleon, Fontaine found himself negotiating his authority with both Bruyère's Travaux de Paris and the Bâtiments Civils, the authorities that fifty years later would manifest themselves in Baltard and Duban.[24]

It might be more accurate to say that Duban's post as vice president of the Conseil was central because he accepted it as implying a duty to continue the completion of the monumental form of the capital, Paris. Contemporary depictions of Duban play down his administrative role, emphasizing the "romantic" innovations of his first Ecole des Beaux-Arts building of the 1830s and expressing woe at his not being given a major commission afterward, especially his loss of the Louvre in competition with Visconti.[25] Ernest Beulé observes, "If the group to which Duban belonged had built monuments that have been admired – cathedrals [Vaudoyer], libraries [Labrouste], law courts [Duc] – Duban was not so fortunate; he could only finish buildings already begun."[26] Beulé goes on to depict the debilitating effect losing the Louvre commission had on the architect. "These failures could not heal an already melancholic heart. Duban withdrew, his health deteriorated; he suffered long, a victim of excessive sensitivity."[27]

Looking at Duban's career through the administrative lunette, however, things do not appear so dire. He seems to have seen the Louvre project on two planes, as a matter of filling out the microcosm of the palace itself and also as a matter of reshaping central Paris around it. If Visconti's appointment blocked success in the first area, Duban's function on the Conseil des Bâtiments Civils from 1854 (and vice president from 1862) with his *inspection* this very quarter, placed him in the best position to push forward the latter. He could be firm. Napoleon referred to the uncomfortable necessity of dealing with Duban "de puissance à puissance" – "as one great power to another."[28]

Duban had been named architect of the Louvre on October 12, 1848, following Fontaine's resignation on September 24, and carried forward restoration work with a 200,000 franc appropriation of December 12 of that year.[29] He remained in the post to March 1854, after his projects of 1848 and 1851 to join the Louvre and Tuileries had been rejected in preference to Visconti's.[30] The letter book of his *agence* survives, and we see that from the start – when the building was still the "Palais du Peuple" rather than a royal residence – he understood it as an urbanistic as well as an architectural problem. In a lengthy letter of December 22, 1849, to the ministre des travaux publics he underlines this on his own initiative:

Now . . . that the state will complete and restore those parts of the Old Louvre that especially ornament its urbanistic aspect I feel it my duty to point out to you these areas where the cooperation with the city can be requested, so that large expenditures undertaken for a noble end should not later be the object of regret. . . .

Perhaps no other building from the past demands more imperatively than the Old Louvre that isolation on all exterior sides, isolation that was the assumption of the architectural shaping of the successive creation of the buildings that compose it.[31]

He cites specifically the moat originally in front of Perrault's Colonnade. The most immediate issue in the Louvre *entourage* was that monumental space before the eastern facade. We noted in Chapter 3 that dramatic plans had been sketched for this beginning with the original construction in 1670–1672, but that the space actually remained a narrow, irregular void filled with wooden shanties beyond which rose the gothic facade of Saint-Germain-l'Auxerrois, to one side and slightly akilter. On November 15, 1853, the clearing of this space was declared *d'utilité publique*. Simultaneously Duban proposed to regularize it and to scale it up to match its noble western side by the imposition of a giant order of pilasters, evidently in the manner of Hardouin Mansart's place Vendôme.[32] It was only after Duban's departure, however, that Haussmann began seriously planning the space, and Hittorff was consequently asked to extend his architectural management eastward down the west axis from the Champs-Elysées and the place de la Concorde and to produce the peculiarly unimpressive composition that confronts the Colonnade today (Figures 115 and 116).[33]

Duban had already put his conception of the centrality of the Louvre in the monumental shape of Paris before the Conseil in a report on the *entourage* of the Louvre dated February 20, 1854.[34] It is a critique of the plan approved by the Conseil Municipal on January 16, 1854, for the area between the place du Carrousel and the Théâtre Français (Figures 79 and 80). The issue was the narrowness of the new streets and the lack of a monumental square before the theater. Duban judged the proposed arrangement insufficient and inappropriate.

Figure 79. Plan of the meeting of the avenue de l'Opéra, the rue de Rivoli, and the rue de Richelieu as initially projected, c. 1852.

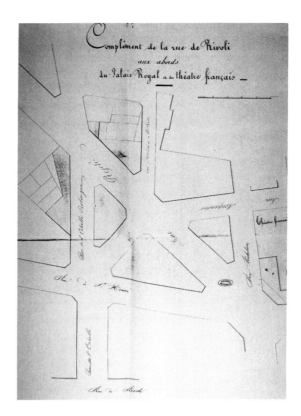

Figure 80. Place du Théâtre Français as erected, 1864–1868, looking north on the rue de Richelieu, the Théâtre Français (Victor Louis, architect, 1786–1790) at the right, typical facades (Gabriel Davioud, architect, Henri Blondel, contractor) to left.

Alone perhaps among all the monuments of this sort in Europe, the Théâtre Français is without the [urban] space necessary for its function and its dignity.

The widening of the rue de Richelieu shown on the plan is an insufficient concession made to its [the theater's] dignity. Exposed to view on a broad plaza, its facade, the work of a celebrated architect [Victor Louis], would be an ornament to the city. . . .

It is indisputable that the agglomeration of buildings produced by different interests that must be reconciled cannot produce anything completely regular. But, at least, in this quarter of luxury, a center of the advantaged population, in the vicinity of several palaces and the first theater in the world, our eyes should not be assaulted by defects that one would regret to find along the new rue de Rivoli; that a monumental appearance, if not a regular one, might result from the intelligent arrangement of masses and voids. Let us beware, finally, that disorder on a grand scale does not replace the disorder of the quarters that one so correctly desires to regenerate.

Were one to object to this proposal of a square because of the proximity of the Palais Royal, one may respond that the location of these spaces in the neighborhood of the Palace of the Sovereign announces it, in a way, and increases the convenience and dignity of its surroundings; that these two squares are quite distinct in their appearance and function, one monumental and serving as a link between two important palaces, the other the center of sophisticated commerce and the only passage for carriages between the place de la Concorde and the Pont Neuf.[35]

Brought back to the subject of the monumental order of Paris by the Opéra site project of 1860, Duban's regrets in another report the building being oriented on the boulevard des Capucines (as had the *enquête* a few weeks before) because to him the most important axis intersecting the site will be that of the rue de la Paix north from the west axis of the Tuileries. "One cannot sufficiently deplore that the rue de la Paix, which owes its splendor to the sovereigns of two great reigns, completely monumental by the very variety of its tableaux, linked by the Tuileries to the palace of the sovereign, in the reorganization of Paris might receive for termination and *point de vue* at the boulevard only an angled facade or, at best, the rounded corner of private constructions."[36] (As we saw in Chapter 1 the solution was to use the avenue de l'Opéra to create a local subcomposition symmetrical to the boulevards.)

Duban envisioned the city center as a monumental whole according to familiar principles that consistently inform his work at the Louvre (1848–1854), at the Conseil des Bâtiments Civils (1854–1870), and as inspecteur général of the first circumscription (1861–1870). First, there was the rule set by axes of orientation fixed by that of the Louvre and Tuileries; second that representational institutions should articulate this structure by assuming a proper scale and degree of embellishment set off in ample squares; third, that such foreground buildings should freely achieve the shape appropriate to and expressive of their functions. In this he was carrying on the grand tradition of Louis XIV and he cited it liberally and admiringly.

The *traité* between the city and the state of May 28, 1858, produced in the years immediately afterward a series of monumental City projects arriving before the Conseil des Bâtiments Civils. Duban took charge of the evaluation of the important ones, Davioud's theaters of the Châtelet and Bailly's Tribunal de Commerce at the crossing of the rue de Rivoli and the boulevard de Sébastopol, Garnier's Opéra, and Ballu's church of La Trinité.[37] Duban was severe, reiterating in various ways his criticism of February 20, 1854, that the city was too niggardly in opening spaces around monuments and too hesitant in developing them architecturally. He also indulged in a practice that had previously only been very sparingly used in the criticism of provincial buildings by the Conseil, that of the redrawing of the submitted design by the inspecteur général – Duban himself – to demonstrate graphically just how it should be reshaped. In the case of the Tribunal de Commerce it was the plan that he rearranged, in that of La Trinité it was the shaping of its conventional ecclesiastical mass to show how its single facade tower should terminate the axis up the rue de la Chaussée d'Antin, to achieve frankness ("franchise") in the expression of the interior volumes on the outside and to imprint a religious as opposed to a "civil" character on the facade in the choice of details (Figure 148). We noted in Chapter 2 that this practice of the inspecteurs généraux of the Conseil of redesigning the submitted projects is documented and defended by de Gisors in his unpublished collection of such designs, mostly from the late Empire and the Restoration and all provincial.[38] De Gisors notes in his text, however, that this was done infrequently – in 88 cases out of 1,441 considered, to be precise – and even then criticized by "plusieurs architectes distingués de la capitale" – "a number of distinguished architects of the capitol." Duban was doing de Gisors one better: He was reshaping the designs of the leading architects of Paris, Bailly and Ballu.

Beyond these dramatic instances of interference, Duban gave day-to-day advice on design and construction to the architects in his circumscription. The most remarkable of these, Charles Garnier, was warm in his acknowledgment (although not quite on the points that the record of the Conseil des Bâtiments Civils would indicate).[39] Christopher Mead has shown that Duban seems to have actually contributed to the design in two important details, first by demanding that the giant order of the facade be closed and scaled down by the introduction of what became the polychrome marble minor order within it, second by suggesting the elimination of the galleries around the stair hall on the south to link it with the grand foyers and to open the great tableau which since has been repeatedly reproduced as the image of the monument. Writing in his *Nouvel Opéra de Paris* a decade after Duban's death Garnier is warm in his acknowledgment.

Duban, who had a truly paternal affection for me, was, in fact, the inspecteur général charged with the surveillance of my works. . . . He liked to talk with me, as a colleague as he put it, . . . and the position he took was to encourage me, to support me in all the frustrations I faced. . . . He spoke to me as if he was my admirer and disciple.

Once he . . . put aside his reserve, and that was on the subject of the *avant foyer*. He said to me with great hesitance . . . that it seemed to him that the suppression of the galleries at the second and third stories on the side toward the vestibule, in making the space higher, more noble, would prepare for the entrance into this hall better than would low ceilinged corridors. . . .

[Duban] was a correct, elevated, animated, passionate character! He put art above all other human powers; he had faith, conviction, and never, himself so sensitive and generous to his colleagues young and old, did he give one inch to even the most powerful in order to entertain a delusion that would, in his eyes, constitute an artistic crime.[40]

Upon the removal of the scaffolding concealing Garnier's facade in 1867 Duban wrote him a note praising the achievement but implying some unspoken collusion between them.

Works such as these are not to be analyzed; they must be admired as a whole, so homogeneous and distinct are they.

You must be satisfied and you are right to congratulate yourself in contemplating this masterpiece, an honor to our time. As for me, I have reasons *that I know* to be pleased by such a rejection of the recriminations as you know. (Duban's emphasis)[41]

The Opéra will, Duban continues, "persuade our time that it cannot question whether architecture in its means of expression, of splendor, of magnificence, disciplined by taste, is the first of the arts."[42]

By this point, with Duban not only using his powerful position in the Conseil des Bâtiments Civils to inflect Haussmann's transformation of central Paris according to his sense of the "Grand Design" but also actually redrawing certain city projects to bring them into line with it, we have Duban assuming the authority of the premier architecte du roi in succession to Hardouin Mansart and the Napoleonic Fontaine. Only one thing would seem to be lacking, the actual authorship of some part of the ensemble. However, although the selection of Visconti and then Lefuel as architects of the New Louvre was a bitter disappointment to him and while his project for the place du Louvre was unexecuted, Duban was able to insinuate a model of his conception into this context when in 1856–1862 he built the monumental treatment of the part of the quai Malaquais facing across the Seine toward the palace (Figures 81 and 82), just west of Le Vau's contribution, the Collège des Quatre Nations.[43] This commission began in 1856 as merely the monumental arrangement of government property that was to be sold for private construction. By 1858 it had been transformed into the construction of a series of studio and exhibition halls for the Ecole des Beaux-Arts, which was contiguous to the site at the back. Although disciplined by the same *alignements* as the house facades beside it, Duban's front inflates its parts to urban scale in its two tall stories, in the subtly indented trace of the facade line, in the broad gallery openings, and most powerfully in the three *oeils-de-boeuf* carrying the pilaster order through the cornice line and snapping the roof masses into three dimensions. It is shaped and scaled to be seen next to the Collège des Quatre Nations from the Louvre across the Seine (Figure 82) and, in fact, is constituted of details from the Galerie d'Apollon there, which Duban himself had rebuilt in 1848–1854, reerecting the *oeils-de-boeuf* documented in engravings but subsequently destroyed

Figure 81. Ecole des Beaux-Arts. Facade on the quai Malaquais (Félix Duban, architect, 1856–1862).

Figure 82. Ecole des Beaux-Arts. Quai Malaquais facade seen past the west wing of the Collège des Quatre Nations (Louis Le Vau, architect, 1662).

Figure 83. Palace of the Louvre, Galerie d'Apollon (erected by Louis Le Vau, 1661–1663; restored by Félix Duban, 1848–1854).

(Figure 83). Here in this one fragment is the mirroring entourage that Duban would have created around the palace, more sympathetic in style and stronger in scale than the rue de Rivoli model extended around it by Visconti and Hittorff.

*   *   *

This narrative of Duban's interventions is impressive. He made himself the shaper of monumental Paris as no one had since Bruyère and Fontaine fifty years before. But how does it square with the received depiction of Duban as a radical "romantic," building the Ecole des Beaux-Arts as a summation of the history of French architecture, setting the stage for Labrouste (his *inspecteur* in the work at the Ecole), Duc, and Vaudoyer?

One of the fundamental principles of that "romantic" architecture was structural and functional inflection which, in the cases of Labrouste and Vaudoyer, resulted in a categorical hostility to the academic architecture of Louis XIV and Napoleon and its formalism of the Orders.[44] It thus has always been puzzling that one of the group's earliest and most intelligent advocates, Hippolyte Fortoul, characterized their accomplishment – especially as it was manifested in Duban's Ecole buildings – as returning architectural development to the early seventeenth century.[45] This sounds confusing in the face of the gothic and early Renaissance architectural fragments with which Duban clothed his courtyards, but it is perfectly accurate in characterizing the basic quality of his spatial composition, curved and canted and opening to trick perspectives. It is the quality evoked in the first paragraphs of this book as setting the stage for the urbanism of Garnier's Opéra.

Duban understood the art of shaping space and modulating volume that had been established in *Grand Siècle* (although perhaps more richly and subtly by François Mansart than by his nephew, Hardouin, as Fortoul implies). He had displayed this skill in his Grand Prix design of 1823 (Figure 84). He developed it further in his Ecole courtyard composition (Figure 2), in his project for Napoleon's tomb under Hardouin Mansart's dome, and for the restoration of François Mansart's wing at Blois. One is left very curious how he proceeded in his lost projects to extend the chateau at Chantilly (1845–1848) and to unite the Louvre and the Tuileries (1849, 1851). Ernest Beulé was to end his necrology (1872) by asserting that Duban, "a contribué à maintenir l'architecture dans la voie qu'elle a parcouru depuis un siècle" – "Duban has contributed to maintaining architecture in the path that it has followed for the last century."

It would seem that we are wrong in seeing the four "romantic" *pensionnaires* of 1830 as a monolithic group. Contemporaries understood Labrouste and Vaudoyer as more rigid rationalist designers and Duban

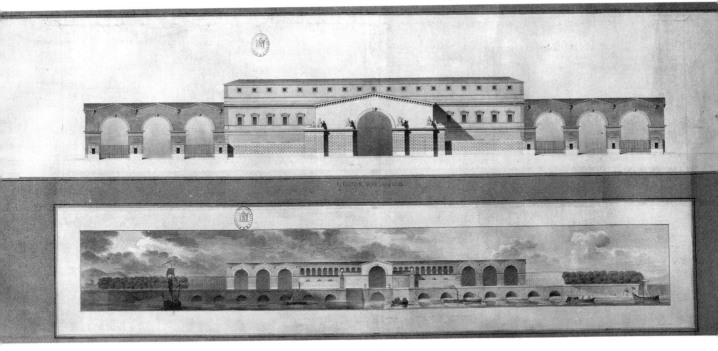

Figure 84. Félix Duban, project for a custom house, Grand Prix de Rome, 1823.

together with Louis Duc (1802–1879) as more traditional and expansive. Interestingly Duc's great west facade of the Palais de Justice of 1852–1868 would have formed another part of the entourage of the Louvre had the place Dauphine been demolished as Duc contemplated and in its scale and siting is even more obviously a response to that seventeenth-century monument, especially Perrault's Colonnade, which it confronts and repeats (Figures 85, 86, 87, and 88). In the terms of Charles Blanc, cited at the end of Chapter 3, one can read it too as a nineteenth-century reformulation of the seventeenth-century paradigm.[46] As in Duban's quai Malaquais facade the windows have expanded and the columns retreated into the wall piers to produce a skeletalized volume, here necessarily scaled up one notch further and their columnar quality made more emphatic. As Duban's facade transforms the Galerie d'Apollon, so does Duc's facade transform Perrault's Colonnade (Figure 88) but more concentratedly, as the segmental arches of Perrault's basement story rise and are overlaid with the colonnade to produce a single motif above the heavily rusticated base that remained buried (in spite of Duban's efforts) below Perrault's facade on the filled-in moat. Perrault had sought to invent a new "French" order and Duc has done so, but here specifically expressive of the institution it decorates in its Doric-Corinthian evocation of force and equity.[47] Blanc read the engaged half columns as buttresses and Duc's details as constructed around the expression of structural fact. "The columns engaged in the piers indicate that they function as buttresses, that thus the spaces in between constitute the bays of the vault inside. . . . The architect, having taken this *parti,* has had to break the entablature, that thus, on each half column the entablature projects."[48] Viollet-le-Duc also admired Duc's integration of structure and decoration, writing in his *Entretiens,* "La décoration tient à la structure, l'appui même" – "the decoration adheres to the structure, in fact, supports it."[49]

Perrault's simple-seeming colonnade was a remarkable feat in the construction of the broad lintels and the flat stone ceiling behind. Elaborate cutting and pinning was necessary in the tradition of gymnastic stone building "à la française."[50] That tradition reached its culmination a century later in Soufflot's Panthéon and was consciously resuscitated by Duc in the stone vaulting he con-

Figure 85. Palais de Justice. Vestibule and facade on the rue de Harlay (Louis Duc, architect, 1852–1868).

Figure 86. Palais de Justice. Vestibule on the rue de Harlay (Louis Duc, architect, 1852–1868). Interior.
(Opposite above) Figure 87. Aerial view of the projected rue de Harlay facade of the Palais de Justice with the reconstructed center of Paris in the background, 1858.
(Opposite below) Figure 88. East colonnade of the Louvre Palace (Claude Perrault, architect, 1667–1670).

structed behind the column buttresses of his Palais de Justice facade.[51] His building was the latest term in that tradition, but in its display of buttressing and curves more conscientious in the balancing of composition and construction.

Here on the *terre-plein* of the Pont Neuf, axed on the reerected equestrian statue of Henri IV, was the reestablishment of the scale and modulation of the "Grand Dessin" of absolutist Paris. Neil Levine has observed that the scale and vocabulary was carried over to the Opéra where Garnier worked in collaboration with Duban and in acknowledgment of Duc.

*   *   *

This, then, is what Duban had to put against Viollet-le-Duc's grand plan: in fact, a great deal, the continuity of the representational urban shape of Paris, now in the hands of the vice president of the Conseil des Bâtiments Civils rather than those of the architecte de l'empereur. Yet Duban shared with Viollet-le-Duc a sense of his own rationalizations as superior to the immediate wishes of politicians (and especially sovereigns). On this issue he faced down Fontaine and later Lefuel, and Baltard as well, although this latter was the servant of an administrator, Haussmann, not a monarch.

Duban also had a sense of mission, to keep Paris from losing its scale and shape, and in this perspective his misanthropy may seem justified: He was sorely embattled and little understood. His tool, however, was not an idea, but a sense of form implicit in the actual urbanistic and architectural materials he was manipulating.

In one sense Duban had the better of Viollet-le-Duc. The history that Duban rewrote was political. Viollet-le-Duc was never permitted to touch the Louvre (beyond advising on its ornamental sculpture at Duban's request). Viollet-le-Duc's domain was, it turned out, ecclesiastical rather than representational. If he was to create a base for his projected transformation of French architecture it had to be in this tangential area. The central political monuments were the domain of the Bâtiments Civils. It was from this body, especially under the leadership of Duban, that a renewal of the old order was launched.

But there was one even more massive point of resistance to Viollet-le-Duc's skillfully managed campaign, the city of Paris itself, partly under the control of Baltard as we explore in the next chapter, partly the spontaneous product of the most pervasive but unacknowledged part of the French architectural profession, the private architects creating the flesh of the city for commercial development. These we must examine next.

II

One of the Fourierist César Daly's innovations was to emphasize private construction in his *Revue générale de l'architecture* (1840–1889)[52] and to make it the subject of his splendid and seminal *Architecture privée au XIXe siècle* (1864–1872). In giving private architecture its due Daly was exploring a perception that Félix Pigeory, a government architect writing for the city of Paris, had already chosen to end his 1847 *Monuments de Paris*:

It is clear that private investment, protected [and] encouraged by peace, has contributed a goodly amount to the magnificence of modern Paris. . . .

Small fortunes, gathered together to become millions, have thrown bridges across the Seine, founded numerous businesses, built the railroad stations, opened streets, quarters, squares and *passages* all over the modern Babylon. . . .

This civil architecture – or if you prefer, this *style bourgeois* – emerging as a result of social progress and the infinite division of property to replace the great works of the Renaissance, the ceremonial habitations of Louis XIV, this style of five stories with the inexorable envelope of seventeen meters fifty, is unquestionably the exact artistic expression of our time, it summarizes its tendencies, its combinations, its means.[53]

A glance at the careers of private architects, for example, Alfred Armand (whom we met in Chapter 1 as architect of the Pereires' Grand Hôtels) or Hippolyte Destailleur puzzles one as to how they could have been written out of the conventional architectural history. They would have been central figures in the Anglo-American context. Yet right at the outset, in introducing them, we suffer an inconvenience because there exist no necrologies read before the Académie or personnel dossiers in the state archives. Aside from one obscure Second Empire biographical dictionary compiled by the private architect Alexandre Dubois and abandoned after the letter "A" (thus, fortunately, covering Armand)[54] and the records of the Société Centrale des Architectes (kept with some care by the secretary, Charles Lucas),[55] all we have in these two cases is two biographical sketches from the unlikely hand of the print collector Georges du Plessis.[56] But here is just the point: Both Armand and Destailleur had the time and money to be prominent *mondains* and collectors – indeed, to be able to retire to such pleasures at all. It was remarkable for a government architect to be retired by a municipality or a service; most maintained their posts until they died, having no other steady income.[57] The Armand collection of old master drawings, bequeathed to the Ecole des Beaux-Arts, and the Destailleur collections of prints – one sold to the Berlin Kunstgewerbeschule in 1879, another given to the Bibliothèque Nationale in 1890–1894 – are valued to this day.

Both of these men owed their prosperity to the practice of private architecture. Armand (1805–1888) began in 1827 as a student at the Ecole des Beaux-Arts, in the unobjectionable ateliers of Provost and then Leclère, but never progressed past the lower *seconde classe*. Already in 1836 he was named architect for the stations of the first Paris railroad lines, those to Saint-Germain-en-Laye and Versailles. Here he displayed great ingenuity and was subsequently awarded a series of major railroad commissions: the first Gare Saint-Lazare (1842), the stations of the Rothschild's Chemin de Fer du Nord erected between 1845 and 1851 (especially those at Amiens,

Arras, Lille, Calais, Saint-Quentin, and Douais), and finally, for the Pereires' Chemin de Fer de l'Ouest, the second Gare Saint-Lazare (with the engineer Flachat, 1851–1853). Having proved himself useful to these two leading banker-entrepreneurs of the time, in 1853 Armand switched from railroad work to urban development, directing the Pereire projects around the Grand Hôtel du Louvre (1853–1855) and the Grand Hôtel de la Paix (1861–1862), as well as rebuilding the Pereire city house, 35, rue Saint-Honoré (1855–1857).[58] These two hotels, as we saw in Chapter 1, were among the most extraordinary and expensive constructions of the Second Empire.

In 1862, upon the completion of the Grand Hôtel de la Paix, Armand retired, at the age of fifty-seven, to what turned out to be twenty-six years of collecting and bonhomie before his death in 1888.

The one qualification one might have about Armand's admirably successful career is that he functioned as an organizer and engineer leading a large and changing stable of designers (whom Alexandre Dubois is careful to specify in his biographical note).[59] He was a builder, not an artist. Destailleur (1822–1893) is not open to this criticism, having devoted himself to the quieter and more leisurely enterprise of the practice of domestic design of the very highest class.[60] His father had been a respected palatial designer during the Empire and the Restoration.[61] The son began at the Ecole, also as a student of Leclère, but left just after gaining admission to the first class to marry (an Englishwoman) and to take up the paternal practice. He became the domestic architect of the oldest families of France – the de Luynes, de Nouailles, the Hussonville. He did work for Eugénie at Farnborough and a monument to the prince imperial. He designed the London Rothschild's mansion at Waddesdon and the Vienna Rothschild's city house. The photograph he submitted to the Société Centrale des Architectes contrasts with those of all the other members: Instead of depicting himself in frock coat amid cluttered professional surroundings he shows himself in a fur-collared coat in portrait-like isolation (Figure 89).

* * *

Behind these two paradigms of private practice – one of its entrepreneurial, the other of its artistic, domestic aspect – come a mass of quite considerable designers pursuing these and other career scenarios.

First of all there were the railroad architects, Alexis Cendrier (1803–1892), heading the architectural office at the Chemin de Fer d'Orléans (1837–1840), then of the Paris et Lyon (merged in the Paris, Lyon, Méditerranée) from 1840 to 1859; Félix-Emmanuel Callet (1792–1854) also of the Orléans; Victor-Benoist Lenoir (1805–1863) executing the stations on the Rennes and Cherbourg lines as well as the Gare Montparnasse, 1848–1852. These men, like

Figure 89. Portrait photograph of Hippolyte Destailleur.

Armand, did not restrict their efforts to railroad work: When the city of Paris recommenced construction of the Halles Centrales in 1851 Baltard was required to accept Callet as collaborator (raising questions about effective authorship of the huge scheme).[62] Lenoir had begun his career with the iron-and-glass-roofed Bazar Montesquieu and maintained an extensive practice in private house construction, especially designing the elaborate chateau and gardens at Nardes near Clermont-Ferrand for the Duc de Morny, supposed to have cost twelve million francs.[63] Cendrier, Callet, and Lenoir had all been trained at the Ecole des Beaux-Arts (ateliers of Vaudoyer, Delespine, and Leclère, respectively), and Callet had won the Second Grand Prix in 1818.

There were other specialists in Armand's second expertise, urban development, which in Second Empire Paris meant blocks of *immeubles* or *maisons de rapport*. César Daly considered this type, along with railroad constructions, the great challenge to modern design, and published his *Architecture privée* to document and study it. J.-M.-A. Lesoufaché (1804–1887) in particular was credited by Daly and others with perfecting the type.[64] César Daly wrote, "There are few architects who have built [apartment] houses so profitable to their owners as M. Lesoufacher [sic], and a few private residences built in Paris during the last twenty years have received from their authors an appearance so generally admired by our colleagues and by the public through the numerous changes of fashion and taste."[65]

Lesoufaché had abandoned a promising career in the Bâtiments Civils. He had been Duban's student, then Vaudoyer's *inspecteur* at the Conservatoire des Arts et Métiers, then, from May 1852 to early 1853, inspecteur-enchef of one of the six divisions of Visconti's huge *agence* at the New Louvre. Yet by 1874 he was sufficiently committed to, and sufficiently wealthy from, private practice to fund an annual prize for excellence in private construction, instituted tentatively by the Société Centrale des Architectes in the previous year and awarded to himself. His efficiency also attracted important domestic commissions, especially that from the Duc de Trévise to rebuild the seventeenth-century Château de Sceaux (1858–1862), demolished during the Revolution.[66]

Next to Lesoufaché should be placed Théodore Belle (1819–1879) and Louis Ponthieu (1822–1879), the first the designer for the Compagnie Immobilière du Luxembourg of most of the blocks built in 1862 along the rue Claude Bernard (then the rue des Feuillantines, (Figures 66 and 67), the second the architect of the Pereires' Compagnie Immobilierè de Paris executing the blocks along the rue Marignan (1859–1862) and the quartier de l'Opéra as well as the spectacular (and financially disastrous) rue Impériale at Marseilles.[67] Both of these men, like Lesoufaché, had excellent professional credentials – Ponthieu having been *en loge* twice (1845, 1846) and winning the Second Grand Prix – but left promising careers in the government services, Belle as *auditeur* to the Conseil des Bâtiments Civils, Ponthieu as Théodore Labrouste's *inspecteur* in the administration of the Assistance Publique. Beside them one should place others, equally successful if more humble in training (and radical in ornamental inclinations), especially the mysterious Amoudru who in 1852–1858 executed all the blocks along the new boulevard de Strasbourg for the entrepreneur Jules Ardoin in the "Neo-Grec" style (Figure 90), afterward retiring to an elegant villa of his own design near Pigalle.[68]

As new building types evolved, certain architects addressed themselves to these special problems, as Armand had in the Pereire hotels. Jules Sédille (1806–1871), a builder and specialist in apartment blocks, erected the first Printemps department store (1865) on the rue de Rouen leading from the Gare Saint-Lazare. When it burned in 1881, his son, Paul (1836–1900), reerected it as the extraordinary colorful "bazaar" we see today (Figure 25).[69] L.-C. Boileau (1837–1914) was employed by Boucicaut to erect the Bon Marché, in collaboration with Gustave Eiffel for the interior ironwork and Alexandre Laplanche for the facade design.[70] Bouwens van der Boyen (1834–1907) was tapped by the Crédit Lyonnais for their headquarters with

Figure 90. Boulevard de Strasbourg, apartment facades (Amoudru, architect, 1852 ff.).

its iron and glass banking hall (Figures 23 and 24), built in stages from 1876 on the boulevard des Italiens, as we saw in Chapter 1. Alexandre Dubois (1785–1866) was architect for the Pereires' Compagnie du Gaz and designer of a number of factories and workers' housing blocks.[71] Dubois, like Armand and Destailleur, was a respected print collector as well as a bibliophile and historiograph, collecting notes for the abortive biographical dictionary we have noted.

There were also the decorators, a specialty as important as it was ill-defined. During the years 1830–1870 this field was dominated by Aimé Chenevard (1798–1838), dead young in 1838, and Charles Séchan (1803–1874), the former trained as an architect in Lyon, the latter as a theater designer under Ciceri in Paris.[72] From 1831 to 1841 Séchan worked in collaboration with the architect Léon Feuchère (who in 1842 published a

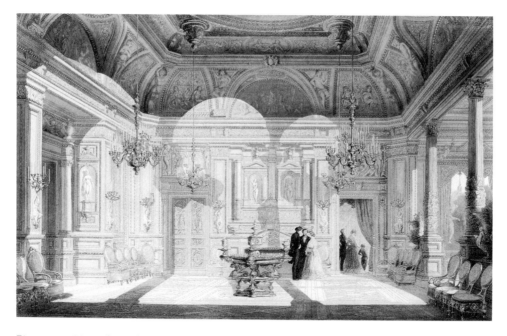

Figure 91. Hypothetical design for a salon from Léon Feuchère, *L'Art industriel,* 1842, plate 61.

remarkable folio of designs, *L'Art industriel* (Figure 91), then set up with Jules Dieterle and E.-D.-J. Desplechin before going out on his own in 1848. In 1844–1846 they worked with the architect Pierre-Anne Dedreux (1788–1849) to build and decorate the Théâtre Montpensier.[73] Dedreux had won the Grand Prix in 1815 but – alone among his generation of ex-pensionnaires – devoted himself to private practice in theaters and chateaux. In 1838–1841 Gottfried Semper in Dresden imported a team of French decorators led by Dieterle to execute the interiors of his new opera house.[74] There was a great deal of money to be made in this area. With Parisian leadership in decoration and art industry and with the importance of *fêtes,* both state (as described in Chapter 3) and private, this was a central field, drawing to it leading architects like Visconti, Duban, and Baltard organizing state affairs, as well as other artists of most varied training. From this central position decorative artists ventured out to offer solutions to new nineteenth-century problems, as the theater decorator C.-A. Cambon did in designing the casino at Dieppe in 1855.[75]

This was just the big business side of private practice, however, that exemplified by Armand. There was also Destailleur's more quiet domain, the architects designing or altering the dwellings of the rich and (like Destailleur) the richest. The Rothschilds' patronage was extraordinary.[76] After establishing himself on the rue Lafitte in 1811, Baron James employed for *fêtes* and decorations the brilliant Louis-Martin Berthault (garden designer in particular and architect of Napoleon's landscaping of the Palatine in Rome).[77] His great work was the chateau at Ferrières (1853–1859), designed externally and in the technical department by the Duke of Devonshire's gardener and engineer, Joseph Paxton, and decorated internally following the advice of the watercolorist, *mondain*, and intimate of the imperial circle, Eugène Lami.[78] These were not so much architects as advisers, each one offering the best advice possible in his particular department.

*   *   *

Having commenced this survey of private practice by outlining of the prototypical careers of Armand and Destailleur, let us end it here with three more that are less simple, those of Jules Saulnier, Henri Blondel, and Paul Sédille.

Saulnier (1817–1881) is one of the best known names of the modern history of architecture as the architect of the Menier mill of 1872 (Figure 92) but also a most minimally understood personality. He is simply the name attached to this extraordinary iron-framed and tile-clad mill floating on four piers over the Marne River at the Menier chocolate company town of Noisiel, east of Paris. When he died the professional press took no notice at all. (Modern scholars often confuse him with his brother, Charles-Emile, who died to some small notice in 1900.) Bernard Marrey has established that Jules Saulnier was the son of a Paris *mécanicien*, apprenticed first to a surveyor, then to one Bonneau, factory architect to the Menier company. When Bonneau died Saulnier took his place, working in contented security for Menier during the rest of his career, first erecting the structures in the company complex at Saint-Denis, then – after the war in 1870 – the factory and new town at Noisiel.[79] In spite of this modesty, Viollet-le-Duc had been publishing his work at Saint-Denis in the *Gazette des architectes et du bâtiment* and Adolphe Lance continued to do so for Noisiel in his sympathetic *Encyclopédie d'architecture*. In the 1920s the mill at Noisiel was made one of the icons of modern architecture by Sigfried Giedion in his *Bauen in Frankreich*.

Henri Blondel (1821–1897), if remembered at all today, is also confused with his namesake the academician Paul Blondel, to whom he was unrelated but who also died in 1897. Yet he was notorious beyond few of his professional colleagues in his own time, dying thirty-two million francs in debt.[80] He had been born in obscurity in Rheims and trained at the local Ecole des Arts et Métiers at Chalons-sur-Marne. Arriving in Paris at the beginning of the Second Empire, he is said to have worked in some capacity in the *agences* of Henri Labrouste and Caristie as well as François Rolland (architect of the department store Au Tour Saint-Jacques, Figures 64 and 65) before setting up on his own about 1855. He started designing apartment

Figure 92. Menier chocolate factory (Jules Saulnier, architect, 1872).

blocks, several of which on the boulevards de Sébastopol and Saint-Michel as well as on the place du Théâtre Français César Daly selected for publication in his *Architecture privée*. Then he moved into bigger projects, working as designer and contractor, executing the dramatic building for the Cercle Agricole facing the Chamber of Deputies (Figure 93), the headquarters of the Dépôts et des Comptes Courants on the place de l'Opéra (1868–1869, Figure 16), and the Belle Jardinière department store (1866–1867) on the quai west of the Châtelet.[81] These were among the great private monuments of the Second Empire, impressive jobs for a man without Beaux-Arts credentials (although we hear of a sage choice of designing assistants in a contemporary source).[82] At some point he moved from construction to investment, especially in his rebuilding of the Ministère des Finances (burned in the Commune) as the third great hotel of Paris, the Hôtel Intercontinental

Figure 93. Cercle Agricole, boulevard Saint-Germain (Henri Blondel, architect, c. 1868).

(1877–1878, awarded the Société Centrale des Architectes Prix de l'Architecture Privée in 1878) and in his development of the rue Marbeuf (1882) in apartment blocks. High expropriation costs on the rue Marbeuf project caused losses that Blondel concealed in his Société de l'Hôtel Intercontinental. In 1886 he was the only bidder to construct the Bourse de Commerce next to the Halles Centrales and the two blocks west of it on the new rue du Louvre (Figures 94 and 95) for the city of Paris. His financial edifice crumbled as the construction rose until in 1892 he was declared bankrupt, 32,114,036 francs in the red.[83] When he died five years later the French professional journals allotted no more than a discreet sentence to the fact (as well as a good half-dozen sentences to the academic accomplishments of his homonym Paul Blondel, who trained Tony Garnier – otherwise sometimes wrongly pictured as the student of the designer of the cavernous Bourse de Commerce).

Paul Sédille (1836–1900), our last exemplum, was more careful. His father, Jules of the first Printemps, was a successful builder-architect, active as a technician in arrondissement affaires.[84] Paul was sent to the Ecole des Beaux-Arts in 1857, student of his father and the practical *voyer* Guénepin. His record there was solid but not brilliant and he soon joined his father's practice, in 1871 replacing him. During the 1870s he emerged as a domestic architect of particular subtlety, practicing a sort of Dubanesque neoclassicism, quite distinct from Destailleur's neo-François Premier. In 1881–1883

Figure 94. Buildings surrounding the Bourse de Commerce on the rue du Louvre (Henri Blondel, architect, 1886–1892).

he erected the new Printemps (Figure 25). He was paid the compliment of being asked to design the entrance and rooms of the Société Centrale des Architectes on the rue Danton. He was rich, like so many leading private practitioners, and had time to write, sometimes unobjectionable critiques and biographical profiles, sometimes, as in his *Architecture moderne en Angleterre* (1890, originally a series of articles in the *Gazette des beaux-arts*, 1886–1887),[85] to present private architecture in freer contexts. His biographer quotes him:

Thus freed from the modern encumbrances [of the restrictions of *voirie*] our private architecture will assume in the near future a physiognomy the new character of which will impose itself on even the haughtiest effects of modern art. . . . As in times past the new customs of a new generation – its new needs, and new well-

Figure 95. Buildings surrounding the Bourse de Commerce (Henri Blondel, architect, 1886–1892).

defined aspirations, its overweaning tastes and at the same time its constantly evolving means of construction – will influence private architecture clearly and inevitably so that it will remain the truest and most sincere testament of past generations.[86]

He was interested in new materials and especially in colored decoration (used so effectively in the Printemps) and in 1889 he designed the impressive Sèvres pavilion at the Exposition Universelle and the tile frontispiece now

Figure 96. 20, boulevard Malesherbes, house of the architect Paul Sédille.

reerected in the garden of Saint-Germain-des-Prés. He was the personal architect of President Carnot. He lived in a splendid house of his own design at 20, boulevard Malesherbes (Figure 96). He composed poetry.

Sédille's most remarkable accomplishment was in becoming, bit by bit, the spokesman for the profession that previously had been spoken for exclusively by the government designers. What is telling is that Sédille could have been a successful government architect but preferred to stay in private practice and formulated the beginnings of a theory of it.

III

The government architect claimed to elevate his art in serving the state; the state asked that the artist shape himself for that high calling. We read in Edouard Charton's *Guide pour le choix d'un état* of 1842 (in the section "Architecte" written by Léon Vaudoyer) that the government architect stands *au premier rang* in the profession and is an *architecte-artiste* with profound theoretical knowledge, opening an atelier for the Ecole des Beaux-Arts, preparing himself for government building projects or oversight functions, serving on scientific commissions.[87] We have noted that Haussmann in his *Mémoires* asserts that a public architectural position should be "une sorte de sacerdoce" – "a sort of priesthood."[88] Letters of candidacy for election to the Académie mention only government work, dismissing private production with a self-deprecating formula. Private architecture was primarily economic, no field for the traditional science of design. Charton notes that a student intending to enter this branch need only spend two or three years at the Ecole, although he admits that one might "acquérir une belle réputation" – "gain a good reputation" were one to treat private work as "plus qu'un simple moyen de faire fortune" – "more than simply a way to make money."[89]

The life and cityscape of nineteenth-century Paris was depicted voluminously in contemporary literature and the architect did not escape having a role. Gourlier's and Charton's ideal – the "architecte-artiste" working on the broadest plane with access to the highest officials – however, makes no appearance in this essentially realist literature. We must go back to Victor Hugo or forward to fin-de-siècle utopianism to find the architect depicted as the leader of the community building monuments to common ideals.[90] The mid- and late-nineteenth-century fictional architect is in private practice building the texture of the city, often stupidly or corruptly. The settings are usually private, not public, monuments, like Nana's and Saccard's dwellings and Mouret's department store in Zola. The architect of

Figure 97. J.-I. Grandville, the architect, from *Jérôme Paturot à la recherche d'une position sociale,* 1843.

Paturot's neogothic house in Reybaud's *Jérôme Paturot à la recherche d'une position sociale* (1846) is a bearded, gesticulating buffoon fixated on style and decorative detail (Figure 97).[91] The son of the academician in Daudet's *L'Immortel* (1888) frustrates his father by leaving the Ecole after short and mediocre studies, gets off to a brilliant start with several decorative and domestic commissions, then loses everything building a rental block around an exotic studio for himself. Henri Begue's Lefort in his play *Les Corbeaux* (1882) is worse in some ways, but – on the model of Henri Blondel – he knows how to make money. Begue's stage directions describe him: "il a les manières communes et la voix forte" – "he has bad manners and a loud voice," as his name implies. He is one of the crows of the title. The late M. Vigneron has bought land in the outer arrondissements, either from the railroad hoping it will be expropriated by the city or from the city hoping it will be expropriated for the railroad – the characters, his family straightening out affairs after his death, are not sure which. Lefort forced himself upon M. Vigneron, "je ne le quittai plus qu'il ne m'eut confié les travaux" – "I will not leave until he gives me the job." Now structures – in a distant part of Paris, "soumis . . . à mille servitudes," "controlled by a thousand restrictions" – are begun and Lefort proposes to continue but Mme Vigneron's advisers drive him out, saving her from sending good money after bad.

When writers of this period placed architects in government service it was merely to underline their empty pretenses, like the doddering Quatrebarbes of Anatole France's *L'Orme de Mail* (1897) or the repulsive Campardon in Zola's *Pot-Bouille* (1881), both architectes diocésains.[92]

Zola's Saccard in *La Curée* (1871), although starting as a commissaire voyer, is really a speculator, playing the games mentioned by Begue and more. He is tremendously successful as long as he buys lots to be expropriated but does not actually build. When he builds, his contractors, two wily provincials, swindle him. Zola's Louis Dubuche in *L'Oeuvre* (1886) really is a trained architect. Seeking security, he marries the daughter of a contractor understanding that he will design for his father-in-law, but his academic training proves useless in practical construction and he is sent into exile at the family chateau.

The only one of Zola's architects to display brilliance is the unnamed author of the department store in *Au Bonheur des dames* (1882), modeled on the writer's friend Frantz Jourdain.[93] Jourdain himself published a novel of architectural life, *L'Atelier Chantorel* (1893), that pivots on the contrast of public and private careers and is very black. The hero, Drosner, resists the rarified training at the Ecole des Beaux-Arts in the atelier of the bluff provincial Chantorel and is consequently blocked from employment in the Bâtiments Civils. He survives by building for contractors, architect-builders

of cupidity and ignorance. He conceives an ideal modern house design –
"No more thick walls, no more obligatory axes, no more useless pilasters,
no more proportioning by eye, . . . Each room will have its own character,
its distinct furniture that will consecrate the harmony of the body and the
spirit in obliging the mind to submit itself to the influence of the environment."[94]

He hopes to reach the public through its display at the Salon, but it is
rejected. In despair he becomes involved with a speculator and is ruined.
The novel's last scene is a dinner of the "Association Amicale des Anciens
Elèves Architectes de l'Ecole des Beaux-Arts" at the Hôtel Continental
about the year 1880. The directeur des Beaux-Arts and the chiefs of the
Bâtiments Civils and the Travaux de Paris (the last identified by name as
Alphand) sit at the *table d'honneur*. Looking around the room, one old student of Chantorel, who has been away three years on an archeological mission, asks another to tell him what has become of their studio mates. He is
told that one is now a prefect, another director of a chemical company, a
third a Grand Prix winner who is in Turkey pursuing historical studies. A
fourth has been named architect of the department of the Gironde through
family connections with the de Broglie; a fifth is drawing for other architects and for publishers but is clever and doing well; a sixth is at the *table
d'honneur* right then having won a string of medals at the *salons* and at the
Exposition Universelle of 1878 and being named expert au tribunaux as
well as architect of the Ministry of War. What about Drosner? the first
inquires. "Mais c'est un monsieur qu'on ne salue plus, un homme à la mer,
un foutu" – "but he is someone one no longer greets in the street, a man at
sea, a bum," comes the reply, a shabby misanthrope who crosses the street
to avoid encountering his own friends.[95]

IV

The literary suspicion of the pretenses of the government architect was justified
by a number of qualifications in commitment by the architects themselves.

The advantages of government practice were great in the early and mid-
nineteenth century. In the *service ordinaire* architects could enjoy permanent
responsibility for the upkeep of buildings with an *agence* in the building
staffed at state expense as well as sometimes a dwelling there. (Lebas spent
his many declining years in such an apartment in one of the pavilions of the
Collège des Quatre Nations overlooking the Seine.) Architects were
expected to receive important visitors to their buildings almost as if they
owned them.[96] Fontaine's diary records his showing the emperor of Brazil
around the chateau at Neuilly – and then joining the party for a formal
dinner.

A few state positions carried with them an interdiction of private practice, for example, the inspecteur général of the Bâtiments Civils (by the decision of October 1812) or architecte d'arrondissement of the city of Paris in the reorganization of 1860. Yet the architects were willing to go only so far. We have noted that Fontaine's diary records a proposal that the architects of the Palais Impériaux should wear livery and its adamant rejection. At state ceremonies the engineers of the Ponts et Chaussées wore uniforms; the architects, black frock coats.[97] They depended on the state but asserted their independence, like the notaries.[98]

Administratively, there is a whole history of efforts to combine the Ponts et Chaussées and the architects or at least to organize them parallel beginning with the first inception of the service in 1791.[99] Alexandre de Laborde offered the proposal in 1819–1820, as we have noted.[100] Suggestions were analyzed by the Conseil Bâtiments Civils in 1841 and 1856 to establish a diploma to certify architects as qualified by government examination and to require this for government service.[101] In 1846 the newly founded Société Centrale des Architectes discussed a report on the virtues of such a diploma presented by a committee comprising Gourlier, Blouet, Baltard, Constant-Dufeux, and Brunet des Baisnes.[102]

Before the Revolution state construction was reserved for the architectes du Roi, qualified by training by the Académie and, sometimes, also by study at the French Academy at Rome.[103] Minor state positions like commissaire voyer or expert au tribunaux were purchased. The Revolution ended venality, and entry into the Bâtiments Civils was open to any qualified architect, although a clear preference was given to successful products of the Ecole des Beaux-Arts, founded specifically to provide a cadre of state designers.

The interesting thing is that the architects did not permit themselves to be made *employés* like the engineers of the Ponts et Chaussées. Within the administration, the *fonctionnaires* were almost always bureaucrats – like the *chefs de bureaux* of the Bâtiments Civils, Louis Guizard (1834–1837), Jean Vatout (1837–1848), and Jacques-Etienne-Marie de Cardaillac (1853–1863, then directeur des Beaux-Arts) or those of the Edifices Diocésains, Jean-Philippe Schmit (1827–1840), Auguste Nicolas (1849–1854), and Victor-Hamille (1854–1870).[104] Viollet-le-Duc served for a short time as chef de bureau of the Monuments Historiques between the regimes of Grille de Beuzelin and Henri Courmont in 1846–1847 but it is unclear that much transpired. Blouet was inspecteur général des prisons. Baltard was named to the new post directeur des travaux de Paris in 1860 but by 1866 it was deemed necessary to add to his office a *service administratif* with a *fonctionnaire*, Michaux, chef du service.[105]

The *fonctionnaires* themselves connected (or failed to connect) with their areas of responsibility from a variety of angles manifesting traditions distinct, again, to each service. Those overseeing the sovereign's palaces tended to be military engineers in background, in the seventeenth-century tradition that continued until 1870: Fleurieu (1805–1810), Costaz (1810–1813), Montalivet (1830–1848), Walewski (1860–1865). Those heading the Travaux de Paris were often civil engineers: Bruyère (1811–1820), Hely d'Oissel (1820–1823), Héricart de Thury (1823–1830), Belgrand, and Alphand. Those administering the Beaux-Arts tended to be historians and critics, sometimes even modest practitioners: Charles Blanc (1848–1852, 1871–1873), Frédéric de Mercey (1853–1860), Philippe de Chennevières (1873–1878).[106] The parallel administration of museums enfolded more critics and practitioners – the sculptor Nieuwerkerke, directeur des musées, 1852, then surintendant des Beaux-Arts, 1863 – and provided minor sinecures for a brilliant group of *employés* – Daudet, Clément de Riis, Félix Ravaisson, Léon Heuzy.[107]

The Bâtiments Civils and the Edifices Diocésains, however, were administered by full-time bureaucrats, men like Alfred Blanche and Louis Guizard who moved back and forth from one service to another building up distinguished careers, or like Vatout and de Cardaillac, efficient if narrow in their restricted areas of authority.[108] These services seem to have been seen as institutional, part of a larger professional organization. The exception, however, is the Commission des Monuments Historiques that in Grille de Beuzelin, Viollet-le-Duc, Henri Courmont, and Emile Boeswillwald enjoyed knowledgeable and committed administrators. In this one instance architects and *fonctionnaires* alternated to direct an enterprise that lay between their expertises, neither entirely literary or entirely architectural.

The usual link of the profession to the administration was tangential, the architects either providing professional services as designers of specific buildings or serving as members of advisory committees – the Conseil des Bâtiments Civils, the Commission des Monuments Historiques, the Comité des inspecteurs généraux des Edifices Diocésains – reporting directly to the minister on the formulation of final decisions but not broaching matters on their own initiative. For example, an illuminating incident took place immediately after the reorganization of the Conseil des Bâtiments Civils of January 1, 1854. As a result of Blouet's departure from the office of inspecteur général des prisons (1848) and the rescinding of the cellular regime of prison design, the minister of the interior sent a request to the Conseil for them to provide model prison plans of four different sizes.[109] To the *fonctionnaires'* surprise, the architects on the Conseil refused on the ground that local climate and available building materials should determine the form of such buildings. De Cardaillac pleaded, "the administration that consults you absolutely has need of your advice, it has confidence only in you and it is to you that it addresses itself."[110] Two weeks later the matter was raised again, and again the architects refused.

The architects kept their distance from the administration, in part for the practical reason of maintaining some private practice, in part because their vision of the art of architecture never became that of specific services rendered to the state rather than a general humane ideal. In 1867 Ludovic Halévy, the author of the popular "La Belle Helène" and *secrétaire perpetuel* of the Académie, could write thus sincerely and privately in his diary upon the death of his grandfather, the architect Hippolyte Lebas (1782–1867), *membre de l'Institut* and chief of the leading atelier of the century:

My grandfather was a very talented artist and an *honnête homme,* in the highest sense of the word. But he was something even rarer than that, because in this time of self-effacement, he was a *caractère* . He lived entirely for his art, loving it with a narrow affection, one violent, passionate, exclusive, disdaining fortune and fame, living in his atelier among his students or alone at home in a spacious office where, morning and evening, he drew. His colleagues, ambitious, threw themselves into lucrative business affairs. They lived in nineteenth-century Paris amid *hôtels meublés* and railroad stations; he lived in Rome, in Athens, in the time of Augustus, in that of Pericles. . . .

He was about eighty-six but until eighty he remained young. He was happy as long as he could go to his atelier each morning, to the Ecole every Tuesday evening, and to the Institut every Saturday.[111]

*   *   *

Around 1870 this system dissolved. The government moved away from awarding so much opportunity to certain academic architects while permitting them to determine their own qualifications and ethos. A diploma was instituted at the Ecole des Beaux-Arts (1867), and government positions came increasingly to be awarded by competition, occasioning much professional discussion in the early 1870s.[112] Beginning in 1884 entry into the Edifices Diocésains was by examination.

Work now was awarded not by seniority and preferment but by merit. Architects could move back and forth between the public and private sectors. The monopoly of the Ecole des Beaux-Arts on preparation was eroded, first by the architectural course at the Ecole Centrale des Arts et Manufactures (founded in 1829 and made a state institution in 1855), then by the founding in 1864 of the private Ecole Spéciale d'Architecture.[113] With the regularization of qualification for government service in the 1870s diplomas from all three schools seem to have been accepted as equal.[114]

A sign of the erosion of the government service's exclusive right to "high" architecture and of the Ecole's monopoly was the institution of an annual triple prize for superior private construction by the Société Centrale des Architectes in 1870. In that year Jules and Paul Sédille gave two hundred francs for the Société to award a prize for the three model examples of private architecture, two Parisian, one provincial.[115] At the meeting of the Congrès des Architectes Français on June 20, 1874, the prizes were awarded to J.-M.-A. Lesoufaché, François Rolland, and C.-A. Benoit of Lyons. Lesoufaché then founded the continuation of the prize on an annual basis as we have noted. In 1875 D.-L. Destors was recognized for the Hôtel Camondo, rue Monceau, and Bouwens van der Boyen for the Crédit Lyonnais; in 1876 it was Paul Sédille himself and Théodore Belle; in 1878 Henri Blondel was recognized for the Hôtel Intercontinental; in 1880 Henri Dubois, and so on.[116]

Although about a decade behind, this emergence of private practice as the equal of public architecture parallels the development in painting traced by Patricia Mainardi in her comparison of the art sections of the Expositions Universelles of 1855 and 1867.[117] After the monopoly collapsed, the distinction between private and public architecture blurred. By 1910 Albert Louvet's *L'Art d'architecture et la profession d'architecte* treats private and public practice as simply two equal options. The idea of a specific link between a certain style of architecture and the building of the state had evaporated, replaced by the conception of a general democratic social mission or an irrespective eclecticism.

HAUSSMANN, BALTARD, AND MUNICIPAL ARCHITECTURE

I

With the astounding transformation of Paris under the prefect Haussmann, the center of architectural power moved in the Second Empire from the sovereign and the Bâtiments Civils toward the municipality. The New Louvre (1852–1857) was the last great exclusively state project. However, as we have noted in citing Pigeory and Horace Say, the municipality saw itself as distinct from the state in its building principles. This was the domain of the bourgeoisie – both the traditional bourgeoisie and the new "Grande Bourgeoisie" of finance and industry – and they saw their tradition as more practical and less monumental than the essentially monarchical representation of the central state authority. The suggestions of Pigeory and Say as well as the conceptions of urban character summarized in Chapter 4 – those of the Saint Simoniens and Horeau – sketch possibilities, but Haussmann with his services des Travaux de Paris under Baltard and des Promenades et Plantations under Alphand actually produced a systematic recreation of Paris.

Haussmann seems to have conceived his initial transformation of Paris all as a piece extending the projects underway – in spite of the designation of three "networks"[1] – and almost immediately after his inauguration on June 29, 1853. The fragmentary documentary record indicates that all the basic projects – the north-south axis, the quarters of the Opéra, of the place du Prince Eugène (now de la République), of the Gare du Nord – were outlined at the outset, simultaneously with Haussmann's other basic projects, the annexation of the suburbs to make them the outer arrondissements, the sewer system, and the water supply. He had a remarkably complete vision of the "Nouveau Paris" in all its aspects. But we must acknowledge that Haussmann was working with a city whose history and socioeconomic organism was remarkably solid, suggesting by itself certain transformations many of which had already been set in motion before his arrival – the east-west axis down the rue de Rivoli to the Hôtel de Ville, the Bois de Boulogne, the Halles Centrales, the rebuilding of the Palais de Justice, and the restoration of Notre-Dame. The great plan of late 1853 was not one drawn on a blank sheet of paper but on the contrary was engendered from a web of ideas and interests asserting themselves around the prefect. A second thing we should note is that in the early 1860s, when the initial projects of 1853 were finished or well underway, something happened – scale changed, focus was lost, coordination lapsed – as new projects were undertaken that were inflections, elaborations, and extensions of the original project (especially in the outer arrondissements annexed in 1860), which the amazing success of the first decade of work made seem possible, but that now got out of control and led to the financial crisis of 1867–1869 and thence to Haussmann's ouster.

Haussmann was a practical man. In attempting to define the elusive, if impressive, consistency and character of his Nouveau Paris it might be best to depict it as the solution to problems rather than the imposition of an ideal. The first of these problems, of course, was that the city was still held to be the backdrop for the sovereign's representation. Haussmann's transformation had to frame and link the imperial monuments of the nation. The second problem was that this particular sovereign, Napoleon III, drew his power from a compromise with the new capitalist economic forces. Thus the city had to adapt itself to its recreation as a place of exchange of goods, industrial in some quarters, luxury in others. There was also a third problem: the slow evaporation of central authority, which Theodore Zeldin has documented as a part of Napoleon III's reign and which appears in the cityscape as a massive movement of Paris to realize itself by restoring and enframing the jumble of its own monumental history. If we so view Haussmann' transformation as reactive we can appreciate that his (and his administration's) solutions were increasingly characterized by inclusion and juxtaposition – a strange sort of picturesque – as much as by any inflection of a consistent system of form.

*   *   *

Haussmann's depiction of the start of his tenure as prefect we have already mentioned.[2] He called on the emperor on June 29, 1853, immediately before his official assumption of office. In his *Mémoires* Haussmann relates that Napoleon III handed him a plan of Paris with a network of new streets drawn on it in four colors indicating urgency of construction – "A map of Paris upon which one sees drawn by Himself in blue, red, yellow and green, following their degree of urgency, the different new streets which he proposed to have executed."[3] (The topos, in other words, of the emperor designing his own representation and laying the sketch in the hands of his loyal assistant).[4]

That map is supposed to have hung on Haussmann's office wall at the Hôtel de Ville as a symbol of his charge and achieved mythic force (for example, as it appears in Zola's *La Curée* of 1870–1871).[5] We should take it seriously.[6] The actual sheet is lost today, but a purported copy exists, given to Friedrich Wilhelm of Prussia in 1867 (Figure 98), as well as a reconstruction by Charles Merruau (secretary general of the prefect) published in 1875 and, we are told, checked by the emperor before his death (Figure 99).[7] These are essentially the same as the plan included with the text of *Traité* of 1858 funding the Second Network (that plan dated by hand in the Archives Nationales, "1854," Figure 100).[8] The basic scheme was never in doubt: the parallel east-west *percements* on the two sides of the Seine, the rue de Rivoli, and the boulevard Saint-Germain; the north-south axis of the boulevards de Strasbourg, de Sébastopol, du Palais, and

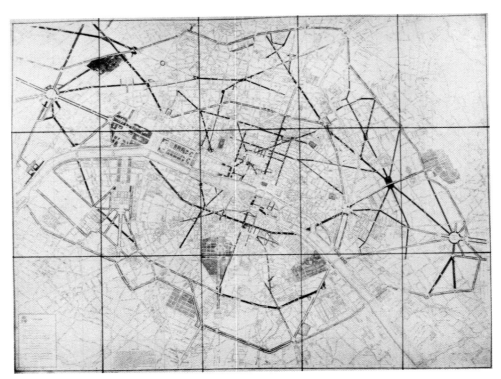

Figure 98. Plan of Paris with the Second Empire transformations marked (darker lines) given to Friedrich Wilhelm of Prussia by Napoleon III, 1867.
(Opposite above) Figure 99. Plan of Paris with the Second Empire transformations marked (darker lines) by Charles Merruau and checked by Napoleon III. From Merruau, *Souvenirs de l'Hôtel de Ville*, 1875.
(Opposite below) Figure 100. Plan of Paris with proposed streets marked accompanying the *Traité* of 1858 (dated, in pen, 1854).

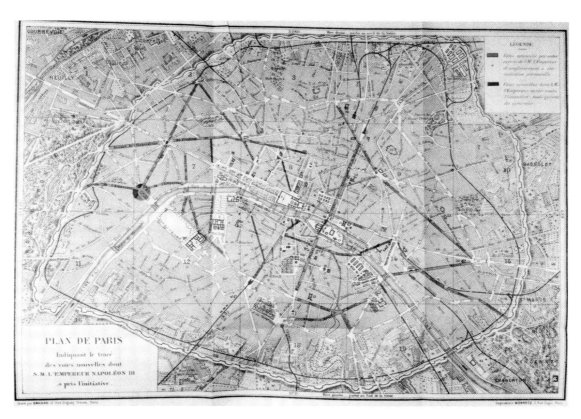

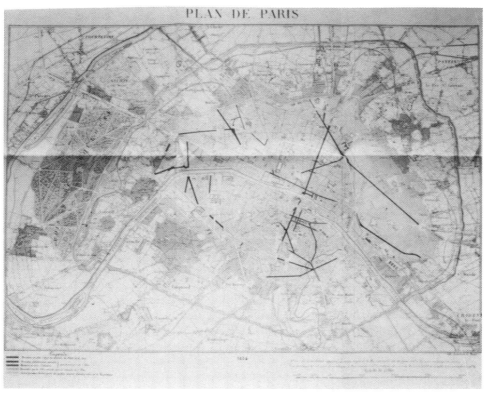

Saint-Michel meeting the rue de Rivoli at the place du Châtelet; the new *places* on the Right Bank boulevards – of the Opéra and Prince Eugène – linked to the railway stations by the rues de Rouen, Lafayette, and the boulevard du Nord (Magenta); the diagonals cutting into the city center from these, the rue de Turbigo and avenue Napoléon (de l'Opéra); the peripheral sprays of avenues at the place de Trocadéro, de l'Etoile, du Trône, Saint-Médard, and the Pont d'Alma, joining the old center of the city to the developing outer arrondissements.[9]

There is a story, of course, to this brilliant solution seemingly sketched in a moment, that of Napoleon III's personal conception of economics and urbanism matured during two decades of exile and imprisonment and – perhaps even more important – that of the evolving shape of Paris itself.[10] This latter, as we have seen, had suggested the west axis since the sixteenth century. The overcrowding of the Halles quarter had suggested the rebuilding of the central markets and their surroundings since the late eighteenth century.[11] Natural topography had determined the entry points of the railroads.[12] Indeed, the Halles project had been authorized by ordonnance royale of January 17, 1847, and the Louvre-rue de Rivoli project by decrees of March 24, 1848, and October 4, 1849 (these constituting most of the First Network). Special funding for the projects had been under discussion before the Conseil Municipal in 1847 and a loan of twenty-five million francs was contracted in 1848, in part to create employment after the Revolution.[13] However, the prefect Berger, assuming office in December 1848, was hesitant to push work beyond the immediate resources of the city or a cautiously contracted loan of fifty million francs of 1852. After months of disputes, Persigny (minister of the interior) and Napoleon III eased Berger out and appointed Haussmann specifically because of his boldness and craft.[14] The project came first; the prefect was appointed to execute it.

II

By 1854 the transformation of Paris was on paper, even if its conception had predated Haussmann's arrival in 1853. What there is of a history to Haussmann's work is the funding and the detailed shaping of this schema – that is, the theater and the economic reality of its implementation.

Haussmann did not begin his administration publicly brandishing Napoleon's multicolored sheet and setting to work on all sides. The Rambuteau-Berger projects were incomplete and in technical or financial trouble. The Municipal Council was wary and cautious.[15] Haussmann speaks in his *Mémoires* of the need to proceed carefully. First he had to clear the slate. He fired the garden planner Varé at the Bois de Boulogne and replaced him with Adolphe Alphand to get the water level in the lake correct and to push the project to rapid completion. Then he pushed Victor Baltard's revised project for the Halles, that in iron. He kept work going on the Champs-Elysées, the avenue de l'Impératrice, the entourage of the New Louvre and the rue de Rivoli – all the while assuring the Conseil Municipal there were ample resources in the existing budget.[16]

Then he began to expand beyond his predecessors' limits. On September 29, 1854, the emperor decreed of "utilité publique" the boulevard du Centre (on September 25, 1855, renamed boulevard de Sébastopol in celebration of that Crimean War victory) cutting from the Seine to the boulevard Saint-Denis, as well as the extension of the rue de Rivoli past the Hôtel de Ville to the rue Saint Antoine.[17] (An *enquête* had been held the previous May.) On August 11, 1855, this was done for the extension of the boulevard du Centre across the Seine to the Observatory (in 1867 renamed the boulevard Saint-Michel).[18] This completed the First Network.

The first percements and regularizations were paid for piecemeal, usually with a state subsidy of about a third, on the grounds that the streets of the capital were of national strategic importance. The city was thus given 2.1 million francs to partially defray the costs of the opening of the Louvre's surroundings by agreement of August 2, 1849. The cost of the opening of the boulevard de Strasbourg was divided between the state (one third) and the city (two-thirds) by agreement of September 8, 1852. The Left Bank extension of the boulevard de Sébastopol (the boulevard Saint-Michel) was similarly divided (up to a total cost of 23.5 million francs) by agreement of October 18, 1854.[19] Further state assistance came with an agreement that the national government would pay for the maintenance of the new streets beginning on January 1, 1856.[20] Later the city traded land in the quartier de l'Opéra for state tracts in what became the Trocadéro.[21]

More money, however, was needed. The rue de Rivoli proved much more expensive than projected. In 1855 a city loan of 50 million francs was opened for public subscription and oversold on the first day. On March 19, 1858, Haussmann presented a *mémoire* to the Conseil Municipal outlining the Second Network, projecting a cost of 180 million francs, and proposing that the state should pay for a third (60 million).[22] This was approved by the Corps Législatif (with the state contribution reduced to 50 million francs) on May 28. On November 14 of that year the state authorized the creation of the Caisse des Travaux de la Ville de Paris, a city-run bank to hold expropriation and resale moneys but one issuing bonds so that it effectively contracted further loans for the municipality.[23] Finally, now, with the printed map that accompanied the *Traité* of 1858 (Figure 100) Napoleon's basic intentions were published, sanctioned, and put under construction constituting the Second Network.

But at this point, just when things seemed clear, new complications arose. There was, in fact, much more to Napoleon III's and Haussmann's tranformation of Paris than this map. Already, in April 1854, they had discussed rebuilding the city's sewer and water systems, and these projects were authorized in 1857 and 1860. Now the expansion of the city limits to the fortifications was promulgated for January 1, 1860. New municipal buildings there had to be projected: schools and *mairies* for the new arrondissements; hospitals (the Hôtel Dieu, the Asile Sainte-Anne, and the Hôpital Tenon); churches. (From the 1859 budget the church appropriation was doubled from one million francs to two.)[24] More money was needed. In 1860 a huge loan of 130 million francs was floated, partly because of the cost of the new arrondissements, partly to complete the Second Network.[25] Construction work picked up all over Paris, to the amazement of Parisians who thought it already awe inspiring: Condemnations mounted from 129 in 1858 to 398 in 1860 to 848 in 1866.[26] In 1865 yet another loan was floated – now of 300 million francs – to finish the work in five years, but it was not enthusiastically subscribed. In the meantime Haussmann had begun work on a mass of street openings like those around the Opéra on the city's sole account, the Third Network. He also began to practice financial tricks moving around funds between contractors and the state Crédit Foncier made possible by special notes, the notorious *bons de délégation*.[27] Already in 1865 conservative voices spoke out to unveil and criticize Haussmann's financial dealings, and by 1868 they reached a crescendo with Jules Ferry's *Comptes fantastiques d'Haussmann* and the consolidation of the city's debt to the Crédit Foncier in a single 398 million franc loan.[28] Now Haussmann was on the defensive. He continued to push his mass of underfunded projects toward completion, but was scrutinized and criticized at every step. In 1869 he was forced to liquidate the Crédit Foncier loan with a 250 million public bond offering. On January 6, 1870, he was replaced upon the appointment as prime minister of the liberal Emile Ollivier.

* * *

There is also another kind of "history" to Haussmann's implementation of Napoleon's sketch of June 1853, its theatrics – the timing and gestures of proclamation and inauguration of the various parts.

Something very visible and concrete was being done to change Paris. People could not mistake it, and they were amazed and profoundly troubled. They became aware of their city and its architecture as never before. The experience of a transformation so huge could not be completely scripted or controlled, but some sort of text could be imposed on it to gain political advantage and to retain momentum to carry it through. At first the emperor imposed Napoleonic imagery on the city, to appropriate it for his own representation, but by 1860 it was the city itself and its transformation that had become the subject of this theater, with the emperor increasingly appearing merely the instrument of its self-realization.

It was the *Traité* of 1858 that finally made Napoleon III's grand scheme clear, and a telling series of events accompanied its negotiation. It coincided with the completion of the boulevard de Sébastopol. The central moment was, literally, that of the ceremonial opening of a curtain, a huge one "en étoffe d'or, semé d'étoiles d'or, bruni et orné d'un réseau de guirlandes" – "on cloth of gold, dotted with golden stars, burnished and decorated with a network of garlands,"[29] drawn across the boulevard just below the boulevard Saint-Denis.[30] The *Moniteur universel* primed the public with a series of breathless articles on March 26, 27, and 30. We read, for example,

> For several days an immense crowd has, in all directions, traversed the boulevard de Sébastopol whose formal opening will occur shortly. Very soon, one says, an immense velum will fall at an appointed moment to reveal the endless perspective of this grandiose avenue beside which the Via Sacra of Rome pales.
>
> • • •
>
> Bright satisfaction can be read on all faces at the sight of these numberless houses, spacious, elegant, already animated by commerce, having shot up from the ground as by enchantment, where there once stood those labyrinths of streets and alleys that never enjoyed the benefit of light and air: the Parisian population thus testifies to the high value of the creation of this street, unrivalled in the world, the most gigantic work of slum clearance [*assainissement*] ever accomplished in the capital of a great empire.[31]

At 2 P.M., April 5, 1858, the prefect and the emperor with their suites met at the crossing of the boulevard de Sébastopol and the rue de Rivoli. The curtain was opened, "et l'oeil a pu suivre dans tout son développement l'admirable voie publique" – "and the eye could embrace in all its length this admirable public thoroughfare."[32] Between lines of troops they rode up the boulevard – decorated by Baltard with Venetian masts bearing long banners (diverting the eyes from the hoardings covering large gaps in construction defining the sides) with two 90-foot pairs at the ends at the rue de Rivoli and the Gare de l'Est – and were received by the Conseil Municipal before the station (Figure 101). The emperor gave an address and the cavalcade then descended to the boulevard again, followed the boulevards de Saint-Denis, des Italiens, and des Capucines to the place Vendôme and thence to the Tuileries. In the evening the boulevard de Sébastopol was illuminated to make it a festive promenade.

This ceremony was only part of a larger series of events, as we indicated in sketching Haussmann's financial history earlier. It was immediately preceded by Haussmann's *mémoire* presenting the Second Network, dated March 19. This was read at the Corps Législatif the day after, April 6,[33] and was fol-

INAUGURATION DU BOULEVARD DE SÉBASTOPOL, LE 5 AVRIL 1858.
Passage du cortège après l'abaissement du *velum*, à l'intersection du nouveau boulevard et du boulevard Saint-Denis. — D'après des documents photographiques de M. Richebourg.

Figure 101. Inauguration ceremony of the boulevard de Sébastopol, April 5, 1858 (Victor Baltard, architect).

lowed by its acceptance with the state's commitment of 50 million francs (May 28) and the creation of the Caisse des Travaux (November 4). The First Network – the New Louvre and the completion of the west axis through it to the Hôtel de Ville, the cross axis of the boulevard de Sébastopol (Right Bank), and the regularization of the Halles Centrales – had had a certain kind of theater, that of accomplishing a task long recognized but delayed. Upon inaugurating the New Louvre in 1857 the emperor proclaimed, "The completion of the Louvre, which you have honored by contributing with such zeal and skill, is not the caprice of the moment, it is the realization of a plan conceived for glory and sustained by the instinct of the nation for more than a hundred years."[34] The significance of these projects spoke for themselves The emperor's genius was not in conceiving them but in accomplishing them.

Haussmann's *mémoire* of March 19, 1858, and Napoleon III's address at the inauguration of the boulevard de Sébastopol of April 5 present a different kind of project, that of expanding the city by linking its core to new, outlaying districts, by integrating the railroad stations into the city communications, and by encouraging private enterprise to produce an immense amount of housing to respond to the increase in prosperity and population that should result. The emperor intoned:

We live at a time when the creation of railroads changes all the economic parameters of a nation because not only do they absorb the majority of available capital for their construction but also because, once built, they favor the accumulation of the population in cities and modify the relationship between the producer and the consumer. The Municipal Council thus has a multiple task to accomplish: it must first of all insure the financial resources of the nation, [then] support new construction to lodge the sudden increase in population, so that, on the other hand, it must demolish in order to create new streets which permit light and air to penetrate the unhealthy quarters and build great arteries helping the development of the city, linking the center to the extremities.[35]

The conception of 1858 was a new one. It implied the destruction of the old, heterogeneous quarters in the city center (for reasons of public order, Haussmann clearly states) and the creation of large new quarters implicitly dividing the population by economic status.[36] The need for this transformation was not self-evident to the Paris population who from the very start were worried about it. Starting with the ceremony of April 5, 1858, these projects became the subject of a strange theater previously left to the celebration of the inauguration of palaces or royal family occasions.

In 1860 the Fontaine Saint-Michel (Figure 102) terminating the axis down the boulevard du Palais across the newly rebuilt ponts au Change and Saint-Michel was unveiled in the same manner as the boulevard de Sébastopol, but more dramatically, since here the velum was hung immediately over a monumental facade and its decorative sculpture had been completed unobserved. The day chosen was August 15, the "Jour du Saint-Napoléon," Napoleon I's birthday and the Second Empire national holiday. The official *Moniteur universel* followed the preparations with anticipation.[37] On the day itself the Pont au Change at the Châtelet was inaugurated and the cover in front of the Fontaine Saint-Michel removed, presenting the composition in its entirety. (Unfortunately, critics felt the fountain, designed by Gabriel Davioud, did not meet the expectations raised by its site and by these formalities.)[38]

August 15 the next year saw an even more theatrical inauguration, that of the long boulevard Malesherbes, leading from in front of the Madeleine up to the new wealthy quarter being developed around the Parc Monceau.[39] As in the case of the boulevard de Sébastopol three years before, Baltard marked the route with Venetian masts and in addition transformed the building site of his own church of Saint-Augustin at the midpoint into a tall openwork trellis outlining the monument's contemplated mass, decked with flags, medals, and insignia (Figure 103). This was important because even less construction was to be seen along the sides than at the boulevard de Sébastopol, especially north of Saint-Augustin. The emperor rode up the boulevard's length from the Madeleine to a large tent set up at the edge of

Figure 102. Fontaine Saint-Michel (Gabriel Davioud, architect, 1856–1860).

Figure 103. Inauguration ceremony of the boulevard Malesherbes, August 15, 1861, the decorated scaffolding of the church of Saint-Augustin in the foreground (Victor Baltard, architect, 1860–1868).

the Parc Monceau amid stands for spectators and a temporary triumphal arch. Haussmann then made a lengthy address about the transformation of Paris, declaring this the first part completed of the Second Network and a demonstration of the linkage of the center and the undeveloped and previously inaccessible outer arrondissements. The emperor replied supportively, then rode through the Parc Monceau to the Etoile and back to the park and down the boulevard. Journalists did not fail to note that Emile Pereire's own mansion on the park was one of the few as yet standing in the quarter.

The greatest bit of this theater came the next year. On December 5, 1862, the boulevard du Prince Eugène was inaugurated in the proletarian east, leading outward from the place du Prince Eugène to the place du Trône, a distance almost equal to that from the Louvre to the Arc de Triomphe.[40] After a triple velum was opened at the place du Prince Eugène, the imperial suite rode down the boulevard's considerable length between lines of troops and past a decorative composition at the mairie under construction at the midpoint. At the place du Trône, Haussmann delivered another lengthy sur-

Figure 104. Inauguration ceremony of the place du Trône, December 5, 1862, with temporary arch and porticos (Victor Baltard, architect).

vey of the transformation of Paris, and the emperor responded. But here there was something new: Instead of masts or trellises, Baltard had erected a full-scale arcade around the immense *place* as well as a huge temporary triumphal arch at the center (Figure 104). This, Haussmann revealed, was a suggestion of a permanent monument he was proposing to build here commemorating the imperial victory over the Austrians in north Italy in 1859.

When one glances at the map of Paris, one is struck to find at the two most distant extremities of the city, at the end points of the two most magnificent avenues, from which spread magisterial avenues penetrating [the agglomeration] in all directions, those of Neuilly and Vincennes, two almost symmetrical plazas that correspond to each other at the east and the west and which seem ready for the same function in the monumental layout [*ordonnance générale*] of the city. The idea of elevating a monument to the military glory of Your Majesty's Reign at the place du Trône is something for which no one can claim the initiative because it presents itself naturally to all minds.

We do not pretend to have resolved, in the hasty works of a temporary decoration, the very complex artistic questions raised by such a conception; but we are certain to have been the faithful interpreters of popular sentiment when we think to dedicate this very spot with a triumphal arch dedicated to the victor of Solferino and to his valiant soldiers where Your Majesty, returning from Italy, reentered Paris at the head of Your troops.[41]

(He failed to mention the arch Perrault had begun on this spot for Louis XIV in 1662.) Presumably this arch was to be on a scale to be visible from and respond to the first Napoleon's Arc de Triomphe across the city.[42] Almost no permanent construction had been carried out around the *place*; Haussmann praised a real estate developer who was soon to make a large commitment to the area, presumably the Compagnie Immobilière.[43]

With this Haussmann acted out the final imaging of the Nouveau Paris – vast in extent, bound together by the new boulevards, dominated by symbols of the two Napoleons. Strangely, at this moment Haussmann's theatricalization of the Nouveau Paris ended. There were no more such ceremonies. The arch at the place du Trône was never executed. In 1862 Viollet-le-Duc's restoration of Notre-Dame was inaugurated on Christmas Day with little special ceremony.[44] In 1865 the Tribunal de Commerce was quietly opened with the annual opening of the tribunal.[45] This now became the time of a new sort of theater, that of bourgeois life in the Nouveau Paris as it drew to completion – that depicted by Baudelaire, Zola, and the Impressionist painters. In October 1868 the extension of the Palais de Justice was inaugurated with no ceremony beyond a formal visit by Haussmann.[46] This was the most magnificent piece of architecture completed in the prefect's transformation of Paris, and it was immediately awarded the Grand Prix de l'Empereur as the greatest work of art produced in France in the decade. August 15 returned to being a carnival holiday instead of a time for official solemnities. The one last piece of theater in the Empire was the opening of the Suez Canal on November 16, 1869 – wonderful with the royal yacht *Aigle* carrying Empress Eugénie down the waterway at the head of an international flotilla. But this was not in Paris. In 1870 Napoleon III left to lead his troops upon the outbreak of the Franco-Prussian War by slipping out from Saint-Cloud without ceremony.[47]

As a kind of footnote and commentary on this we must note that during the night before August 15, 1867 – the Exposition Universelle year – Charles Garnier had the scaffolding removed from the facade of his Opéra.[48] (At the beginning of construction it was projected to be complete in 1867.) Though a skeleton internally, most of the decorative sculpture had been executed, and it was gorgeous. But this was Garnier's own performance on the Jour du Saint-Napoléon and there were no speeches or official recognition.

✱　　✱　　✱

One last qualification is necessary to Haussmann's story of the transformation of Paris: the significance of the extension of the city to the fortifications (effective January 1, 1860) – the doubling of its area and its reorganization into twenty arrondissements.[49]

In November 1861, the municipal Commission des Beaux-Arts was asked to formulate a decorative program for the Salle du Conseil Municipal at the Hôtel de Ville.[50] The Commission proposed that four scenes be depicted: Clovis naming Paris his capital; Saint Louis departing for the Crusades putting his children in charge of the city; the inauguration of the relief of Henri IV over the Hôtel de Ville door; Napoleon III signing the decree enlarging Paris. At that moment the annexation seemed the most significant moment in the whole epochal transformation.

From a general European perspective this makes sense. City extension rather than internal *percements* were then the primary concern in Vienna (the Ringstrasse, planned 1858), Berlin (Hobrecht plan, 1858–1862, Figure 105), Barcelona (Cerdà plan, 1859), and Amsterdam (van Niftrik plan, 1864) not to mention Lyons, Geneva, and Brussels. Economically it was recognized that extension was the fundamental problem, and the celebrated first two treatises on "urbanism" dealt with this, Cerdà's *Teoría general de la urbanizacion* of 1867 and Reinhard Baumeister's *Stadt-Erweiterungen in technischer, baupolizeilicher und wirtschaftlicher Beziehung* of 1876.

The question is to what degree this held also for Paris. When the Commission des Beaux-Arts presented the program for the Salle de Conseil,

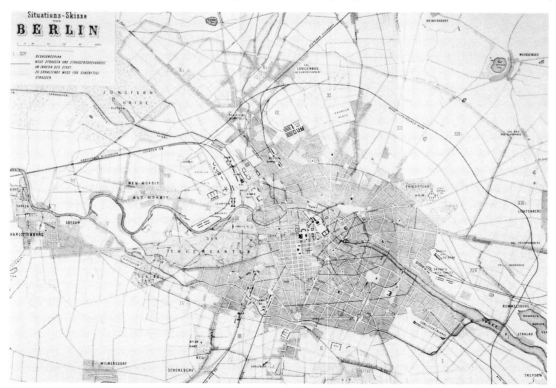

Figure 105. Plan for the extension of Berlin by city engineer James Hobrecht, 1861.

Haussmann and Baltard objected that a formal signing of an extension decree had never taken place and so, for historical veracity, they proposed a representation of the inauguration of the boulevard Malesherbes instead ("Napoléon III inaugurant le percement du boulevard de Malesherbes, agrandissement de Paris jusqu'aux fortifications" – "Napoleon III inaugurating the cutting of the boulevard Malesherbes, the Extension of Paris to the Fortifications"). That is to say, in their minds the Second Network linked the city core to the annexed areas (rather than just to the railroad stations as usually assumed today) and the boulevard Malesherbes leading to the Pereire developments on the Plaine Monceau stood in Haussmann's and Baltard's minds for the whole enterprise. The Commission accepted the proposal.

There had been strong resistance to the extension of the city's limits, however, and there were reasons why reference to the project should have been oblique until it was an accomplished fact in 1860. Such an extension was implicit in the ring of fortifications decreed in 1837 and erected in 1841–1847, but the advantage of escaping city taxation (both for residents and for visiting workers enjoying the cheap wine available beyond the *barrières*) made it impracticable. In 1852 anti-Bonapartists spread the rumor that Louis-Napoleon wished to extend the city, and the prince-president issued a categorical denial.[51] It was only slowly and amid considerable outcry that the project was pushed through in the late 1850s.[52]

Another reason besides political sensitivity for the confusion about the importance of the annexation of the outer arrondissements is that this would seem to have been Haussmann's greatest failure. C.-A. Delangle's first economic projections in 1859 showed that the resulting tax income would equal the city's expenses in extending services to the area.[53] Yet already in a *mémoire* to the Conseil Municipal of June 15, 1860, Haussmann acknowledged that this had been quite naive.[54] In a second *mémoire* of April 21, 1865, he projected the cost at 160 million francs in addition to the 136 million francs already spent.[55] It was this ballooning bill for streets, services, and institutions in the outer arrondissements – constituting much of the Third Network – that wrecked Haussmann's financial calculations and caused the bitter controversies of 1865–1870 leading to his dismissal. Yet, for having risked so much in spending these huge sums, he had very little to show for it in the old suburbs (in contrast to the situation in the city center). Even before the protests about city finances, newspapers and pamphleteers had set up a barrage of exposés of the city's tardiness and neglect in these areas.[56] Although the city responded with lists of buildings erected, roads paved, and sewer and gas mains laid,[57] the reality of the situation was notoriously visible on the ground and in 1870 was depicted in Louis Lazare's adamant *Quartiers de l'est de Paris*.

III

Let us pause a moment in delineating the "histories" of Haussmann's initial transformation to again underline the consistency of the conception. This appears most subtly but most decisively in the style of the new cityscape. Whatever Haussmann did, right from the start it had a certain look, and this look extended far beyond the individual *percements*.[58] With the expansion of cities in the mid-nineteenth century, they became the entire theaters of their populations' lives, and it was a new kind and "style" of life that Haussmann imposed, as we suggested in Chapter 1.

Haussmann describes in his *Mémoires* the more visible ways in which he transformed Paris: the survey of the city; the provision of fresh water through long-distance aqueducts; the creation of a network of sewers; the paving of streets with macadam and their illumination with gas; the development of the Assistance Publique; the control of bread prices by the Caisse de la Boulangerie; the proposition of a huge central cemetery hygenically outside the city limits. One should, however, expand this to embrace a slightly subtler series of initiatives not signaled in the chapter headings of Haussmann's book. We noted in Chapter 1 the network of barracks sited around the city even before Haussmann's appointment and his plan of 1858 to disperse the theaters. He also neatened the cityscape by leveling streets, ordering the regular cleaning of house facades, enforcing the existing *servitudes* (as well as imposing new *servitudes* on newly created spaces), by planting trees in all the major thoroughfares, by furnishing the city spaces with a new array of specially designed public conveniences, and finally by creating a series of inner-city parks of uniform design, some new, some appropriations of existing spaces. As a result the spatial experience of the city was transformed – more subtly, generally, and (in the end) profoundly than by Haussmann's other interventions. It made the Paris of the Impressionists – airy, green, safe (with its broad sidewalks and fenced gardens) for strolling.

The project of leveling, cleaning, and enforcing of *servitudes* was, in fact, just the implementation of two articles in the fundamental (but mysteriously authored) decree of March 26, 1852, that was also permitting Haussmann's generous expropriations. "Henceforth any plan of street *alignements* must include levels and these last will be submitted to the same formalities that regulate *alignements*. Building facades will always be kept in a proper state of cleanliness. They will be scraped, painted, or whitewashed at least every ten years. . . ."[59]

The legislation dates to Berger but it was Haussmann who enforced it. Beginning with *arrêtés* of March 30 and April 10, 1854, the streets of Paris began to be individually surveyed for leveling and the proposed plans displayed in the *mairies* for the required fifteen days before an *enquête* and promulgation.[60] This work of leveling was not just a matter of squaring up the city: It was preliminary to the laying of a system of local sewers and street cleaning outlets that permitted (and still today permits) the periodic washing of the streets.[61]

Facade cleaning was set in motion by an *arrêté* of May 3, 1854, citing the decree of March 26, 1852, and specifying streets to be refurbished before the end of the year: the boulevards and the quais; the places Vendôme, des Victoires, des Vosges, de la Bourse, and Saint-Sulpice; the garden facades in the Palais Royal; the rues Royale, de la Paix, Saint-Denis, and Saint-Martin, de la Chaussée d'Antin, de Richelieu, Bonaparte, Vaugirard, and so on.[62] The commissaires voyers were to notify all the owners and supervise the campaign. In subsequent years the project was extended to include every street in Paris.

The imposition of order was thoroughgoing. By *arrêté* of June 27, 1857 (confirmed and elaborated October 10, 1863), proprietors' buildings along planted avenues were enjoined to make sure their carriage entrances were aligned to the spaces between the city's trees.[63] To ensure compliance the confirmation of this in 1863 required that facade drawings be included in applications for building authorization.

Haussmann's enforcement of the existing *servitudes* is perhaps a bit surprising: One might assume that the main avenues always were as neat and imposing as they seem today. But signs, windows, and temporary constructions encumbered the regular architectural lines at many points. By another *arrêté* of late spring 1854 (June 15), Haussmann set a process in motion to disengage these fronts and return them to what he imagined to be their original pristineness.[64] He cites the *arrêté* of May 3 requiring cleaning and the decree of March 26, 1852, and specifies that owners of buildings on the places de la Concorde, Royale, Vendôme, des Victoires as well as on the rue Royale shall be convened by the commissaires voyers at the local *mairies*, "under the presidency of the mayor . . . in order to discuss . . . the uniform system to follow in order to put these houses in a proper state of cleanliness."[65] At this time the precise alterations necessary were to be specified to them. The *Journal des débats* subsequently noted the execution of this order – and a few years later began to publish articles nostalgic for the old signboards and inflections of Paris facades.[66] In 1858–1859 the monumental fountains of the city – those of the place de la Concorde, the square Louvois, and others – were systematically dismounted, rebronzed by a new and superior process, and remounted.[67]

The leveling of streets, cleaning of facades, and enforcement of *servitudes* was a negative project, like the contemporaneous *percements* – they cleared the field but did not fill the spaces with the signs and equipment of life of the Nouveau Paris. To accomplish this second task Haussmann strengthened the powers of the commissaires voyers (as we noted in Chapter 2) and established a new administration by *arrêté* of December 12, 1854,[68] that of the Promenades et Plantations, headed by the engineer Alphand (who thus expanded his purview from the Bois de Boulogne to the whole of Paris) with an architecte-en-chef detached from the bureau of the Plan de Paris, Gabriel Davioud.[69] An immense campaign of tree planting was begun that left not only the canopied boulevards that we know today but also lines of trees now missing on the rue Royale and the boulevard Haussmann.[70] These trees were protected from traffic by broad sidewalks that Haussmann spread across Paris (authorized by a decree of 1836). They were interspersed with benches of new and superior design that would eventually number 8,428; kiosks for posters (which otherwise would have found their way to building walls), newspaper stalls, and, of course, the celebrated "Vespesiennes" of various and scientific plans.[71] Among the views Caillebotte painted from his balcony in the quartier de l'opéra in 1877 are two of stretches of the pavement below showing the curbs and a pedestrian island furnished with a bench, street lamps, and a tree set in a protective grate, looking like the technical plates in Alphand's *Promenades de Paris* (Figures 31 and 106).

Figure 106. Paris street furniture (Adolphe Alfand, *Promenades de Paris).*

The streets were covered with smooth macadam, like carpeting, and electric lighting was experimented with on the Champs-Elysées.[72]

The kinds of business permitted in certain areas was now set by the city authorities. The *Journal des débats* of February 29, 1856, reports the restrictions proposed for the new blocks flanking the avenue Victoria in the Châtelet: "It . . . is forbidden to rent to butchers, *charcutiers*, bakers, or sellers of wine or liquor, for shops of workers using hammers or for any other obtrusive or unhealthy occupation. . . ."[73] (The quarter had traditionally been that of the butchers.)

The result was a new and different sort of urban space. A series of existing open spaces that had been markets (like the square des Innocents, Louvois,[75] and the area around the Tour Saint-Jacques) or street crossings (like the square Montholon) had their centers filled with curbed islands of grass, trees, and flower beds, protected with a grill (locked, in the case of the Tour Saint-Jacques) with traffic channeled around them.[75] New squares were also created of similar design, for example, in front of La Trinité (with a diminutive *jardin anglais*), Saint-Germain-l'Auxerrois, or the Conservatoire des Arts et Métiers (Figure 115). They were supposed to reproduce the British squares of London's West End, but in the dense texture and monumental shaping of Haussmann's Paris they appear coquettish and more pieces of entourage with nannies shepherding young children around picturesquely shaped bits of gravel and grass.[76]

In Chapter 1 we cited Zola's evocation of the streets of the Nouveau Paris as the carpeted corridors of a sumptuous mansion. This image had power, for there was a tradition of transforming city spaces into interiors on special occasions, as the Marché des Innocents had been into a *bal* by the theater designer Séchan for the Jour de Saint Napoléon (August 15) in 1852.[77] The delimiting, enclosing, planting, and manicuring of these spaces made an approximation of this permanent. What lacked, of course, was a roof – which Hector Horeau would propose in the 1860s for the projected avenue de l'Opéra and, alternatively, the boulevard des Capucines in front of the Grand Hôtel (Figure 30) and which Baltard would actually erect between his pavilions at the Halles Centrales (Figure 111).[78]

The illuminating overlay plans in Hoffbauer's *Paris à travers les ages* (1875–1887) not only indicate the old and the new street patterns but also the sidewalk curb lines and sometimes the tree placement. They thus show the public space being subdivided, differentiated, and furnished. The voids in the plan of Paris, as they broadened under Haussmann, filled with something new – all that constituted light, space, and order. This appeared throughout Paris, but it was particularly concentrated in the elegant western quarters. In 1878 Alphonse Daudet began his novel *Le Nabab* with an evocation of the streets near the place Vendôme.

In this spacious and grand part of Paris . . . on these broad, tree-lined boulevards, these quiet quais, the mist floats immaculately, in numerous sheets, with wisps and balls of cottonwool. It is closed, discreet, almost luxurious, because the sun in its hesitation to rise begins to spread its soft purple colors, which lend to the mist enveloping the neatly aligned *hôtels* up to their rooftops the appearance of white muslin draped over scarlet cloth. One might describe it as a great curtain protecting the tardy and delicate slumber of wealth, a thin curtain through which nothing is heard but the discreet closing of a carriage entrance door, the tin rattle of the milkman, and the tinkle of a train of she-asses trotting past followed by the short, broken breath of their herdsman.[79]

*   *   *

Daudet goes on to contrast this to the dense, active urban texture of the humbler workers' quarters. Paris was coalescing into contrasting zones of distinct urban physiognomy. At the same time that Haussmann was formulating the new spatial *servitudes* that so transformed the "West End," the quartier des Halles was being given a contrasting but equally coordinated form, one to have great influence on future urbanism, although here the prefect was more clearly the instrument for clarifying and regularizing a vision already evolved by his predecessors. As we noted earlier, Haussmann in his *Mémoires* relates how he took Victor Baltard in hand after his first stone pavilion had proven a disaster and pushed him to redesign the structure all in iron – "du fer, du fer, rien que du fer!"[80] (Christopher Mead has found that the prefect exaggerates.[81]) This anecdote is usually presented in the context of the cosmic evolution of architectural design – the practical Haussmann breaking down the academic Baltard's resistance to architectural progress. But there is another transformation of the project evident in the drawings that raises a different issue. We see that in the final drawings the whole quarter has been leveled and recreated so that the system of interior streets organizing the pavilions of the market itself extends unbroken out across the surrounding quarter "en prolonguant les rues couvertes du grand corps des Halles" – "extending the *rues couvertes* of the great mass of the market,"[82] and creating a grid of housing blocks (Figures 107–110). *L'Illustration* in 1857 published a two-page spread of the perspective through one of the covered streets arranged to show its continuation out in the quarter around (Figure 111).[83] Zola's famous contrast of the old Paris with the new in his *Ventre de Paris* (1873) revolves around the vista up the north-south *rue couverte* enframing the transept of Saint-Eustache.[84] A grid of hand-car rail lines in the Halles basements was linked in one projection to a subway line under the boulevard de Sébastopol and thus to the Gare de l'Est and La Villette.[85]

Haussmann's and Baltard's project was one not of just rebuilding the markets, but of creating a whole new kind of commercial quarter in the heart of medieval Paris.[86] From its inception in 1845 the Halles project was

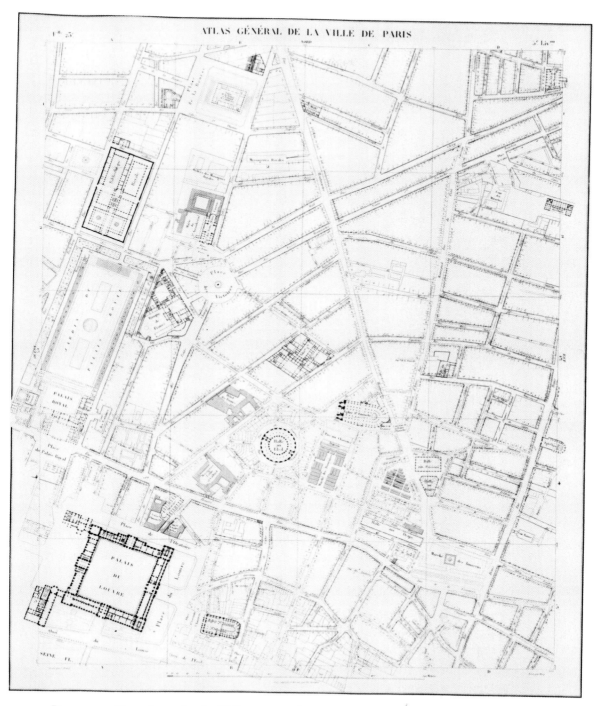

Figure 107. Plan of quartier des Halles c. 1840 from Jacoubet, *Atlas général de la Ville de Paris.*

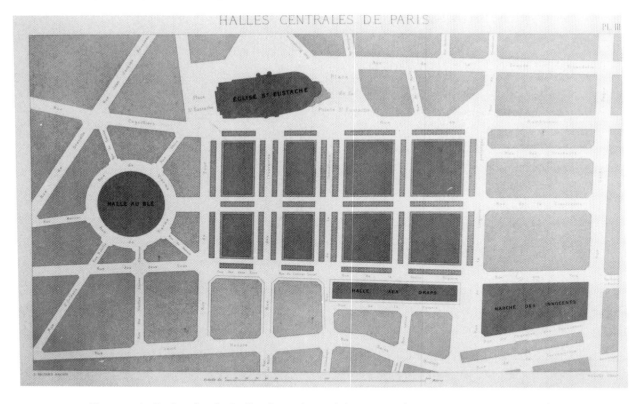

Figure 108. Project for the Halles Centrales and the surrounding streets, 1845 (Victor Baltard, architect).

seen as part of a broader campaign of opening and regularizing the whole quarter down to the Seine.[87] Baltard's three projects for the Halles included three successively more geometric rectifications of the quarter's *alignements,* that of June 1845 (decreed January 7, 1847, Figure 108), of August 1851 (decreed March 10, 1852, Figure 109), and that of March 1854 (decreed June 21, 1854), which was now almost identical to that illustrated in the *Monographie des Halles centrales* (Figure 110).[88] This last was embodied in a three-dimensional model viewed and approved by the emperor at the Hôtel de Ville on May 19, 1854.[89] The preexisting street pattern (fortuitously right angular) determines the basic grid, but with each plan the streets become wider and more equal while the blocks move toward a regular checkerboard of cubes (with canted corners) and the market pavilions arrange themselves until they carry on the dimensions and proportions of their surroundings perfectly. This plan was further refined and put into effect by the decree of August 23, 1858 declaring the rue de Turbigo of "utilité publique."[90] Further *arrêtés* followed in 1860 determining the rue du Louvre and the area northwest of Saint-Eustache.[91] The "Deschamps"

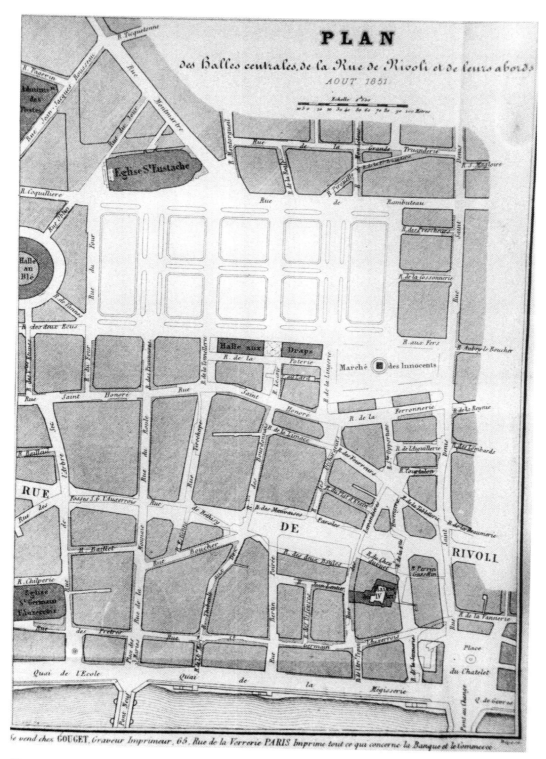

Figure 109. Project for the Halles Centrales and the surrounding streets, 1851 (Victor Baltard, architect).

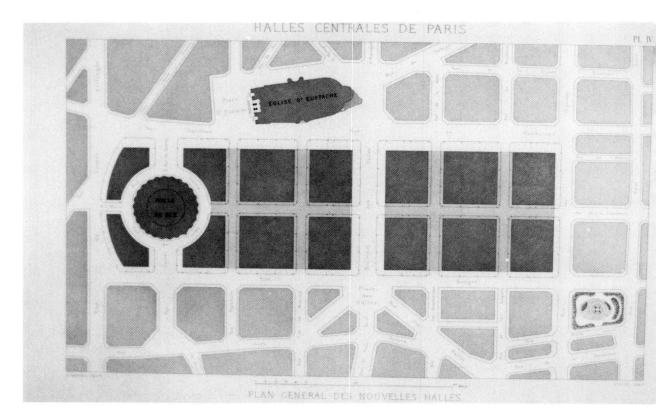

PLAN GENERAL DES NOUVELLES HALLES

(Opposite above)
Figure 110. Definitive project for the Halles Centrales and the surrounding streets, 1854 (Victor Baltard and Félix-Emmanuel Callet, architects).
(Opposite below)
Figure 111. Halles Centrales: view down the central covered street toward the east.

Figure 112. Rue Etienne Marcel (decreed 1860, 1880) looking west past the Hôtel des Postes (Julien Guadet, architect, 1879–1886).

map shows the gridded street pattern in dotted lines extended over the whole area south of the projected rue Etienne-Marcel.

The Halles scheme was not just a new kind of architecture, it was a new concept of commercial urbanism. The entire rectangle defined by the Palais Royal and the future rue Etienne-Marcel, boulevard de Sébastopol, and rue de Rivoli was to be gridded by streets extended from the gridded Halles implying the same system of served and serving space. Every block would have been rebuilt, a new proportion of street to block would have been imposed. One block was actually built, complete, at that time, the "Massif des Innocents" placed in what had been the western half of the Marché des Innocents by investors including Henri Germain (soon to be president of the Crédit Lyonnais).[92] It was a dense, square block sparely and uniformly articulated externally, divided into ten *immeubles* internally open only in narrow light courts. The *Revue général de l'architecture* felt it worthy of remark: "This immense construction, very simple but in good taste, already shelters a world of merchants and agents of the Halles."[93]

This would have produced a whole new city texture carrying the "dégagement" of Napoleon III's sketches and the orderly "style" of Haussmann's furnishing of the city to a surrealistic level far beyond that of the quartier de l'Opéra and approaching the frightening caricature of Victor Fournel's *Paris futur.*

Enough of this rebuilding was actually executed to indicate that it was serious – and little enough to indicate that it was very bold.[94] The blocks east of the Halles abutting the boulevard de Sébastopol were rebuilt on this pattern. Part of the northern perimeter was regularized with the cutting of the rue de Turbigo, begun in 1858. The blocks around the Marché des Innocents (now made a grassy "square") and the the new rue des Halles were rebuilt beginning in 1854 and completed around 1860.[95] In 1860 and 1880 the rue du Louvre and the rue Etienne Marcel were outlined with the ample width of 20 meters[96] defining the western and northern edges of the quarter, followed by the erection of the massive blocks of the Hôtel des Postes (1879–1886, by Julien Guadet, Figure 112) and the Bourse de Commerce with its two accompanying blocks filling out the urban texture (1886–1888, by Henri Blondel, Figures 94 and 95).

Zola used the Halles Centrales to embody the Nouveau Paris in his *Ventre de Paris* of 1873. His hero, Florent, caught up in the resistance to the *coup d'état* of December 2, 1851, was arrested in the streets around the old Halles, and transported to French Guinea. He escaped some five years later and, in the first pages of the novel, arrives back in Paris, asleep on a vegetable cart whose driver picked him up unconscious from beside the road. Now he is moving toward those Halles in the middle of the night. He passes places significant to him from the disturbances: where he was arrested; where he saw four men summarily executed against the wall of Saint-Eustache. Then they stop but, "au bord d'une large rue qu'il ne reconnaissait pas" – "in a street he does not recognize." Above the hubbub and lanterns that seem to dance among piles of vegetables, Florent starts to discern the unexpected profile of the new Halles.

But what surprised him was, on each side of the street, gigantic pavilions, the superposed roofs of which seemed to grow, to extend, to lose themselves in a cloud of reflections. He dreamed, in his fatigue, of a line of palaces, enormous and square, transparent as crystal shining on their facades with the thousand slits of the ventilators, continuous and unending. Between the sharp edges of the supports the thin yellow bars created ladders which mounted the pyramiding roofs. . . .

When he came out in the great central street, he thought of some immense, unfamiliar city, with various quarters, suburbs, villages, promenades and highways, plazas and street corners, placed in entirety under a roof some rainy day by some gigantic whim. Shadows slept in the corners of the roofs, multiplying the forest of pillars, enlarging infinitely their delicate network of open galleries and transparent screens; and beyond the city, in the depths of the shadows, a whole vegetation, a flowering, monstrous, of metal, of which the trunks rose like rockets, the branches spread and intertwined, to cover a world with the light leafings of an ancient jungle.[97]

The rest of the action of the story unfolds in and around this immense building, depicted in its spaces, its basements, and roofs as a city all by itself. The Halles Centrales is the Nouveau Paris – and, for Zola, a terrifying vision.

*   *   *

The intensity of exploitation in the dense, gridded quarter projected here reflects an increasing differentiation and specialization of the parts of the city. Although this was noted by contemporary critics (especially the Lazare brothers), it was not clearly proclaimed by Haussmann. However, contemporaneously, in Lyon, the prefect Claude-Marius Vaisse and his city engineer Joseph Bonnet articulated these distinctions in the conception of their transformation of the city.[98] (The Paris newspapers kept close track of these developments in the country's second city.)[99] They proposed to develop the city in four zones: a spacious middle-class residential quarter expanding unimpeded across the flats east of the Rhône near the park of the Tête d'Or; a dense, gridded commercial zone transforming the old city center between the Rhône and the Saône; an untouched historic quarter around the university and the cathedral against the heights west of the Saône; and finally a workers' zone spreading over the heights of the Croix Rouge on the north, linked to the commercial center by a tramway.[100] Bonnet had explained the principle in a report to Vaisse on September 1, 1858.

Business is concentrated in a very small quarter limited at the north by the rue des Capucins, at the south by the place Bellecoeur, at the east by the Rhône, at the west by the Saône, and we are seeing before our very eyes a *ville des affaires* establish itself, if I might use a word that in France [lacks] the precise meaning which it has acquired in London. It is here that the bankers, traders, merchants, in a word all the businessmen are obliged to maintain their offices and warehouses. But habitation in the formal sense is moving to Perrache and especially Brotteaux, near the park, the great public walks, the broad quais and avenues, [so that] there where lots have not attained the high cost that they necessarily acquire in a very central location, sought by commerce, one may properly lodge one's self cheaply.
  Such is the tendency of our time. . . ."[101]

The relegation of the Lyonnais workers to their traditional slum on the slopes at Croix Rouge is a grim note, especially in the provision of a swift but narrow link in the tramway. It returns us to the differentiation operating with a less clearly articulated strategy in the Paris Halles quarter where the engineers Brame and Flachat had proposed to bring workers in from the northern suburbs by their projected subway under the boulevard de Sébastopol. "It can, to a certain extent, be used to transport people and especially workers who, as a result of the transformations affected in the quarters in the center, will be obliged to live at the extremities of the city."[102] The ultimate result of this differentiation and concentration was suggested in Henri-Jules Borie's utopian "Aérodomes" of 1865, a city center of twenty-story blocks of construction linked by terraces and bridges, towering above the remains of the old Paris spreading around.[103] In the 1880s such a place actually came into being in Chicago, with its grid of "skyscrapers" compressed within the "Chinese Wall" of railroad lines. It was a Parisian, Paul Bourget, who gave that cityscape the most telling evocation. "Its appearance, when one studies it closely, shows so little trace of individual will, there is so little caprice and fantasy in its buildings and streets, that they seem the work of some impersonal, irresistible, unthinking power, like a force of nature in the service of which man has only been the obedient tool."[104]

*   *   *

The quartier des Halles represented this new economic concentration and regularization manifested as an architectural-urbanistic artifact. To refer back to the question posed in Chapter 5, this is what Baltard had to put against the ideas of Viollet-le-Duc. This too was a very great deal, as Zola insists, at least as much as the vision of representational monumental continuity embodied in Duban or the service to the vanities of sovereign power embodied in Fontaine and Lefuel. Baltard's power was that most important one of all: control of the city's functions and texture, the legitimate sphere of the municipal service as we saw in Chapter 2.

Baltard's power was great and it produced something new but – as in the cases of Viollet-le-Duc and Duban, Fontaine and Lefuel – his manner of exercising it was distinctive. That manner is summed up in the most famous anecdote about him, that he was one way or another only someone else's instrument in designing the Halles Centrales. Unlike Viollet-le-Duc and Duban who pursued grand intellectual projects struggling to be faithful to their conceptions against resistance, Baltard would seem to have sought to do as he was told, to balance and satisfy conflicting demands, to be practical and thus "municipal" (in Pigeory's and Horace Say's sense) but also artful (if not artistic), to build a span of very different buildings each individually characteristic – markets, churches, administrative offices; restorations, new buildings, *fêtes*, decorations – yet all integrated into a tightly controlled cityscape. The architectural quintessence is the juxtaposition of the Halles Centrales and Baltard's restored church of Saint-Eustache (Figure 113).

Beginning in 1843 Baltard elaborately furnished, decorated, and restored that huge gothicizing Renaissance-baroque church with an incrementally increasing budget permitting massive renewal.[105] In 1862 he drew up a fur-

Figure 113. Church of Saint-Eustache, interior (Victor Baltard, restorer, 1843–1862, the pulpit his design).

ther project to demolish its eighteenth-century facade bays and towers and to rebuild the west end in his own version of the structure's already finicky and fantastic style.[106] In between times he projected and, in 1860–1867, erected the western group of pavilions of the Halles Centrales with the north-south *rue couverte* aligned to perfectly enframe his own reconstitution of the church's transept facade.

Florent's first encounter with the Halles Centrales in Zola's *Ventre de Paris* ends with him recognizing where he is by seeing Saint-Eustache. "He turned his head, frustrated not to know where he was, worried by this colossal and fragile vision; and when he raised his eyes, he saw the illuminated clock of Saint-Eustache. He was at the Pointe Sainte-Elizabeth."[107]

Later in the novel Zola muses on the tableau of the *rue couverte* – Baltard's Nouveau Paris putting Baltard's Vieux Paris literally in perspective.

That is a curious juxtaposition, he said [Claude, a painter, to Florent], this glimpse of a church enframed in this avenue of iron. . . . *Ceci tuera cela,* iron will kill stone, and the time approaches. . . . Mark you, it is a manifesto: it is modern art, realism, naturalism, as you like to call it, which has matured in the face of the old art. . . . The masons of the *bon dieu* are dead, wisdom will be to no longer construct these ugly carcasses of stone where no one will live. . . . Since the beginning of the century only one original building has been built, a single monument not copied somehow, which has developed naturally, from the soil of the times; and it is the Halles Centrales, mark you Florent, a work of thought, which is yet only a timid intimation of the twentieth century. . . .[108]

The striking juxtaposition of iron and stone might seem fortuitous (as Zola's characters imagine it to have been) except that Baltard repeated it as the solution for a single building in his most important construction after the Halles, the church of Saint-Augustin (1860–1868) on the boulevard Malesherbes (Figures 114 and 147) of which he had appointed himself architect. Let us save the complicated matter of its exterior form for the next chapter. What is important here is Baltard's blunt, self-conscious juxtaposition of an iron frame and a masonry envelope in the structural system gridding it on the interior and articulated with metal angels at the joints at the clerestory. This, finally, was the iron parish church Rambuteau and Say had been projecting since the 1830s.

The challenge to conventional architectural rules was unmistakable and central. The critics understood this but struggled with their evaluations.[109] The rationale was that the trapezoidal site obliged Baltard to reduce the depth of the nave chapels toward the front so they would not be able to carry to earth the thrust of a heavy main vault in stone. The objection to Baltard's consequently slipping a metal colonnade and vault frame into his thick, arcuated nave and chapel structure was that it was discontinuous and furthermore that only substantial sculpted stonework could assume sufficient visual emphasis to be aesthetically effective (Bouchet) and proper constructive primitiveness to make such a span seem an accomplishment (Sédille). Bouchet summarized his objections: "In my opinion, a character of meditation and contemplation should predominate in all parts of a church. Thus, one way to distinguish between the special character of a religious monument and that of any other building is to reserve for the former all the characteristic marks which do not appear in any building where industry plays any role."[110] Viollet-le-Duc *fils,* however, questioned the intelligence of Baltard's engineering, observing that he used masonry to stabilize a metal system which should have been made stable in itself and, in fact, really just used the skeleton to lighten an essentially lithic conception and composition. For Charles Garnier, however, it was this very division of labor between stone, used for stability, and iron, to span voids, that was the design's fundamental virtue.

Charles Garnier spoke in a remarkably (and, for Garnier, characteristi-

Figure 114. Church of Saint-Augustin, interior (Victor Baltard, architect, 1860–1868).

cally) frank necrology of Baltard read before the Institut in 1874. "M. Baltard," he states,

knew . . . how to unite all the capacities recognized necessary for our art, and what Augustus's architect [Vitruvius] demanded has been amply provided by the architect of M. Haussmann. . . . M. Baltard, in fact, is a distinguished writer, an accomplished orator, a skillful draftsman, a judicious administrator and an ingenious builder. He possesses nicety of judgment, speed of decision, knowledge of human nature, the loyalty of a soldier, and the courtesy of a *grand seigneur*. . . .[111]

In this very breadth of competence, however, Garnier observes that Baltard could have followed many careers.

If circumstances had led M. Baltard to pursue another career, . . . our excellent colleague might have been a skillful doctor or a remarkable politician; he might have become a scholar or a businessman, a poet or a merchant. . . .

In spite of all these qualities, or better because of them, M. Baltard has been condemned to not surpass in art what it is common to call a respectable medium; in fact, the very weight of his thoughts and his inclinations have become an obstacle to the production of extraordinary works. . . .

Baltard might have been included among the [greatest artists] if he had had the luck to have some defect that prevented him from being perfect. He loves what is complicated, he knows he can overcome difficulties and sometimes amuses himself to create new ones solely for the honor and pleasure of winning out."[112]

He ends with the observation that Baltard's principal work, the Halles Centrales, is, in a sense, too successful because it established a type so immediately and broadly adopted that the originality of the prototype has become obscured.

Thanks to the Halles, Baltard's name will never be forgotten; but nevertheless one might fear that, by its very excellence, this edifice might be incapable of preserving, at least for the mass of people, the memory of its builder. I shall explain myself. I have said that the Halles has already several times been copied; a few artists have only been inspired by it, but more than one architect has followed the ideas of M. Baltard almost point by point. This sort of plagarism is spreading more and more, and it suggests that this is almost inevitable because, at this moment, it is this way of conceiving a market that is really practical. But this plethora of similar structures, which threatens to increase further, is destined to overwhelm the initial monument. The creation of a single man one day soon will appear the creation of all, and when, in the future, one admires all these great constructions, one perhaps may not be able to distinguish the original building, nor recognize the name of the eminent architect who had been the creator of the original model.[113]

What Baltard represented to the architects of the Second Empire was, in the end, a threat: that of the loosening of the consistencies of art in the face of anonymous technology – of unresolved juxtapositions – empowered by the concrete needs of the municipal architecture and made plausible by the shadow of adherence to the niceties of traditional design. That may be why Baltard's nomination for the Grand Prix de l'Empereur in 1869 was so strongly resisted. His work, seen summarized in Saint-Augustin and the Halles Centrales, was neither one thing nor another.

IV

In Chapter 1 we sketched the experience of the quartier de l'Opéra as created around 1860, indicating that the shaping of a city creates blocks and spaces of many sorts as well as most varied impressions. Napoleon III's *percements* by their very existence, by their size and extended length, and by the disruption caused by their construction became powerful urban experiences. Haussmann's neatening and furnishing of the city created equally powerful ones on an intersecting plane. The spontaneous social and economic colonization of these new areas worked forcefully on a third. But, as in the quartier de l'Opéra, there was also a plane of aesthetic intention, tilted again in relation to these others – an effort to give conventional value to this transformation by shaping its results into urban tableaux. Here the work penetrated another area of established patterns and categories where Haussmann and his architects could try to make the city "say" something.

In spite of the powerful subjective impact of the Halles Centrales and of those gridded spaces extending from it that were executed, there was nothing conventionally monumental about the project. (Indeed, it was to obtain such monumentality that Baltard had originally proposed to clad the pavilions in cut stone.) Napoleon III's city plan of 1853 was fundamentally monumental in the traditional representational sense, as was his manner of presenting it to the public in 1858. In one instance that we began to sketch in Chapter 5, Haussmann had to create his own version of traditional monumentality soon after his inauguration on June 29, 1853: the erection of the entourage east and north of the New Louvre and the extension of its constituent rue de Rivoli to the Hôtel de Ville. Concomittantly he had Hittorff formalize the Champs-Elysées to the place de l'Etoile to articulate the great west axis and prepare for the Exposition Universelle of 1855, decreed on March 8, 1853.[114] We have noted that this work was to be complete by the time of the opening, May 15, 1855. (This was only achieved along the north side; the east was not completed until 1860.)

The Louvre entourage was set in two parts, by plans agreed upon August 2, 1849, and decreed on October 4, for the north, and on November 15, 1853, for the east. We saw in Chapter 5 how Duban tried to control this project and to shape and pilaster the walls of the public space confronting Perrault's Colonnade. He withdrew as architect of the Louvre in March 1854, leaving Haussmann a free hand to appoint the city architect, Hittorff (1792–1867), to extend his purview eastward from the Champs-Elysées and the place de la Concorde to the new place du Louvre (Figures 115 and 116). The result was the peculiarly underscaled composition one sees today: two blocks of houses in the modest system of the rue de Rivoli enframing the kiltered facade of Saint-Germain-l'Auxerrois and its reproduction in Hittorff's mairie of the first (once fourth) arrondissement.[115] Haussmann took much credit for himself in his memoirs. He writes that Achille Fould, the ministre d'etat et de la maison de l'empereur, proposed to demolish the church because of its misalignment and scale.

It was after this conversation that I sought, not without difficulty, an arrangement of the new square in which Saint-Germain-l'Auxerrois might play its part. I believe I found this in the erection of the *mairie* along an angling *alignement*, mirroring that of the church and in the construction of a tower facing the principal entrance of the Louvre that would link them [the *mairie* and the church] and set them off as a belfry.

To enframe this square, two blocks of houses, built up to the [zoning] limit, on one side at the corner with the quai de l'Ecole, on the other at the corner with the rue de Rivoli, on the *alignement* of the rue du Louvre, parallel to the Colonnade, would set off the graceful proportions of these [structures] which the great void had threatened to overwhelm. . . .

In order to justify this addition to Saint-Germain-l'Auxerrois, whose historic belfry was still sufficient for its religious function, I had a model carillon installed, with the advice of a commission composed of scholars and artists, presided over by M. Dumas.[116]

This precious tableau was Haussmann's first monumental (rather than practical) urbanistic solution during his tenure as prefect, and he was proud of it. But, as we saw, the story was more complex and the results not entirely applauded. It was out of character and scale with Perrault's Colonnade (Figure 88). The Conseil des Bâtiments Civils never liked the scheme and it was they, not Haussmann, who insisted on the central accent, the belfry, to draw the composition together. The prefect's relations with Hittorff, furthermore, had become so strained that the design of the belfry was given to Théodore Ballu (1817–1885) who had just distinguished himself finishing

Figure 115. Place du Louvre: east side. Belfry on axis (Théodore Ballu, architect, 1857–1862) with *mairie* of first arrondissement to the left (J.-I. Hittorff, architect, 1855–1861) and Saint-Germain-l'Auxerrois to the right.

Figure 116. Place du Louvre: east side. Belfry, *mairie*, and Saint-Germain-l'Auxerrois enframed by blocks of apartments (1856).

Sainte-Clothilde and restoring the Tour Saint-Jacques. The result was neither practical nor popular. Saint-Germain l'Auxerrois already had a belfry, attached to the south side of the *chevet*, which had a place in history for having rung the signal on Saint Bartholomew's Night (Haussmann notes this, mentioning his own Protestant origins). The new belfry was given an elaborate carillon (assembled with the advice of a committee of experts) emphasizing its purely decorative nature.

*   *   *

Haussmann's pseudomedieval carillon tower facing Louis XIV's resounding representational colonnade is such an anticlimax that one is surprised to see the prefect pointing to it at all in his *Mémoires,* much less with pride. How could the man who regularized the quartier des Halles with the firm hand we have witnessed have been satisfied with the tinkling of bells in a tree-dotted square before the manifestation of the Sun King? Yet this peculiar marriage of the economic and the sentimental was implicit in Saint-Eustache's presence in the quartier des Halles and it extends to the larger urbanistic projects initiated immediately afterward: the cutting of the boulevard du Centre and the creation of the quartier du Châtelet at its intersection with the rue de Rivoli.

Figure 117. The quartier du Châtelet seen from the Ile de la Cité, c. 1862 (the Tribunal de Commerce incomplete to the left), showing the théâtres Lyrique (right) and Cirque Impérial (left; both Gabriel Davioud, architect, 1859–1862), and the Tour Saint-Jacques (Théodore Ballu, restorer, 1853–1856).

By steps, in 1852–1858, the Châtelet area was completely razed and rebuilt in a rectangle some 275 yards north-south from the rue de Rivoli to the quai and 600 yards east-west from the Hotel de Ville to the rue Edouard Colonne (Figures 117 and 118).[117] Haussmann inherited a framework: the rue de Rivoli (the houses along which were already under construction in June 1853),[118] the line of the "boulevard de Strasbourg prolongé" already

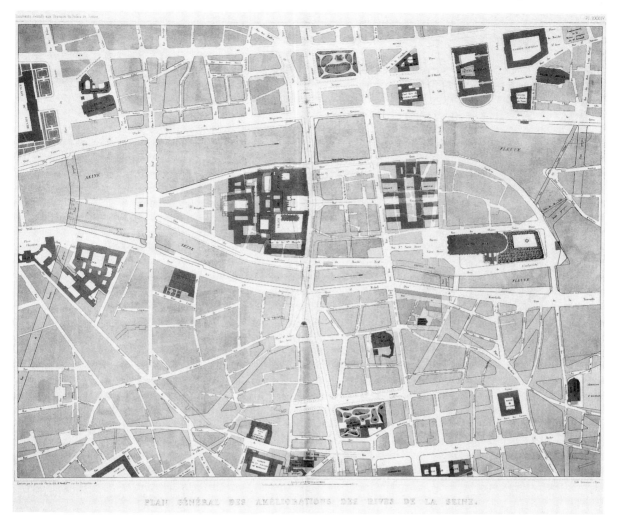

Figure 118. Plan of projected transformation of the Ile de la Cité, the quartier du Châtelet, and the Latin Quarter, 1858.

fixed by his predecessor Berger, their intersection near the Tour Saint-Jacques (ordered restored and surrounded by a fenced "square" in March 1853),[119] and the tight old place du Châtelet at the Pont au Change. Although initially just a narrow cut in the tightest hodgepodge of medieval Paris, this spot was going to be the center point in the Nouveau Paris – the crossing of the *cardo* and the *decumanus*, the Oxford Circus.[120] It cried out to be shaped and be made to speak monumentally and that Haussmann did, very peculiarly.

The Grand Prix program of 1850 had been for the conception of a grand "place publique" (Figures 119 and 120), but never had academic projections seemed so far from practical reality as in the contrast between this and Hauss-

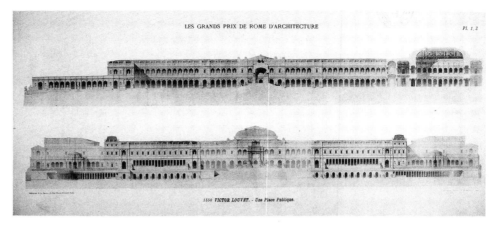

Figure 119. François-Philippe Boitte, project for a public square, competition for the Grand Prix de Rome, 1850.

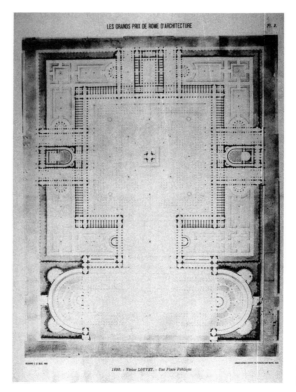

Figure 120. Boitte, project for a public square, plan.

mann's Châtelet. The plans were formulated by April 1854. By decree of June 21, the place du Châtelet was broadened from 75 to 90 meters east-west and extended 20 meters further in from the quai to a new street paralleling the rue de Rivoli.[121] By decree of July 29, 1854, this new street (really a monumental vista) was shaped into the boulevard de l'Hôtel de Ville, 30 meters wide, from the Châtelet to the center of the city hall's facade, "de façon à ce que la façade du monument puisse être aperçue de la place du Châtelet" – "so that the facade of the monument could be seen from the place du Châtelet."[122] (When Queen Victoria visited Paris in 1855 this avenue was renamed to honor her.) The enlarged Châtelet opened west of the boulevard de Sébastopol while the "square" around the Tour Saint-Jacques was defined east of the boulevard between it and the rue de Rivoli. As later at the places du Palais Royal and du Théâtre Français, these two spaces linked diagonally, checkerboard fashion, here with the Tour Saint-Jacques pinning down the vista diagonally from the quais very picturesquely (Figure 121). A new Hôtel des Postes designed in the style of the New Louvre by J.-L.-V. Grisart was to occupy the west side of the place du Châtelet (Figure 87) – until it was eliminated in the *Traité* of May 1858; the Chambre des Notaires (which would thus be displaced from its traditional home at 1, place du Châtelet) would be moved to the narrow block at the north defined between the rue Saint-Denis and the boulevard de Sébastopol where Rohault de Fleury designed a new monumental establishment (Figure 121, far left).

There was one final step in the shaping of this space, one Haussmann again takes considerable credit for in his *Mémoires* (and about which contemporaries again were quite dubious): the definition of two further monumental vistas after the *Traité* of May 1858, by the relocation of the Napoleonic Fontaine de la Victoire to the revised axis of the Pont au Change extending that of the boulevard du Palais, setting it silhouetted against Rohault de Fleury's facade, and the erection of the Tribunal de Commerce by Antoine-Nicolas Bailly (1810–1892) in 1858–1865 with its

Figure 121. Tour Saint-Jacques (Théodore Ballu, restorer, 1853–1856).

strange off-center dome intended by Haussmann to pin down the vista along the boulevard de Sébastopol (Figure 122).[123] We read in Félix Narjoux's *Monuments élevés par la Ville* (1881–1883),

The element of the palace that most attracts attention is the dome . . . perhaps useless to the monument in itself [but] it serves for the adornment of the ensemble and as a terminal point of the axis of the boulevard de Sébastopol. . . . The Tribunal de Commerce provides from afar a decorative accent which defines itself among the group of new streets linking the quarter of the Right Bank of the Seine to those of the Left. It is not overwhelmed by the immense constructions of the Palais de Justice, to which it is so close, and whose vicinity is so intimidating.[124]

Haussmann concurred:

I have never fixed the lines of any street without keeping in mind the terminal feature [*point de vue*] one might give it, especially in the case of one of the principal arteries of Paris. Thus, the examination of the plan of Paris showed me that M. Berger might have changed the axis of the boulevard de Sébastopol very slightly, a change that would have resulted in a swerve of several meters at its end at the place du Châtelet. By this one could have had the dome of the Sorbonne as terminal. Obliged to renounce that, I particularly recommended to M. Bailly that he arrange a dominant motif in his project for the commercial palais de justice distinguishing itself forcefully from its mass, which would establish it when seen from the Gare de l'Est down the axis of the boulevard de Sébastopol.[125]

Two theaters, designed by Gabriel Davioud (1823–1881), were simulta-

Figure 122. Tribunal de Commerce seen from the place du Châtelet (Edmond Bailly, architect, 1857–1865).

neously placed on the east and west sides of the place du Châtelet as part of Haussmann's relocation of public entertainments after the *Traité* of 1858 (Figure 117). Haussmann insisted that thin blocks of rental apartments sandwich the two theaters and that commercial space occupy the street floor of the Tribunal de Commerce along the boulevard du Palais.[126] The facades and cornice lines of all three were simply pushed up to the *alignements* set for the avenue Victoria and the boulevard de Sébastopol by decrees of July 29 and September 29, 1854. The only monumental spatial distinction made in the facades around the *place* was the inset arcades permitting more ample access to Davioud's two theaters.

The architects Davioud and Bailly seem to have struggled for solutions to this new Haussmannian urban situation. The shapes they were given were indecisive (or, in the case of the Tribunal dome, inappropriate); the masses inarticulate and pressed hard up against the street lines; the decoration desired was finicky. Duc, working out his design for the facing corner of the Palais de Justice around 1850, chose to continue the severe gothic style of the old buildings of the Châtelet in his rebuilding of the Tour de l'Horloge and the Conciergerie (Figure 123) but this solution was specifically denied Bailly and Davioud by the prefect.[127] Bailly's design seems the most successful of these three and is the most central, located at the bottom of the boulevard perspective. The architect's necrologist tells a peculiar story about it.[128] During the Italian campaign in 1859 Napoleon III had been deeply struck by a piece of Renaissance architecture he had encountered. He expressed to

Figure 123. Palais de Justice, Conciergerie (Louis Duc, restorer, 1853–1857) flanking the boulevard du Palais across from the Tribunal de Commerce.

Haussmann his desire to see it reproduced in the Tribunal de Commerce, but could not remember what it was. Haussmann laid the matter before Bailly and the latter requested an audience with the emperor, bringing reproductions of possibilities. Reviewing these, they came upon the city hall of Brescia, and Napoleon III recognized his model – an elegant late Quattrocento one with grotesque pilasters and a quasi dome – bidding Bailly reproduce it as best he could. The result did not please the Conseil des Bâtiments Civils, as we have seen, although it arrived before them with a letter from Haussmann explaining the special circumstances.[129] They recommended the elimination of the commercial space and the rearrangement of the plan and the dome as well as the toning down of the decoration. (This was not done.)

Bailly was well connected and self-confident. He had been an *inspecteur* at the Hôtel de Ville and then Visconti's assistant on the Fontaine Molière. He had a large and prestigious private practice.[130] At this point he had just rearranged the Crédit Foncier's *hôtel* on the place Vendôme and built the Jockey Club's hippodrome at Longchamps. He would seem to have known how to oblige Haussmann and the emperor. His Tribunal came out an elegant bit of urban furniture, strikingly distinct from Duc's Palais de Justice across the boulevard du Palais. The more careful, principled Davioud did not carry off the Châtelet theaters with such style. The integration of apartment blocks and the subordination of his two structures to the domed Tribunal de Commerce did not permit him to develop his compositions in mass. He tried to abstract Renaissance details into a flat, rationalist wall treatment, but the results were indecisive and confusing to contemporaries.[131]

✳   ✳   ✳

This, then, when it was completed around 1862, was Haussmann's new center for Paris. We see it clearly in Figure 117, a photograph of about that year with the blocks of houses around the avenue Victoria complete but still unoccupied and shuttered. This view shows the new height and density of Haussmann's "architecture règlementaire" contrasting to the lower, heterogeneous housing around (today destroyed and replaced by blocks filling the Second Empire envelope). As in the projected quartier des Halles and in the later quartier de l'Opéra a new proportion of street to *îlot* appears, varying between 1:3 and 1:2. As later department stores were drawn to the new quarter so here "Au Tour Saint-Jacques" already occupies the block between the boulevard de Sébastopol and the rue Saint-Martin north of the square (Figures 64 and 65).[132] Comparing the photograph to the plan, we see that Haussmann was clever in dotting incidents around his new spaces – the axial tableaux of the Hôtel de Ville, the Tribunal de Commerce, and the Fontaine de la Victoire enframed by the Chambre des Notaires – but also that all are very carelessly executed. Comparing the enframement of the Hôtel de Ville by the otherwise useless avenue Victoria to careful tableaux of the decades before like the place du Palais Bourbon or Duban's Ecole des Beaux-Arts courtyards or even Visconti's Louvre axes, we see that Haussmann's shapes and dimensions are not effective in producing a specific effect. The Tribunal de Commerce is too far away across the Seine to close the south side of the place du Châtelet (and its asymmetrical dome confuses as much as composes); the Fontaine de la Victoire is weak and Rohault de Fleury's facade weaker. The most memorable passage in the series of pictures is the diagonal vista of the Tour Saint-Jacques, and it is this to the exclusion of the more "classic" and self-conscious tableaux that is familiar in photographs and graphic reproductions (Figure 121). When the restoration work was begun in 1853 the *Moniteur universel* published a lengthy article exploring what uses it might serve.[133] The author proposes four fountain basins at the base ornamented with four statues of eminent residents of the old parish of Saint-Jacques-la-Boucherie and at the top a public clock with four faces and a carillon, giving the tower a nonreligious function appropriate to its new state. "One will thus follow the very picturesque manner adopted some time ago already for the ornamentation of plazas and street intersections."[134]

The dominance of the Tour Saint-Jacques, picturesquely sited, sets a note that conflicts with Haussmann's proclaimed search for monumental vistas but that harmonizes with a perhaps less conscious aspect of his project: the unimportance of the actual institutions assembled here at the heart of the Nouveau Paris as well as the muteness of their symbolic keying. The institutions are four of indeterminant public or private status and two minor historical curiosities – the fountain and the tower. The notaries were a private body with public authority to legalize transactions and to hold money;[135] the Tribunal de Commerce was a municipal court with authority over matters of commerce (especially bankruptcy) and was self-governing. It formerly occupied the anonymous upper floor of the Bourse. Theaters were a regulated private enterprise functioning in buildings erected by the state. That is to say, the structures defining the Châtelet were monuments to money, pleasure, and historical curiosity. Tourists knew the Châtelet for another reason: It was through an obscure public stairway descending into the ground in a corner that on two days a month expeditions departed for a guided tour of the new sewer system. This is very different from the traditional city square conjoining the church, the law courts, and the city hall or prefecture. (In Paris all of these retained their historic positions and were a short walk from the Châtelet and, in the case of the Hôtel de Ville, visible from it.) Nor was there anything powerfully symbolic or timely in the decoration, inscriptions, or nomenclature in the quarter, except perhaps the name Victoria commemorating the visit of that foreign and sometimes hostile sovereign. Napoleon III appeared nowhere.

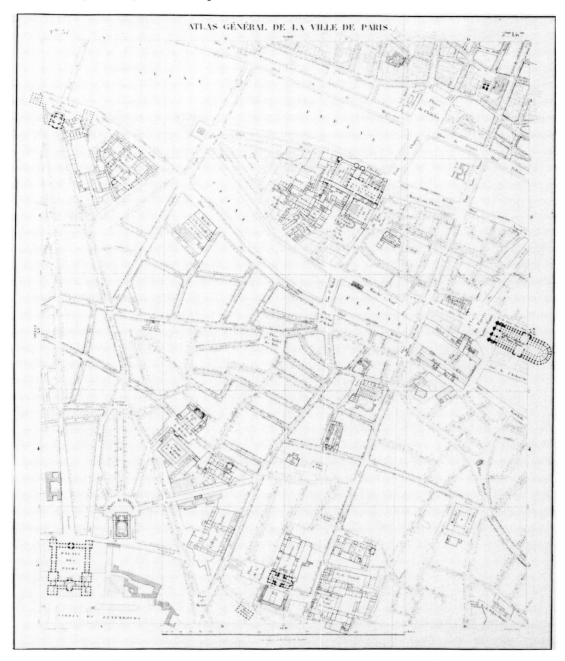

Figure 124. Map of the Ile de la Cité and the Latin Quarter, c. 1840. Jacoubet, *Atlas général de la Ville de Paris.*

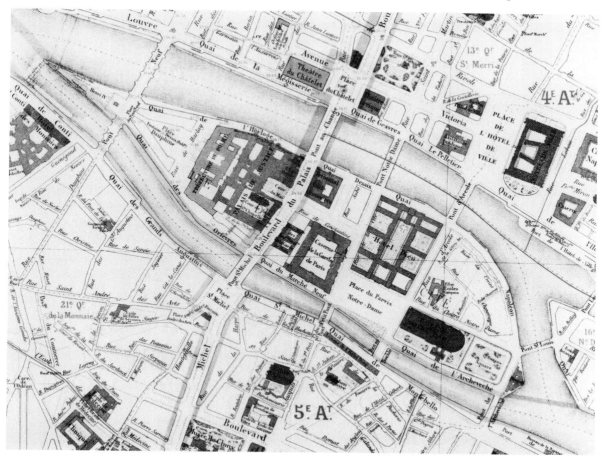

Figure 125. Map of the central portion of the boulevards de Sébastopol, du Palais, and Saint-Michel, 1868. "Plan Deschamps."

* * *

In the case of the boulevard du Centre – eventually divided into the boulevards de Strasbourg, Sébastopol, du Palais, and Saint-Michel – this strange inexpressiveness of Haussmann's urbanism is clearer while the picturesque asserts itself even more. Although projected with the construction of the boulevard de Strasbourg in 1852, the Right Bank section was laid out in detail by decree of September 29, 1854, the Left Bank section by that of August 11, 1855, and the linking stretch on the Ile de la Cité by decree of September 23, 1858.[136] All these decrees set the width and placement of cross streets so that they fixed the framework of the whole urban transformation (although the rue de Turbigo was omitted until the *Traité* of 1858). We see the plan for much of its length in the publication of the Palais de Justice documents of 1858, where vistas and axes are helpfully marked with red lines (Figure 118). What is interesting is that the boulevard's length is

243

paced with a regular succession of incidents, here imposed as they did not have to be along the rue de Rivoli extending the west axis (Figures 124 and 125). Proceeding from north to south one finds the square de la Conservatoire des Arts et Métiers opening the tableau of Vaudoyer's carefully composed institution with Cusin's Théâtre de la Gaité embedded in its south side (Figure 126);[137] Saint-Leu, composed and rebuilt by Baltard (1857–1860, Figures 145 and 146); the Châtelet; the Cour de Mai of the Palais de Justice opening westward at a kink in the axis (two more theaters were to have been embedded in the facades facing it);[138] the place Saint-Michel with Davioud's monumental fountain marking a crook in the axis and the beginning of the rue Danton (Figure 102); the square to be opened around the Hôtel de Cluny at the intersection with the incipient boulevard Saint-Germain (Figure 127); and that opening at the brow of the Montagne Sainte-Geneviève west into the extended Luxembourg Gardens and east now the widened (decreed July 30, 1859) rue Soufflot enframing Soufflot's mighty Panthéon. The south end then terminates in Perrault's Observatory.

A great deal of planning, money, and design went into the conception of this busy and eventuated thoroughfare. But what sort of urban experience results? The content of all the tableaux along it is heterogeneously historical, saying nothing about the Second Empire (in contrast to the west axis): gothic fragments like the Hôtel de Cluny, the Tour Saint-Jacques, Saint-Leu; classical ones like the Panthéon, the Cour de Mai, the Luxembourg, and the Hôtel de Ville; heterogeneous composites like the Conservatoire des Arts et Métiers; theaters. The chief exceptions – the Tribunal de Commerce and the Fontaine Saint-Michel – are equally indecisively keyed.

We have noted the dramatic unveiling of the boulevard de Sébastopol in 1858 and of the Fontaine Saint-Michel in 1860. The city put special effort into the shaping of the place Saint-Michel with its uniform facades squared up to enframe the isolated *îlot* on axis with its great architectural signboard around the fountain itself. Hostile critics squeezed embarrassing meanings from it, refusing to accept that such a prominent monument could be so mute, but the story of its iconography seems to be that of a crisis in making an architectural declaration.[139] The first design by Davioud of November 21, 1856, centered on a statue of France and bore the inscription, "Fontaine de la Paix." (The Crimean War had ended by a treaty signed in Paris on March 30 of that year.) F. Camus later explained the design and symbolism as it then stood in the *Journal des débats*:

At the back of a broad niche embracing the center of the edifice will stand a colossal statue of France surrounded by Peace and War depicted as geniuses. To the right and left of this group, which will be in bronze, will be set up four columns of red marble with capitals also in bronze, surmounted by statues in white marble representing Force, Wisdom, etc., the whole [construction] covered by a roof in slate of

Figure 126. Théâtre de la Gaité on the place de la Conservatoire des Arts et Métiers (Alphonse-Adolphe Cusin, architect, 1860–1862).

Figure 127. Garden of the Hôtel de Cluny at the intersection of the boulevards Saint-Michel and Saint-Germain.

the Renaissance style. Below, water, flowing from masks into vases, will proceed to collect in basins ornamented with bronze figures personifying commerce, the arts, agriculture, and industry. Finally the pediment will be ornamented with a plaque of marble upon which an inscription will set itself off in letters of gold:

IN THE REIGN OF NAPOLEON III

THE CITY OF PARIS ERECTED THIS MEMORIAL

TO PERPETUATE THE MEMORY

OF THE GLORIOUS PEACE

SIGNED BY PLENIPOTENTIARIES

AT THE CONGRESS OF PARIS

MARCH 30, 1856.[140]

The bronze was to be that of captured Russian canons – a parallel, Camus notes, with Napoleon I's Colonne de la Grande Armée. The name would be either "Fontaine de la Paix" or "Fontaine Sébastopol."

By the time the Fontaine Saint-Michel had been completed in 1860 another war had been fought – with Austria in Italy – and the administration chose to erase immediate political meaning, elaborating instead the innocuous theme of the old place Saint-Michel on this site. We read a puzzled explanation in the *Moniteur universel:* "Certain circumstances . . . have produced a change in the program of the edifice and significantly modified the character of its original ornamentation."[141] Critics asserted that the real import of the traditional subject depicted in the fountain, St. Michael killing the dragon, was a veiled reference to Napoleon III's imposition of public order.[142]

Just as the place Saint-Michel says very little symbolically, so it is – in spite of much effort and expense spent to gain uniformity and symmetry – indecisive monumentally. As Adolphe Lance noted in the *Encyclopédie d'architecture,* the need for traffic to flow smoothly up the broad streets intersecting here forced the three *îlots* composing the tableau to be set too far apart to create an effective composition. When Charles Fichot drew it just after the unveiling in November 1860, he widened the streets and compressed the *îlots* even further, transforming it from a composition of masses to one of spaces and perspectives (Figure 128). He saw that this urbanism was about space dominating architecture, destroying conventional methods of composition and symbolization.

The story of the symbolic silencing of the Fontaine Saint-Michel is part of a longer history of Second Empire representational hesitation. We have noted the magnificent triumphal arch Haussmann proposed at the place du

Figure 128. Fontaine Saint-Michel as drawn by Charles Fichot, dated October 25, 1860.

Trône to commemorate the North Italian war – sketched in wood and canvas in 1862 but never executed. Immediately after the Crimean armistice in July 1856, the Senate similarly had proposed a bronze column (again fabricated from captured Russian canons) atop the Montagne Sainte-Geneviève where the new boulevard de Sébastopol (Left Bank) would cross the axis of the rue Soufflot leading to the Panthéon.[143] The north face of the base would represent the Crimean army triumphantly returning to Paris, the east face the army driving Garibaldi from Rome, the south face the Army of Algeria. At the top would be Napoleon III, like his uncle on the Colonne de la Grande Armée, visible across the city. "From a distance the arriving traveler," wrote the Senate committee, "will see at the same moment two monuments that recall the grandeur and the glory of two generations and of two Empires."[144] Again, it was two years before that Hittorff had drawn a project for the place de l'Etoile defining the Arc de Triomphe with a circling plane of smooth walls and a composition of statues of Napoleon I's marshalls filling the space to make more specifically Bonapartist the signification of the Arch. This, like the column on the Montagne Sainte-Geneviève and the triumphal arch at the place du Trône, was set aside. As at the Fontaine Saint-Michel, Hittorff finally executed a ring of mansions around the Etoile transforming it into a bourgeois promenade. One after another great symbolic gestures in the style of Louis XIV and Napoleon I failed to be executed. What there is of Napoleon III in the heart of the city, at the Châtelet, is his sentimental reminiscences of Brescia embodied in the Tribunal de Commerce and the feminine elegance of the courtyard at the Hôtel de Ville (Figures 52 and 53).

V

The boulevard du Centre and the abortive forum at the Châtelet were the watershed. The implications of Haussmann's transformation of the quartier des Halles and his shaping of the place du Louvre combined and elaborated themselves into a concrete piece of the Nouveau Paris that then spread across the city after the *Traité* of 1858 – as well as across Europe and the world during the last quarter of the century.

The *Traité* created a further series of spaces for Haussmann to shape. Most of these are less extraordinary than what we have already examined, being now variations – and exaggerations – of established themes. Haussmann himself has little to say about these later projects in his *Mémoires:* They seem not to have involved the struggle – both conceptual and political – that the first projects did.

The *Traité* of May 1858 designated two great *places* to be cut out of the concentrated texture of the city along the boulevards, the place de l'Opéra and the place du Prince Eugène, as well as the creation or elaboration of several on the edge of the suburbs, the places d'Alma, du Trône, d'Italie, and that at Saint-Médard. The *places* on the boulevards were built up in tight, tall *îlots* with uniform facades marked by the giant order introduced by Hittorff at the Etoile (Figures 1, 129–131). They were dominated by symmetrical institutions – the aristocratic Opéra on the boulevard des Capucines; the projected popular Orphaeum on the old "boulevard du

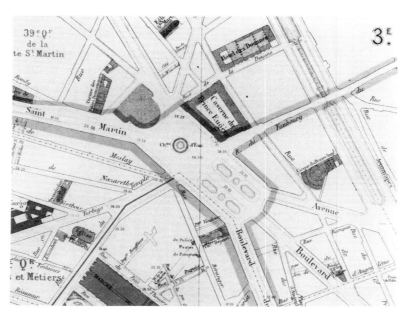

Figure 129. Plan of the place du Prince Eugène (now place de la République), "plan Deschamps," 1868.

Figure 130. Place du Prince Eugène (now place de la République), north side, Caserne du Château d'Eau to left (Legrom, architect, 1857–1860), Magasins Réunis to right (Gabriel Davioud, architect, 1865–1870).

Figure 131. Place du Prince Eugène (now place de la République), south side at exit of the rue de Turbigo.

Crime." These were to be in contrasting gorgeous and severe style responding to their social context, like Ballu's contemporaneous parish churches of La Trinité, splendid in the "West End," and Saint-Joseph, severely Romanesque for its location in the workers' east.[145] The Opéra and the projected Orphaeum drew to themselves appropriate commercial establishments, the Grand Hôtel de la Paix and the Printemps in the west, the Magasins Réunis in the east. In addition, a barracks loomed over the northeast side of the place du Prince Eugène.

Neither *place,* however, was so subtly shaped or proportioned, the Opéra squeezing itself into its entourage; the place du Prince Eugène unhappily large and spreading, as if for troop maneuvers in front of the barracks. The decorative keying of both followed from the great failure of nerve at the Fontaine Saint-Michel. Napoleon III is absent from the ornamentation of either the Orphaeum or the Opéra, although there is an imperial pavilion at the latter with eagles and laurel-brandishing caryatids. The center of the place de l'Opéra was a void; that at the place du Prince Eugène had a fountain reminiscent of one once located nearby, the Château d'Eau.[146] The symbolic subject of Napoleon III's transformation of Paris was merely Paris itself, its history, and its institutions – or rather, a highly reconstituted version of it.

A number of secondary spaces shaped during the 1860s perhaps were more successful. The place d'Estienne-d'Orves and La Trinité, laid out in 1860 at the head of the rue de la Chaussée d'Antin, took the classic problem of the square before the church and rendered it in tall defining blocks bearing Haussmann's giant order, centering on a fenced *jardin anglais* and a richly picturesque parish church (Figure 132).[147] It is a urban, sophisticated reworking of the parish squares earlier laid out in front of Sainte-Clothilde, Saint-Vincent-de-Paul, and Saint-Lambert (as well as Haussmann's later work at Saint-Joseph and Saint-Bernard), more elaborate in its form and more humane in the provision of a neighborhood garden, but again lacking stern monumental coordination. At this same time (1860) the place du Théâtre Français got its final form, with Henri Blondel's north and west frontages overspread by the Haussmannian giant order, and Davioud's elegant paired fountains, topped by Carrier-Belleuse's nymphs (Figure 80).[148]

*   *   *

There was one last great "passage" in the central thick texture of Haussmann's Nouveau Paris, the quarter of the Gare du Nord (Figures 133–135).[149] This is a somewhat complex case since although the architect, Hittorff, was prominent in the municipal service and the project was part of the reshaping of this quarter of the city under Haussmann's close scrutiny, the institution itself was a private company (albeit one operating under cen-

Figure 132. Church of La Trinité with flanking apartment facades and place Estienne-d'Orves (Théodore Ballu, architect, 1860–1867).

tral government supervision). Railroad travel has lost all its wonder since World War II: The modern visitor hurries away from this encumbered and chaotic old station as quickly as possible. (At least before the arrival of the TGV.) But in the mid-nineteenth century this was the Rothschilds' railroad to Belgium and England, the busiest and most profitable of all.[150] In 1858–1862, when it was totally rebuilt by the railroad's engineers after Hittorff's designs, it was the great station of Paris – about which Frances Willard in 1869 would exclaim in her diary, "hardly an opera house in America is so gracefully adorned"[151] – and the center of a whole rebuilt quarter of new *percements* and *îlots*, much of which (Karen Bowie has found) was owned by Rothschild.[152]

Haussmann cared enough about this development to include an anecdote in his *Mémoires*. Interestingly, it is that (as at the Halles Centrales) the street plan of the quarter was laid out by the city to match that of the building itself, so the *arrivées* would have gone straight down the rue de Saint-Quentin and the *départs* straight up the rue de Compiègne, but that Hittorff changed his plan unilaterally and spoiled the scheme.[153] (Karen Bowie has documented that Haussmann here again exaggerates.)

The quarter otherwise consisted of the extended rue Lafayette and the boulevard du Nord crossing at right angles in front of the main axis of the

Figure 133. Gare du Nord (J.-I. Hittorff, architect, 1858–1862) seen up the avenue de Denain.

Figure 134. Gare du Nord and place de Roubaix (now place Napoléon III). Seen from the east.

Figure 135. Facades on the south side of the place de Roubaix (now place Napoléon III).

station so they could extend beyond it at the corners. The triangle of ground thus left between the streets and the facade was divided into four *îlots* by the streets serving the *arrivées* and the *départs* plus the 30-meter avenue de Denain on the axis (Figure 133). There was orignally to be a broad, circular *place* at the crossing, appropriate to the majesty of the situation, but this was restricted and squared in execution. Hittorff's station facade itelf was left as the event of the composition, looming behind the grid of streets cutting toward it from the *place*, marked by the Haussmannian order in its most splendid and impressive manifestation, a file of huge deeply relieved pilasters coupled in pylons staked around an iron and glass shed. The details are big and abrupt – very different from the subtly inflected "Neo-Grec" or Renaissance surfaces of contemporary Paris construction – scaled to read from a distance, urbanistically. Here, finally, was something like an answer to Louis XIV's colonnade of the Louvre. Here masses and spaces work reciprocally as they failed to do in the Châtelet.

Knowing that this is the Rothschild railroad opening to industrial Belgium and Britain and knowing that Hittorff knew and admired British industrial architecture from visits in 1820 and 1855, one might recognize that he has started from the "Euston Arch" erected in 1835–1839. But for all the grandeur of that primordial model, twenty-five years have passed since Phillip Hardwick's conception and the railroad station has been transformed from an open yard for which a free-standing monumental portal would be appropriate to a spreading enclosed space of iron and glass. In response, Hittorff has fragmented the propylaeum model into a line of pilastered pylons that scale up the light industrial artifact without concealing it – a more forceful execution of Baltard's *parti* in Saint-Augustin (Figure 114).

This screen of pylons works urbanistically, as an organizing grid mediating between the *immeubles* of the new quarter facing the station. The lateral sections maintain in their horizontal cornice the line of the bottom of the mansards of the facing houses (Figures 134 and 135). In the giant ionic pilasters of these pylons one has the ultimate Haussmannian order: single shafts embracing the whole facade plane permitted by law from sidewalk to roof angle. One can finally see just how big the scale of the *immeuble haussmannien* really is.

An axial approach route has been provided from the intersection of the rue Lafayette and the boulevard du Nord. From that spot, suddenly visible to carriage passengers as they turn up to the station, only the central bay of the structure appears (Figure 133), breaking with the neighborhood scale to become monumental and to assume the form of a ceremonial arch delimited by pilasters and peopled with caryatids and statues (representing the cities served by the line).[154] It is the "Euston Arch" dematerialized and the arch itself expanded to overwhelm the rectilinear restraint of the orders so as to yawn around a great glass window and the railroad clock.

Mounting to the station the avenue de Denain first splays to reveal the whole expanse of the center of the facade under the raking cornice, then opens fully to the square in front – almost, but maintaining a dynamic splay so the space is nearly pinched shut at the two ends (Figure 134). This is a compressed and dynamic space (compare it to those of the Châtelet) and approximates in big angular planes what Duban had demonstrated more subtly in the Ecole courtyards (Figure 2).

If this analysis is correct, there is one passage in the facade composition that must be read as a gap, the two areas between the central arch and the lateral wings. It is here that the station's scale switches from local – maintaining that of the surrounding *immeubles* – to monumental and axial. These gaps are the key to the multiple, interwoven readings of Hittorff's composition: It is a coordination of fragments across the continuous planes that now constitute the building blocks of Haussmann's city texture which manage to break out of that deadening constraint by allusions and illusions.

Hittorff's long and extraordinary career finally comes to an end with this design, and his last writings explore the problems he seems to broach here. In a "Mémoire sur les ruines d'Agrigente" read before the Académie des Beaux-Arts August 13, 1859 (just as the design of the Gare du Nord was beginning), he presented the combining of architectural elements from different systems as a fundamental principle (for example in the "Tomb of Theron" with its aedicular facades and pyramidal roof) understood in the Renaissance and wrongly rejected by neoclassicist purists.[155] In 1862 (with the Gare du Nord just completed) Hittorff published his "Mémoire sur Pompéii et Pétra" in which he explores the idea that the fragmentation of architectural ensembles in Pompeiian paintings was paralleled by a similar decomposition in Roman monumental facades.[156] His central example is the rock-cut tomb at Petra, the "Karzr Faraoum," which he interprets as a flattening and intermingling of the elements of actual funerary temples consisting of a colonnaded front, a courtyard surrounding a monopteros, and a temple-fronted sanctuary beyond. This is fundamental to classical architecture, Hittorff concludes, and reappears in the Renaissance when Bramante proposed to place the dome of the Panthéon on the vaults of the Basilica of Constantine to produce his design for Saint Peter's. The Romans and the Renaissance shared a single vision, "celle d'élever un édifice sur un autre, et de former les deux édifices ainsi réunis une seule construction d'une heureuse unité" – "That of elevating one monument on top of another and to make of the two edifices thus combined a single construction of satisfying unity." In a sense the Gare du Nord facade is a reassembling of the "Karzr Faraoum" cut into the rock-cut cliffs of Haussmann's Paris.

The Gare du Nord facade is the great colonnade with which Haussmann and Hittorff failed to confront Perrault's Colonnade in the place du Louvre or, to overlay a tangential comparison, a critique of Duc's Palais de Justice facade, which does take up that challenge, because instead of expressing all the nuances of integral stone building in a manner that would even delight Viollet-le-Duc, Hittorff achieves purity through the reduction of traditional stone architecture to a thin veil over the angular iron and glass organism inside.[157] Hittorff is true to the ethos of the Travaux de Paris as it was established in Baltard's work, accepting new technical creations and making them architecture by juxtaposition – always unlikely to some degree – with traditional forms. In his writing Hittorff struggles to raise this dissolution of the unity of traditional building to a theory.

CHURCHES AND HISTORIC MONUMENTS

In the introduction we suggested that whereas the municipal service was expanding, elastic, and aggressive – especially under Haussmann – the Edifices Diocésains was weaker and without strong leadership. This was developed a bit further in Chapter 2. Religious architecture would seem to have failed to organize itself around an idea of Christianity in building and thus became a void into which at least two tangential interests expanded. Many churches and most cathedrals were structures older than Louis XIV, often medieval – and as a group encompassing the whole history of French architecture. When consciousness of history emerged and manifested itself administratively in the Commission des Monuments Historiques, churches became the logical field of appropriation – especially since political monuments were largely denied it. Furthermore, but in contrast, parish churches had always been the central ecclesiastical authority's least concern, so that with the explosive growth of cities during the nineteenth century the municipal architects, especially in Paris, appropriated this ground, redefining the parish church, now not as documents of the history of culture but instead as events in a tightly controlled cityscape.

I

For all of their expansion in numbers and importance during the nineteenth century, we saw in Chapter 4 that institutional buildings found a traditional place in the monumental urban order established around palatial complexes. But there was another new element in nineteenth-century Paris, the historic monument. What was its place in the monumental order?[1]

This was a new question to the designers and administrators around 1800 because until then the whole city was a static monument, massive, unassailable, and inevitably reproducing itself in a relatively stable order. There was no clear distinction between "now" and "then."

This is also a question to which we do not have the most direct bureaucratic answer because the administration of the city of Paris did not explicitly recognize this category of building until 1860, with the creation of the municipal bureau of Travaux Historiques, expanded in 1865 to embrace the Commission des Travaux Historiques, the *Histoire Générale de Paris*, and the Musée Carnavalet.[2] Before that the designation and advocacy of the preservation of "monuments historiques" was left to private citizens, led by the Abbé Grégoire from 1794 and Arcisse de Caumont a generation later, then the responsibility of the Ministry of the Interior after the creation of the Inspection Générale de Monuments Historiques in 1831 and subsequently of the Commission des Monuments Historiques in 1837.[3] This administration formulated policy and funded model projects, but necessarily from a national perspective, that of a network of especially significant individual monuments. Complexes of monuments in urban centers were not its concern; there the bureaus of Voirie and the administration connected to it was in authority and historic monuments did not yet have a place.[4]

The lack of a place to start with within the administration of the city of Paris, suggests (at least at the outset) that we might turn to that extraordinary architect-functionary in the service des Monuments Historiques of lucid conceptions, Eugène-Emmanuel Viollet-le-Duc. His *Dictionnaire raisonné* (1856–1868) was intended to make relevant matters clear and in the celebrated entry "restauration" (1866) seems to do so.[5] "Le mot et la chose sont modernes" – "the word and the thing are modern," he starts. He depicts restoration of historic monuments as an unusual activity unique to the nineteenth century, paralleling the biological explorations of Cuvier and those of philologists, ethnologists, and archeologists who came after him.

Our time, and only our time, since the first centuries of history, has taken an unparalleled attitude in regard to the past. It has chosen to analyze it, to compare it, to divide it and formulate its real [*véritable*] history, following, step by step, the evolution, the progress, the transformation of humanity. . . . Were our epoch to have nothing else to transmit to the future centuries but this new method of studying the facts of the past, whether of the material order or whether of the moral, it would be worthy of respect.[6]

Significantly, as his citation of Cuvier implies, Viollet-le-Duc's understanding of an historic monument was in terms of its physical structure. The monument's statics – its fundamental physical fact – was the ultimate truth to be discovered and to be displayed in restoration. "Each building and each building part should be restored in the style inherent to it, not only in appearance, but also in structure."[7] Just what this implies Viollet-le-Duc delineates with subtlety and eloquence. The restorer must know all the constructive strategies of the past and be able to grasp the particular nature of any specific monument thoroughly, intuitively – even what Viollet-le-Duc calls its "tempérament." "If the architect charged with the reconstruction of an edifice should know the form, the styles inherent in the building and to the school from which it emanates, he must even more, if it is possible, know its structure, it anatomy, its temperament, because above all he must make it live [*fasse vivre*]."[8] Restoration is a dangerous structural operation that might literally physically destroy a monument if it collapses; the architect must know his monument so thoroughly that he can respond immediately to subsidences, or structural weakening, and give confidence to his workmen (p. 28). Above and beyond all a properly restored building is a structurally strengthened one. "In restoration there is one dominant condition that must always be kept in mind. This is to substitute for parts removed only superior materials and stronger and better construction. The restored edifice must pass into the future, as a result of the operation to which it has been submitted, with a longer lease on life than it has had already."[9] He notes that such attention might reawaken knowledge and appreciation of good construction in the profession generally and thus counter the decline of technique, which he blames on centralization and on the Conseil des Bâtiments Civils (p. 27). His ultimate objective is to prepare conceptually for a synthetic architecture of the future. "Our time is not content simply to cast an analytical glance behind: This retrospective work can only develop the problems occurring in the future and facilitate their solution. This is the synthesis that follows the analysis."[10] However, to follow Viollet-le-Duc's thought beyond the *Dictionnaire raisonné*, that synthetic style has yet to appear so the nineteenth century has no right to leave a trace on any monument beyond its scientifically neutral reconstitution.

If the nineteenth century had a style of architecture particular to it, perhaps one might suggest that it would be good to identify an intervention every time the occasion is presented to finish an old monument. But I doubt . . . that we have arrived at this style. Our epoch, on the contrary, possesses one quality that is peculiar to it. . . . It grasps, by the attentive study of the past . . . how to seize the spirit, the origin of its forms in the conditions controlling the artists of these ancient times. . . . Thus in order to be of our time we must conserve buildings in their original form.[11]

❊   ❊   ❊

A good deal has been written about the entry "restauration."[12] Here we only examine one relevant implication – how a monument seen thus might function in the city texture – and make a contrast with how other agencies of the administration responsible for what came to be defined as "historic monuments" saw them.

In a sense it is highly anticlimactic that Viollet-le-Duc should present restoration as recreating structural integrity, since physical maintenance was the most indisputable objective of the Commission des Monuments Historiques. What is extraordinary is that he restricts the agency's responsibilities to this and that, elsewhere in his writings, he makes it clear that this presentation of structural artifacts is an important contribution to the reconstruction of the history of culture. In his entry "construction" in the *Dictionnaire raisonné* and especially in his late didactic volumes *Histoire d'une cathédrale et d'un hôtel de ville* (1878) and *Histoire d'un dessinateur: comment on apprend dessiner* (1879), he constructs a detailed social history from the way communities build. In the case of the imaginary cathedral of Cucy depicted in the earlier volume, the building was erected by the citizens of the commune and at first was a broad barnlike structure (like Bourges or Notre-Dame at the beginnings of their histories) serving as a covered market as well as a place of religious ceremony. Only later in a repressive period was the space filled with chapels and shrines and used exclusively for the cult.

A building transformed into a model of engineering (and thus implicitly a political document) assumes a new and peculiar place in an urban texture. It is a separate entity, freed from the evolving, changing life of the city flesh. It is to be seen and examined more than used. Viollet-le-Duc did not propose to convert churches back into part-time market buildings as in the time of the municipal republics. Instead he set them aside from the city texture, as demonstrations of an analysis – in a sense seditious tumors in the city flesh that might inspire impatience with the old to permit the birth of the new.

Political monuments in active function – like the Chambre des Députés, the New Louvre of Naploeon III, and the Hôtel de Ville as transformed by Rambuteau and again by Berger and Haussmann – were designed to present themselves along a processional axis, the axis of movement of the eyes and feet of the political chief. We saw in Chapter 3 that these were highly controlled architectural declarations. Their meaning was patent, and much of their power lay in the very fact that the *pouvoir* could speak architecturally with such lack of qualification.

The restorer's objective is not to prepare his building to receive the sovereign or the people through its door, but rather to lead the attentive observer around it and to reveal intellectually telling viewpoints. The building is a sample of abstract structural thought; it could stand anywhere. The observer is a distinterested scientist; he could be anyone. Viollet-le-Duc explained in a letter of October 9, 1871, "Monuments in general and those of the Middle Ages in particular are not made to be seen straight on [*en géométral*] but from certain angles, and that is entirely natural: The axial point is unique, the others infinite in number. Thus one must make buildings not in anticipation of this one point, but of course with multiple [view]points in mind."[13] Although Viollet-le-Duc's works were either restorations, buildings on open sites, or (in a few cases) *immeubles* inserted in tightly defined *alignements*, there seems no evidence of the scenographic adjustment that we analyzed in the work of Duban and Garnier.[14]

*   *   *

Viollet-le-Duc's restorations provide a very cold, objective experience. In a sense the historic monument raises from another direction the matter of the rationalizing gaze that Foucault brought out in his analysis of institutions like the prison, the clinic, and the asylum – only in this case the building is the object of the gaze and the analyst circumambulates. What these all have in common is their complete disassociation from immediate life and events. Like the hospital or the prison, the historic monument is another dead spot in the urban texture, but in this case necessarily revealed to contemplative view instead of concealed behind an anonymous wall.

We emphasize the monument's opaqueness because, in fact, the insertion of scientific specimens in the socially and politically loaded urban texture was quite difficult to accomplish. This may be why so few pure examples exist in Paris itself. The Commission des Monuments Historiques did not have outright control of buildings which, previous to its creation, had already been attributed to one or another of the initial postrevolutionary bodies – the Bâtiments Civils and the Edifices Diocésains; the department and the commune. The commission's charge was principally to be vigilant and to intervene sporadically to adjust the actions of these other authorities in order to preserve historic evidence. Its restricted budget (100,000 francs in 1833; 200,000 francs in 1838; 400,000 francs in 1842; 800,000 francs in 1848)[15] was to be divided into small contributions to make adequate fuller funding from other agencies and localities. The accomplishment of this charge by the commission is enlightening. Their intervention in secular construction was slight. In the cases, for example, of the Palais de Justice in Paris (or the Conservatoire des Arts et Métiers) reconstruction was funded by other agencies and the Commission contributed only to specific sections, the Sainte-Chapelle and the church of Saint-Martin-des-Champs. Versailles was restored in 1835–1839 by Fontaine at the considerable expense of 4.5 million francs, but as a political monument, funded by the Liste Civile.[16] Nor, considering the millions of francs expended, could the Monuments Historiques have funded the job.

II

Church property had been confiscated in 1789–1791 as *biens nationaux* with the eventual proviso the buildings and staff proportionate to the nation's spiritual needs would be provided by the state.[17] The great churches of France had originally been erected with far more generous financial means. Forty years of the new stringent regime made the creation of the Commission necessary and also made its small contributions unusually significant. The problem was the intervention that came as well.

The administration of the Edifices Diocésains was in a particularly tight position. Until 1848 the Architectes Diocésains were local men appointed by the bishops. They had no expertise in restoration. From its very first meeting the Commission des Monuments Historiques in 1837 discussed taking over part or all of the yearly repair budget of the Edifices Diocésains.[18] That agency, however, had a bureau of building construction, maintenance, and furnishing headed from 1827 to 1840 by the lithographer and antiquarian Jean-Philippe Schmit.[19] The bureau in general and Schmit in particular had very different ideas about what constituted church maintenance. Schmit embodied this in reports, articles, and a series of volumes, *Les Eglises gothiques* (1837), *Cours de dessin d'ornement à l'usage des écoles des arts et métiers d'après les types antiques, du moyen-âge et de la Renaissance* (1842), *Nouveau manuel complet de l'architecte des monuments religieux, traité d'application pratique de l'archéologie chrétienne . . .* (1845). He assumed that – as his bureaucratic position suggests – churches were functioning religious buildings, not documents of the history of construction. His first volume is a small, short, powerful diatribe depicting the symbolic essence of the gothic church and attacking certain modern ideas. Although seeming to address a wide audience, he involuntarily cites what administrators should do. He declares that each architectural epoch has a specific language and that gothic cannot be "read" in terms of the conventional classical grammar. Instead the gothic building is an entirely symbolic, emotive entity, derived not from structure but from analogy with the primeval forest. Its facade proclaims the separation of the worldly outside from the divine within and reminds visitors that they must choose between them by the representation of the Last Judgment in the tympanum. "Cross then this threshold, filled with the emotion that dominates you. Oh the marvel! everything changes suddenly: instead of the solemn and melancholic aspect of the facade, in place of that image of judgment [traditionally in the tympanum], it is the spectacle of glory that surrounds you. . . . In the contemplation of this quality of immensity stamped on the architectural work, one senses that its author is imbued with that of God to whom it has been erected. . . ."[20]

Schmit devotes chapters to each of the symbolic parts of the church – the flèche, tomb monuments, wall paintings, stained glass windows, and so on. He insists that unfinished medieval churches not be completed, only be made structurally sound and be freed from postmedieval intrusions. Lastly, he writes eloquently against the isolation of churches in the cityscape:

The churches of the Middle Ages were not made to be seen thus open all around: they are only properly situated amid silence and retreat; they wish to see themselves surrounded by modest and peaceful dwellings which seem to come and press themselves at their feet; they need especially to be surrounded by those quiet and solitary cloisters, devoted to the habitation of ministers and servants of the temple, who form its guardians. . . .

The moment the church is nothing more than a building accidentally placed on the public thoroughfare like a theater, like a bazaar, like a café, one is led naturally to say: "I will drop in as I pass," as one says, "I will drop in at the museum as I pass."[21]

Schmit also sat on the Comité Historique des Arts established in the Ministère de l'Intérieur in 1835 under the secretaryship of Adolphe Didron.[22] Although the membership included a number of archeologists – Ludovic Vitet, Prosper Mérimée, Albert Lenoir, Charles Lenormant – it was dominated by churchmen and carried forward a very distinct program of monumental preservation. Delécluze, a bemused member, records in his *Souvenirs de soixante années* that the moving force was the eloquent Comte de Montalembert, seconded by Dusommerard of the Hôtel de Cluny, the pious architect Jean-Baptiste Lassus, and Didron (the secretary). The articles in the *Bulletin archéologique* produced by the comité from 1843 to 1853 concentrate on matters of liturgy and symbolism more than sound construction.

Montalembert had emerged around 1830 as an ardent opponent of the "vandalisme" of France's medieval religious heritage.[23] As a proselytizing Ultramontane he was chagrined that it was archeologists (often Protestants like Guizot or atheists like Mérimée and Viollet-le-Duc) who led the way in preservation. He pressed Catholics to make a contribution, especially in the area of liturgical iconographic reconstruction.[24] A group of Catholic students of medieval symbolism gathered around him and Didron: Ferdinand de Guilhermy, Arthur Martin, Charles Cahier, and the architects L.-A. Piel and Lassus. Guilhermy in 1837 worked out the iconographic program for the reconstruction of the stained glass windows of Sainte-Chapelle.[25] Martin and Cahier in 1841–1844 published the extensive stained glass surviving in Bourges Cathedral together with a detailed iconographic explanation.[26] Lassus wrote studies of the stained glass of Chartres and of the sketchbook of Villard de Honnecourt, both published posthumously.[27] Didron edited the comité's *Bulletin archéologique* and then the impressive *Annales archéologiques* (1844–1870, continued after Didron's death in 1867 by his nephew), including several important articles by Viollet-le-Duc on medieval construction, but most devoted to iconography and church furniture. Montalembert (along with Didron and Guilhermy) contributed to the Catholic newspaper *L'Univers* and spoke for the movement in the legislature, as deputy, then as senator.[28] The Comité des Arts was appropriated by this group, discussing matters of liturgy, sending out circulars about church furnishing, and subsidizing Catholic medievalist publications like Lassus's posthumous *Monographie de la cathédrale de Chartres* (1867).

This is a long story and again one that has been recounted elsewhere.[29] What interests us here is that not only did they concern themselves with restoration but also with the projection of new ecclesiastic monuments appropriate to the nineteenth-century city, mirroring their concerns with the treatment of existing structures. The first plates of Didron's *Annales archéologiques* make this clear: a pristine, "correct" French gothic church of the thirteenth century with all the expensive architectural-symbolic parts – transepts, chapelled choir, towered facade – encapsulating the reconstructed liturgy and iconography of the time (Figures 136 and 137).[30] In its neatness and perfection the type resembles the church models that medieval churchmen were depicted presenting to saints in contemporary representations.

That model was erected by Lassus (in succession to Piel, who took orders after the project had been begun) as Saint-Nicolas at Nantes (1840–1848, 1874, Figure 138), then approximated in Paris in the parish church of Sainte-Clothilde,[31] broached (not entirely satisfactorily) in 1839, and begun in 1847 by the Cologne-born Franz-Christian Gau and finished after his death in 1853 by Théodore Ballu in 1857 (Figure 139). Finally Lassus by himself erected the parish church of Saint-Jean-Baptiste in Belleville in 1853–1859 (Figure 140) and began the new cathedral at Lille for Arthur Martin in 1856 (Figure 141).[32] This last commission was obtained only after a competition had actually been won by the English ecclesiologist, William Burges, with a more decorative design.[33] Wall paintings and carved symbolic decoration were a fundamental part of these projects and – by dint of a large special appropriation – they were actually executed at Sainte-Clothilde.[34]

An important implication of this campaign to revive the thirteenth-century type was that the existing gothic structures were not to be restored as scientific specimens of construction but rather to be finished and provided with all the decorative and liturgical trappings as the Rhineland Catholics Sulpiz Boisserée and August Reichensperger were doing in completing Cologne Cathedral.[35] Some – Schmit, evidently, for one – were hesitant. But beginning in 1840 projects were pushed at Rouen to "finish" the facadeless abbey church of Saint-Ouen.[36] In 1843 Jean-Jacques-Nicholas Arveuf, Montalembert's initial choice as restorer of Notre-Dame, prepared such a project of completion including spires on the towers, proposing it at the same time when named architect of the cathedral at Rheims.[37] (In the end, however, Lassus and Viollet-le-Duc received the commission to restore

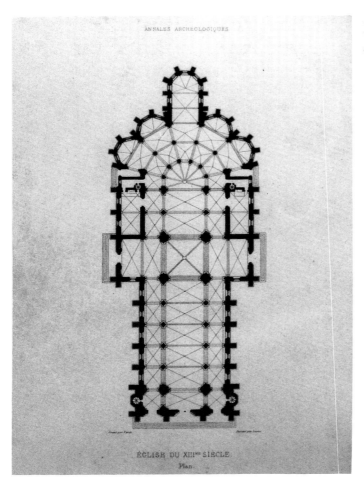

ÉGLISE DU XIIIᵐᵉ SIÈCLE.
Plan.

Figure 136. Model church of the thirteenth century. Plan. *Annales archéologiques*, 1844

Figure 137. Model church of the thirteenth century. Longitudinal cross section.

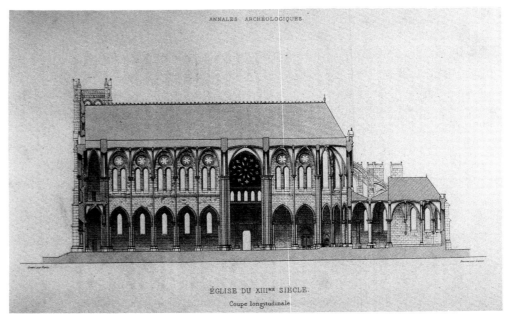

ÉGLISE DU XIIIᵐᵉ SIÈCLE.
Coupe longitudinale

Figure 138. Church of Saint-Nicolas, Nantes (Louis-Alexandre Piel and Jean-Baptiste Lassus, architects, 1840–1876).

Notre-Dame, and Arveuf was sharply criticized by Didron for his project at Rheims.)

A further implication was that such a pristine, symbolically shaped building should assert itself in the cityscape, from some distance, either by having a large *place* cut out in front as at Saint-Jean-Baptiste in Belleville or Sainte-Clothilde, or by rising high above the surrounding houses, as at Lille and Cologne. But as Schmit says, a cathedral gathers schools, cloisters, and other structures around itself and these French buildings need not have been thus isolated, as later nineteenth-century Anglo-American examples like the Englishman Bodley's National Cathedral in Washington, D.C., make clear.

This neo-Catholic architecture has always been treated uneasily. Strict archeologists – including Catholics like Didron – felt it could be exagger-

Figure 139. Church of Sainte-Clothilde (Franz-Christian Gau and Théodore Ballu, archi-tects, 1846–1857).

Figure 140. Church of Saint-Jean-Baptiste, Belleville (J.-B. Lassus, architect, 1853–1859).

Figure 141. Cathédral Notre-Dame de la Treille, Lille. Competition project, side elevation (J.-B. Lassus, architect, 1856).

ated, as Didron made clear in his critique of Arveuf's projects for Notre-Dame and Rheims. Viollet-le-Duc hated the centralized church as much as he did the centralized state; he restored only to display what was physically present and part of the environment. In new church design he emphasized locality, as we see in the projects published in his student, Anatole de Baudot's, *Eglise de Bourgs et Villages* of 1867, especially Viollet-le-Duc's own church of Saint-Gimer at Carcassonne, 1852–1859 (Figures 142 and 143).[38] Being primarily a work of construction, a parish church was a "naive" response to climate and materials and was shaped by local construction traditions and forms.

Today a compact block of thirteenth-century gothic-like Sainte-Clothilde

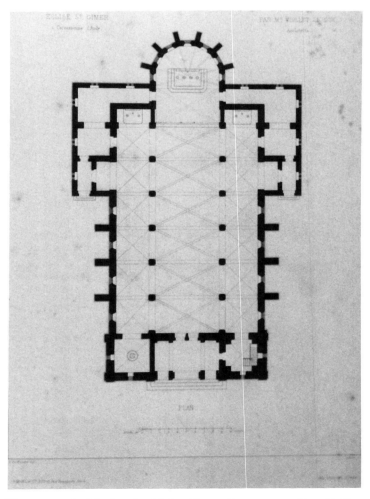

Figure 142. Parish church of Saint-Gimer, Carcassonne. Plan (E.-E. Viollet-le-Duc, architect, 1852–1859).

Figure 143. Parish church of Saint-Gimer (Viollet-le-Duc, architect, 1852–1859).

or Saint-Jean-Baptiste in Belleville seems cold and out of scale in the Parisian cityscape, not unlike the Madeleine. By the fall of the Second Empire iconography was to overcome archeology, and the neo-Catholic movement produced in the Sacré-Coeur dominating Montmartre in Paris and in Notre-Dame de Fourvière looming over Lyons with all their pristineness, symbolism, political assertiveness, and architectural exoticism.[39]

III

The city of Paris may not have had a bureau of historic monuments but it did have to deal with them, either as churches, like Saint-Eustache, or as ruins, like the Tour Saint-Jacques and the Thermes, or again as active political monuments, like the Hôtel de Ville. For political reasons there was little intrusion here on the part of the national Commission des Monuments Historiques. All the city-funded projects were executed by the staff of the Travaux d'Architecture, especially by Victor Baltard, the head and from 1848 architecte-en-chef of its first section, that controlling churches (in succession to Hippolyte Godde). In 1860, Baltard was elevated to directeur des Travaux de Paris and Théodore Ballu succeeded to the direction to the Première Section. (Notre-Dame, as a cathedral, was under the control of the Edifices Diocésains, although in fact until 1843 its architect was Godde as well.) Restoration constituted part of the *service ordinaire* and was thus carried out by the architect of the division. The Commission des Monuments

Historiques protested vigorously against this, as their minutes document, suggesting that separate and specially trained architects be named for each restoration, but in vain before 1877.[40]

There was a campaign of church transformation under Baltard, but it was quite different from those directed by the Commission des Monuments Historiques, focusing instead on religious decoration and urbanistic integration.

Beginning in the early 1840s a movement emerged in the Conseil Municipal to revive the medieval and Renaissance art of mural decoration in the city churches.[41] Its first products were Mottez's paintings in the porch of Saint-Germain-l'Auxerrois (1842–1846, planned 1839) and the chapel murals at Saint-Severin (1839–1841). In 1842 the young Baltard was put in charge of a systematic decoration campaign as Inspecteur des Beaux-Arts of the city of Paris upon the suggestion of Ingres and J.-E. Gatteaux (who sat on the Conseil Municipal). Baltard supervised the work at Saint-Merri and coordinated his friend Flandrin's decorations at Saint-Germain-des-Prés (begun in 1842) with the ornamental decoration of Alexandre-Dominique Denuelle and his own restoration campaign (Figure 144). During the Second Empire this program expanded vastly to produce the restoration and decoration of Saint-Eustache (1851–1854) and Flandrin's nave murals at Saint-Germain-des-Prés (1856–1861). Extensive mural programs were also executed in the newly constructed churches, Gau and Ballu's Sainte-Clothilde (decorated 1855–1859), Ballu's La Trinité (1860–1867), and Baltard's own Saint-Augustin (1860–1868).

This muralist program paralleled the work of the neo-Catholics and the Comité des Arts but was distinct in deriving from the school of Ingres and thus being less concerned with medievalism and symbolism than with a revival of Renaissance monumental classicism. Baltard's work here thus harmonizes with that executed in his other function as architect of the churches of Paris. He proceeded by the application of the conventional "classical" principles we explored in Chapters 5 and 6.

The second problem for Baltard was the compositional integration of existing churches into the transformed monumental cityscape. He offered his initial solution in the rebuilding of Saint-Leu when the boulevard de Sébastopol was projected cutting past its apse in early 1854 (Figures 145 and 146).[42] The *plan parcellaire* shows the church now embedded in one of the regular blocks projected to define the boulevard. In execution, the church spaces fill the whole envelope, expanding outward from the old building on the north and east (boulevard) sides to become a one-story platform above which the characteristic (and ancient) buttressed, traceried physiognomy of the church emerges. (This repeats the arrangement Baltard contemporaneously conceived for the intersection of the Oratory and the

Figure 144. Decoration of the chancel of the church of Saint-Germain-des-Prés (Victor Baltard, architect, Alexandre-Dominique Denuelle, decorator), 1842–1846.

rue de Rivoli).[43] Along the south face of the block, construction is carried up four stories to house the priests' residence in two blocks enframing a large Lady Chapel erected by Baltard on the cross axis of the nave (using concrete arches as an experiment in this new material). A peculiar part-gothic part-Quattrocento ornament (suggestive of Saint-Eustache) relieves the walls. In a word, Baltard has enframed and "packaged" the ancient church here to mediate with its new Haussmannian situation urbanistically and stylistically.

Figure 145. Church of Saint-Leu. Chevet facade on boulevard de Sébastopol (Victor Baltard, architect and restorer, 1858–1862).

In 1862–1866 the facade of Saint-Laurent further up the same boulevard was moved forward and gothicized by Constant-Dufeux in a similar style.[44]

As we noted in Chapter 6, the city had set an example for the treatment of churches as urban furniture in its 1836 purchase of the Tour Saint-Jacques, once the belfry of the church of Saint-Jacques-la-Boucherie, after the Revolution a shot tower, then in city possession a picturesque event along the projected avenues linking the Louvre and the Hôtel de Ville. It extended this in the treatment of Saint-Germain-l'Auxerrois and the Hôtel de Cluny.

Baltard's biggest ecclesiastical job was the church of Saint-Augustin (Figures 147 and 115).[45] Here again he inserts his church in the envelope of the *alignements* (apparently of necessity), producing its odd but fascinating trapezoidal nave and expanded domical crossing space.[46] The building was intended as an episode to break up the monotony of the boulevard Malesherbes, which turned slightly here at its intersection with the boulevard Haussmann (opening up here as the square Laborde). The church's telescoping facade terminates the axis up the boulevard from the Madeleine; its dome closes that down from the Parc Monceaux. As with Saint-Leu the

Figure 146. Church of Saint-Leu. Residences and school rooms on south side (Victor Baltard, architect, 1858–1862).

building continues the abstract urban texture and also forms a mild articulation point. But here it seems more strained, as in Davioud's theaters at the Châtelet, also embedded in a constraining web of *alignements*.

The great achievement of this genre of church-as-urban-furniture was Ballu's La Trinité (Figure 148), closing the Chaussée d'Antin with its single decorative tower, allowing the privacy of a fenced square in front, and enframing rental blocks determined by strict *servitudes* in their mass and decoration (Figure 132).

✳   ✳   ✳

We noted in Chapter 6 that the opening of the center of Paris was only part of Haussmann's transformation of the city. A balancing and equally important part was the 1860 extension of the municipal administration to the fortifications – this latter as large a project as the former, if a less successful one. This extension

Figure 147. Church of Saint-Augustin (Victor Baltard, architect, 1860–1868).

also influenced the evolution of Second Empire church design. Beside the work of transforming existing churches to fit into the texture of the new *percements* was an even larger job of building entirely new parish churches at the edges of the old agglomeration and out in the new arrondissements.[47]

Although this is not among the headings Haussmann so obliging laid out in his *Mémoires,* one would seem to be able to speak of a real municipal church building campaign beginning in 1859. Until 1858 church building had languished in Paris. Sainte-Clothilde, projected under Rambuteau in 1839 and begun in 1847, was completed with its decoration in 1859. A number of existing churches were restored by Baltard, some extensively as in the case of Saint-Eustache. But the only new churches designed and begun were two neogothic projects in the northern quarters, Lassus's Saint-Jean-Baptiste in Belleville (1853–1859) and Auguste Magne's Saint-Bernard behind the Gare du Nord (1858–1862). The municipal budget in 1855 provided 400,000 francs for the work on Sainte-Clothilde, 400,000 for other church work, and 200,000 for decoration (mostly of churches). Indeed the church felt itself quite ill-housed in Paris, and there were a number of individual parish initiatives, especially the erection by Boileau of Saint-Eugène in iron.[48] One should note, however, that in Sceaux and Saint-Denis, the regions of the department before 1860 immediately north and south of the city, the two architectes d'arrondissement were quite busy with church construction, Naissant at Sceaux with Saint-Lambert (1846–1856), Notre-Dame de la Gare (1855) and the parish church of Saint-Pierre at Charenton (1857–1859); Paul-Eugène Lequeux at Saint-Denis with Saint-Jacques-Saint-Christophe (1841–1844) on the Canal Saint-Martin and Notre-Dame-de-Clignancourt (1859–1862).

In September 1858, Haussmann announced a doubling of church construction funds in his budget for 1859 addressed to the Conseil Municipal.[49] He proposed to henceforth spend a million francs annually on church restoration and another million on new church construction. "A higher objective, that of the progress of public morals, obliges us to further as far as we are able the laudable efforts of the clergy."[50] During 1859 projects were commisioned for three large parish churches in the wealthy western quarters, Baltard's Saint-Augustin, Ballu's La Trinité, and Lusson's Saint-François-Xavier behind the Invalides.[51] After the Italian War the central government announced a similar expansion of funds for cathedral construction, and of aid for parish church construction taking money from the unused portion of the war loan.[52]

In 1860 the outer arrondissements became part of the city and a series of large parish churches were initiated there: Ballu's Saint-Ambroise on the avenue du Prince Eugène (1863–1869) and Saint-Joseph further northwest into Ménilmentant (1866–1875); L.-J.-A. Héret's Notre-Dame-de-la-Croix in Ménilmentant (1863–1880); Léon Ginain's Notre-Dame-des-Champs near Montparnasse (1867–1871); Vaudremer's Saint-Pierre-de-Montrouge (1864–1875) almost at the southern city limit at the Porte d'Orléans.[53]

These were all large churches of the same type and they were analyzed together, both by the Conseil des Bâtiments Civils and later by the critics. Yet the issue they raised seemed difficult to focus. Haussmann wanted the most building for the least expenditure, stating in his 1858 budget address, "It is enough to build churches today [that are] reasonably large, convenient for observances, but remarkable more for their propriety of design than for the number of rose windows and statues."[54] In 1866 he impaneled a special commission headed by Chaix d'Est Ange and including Duban (who wrote its report) to examine, "les moyens de construire des églises avec économie" – "ways to build churches economically."[55] Yet it emerged unclear just what constituted economy or whether this was appropriate to metropolitan church construction. The commission reviewed a broad array of opinions including the advocacy of iron construction (as in the case of Saint-Eugène and as had been proposed for Sainte-Clothilde) and especially the adoption of gothic construction techniques that Viollet-le-Duc and Anatole de Baudot defended as uniquely efficient.[56] But they concluded in the end, "that the

Figure 148. Church of La Trinité (Théodore Ballu, architect, 1860–1867).

Figure 149. Church of Saint-Ambroise (Théodore Ballu, architect), 1863–1869.

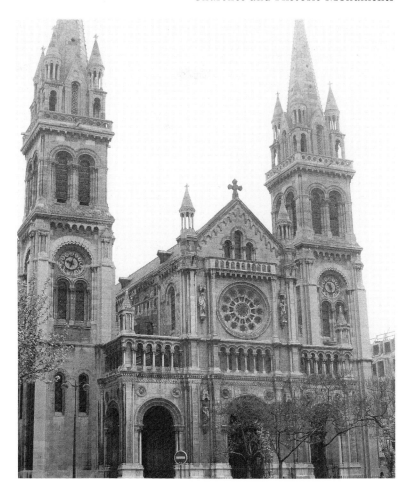

basic objective might be the search for economy reconciled with the elevated function of these buildings, the supreme expression of an epoch. . . ."[57]

The architects of the new parish churches were a heterogeneous group of individuals appointed from within the administration – some respected and recognized, like Baltard, Ballu, and Ginain; some conventional functionaries like Magne, Héret, and Lusson. (Lassus and the young Vaudremer – the latter Baltard's *inspecteur* at Saint-Augustin – were exceptions. Viollet-le-Duc himself produced a design for a parish church at Chaillot under circumstances that were unclear and frustrating to him.)[58] The Paris staff were unsympathetic to the gothic after 1860. All their productions were round-arched with certain hesitant innovations like the iron vault skeletons at Saint-Augustin and Notre-Dame-de-la-Croix.

The designs that impressed contemporaries were Ballu's three (Figures 148–150), not for their composition or structure, but rather for their self-conscious response to social theater – in a sense extending the idea of the

Figure 150. Church of Saint-Joseph (Théodore Ballu, architect), 1866–1875.

church as urban furniture to that of the church as the characterizing leitmotif of the new quarters. This was an issue that could be understood. Ballu's discerning necrologist Paul Sédille saw in his easy eclectic designs an accurate expression of social locality – the decorative La Trinité a theater for upper-class weddings, his simple Romanesque Saint-Joseph in the workers' east an emblem of the faith of the poor.

La Trinité is, in fact, a true Parisian church of the nineteenth century, sufficiently religious and severe, in this century of too tepid faith, suitably luxurious and comfortable to satisfy the worldly expectations of the wealthy bourgeois who frequent this church. Its broad nave is a sumptuous and appropriate setting which receives the smiling hopes of advantageous marriages; and nevertheless we remember that, draped in mourning, this simple nave takes on a great solemnity when you make it the place of ultimate farewell for a departed friend.[59]

Both La Trinité and Saint-Ambroise were published in monographs.[60] The first is introduced with a few words on the character of its familiar location behind the Opéra but the second is introduced with a page of tabulated statistics of mortality and indigents to communicate the humble nature of its parish totally abstractly.

In Ballu's hands the parish church became a distillation of its quarter, a characterizing marker more legible than the page of statistics to which social science was now reducing communities. This was very different from treating a church as a document of the history of architecture and society, but it was also quite distinct from treating it as a place where all are equal before the divine mystery.[61]

CONCLUSION

This book has depicted the distinct cultures of the separate (and often competing) government architectural services controlling the shape of mid-nineteenth-century Paris. It has done so in the context of the rapid evolution of construction there so as to avoid characterizing each service in the abstract, just as the whole project is based on the avoidance of the assumption of a single, consistent bureaucratic mentality or style. The story, as told here, on the contrary, is infinitely complex and fluid, personalities defining themselves within services – Fontaine, Duban, Viollet-le-Duc, Baltard – services defining themselves within the administration, state architecture defining itself against private construction – all shifting, competing, changing as French society moves from the last assumptions of absolutism under Napoleon to the Nationalism of Louis-Philippe and finally (especially with the utopians and Viollet-le-Duc) toward reconceiving itself as a social obligation.

In concluding, there are two generalities we wish to draw forth from the mass of particularities that necessarily compose this story: (1) the problem of architectural vocabulary in this situation, (2) the possible significance of this situation (and the writing of its history) in the broader context of understanding modern architecture.

The point of Chapter 3 – where the story really begins after the evocations of Chapter 1 and the framing of Chapter 2 – is that the government architectural services started around 1800 with a clear duty and manner of speech: the duty to imprint the sovereign's authority on the face of Paris, the traditional rhetorical speech of axes and Greco-Roman details constituting the "goût du roi." The problem dealt with in the four remaining chapters of this volume is how these were reformulated to serve new functions with new vocabularies. The simple "modernist" answer is that architecture was reconceievd rationally, scientifically, as a shell to protect and further social functions. But, regardless of what validity this might have come to have in the twentieth century, we have seen that in the nineteenth things still functioned within a traditional hierarchy of building types (the subject of Chapter 4) or, in the case of Viollet-le-Duc and his restoration campaign, symbolically. The real issue was, with the evaporation of the "goût du roi," what was the language of the new authority? This is the subject of Chapters 5 and 6 and it appears to have been a struggle between the Bâtiments Civils, defining the taste of the nation – denied a living embodiment in the king become retrospective in motif while traditional in scale and axes – and the Travaux de Paris defining a more elastic speech drawing from the third competing force, private construction. The further we move from the "goût du roi" in this hierarchy, the further we get from any consistent system that we today would call an architectual vocabulary – the Greco-Roman style, the styles of history, the "style" in rationalized construction.

C.-P.-V. Marie Haas proposed in 1861 with disarming confidence that, politically, the Revolution of 1789 replaced the government of the king with that already existing in the municipality. Whatever validity this might have had politically, it seems false in architecture: Municipal building – whether in seventeenth-century Holland or in nineteenth-century France – accepted the forms of royal construction, but applied them informally, as if placing itself in a lower order. There was no alternative municipal vocabulary. But there was an execution of the state vocabulary more sketchily, by means of cheaper, more efficient techniques, which (Pigeory remarks) was denied national architecture by the position it had to keep up. Within this, municipal architecture found room for itself to acknowledge locality and inidivduality, which in national architecture would seem mere provincialism.

Our second point in conclusion relates the place of all this in the broader spectrum of recent architecture. This book has recounted the history of the architecture of authority in a single (but very influential) European capital during the first century of our industrial and intellectual era. It passed from being the architecture of the king to that of the democratic administration and showed traces of becoming what it would become in our own century, that of the people as a quantified whole – although we have only had time to focus on the second of these three states. But beyond the architecture of authority in our modern centuries lies that of economics, simultaneously self-effacing and ubiquitous, as we saw especially in Chapters 1 and 5. The greatest objection one might make to this narrative is the slight coverage we could offer of private construction's role. This is a weakness widespread in contemporary building history and practice, the misapprehension that one can understand and command architecture by controlling governmental authority, when the real challenge seems to be to learn to ride the unbroken horses of corporate business and real estate development. Perhaps the Pereire brothers are at least as basic to the story as Baltard and Haussmann.

The recognition of the importance of private economic power, however, suggests the balancing importance of architecture as the theater of social life in many aspects not mentioned in building programs, one emerging for many years after structures are up and the clients and architects have left the scene. When a twentieth-century building is finished, photographers are sent for and they take its "official" portrait for publication before its users have moved in or it has become weathered, chipped, and adapted to what turns out to be its real function. When a nineteenth-century French building was completed the architect's draftsmen produced a set of exquisite wash drawings to serve as models for the steel engravings by which it would be known through the newly established architectural journals. Like this body of visual documentation, our history of architecture slices across the array of monuments at their moment of completion. Yet there is no art more than architecture where its productions are recreated decade by decade, as they are used, fantasized about, experienced, and depicted from odd angles and in surprising fragments. Indeed, one of the great attractions of the architecture of authority is its disconnection from everyday life, which leaves room for the most elaborate and outrageous colonizations. (The romantic architect-writer Petrus Borel has his fleeing hero in *Madame Putiphar* (1839) scratch a secret message for his beloved on one of the pilasters of the Louvre, that ultimate declaration in the king's tongue.) Private architecture is too careful a negotiation with its users to permit such latitude.

If we are to have a more effective architecture not only must we step down from the security of government planning authority to confront economic realities, but we must also define more broadly just what this architecture is – a fixed thing of form? Or one open, in some sense or another, to becoming entwined with the lives of its users. If this volume has succeeded to some extent, at least for the author, it may be in framing the volume that should follow.

NOTES

CHAPTER 1. THE QUARTIER DE L'OPERA

1. The most recent study of the building and the quarter is Christopher Mead's *Charles Garnier's Paris Opera* (New York: Architectural History Foundation, 1991), with bibliography. See also Monika Steinhauser, *Die Architektur der Pariser Oper* (Munich: Prestel, 1969); Charles Garnier, *Le nouvel Opéra de Paris* (Paris: Ducher, 1876–1880), 2 vols. and atlas; and *Le Théâtre* (Paris: Hachette, 1871).

2. Garnier, *Le nouvel Opéra de Paris*, I, p. 102; Haussmann concurred: *Mémoires du Baron Haussmann*, 3 vols. (Paris: Victor-Havard, 1890–1893), III, p. 504.

3. I discuss this in *Designing Paris*, pp. 71–83. Cf. Catherine Marmoz, "The Buildings of the Ecole des Beaux-Arts," *The Beaux-Arts and Nineteenth Century French Architecture,* Robin Middleton, ed. (London: Thames and Hudson, 1982), pp. 124–137.

4. Garnier describes the model theater in terms of one's movement through it in *Le Théâtre* (1871). Cf. Théophile Gautier reviewing Garnier's designs in the *MU*, February 11, 1861; May 13 and 20, 1863; August 5, 1867; Cf. Charles Goodhart-Rendel, "Paris Opera House," *Architectural Review*, 105, no. 630 (June 1949), pp. 303–304.

5. The subject of considerable study: Adeline Daumard, *Maisons de Paris et propriétaires parisiennes au XIXe siècle* (Paris: Cujas, 1965); Jean Castex, *Formes urbaines: de l'îlot à la barre* (Paris: Bordas, 1977); François Loyer, *Paris XIXe siècle: l'immeuble et la rue* (Paris: Hazon, 1987); Françoise Boudon, "La 'Maison à Loyer' de la ville haussmannienne," *Revue de l'art,* no. 79 (1988), pp. 63–72; Jean des Cars, Pierre Pinon, et al., *Paris. Haussmann* (Paris: Picard, 1991), especially the essay by Monique Eleb, pp. 284–296. The nineteenth century was conscious of the novelty: L.-M. Normand, *Paris moderne,* 4 vols. (Paris, Normand, 1843–1853); César Daly, *Architecture privée au XIXe siècle sous Napoléon III,* 6 vols. (Paris: Morel, 1864–1877); F. Barqui, *L'Architecture moderne en France* (Paris: Baudry, 1871).

6. If I might be permitted to use the image with which Henry Blake Fuller begins his of Chicago in *The Cliff Dwellers* (New York: Harper & Brothers, 1893).

7. One of the motifs of Impressionist cityscapes is precisely the brilliance of the newly cut facades – see especially Manet's *Rue Mosnier* series of 1878 (or Claude Monet's *Place du Louvre* in Berlin of 1866).

8. Kirk Varnedoe, *Gustave Caillebotte* (New Haven: Yale University Press, 1987), plate 41.

9. Bernard de Montgolfier, *Les boulevards* (Paris: Musée Carnavalet, 1985); Pierre Lavedan, *Nouvelle histoire de Paris: histoire de l'urbanisme à Paris* (Paris: Hachette, 1975), pp. 186–189.

10. See a number of the volumes produced by the Délégation à l'Action Artistique de la Ville de Paris, among them Pascal Etienne, *Le Faubourg Poissonnière* (1986), and

Françoise Hamon and Charles MacCallum, *Louis Visconti, 1791–1853* (1991, especially pp. 184 ff.).

11. Karen Bowie, "Les Gares parisiennes: historique," *Les Gares parisiennes du XIXe siècle* (Paris: Délégation à l'Action Artistique de la Ville de Paris, 1987), pp. 33–142.

12. F. and L. Lazare, *Dictionnaire administratif et historique des rues de Paris et de ses monuments,* 2nd ed. (Paris: Lazare, 1855), pp. 528–529, 672, 710.

13. Although this relocation of the theaters would appear to have been systematic I have been unable to find any discussion of it in the newspapers or analysis of it in the city archives. Cf. Gabriel Davioud and César Daly, *Les Théâtres de la place du Châtelet* (Paris: Ducher, 1865); Auguste-Joseph Magne, *Monographie du nouveau Théâtre du Vaudeville . . .* (Paris: Ducher, 1873).

14. The literature of the commercial development of Paris in general and this quarter in particular is long and distinguished. See Maurice Halbwachs, *Expropriations et le prix des terrains à Paris (1860–1900)* (Paris: Cornely, 1909); Louis Girard, *La Politique des travaux-publics du Second Empire* (Paris: Colin, 1952); Adeline Daumard, *Maisons de Paris et propriétaires parisiennes au XIXe siècle, 1809–1880;* Pierre Lavedan, *La Question du déplacement Paris et du transfert des Halles* (Paris: Ville de Paris, 1969); Jeanne Gaillard, *Paris, la ville, 1852–1870* (Paris: Champion, 1976); M. Lescure, *Les Sociétés immobilières en France au XIXe siècle* (Paris: Sorbonne, 1980); and *Les Banques, l'état et le marché immobilier en France à l'époque contemporaine, 1820–1940* (Paris: Ecole des Hautes Etudes, 1982); Jean-Pierre Allinne, *Banquiers et bâtisseurs* (Paris: CNRS, 1984); David Harvey, *Consciousness and the Urban Experience: Studies in the History and Theory of Capitalist Urbanization* (Baltimore: Johns Hopkins University Press, 1986). Also Jean Autin, *Les frères Pereire: le bonheur d'entreprendre* (Paris: Perrin, 1984).

15. The company's annual reports were published in their entirety in the *MU* as well as such journals as the *Journal de Chemins de Fer* and the *JD* around May 1 each year.

See especially *MU*, April 25, 1860 (p. 487); April 30, 1861 (pp. 607–608); May 5, 1862 (pp. 653–654).

16. The contract is published – with sharp criticisms – in the *Revue municipale*, May 1, 1861, pp. 124–125. See also *MU*, June 28 and 30, July 3, 1861.

17. *Ill*, October 22, 1855; *Illustrated London News*, October 27, 1855; Niklaus Pevsner, *A History of Building Types* (Princeton: Princeton University Press, 1976), Chapter 11; Jean d'Ormesson et al., *Grand Hôtel* (New York: Vendôme, 1984).

18. "Le centre de Paris, ou plûtot de la vie parisienne, est aujourd'hui sur le boulevard des Capucines, au débouché de la rue de la Paix et du Chaussée d'Antin. Les grands percemens projetés, qui vont faire converger sur ce point de larges voies partant de toutes les extrémités de la capitale, l'y fixeront d'une manière définitive et produiront un mouvement de population dont tout ce que nous avons sous les yeux ne peut donner qu'une faible idée." (*JD*, May 5, 1861)

19. Ensuite les boutiques que nous avons et que nous aurons à louer sur le boulevard des Capucines, dans les rues de Rouen, Mogador et Lafayette prolongée [rue Halévy] prendront d'autant plus de valeur que nous aurons fixé sur ce point une plus grande agglomération de riches voyageurs.
. . .

"En outre, sur le boulevard, les premiers étages se louent cher parce qu'ils conviennent au commerce. Pour les étages supérieurs il en est autrement. Leur situation exceptionnelle porte leur location à un prix généralement trop élevé pour des habitations particulières. Leur affectation à des appartemens meublés peut seule leur donner un utile emploi. Aussi l'établissement du Grand Hôtel de la Paix aura pour effet de faire produire à nos étages supérieurs des loyers plus importans que des locations ordinaires; il est logique en effet que, lorsqu'on n'occupe un appartement que pour un temps très court, on peut les payer plus chers que lorsqu'on l'occupe d'une manière permanente. . . .

"Les terrains du boulevard des Capucines et de la rue Mogador (côté gauche) seront appropriés à des cercles, à des maisons meublés, et à des maisons de location." (Ibid)

20. "Cette location ajoutera à la concentration dans ce quartier d'une clientèle nombreuse d'hommes riches, et y fournira l'aliment d'un grand nombre d'industries de luxe" (*JD,* May 10, 1862).

21. "conviennent parfaitement tant à raison de leurs situation au centre de Paris que de leurs grandes proportions, au commerce, à l'industrie et à commerce" (*JD,* May 10, 1862).

22. As is documented in the Louvre *agence* pay books, AN 64 Aj 65.

23. *L'Architecture,* 1892, pp. 192–193. On Armand's stable, see the illuminating biography of him in Alexandre Dubois and Charles Lucas, *Biographie universelle des architectes célèbres* (Paris: Lahure, 1868).

24. *JD,* March 25, 1878.

25. *Ill,* 47 (January 6, 1866), p. 10.

26. Hilary Ballon, *The Paris of Henri IV* (Cambridge, MIT Press, 1991); O. Zunz, "Etude d'un processus d'urbanisation: le quartier du Gros-Caillou à Paris," *Annales,* XXV, no. 4 (July–August, 1970), pp. 1024–1065; Françoise Boudon, "Urbanisme et speculation à Paris au XVIIIe siècle: le terrain de l'hôtel de Soissons," *Journal of the Society of Architectural Historians,* 32, no. 4 (December 1973), pp. 267–307, and "Tissu urbain et architecture: l'analyse parcellaire comme base de l'histoire architecturale," *Annales,* 30, no. 4 (1975), pp. 773–818; Jean-Louis Harouel, "De l'influence des règles d'urbanisme sur l'aspect des édifices privés," *Cahiers du Centre de Recherche et d'Etudes de Paris et de l'Ile de France,* 18 (1987), pp. 15–35.

27. Léon Daffrey de la Monnoye, *Théorie et pratique de l'expropriation pour cause d'utilité publique* (Paris: Pedone-Lauriel, 1879) reproduces and analyzes the two laws in great detail. The Second Empire legal manual *Traité de l'expropriation* (Paris: Cosse, Marchal, 1866) by Charles de Lalleau (extended by Jousselin) analyzes the implications of the parts of expropriation law globally. See also Léon Bequet, *Répertoire du droit administratif,* 24 vols. (Paris: Dupont, 1882–1914), "expropriation." Jean-Louis Harouel, *L'Embellisement des villes: l'urbanisme français au XVIIIe siècle* (Paris: Picard, 1993).

28. *Bulletin des lois,* 31, pp. 126 ff., especially pp. 139–141.

29. André Brunot and Roger Coquand, *Le Corps des Ponts et Chaussées* (Paris: CNRS, 1982), pp. 291–302. Departmental roads were always planned by the Ponts et Chaussées; communal streets by whomever the locality chose. In the case of Lyons during the Second Empire the city architect, René Dardel, planned *percements* until he withdrew to concentrate his attention on a major building, after which the task fell to the director of the Ponts et Chaussées, Joseph Bonnet. Charlene Marie Leonard, *Lyon Transformed: The Public Works of the Second Empire, 1853–1864* (Berkeley: University of California Press, 1961); André Bruston, "La 'régénération' de Lyon, 1853–1865," *Espaces et sociétés* (1975), pp. 81–103; Gilbert Gardes, *Lyon,* 2 vols. (Paris: CNRS, 1988). In only one case in Paris have I encountered clear documentation, that of the rue de Poulies at the rue de Rivoli, which was *alignée* in 1850 by a three-man commission consisting of the architect of the Louvre, Duban, the commissaire voyer, Vestier, and one Corval, evidently representing the property owners: AN 64 Aj 18, letter no. 18, March 25, 1850. This conforms to the specifications of the law of September 16, 1807: "Quant aux travaux des villes, un expert sera nommé par le propriétaire, un par le maire de la ville, et le tiers expert par le préfet."

30. The final Imperial decree of September 29, 1860, summarizes the preceding legislation: Adolphe Alphand, *Recueil des lettres patentes, ordonnances royales, décrets et arrêtés préfectoraux concernant les voies publiques* (Paris: Imprimerie Nouvelle, 1886), p. 322.

31. AN C 1058: appended to the text of the *Traité* of 1858. Haussmann tells us that upon his appointment the emperor presented him with a map of Paris with the *percements* marked in four colors (*Mémoires,* II, Chapter 2). The original plan is lost but one prepared by Napoleon for Friedrich-Wilhelm of Prussia in 1867 is reproduced in Werner Hegemann, *Der Städtebau nach den Ergebnissen der Allgemeinen Städtebau-ausstellung in Berlin,* 2 vols. (Berlin: Wasmuth, 1911–1913), and another corrected, supposedly, by Napoleon III shortly before his death in Merruau,

Souvenirs de l'Hôtel de Ville de Paris (Paris: Plon, 1875).

32. Cf. *Le Monde illustré,* October 13, 1860.

33. "La rue projetée en face de l'Opéra, de l'autre côté du boulevard, devait avoir une étendue calculée, toutes proportions gradées, . . .

"Il serait de plus fâcheux effet que la salle fut élevée sans qu'il fut bien étendue que, de l'autre côté du boulevard, une large rue doit s'ouvrir directement devant elle. Car, l'Opéra fut-il un chef d'oeuvre, si l'on n'y arrivait qu'*obliquement* par la rue de la Paix, il y aura une *désenchantement universel* et il s'éléverait contre l'administration un concert de *justes* et *sévères* reproches lorsqu'on verrait la rue de la Paix venant seul se briser contre les constructions du boulevard, sans aucun lien et en désaccord complet avec la façade du théâtre.

"La commission pense aussi que pour rendre plus agréable l'aspect de la place, qui doit s'étendre devant l'Opéra, il conviendrait d'arrondir par un décrochement, les maisons formant de chaque côté de cette place, le coin du boulevard des Capucines et de faire disparaître ainsi les angles de la place ouvrant sur le boulevard." (the commission's emphasis) (AN F21 830)

34. "Mais le caractère monumental que le Nouvel Opéra doit avoir, ne permet pas de laisser construire sur les terrains voisins, selon les caprices des possesseurs."

35. Op. cit., pp. 54–60.

36. Ibid., pp. 54–56; AN F21 830; Canadian Centre for Architecture, Montreal, Rohault de Fleury papers.

37. AN F21 830, dated July 28, 1858, "Théâtre Impériale de l'Opéra, bureau de l'architecte"; also projects of 1857 and December 12, 1860, in the Bibliothèque de l'Opéra.

"Construire un opéra définitif; ouvrir une large communication entre le point le plus fréquenté des boulevards et le Chemin de fer de l'ouest, en transformant un des plus beaux quartiers de Paris, tel est le double but qu'on se propose dans les projets que nous avons rédigés.

"l'Opéra doit être dans un quartier riche. Si l'on le déplace, il faut suivre la direction que prend Paris vers l'ouest; c'est d'ailleurs en s'éloignant du centre qu'on trouvera un emplacement suffisant pour les immenses développements actuellement nécessaires au service de ce grand établissement national."

38. "Nous n'avons donc pas hesité à entourer l'Opéra de maisons particulières, animées à rez-de-chaussée par le commerce et les lumières qu'il répond naturellement dans les voies publiques, qu'il élargit encore le soir en mettant pour ainsi dire les magasins dans la rue."

39. "Faisant allusion aux aventures privées d'Haussmann avec une danseuse, et à propos du projet de l'Opéra qu'on désavouait; il est fâcheux que M. le Préfet de la Seine fasse entrer l'Opéra partout où il ne devrait pas être." Emile Ollivier, *Journal, 1846–1869,* Théodore Zeldin and Anne Troisier de Diaz, eds. (Paris: Juillard, 1961), I, pp. 332–333.

40. AN F21 6395.

41. So we read in the company's annual report, *MU,* May 5, 1861.

42. *Recueil des Actes administratifs de la préfecture du département de la Seine,* 9 vols. (Paris: Paul Dupont, 1876), VI, p. 393.

43. AN F21 1830.

44. For example, Léon Vaudoyer's Grand Prix project of 1824: *The Architecture of the Ecole des Beaux-Arts,* Arthur Drexler, ed. (New York: Museum of Modern Art, 1977), p. 155.

45. Bibliothèque de l'Opéra. Canadian Centre for Architecture.

46. *Mémoires,* III, p. 504: He attributes the facades to the "architecte de l'état" that would preclude the commissaire voyer and suggest Rohault.

47. AN F21 830. About this time Rohault designed a facade on the far end of what became the avenue de l'Opéra in a very different scale: *Encyclopédie d'architecture,* 3S. IV (1884), plate 978. This, however, was before the place du Théâtre Français had been conceived and the avenue de l'Opéra was expected to extend unbroken to the rue de Rivoli.

48. This might be inferred from their words in the 1860 report to the stockholders, *MU,* April 25, 1860, p. 487.

49. *RGA,* XI (1853), col. 85.

50. David Jordan at the University of Illinois, Chicago, speculates that Bordeaux was an important model for Haussmann especially because he cited it in a speech of June 6, 1861, before the Senate (*JD,* June 8, 1861).

51. Jane Fulcher, *The Nation's Image: French Grand Opera as Politics and Politicized Art* (Cambridge-New York: Cambridge University Press, 1987).

52. Thierry Kozak, "L'agence centrale de la Société Générale à Paris (1908–1912)," *Histoire de l'art,* 1/2 (1988), pp. 51–60.

53. *JD*, December 11, 1896, "La Soirée Sarah Bernhardt." On the elevators, see Henri-Jules Borie, *Aérodomes* (Paris: Morris, 1865), p. 24.

54. "Ce parti pris d'un luxe vraiment éblouissant, qui rappelle les splendeurs de Versailles, est d'un effet d'autant plus grand qu'il tranche violemment sur la confortable simplicité de toutes les autres pièces." Charles-Emile Yriarte, *Les Cercles de Paris, 1828–1864* (Paris: Dupray de la Maherie, 1864). Yriarte had started his career as an architect, working in Garnier's *agence* at the Opéra. The plan of the club when it was gutted in 1924: AS VO11 489 (it had, by then, already been redecorated by René Sergent). Joseph-Antoine Ray, *Histoire du Jockey Club de Paris* (Paris: Marcel Rivière, 1958).

55. Jean Bouvier, *Le Crédit Lyonnais de 1863 à 1881* (Paris: SEVPEN, 1961), I, pp. 294–298.

56. "avoir sur le trottoir le plus fréquenté une boutique immense. . . . Nous aurons par notre façade la plus vaste publicité qu'on puisse avoir; 200.000 personnes passeront chaque jour devant nous et nous pourrons dire dans toutes les langues que nous leur offrons tous nos services."

57. March 26, 1878.

58. July 20, 1878.

59. "En dix-huit mois le chiffre de nos employés est passé de 250 à 1.000. . . . M. Germain [president of the bank] pense que nous devons aussi songer à la convenance qu'il y aurait pour nous de loger auprès du Crédit Lyonnais un certain nombre d'affaires qui gravitent autour de lui, ou qui graviteront si nos désirs s'accomplissent: les Chemins autrichiens, avec lesquels nos rapports vont devenir plus étroits; le Nord-Espagne, que nous voulons nous attacher; la Foncière Lyonnaise, le Mône, la Caisse Paternelle, le Gaz de Paris, Chatillon-Commentry, Descazeville, sont toutes les affaires que nous voudrions dans notre voisinage. Peut-être même aurons-nous dans l'avenir d'autres affaires à arbiter: une société pour l'industrie du gaz, une houillère, une société métallurgique, une compagnie ferroviaire. Nous pouvons entrevoir de telles créations. Il nous faut un outillage plus complexe, une usine plus vaste." (*Le Crédit Lyonnais,* p. 297, note).

60. Paul Dufournet et al., *Hector Horeau, 1801–1872* (Paris: Académie d'Architecture, 1979), pp. 93–95.

61. Pierre Citron, *La poésie de Paris dans la littérature française de Rousseau à Baudelaire,* 2 vols. (Paris: Minuit, 1961); Walter Benjamin, *Charles Baudelaire: A Lyric Poet in the Era of High Capitalism* (London, NLB, 1973); Michel de Certeau, *The Practice of Everyday Life* (Berkeley: University of California Press, 1984), especially Part III; Susan Buck-Morss, *The Dialectics of Seeing: Walter Benjamin and the Arcades Project* (Cambridge: MIT Press, 1989).

62. Aaron Scharf, *Art and Photography* (Baltimore: Penguin, 1974); Kirk T. Varnedoe and Thomas P. Lee, *Gustave Caillebotte: A Retrospective Exhibition* (Houston: Museum of Fine Arts, 1976), pp. 131–132, 147–160; Marie Berhaut, *Gustave Caillebotte: sa vie et son oeuvre* (Paris: Bibliothèque des Arts, 1978), pp. 114–116; Kirk Varnedoe, *Gustave Caillebotte,* pp. 140–156. This is to touch the tip of a very large scholarly iceberg: See T. J. Clark, *The Painting of Modern Life: Paris in the Art of Manet and His Followers* (New York: Knopf, 1985); Robert Herbert, *Impressionism: Art, Leisure and Parisian Society* (New Haven: Yale University Press, 1988).

63. Chapter 5. See Jean Meral, *Paris dans la littérature américaine* (Paris: CNRS, 1983).

64. "Les amants avaient l'amour du nouveau Paris. Ils couraient souvent la ville en voiture, faisaient un détour, pour passer par certains boulevards qu'ils aimaient d'une tendresse personnelle. Les maisons, hautes, à grandes portes sculptées, chargées de balcons, où luisaient, en grandes lettres d'or, des noms, des enseignes, des raisons sociales, les ravissaient. Pendant que le coupé filait, ils suivaient, d'un regard ami, les bandes grises des trottoirs, larges, interminables, avec leurs bancs, leurs colonnes bariolées, leurs arbres maigres. Cette trouée claire qui allait au bout de l'horizon, se répétissant et s'ouvrant sur un carre

bleuâtre du vide, cette double rangée inter-rompue de grands magasins, où des commis souriaient aux clientes, ces courants de foule piétinant et bourdonnant, les empilis-saient peu à peu d'une satisfaction absolue et entière, d'une sensation de perfection dans la vie de la rue. Ils aimaient jusqu'aux jets de lances d'arrosage, qui passaient comme une fumée blanche, devant leurs chevaux, s'étalaient, s'abattaient en pluie fine sous les roues du coupé brunissant le sol, soulevant un léger flot de poussière. Ils roulaient toujours, et il leur semblait que la voiture roulait sur des tapis, le long de cette chaussée droite et sans fin, qu'on avait faite uniquement pour leur éviter les ruelles noires. Chaque boulevard devenait un couloir de leur hôtel."

65. Jeanne Gaillard has contributed to a short critical overview of the novel *Au Bonheur des dames* (Paris: Hatier, 1982). The archi-tect Frantz Jourdain helped Zola in imaging the department store: Meredith Clausen, *Frantz Jourdain and the Samaritaine: Art Nouveau Theory and Criticism* (Leiden: Brill, 1987), Chapter 7.

66. *Le Bâtiment*, October 2, 1864.

67. "la réalisation moderne d'un palais de rêve, d'une Babel entassant des étages, élargissant des salles, ouvrant des échappées sur d'autres étages et d'autres salles, à l'infini."

68. Jeanne Gaillard discusses this aspect of Zola's *Au Bonheur des dames*.

CHAPTER 2. THE GOVERNMENT ARCHITECTURAL SERVICES

1. On the basic structure of government administration see Nicolas Boussu, *Etudes administratives: l'administration des beaux-arts* (Paris: Baltenweck, 1877); Bequet, op. cit., "Beaux-Arts," printed separately in two volumes; P. Dupré and G. Ollendorf, *Traité de l'administration des Beaux-Arts* (Paris: Dupont, 1885). Jean-Pierre Eperon, *Architecture: une anthologie*, 3 vols. (Liège: Mardaga, 1992–1993).

For a general study of the administra-tion of architecture see William H. White, *Architecture and Public Buildings* (London, P. S. King & Son, 1884). (I owe this refer-ence to Ellen Christensen.) Cf. Gloria C. Clifton, *Professionalism, Patronage and Public Service in Victorian London: The Staff of the Metropolitan Board of Works, 1856–1889* (London: Athlone, 1993); and Geoffrey Tyack, *Sir James Pennethorne and the Making of Victorian London* (London: Cambridge University Press, 1993).

There are a number of modern studies of the administration of the arts: William Underwood Eiland, *Napoleon III and the Administration of the Fine Arts*, Ph.D. dis-sertation, University of Virginia, 1978; Pierre Vaisse, *La Troisième République et les peintres: recherches sur le rapport du pouvoir et de la peinture en France de 1870 à 1914*, thèse d'état, Paris IV, 1980; Michael Marrinan, *Painting Politics for Louis Philippe* (New Haven: Yale Univer-sity Press, 1988); Patricia Mainardi, *Art and Politics of the Second Empire: The Univer-sal Expositions of 1855 and 1867* (New Haven: Yale University Press, 1987). Cf. Bruno Foucart, *Le renouveau de la peinture religieuse en France (1800–1860)* (Paris: Arthena, 1987), pp. 75–92. Jane Roos will shortly publish a volume on state art policy during the Third Republic.

The situation in architecture is more sketchy, although Hautecoeur builds his *Histoire de l'architecture classique en France* in part on this structure. See Annie Jacques, *La carrière de l'architecte au XIXe siècle* (Paris: Musée d'Orsay, 1986), and my "The Nineteenth Century French Govern-ment Architectural Services and the Design of the Monuments of Paris," *Art Journal*, 48, no. 1 (spring 1989), pp. 16–22.

2. On "policing" see Michel Foucault, "La politique de la santé au XVIIIe siècle," *Les machines à guérir* (Liège: Mardaga, 1979), pp. 7–18, with summary bibliography. Cf. Nicholas de Lamarre, *Traité de la police*, 4 vols. (Paris: Cot, 1704–1738); N.-T. Le Moyne des Essarts, *Dictionnaire universel de la police*, 8 vols. (Paris: Moutard, 1786–1790). More broadly, this has come to be understood in terms of the policies of Henri IV and Louis XIV: Louis Marin, *Le Portrait du roi* (Paris: Minuit, 1981); Jean-Marie Apostolides, *Le roi-machine: specta-cle et politique aux temps de Louis XIV* (Paris: Minuit, 1981); Jean-Marie Pérouse

de Montclos, *Histoire de l'architecture française: de la Renaissance à la Révolution* (Paris: Menges, 1989), Chapters 8, 10, and 11.

3. Donald Drew Egbert, *The Beaux-Arts Tradition in French Architecture* (Princeton: Princeton University Press, 1980), pp. 139–160.

4. David Van Zanten, "Architectural Composition," *The Architecture of the Ecole des Beaux-Arts* (Cambridge, Mass.: M.I.T. Press, 1977), pp. 232–242.

5. "le projet d'un monument public de sa composition et conforme aux usages de la France." Académie des Beaux-Arts, *Règlements pour les travaux des pensionnaires de l'académie de France à Rome* (1821), pp. 103–104.

6. As in the case of the Grand Prix programs, there were cases of "radical" (or at least personal) fifth-year *envois*, especially in the years around 1830 from the circle of Henri Labrouste: Van Zanten, *Designing Paris*, pp. 17ff.

7. AN F13 673–677, letter from the minister of the interior of June 9, 1829, insisting on this.

8. The eight members in 1850 were Lebas, Huvé, Gauthier, Caristie, Lesueur, Fontaine, Leclère, and Debret among which Fontaine alone came from another service, that of the Palais Nationaux (and he was once premier architecte de l'empereur); in 1870 they were Léon Vaudoyer, Henri Labrouste, Lefuel, Baltard, Lesueur, Gilbert, Duc, and Duban – Lefuel from the Palais Impériaux (also architecte de l'empereur), Baltard head of the Travaux d'Architecture of the city of Paris.

9. These letters survive in the archives of the Institut de France. Another example recently published is Visconti's 1847 autobiographical manuscript, which makes no mention at all of his extensive private practice (*Visconti*, pp. 22–42).

10. Paul Dufournet et al., *Hector Horeau.*

11. Georges Toudouze, *Gabriel Toudouze, architecte et graveur* (Paris: Le Musée, 1906).

12. From 1844 to 1877 Daly (the director of the *Revue générale de l'architecture et des travaux publics,* 1840–1889) was *architecte diocésain* of the Tarn and thus architect for the restoration of the Cathedral of Albi, executing the extensive (and controversial) work there. (See Marc Saboya, *Presse et architecture au XIXe siècle,* Paris: Picard, 1991.) Chipiez (co-author with Georges Perrot of the monumental *Histoire de l'art dans l'antiquité,* 1882–1914) worked all his career in the Ministère de l'Instruction Publique as one of the inspecteurs principaux de l'enseignement de dessin.

13. Or so we extrapolate, although the evidence is equivocal: Françoise Boudon in *Hittorff, 1792–1867* (Paris: Musée Carnavalet, 1986), pp. 279–295; Van Zanten, "Les collaborateurs de Visconti," *Visconti,* pp. 72–77. Bailly bequeathed his private practice to his assistant Ernest Sanson when he became deeply involved in city work in the 1860s, Sanson and his successor René Sergent making of it one of the great international practices of the turn of the century. See Gerard Rousset-Charny, *Les Palais parisiens de la belle époque* (Paris: Délégation à l'Action Artistique, 1990).

14. Van Zanten, *Designing Paris,* pp. 127–129.

15. One might add Lucien Magne's less formal *L'Architecture française du siècle* (Paris: Firmin-Didot, 1889).

16. *Nouveau Dictionnaire biographique et critique des architectes français* (Paris: André, Daly fils, 1887). Adolphe Lance's similar *Dictionnaire des architectes français au XIXe siècle,* 2 vols. (Paris: Morel, 1872), does not give a substantially different canon, but Charles Gabet's slighter *Dictionnaire des artistes de l'école française* of 1831 (Paris: Vergne) does, interestingly, as would have Alexandre Dubois's and Charles Lucas's *Biographie universelle* had it been completed (only the letter *A* saw publication in 1868). Eugène Delaire's *Architectes élèves de l'Ecole des Beaux-Arts* (Paris, Chaix, 1895, second expanded edition, 1907) distinguishes architects only by their education.

17. Henri Terson, *Origines et évolution du ministère de l'Intérieur* (Montpellier, 1913). Charles Gourlier, *Notice historique sur le service des travaux des bâtiments civils* (Paris: Colas, 1848, with later extended editions). Three modern studies are underway

by Georges Teyssot, Françoise Boudon, and Lauren O'Connell. See the last's dissertation, *Architecture and the French Revolution: Change and Continuity Under the Conseil des Bâtiments Civils* (Dissertation, Cornell University, 1989).

18. Gourlier reproduces the texts of the organizations of 1812 and 1838–1841. That of the organization of 1832 can be found in AN F21 6697. *RGA*, II (1842), cols. 128–133, 159–166; X (1852), cols. 109–112.

19. On the 1863 reorganization: *RGA* (1863), cols. 198–199. Vatout has left a diary. See Henri duc d'Aumale, *Notice sur le comte de Cardaillac* (Paris: Firmin-Didot, 1880).

20. Léon Bequet is confused by this (op. cit., "Bâtiments Civils," p. 619) and quotes Christophle and Auger, *Traité théorique et pratique des travaux-publics:* "Les édifices et monuments ont étés rangés parmi les bâtiments civils par des décisions successives prises, soit à l'époque de la construction, soit postérieurement." An approximate list was given annually in the *Almanach National*.

21. Maurice Block, *Dictionnaire de l'Administration française,* 3rd ed. (Paris: Berger-Levrault, 1891), p. 256.

22. Documents on the New Louvre *agence:* AN Aj 64 65. Garnier, *Le Nouvel Opéra de Paris,* II, pp. 501–503. In the *service ordinaire,* for the upkeep of buildings already erected, an architect's office was maintained within the building itself, as it still is at the Palais de Justice.

23. See Van Zanten *Designing Paris,* pp. 122–123.

24. The fees of the *architectes-en-chefs* could become excessive in the case of large projects – as we see in the fees Léon Vaudoyer received building the cathedral at Marseilles (Van Zanten, *Designing Paris,* p. 127). The percentage usually declined with the size of the project. The architects of large projects like the New Louvre and the Opéra were often paid reduced percentages (as was Garnier at the Opéra, about which his wife complained bitterly in her memoirs, "Charles Garnier par Mme. Garnier," *L'architecture,* 38, no. 21, pp. 377–390), or a flat fee, as were both Visconti and Lefuel at the New Louvre, although this was

40,000 francs per annum coming with the title architecte de l'empereur.

25. F21 1830.

26. F13 638–639; F21 1817. The Visconti papers include an interesting stack of solicitations for positions in the Louvre *agence.* Fontaine in his *Journal* mentions applicants' protectors as a matter of course (e.g., I, pp. 14, 426; II, p. 829).

27. When Blouet's post as inspecteur général des prisons was eliminated in 1848 there was a frantic scurry to find him some sort of other employment (AN, F21 1817). After doing a project to remove the Assemblée Nationale to the Tuileries, he ended his career as architect of the palace at Fontainebleau.

28. *Visconti,* pp. 22–42; Rémusat papers, Archives Municipales, Toulouse (I owe the latter reference to Michael Driskel).

29. AN F21 2484. I owe this reference to Françoise Boudon. It is confirmed in the reorganization of January 9, 1840.

30. Institut de France, MSS 1044, 1045.

31. Terson, op. cit., pp. 88–110; *Enquête parlementaire sur le régime des établissements pénitentiaires,* 8 vols. (Paris: Imprimerie Nationale, 1873–1875); J. Léauté, *Criminologie et science pénitentiaire* (Paris: PUF, 1972); Michel Foucault, *Surveiller et punir* (Paris: Gallimard, 1975); Pierre Deyon, *Le temps des prisons* (Lille: Université, 1975); Patricia O'Brien, *The Promise of Punishment: Prisons in Nineteenth-Century France* (Princeton: Princeton University Press, 1982). See also Robin Evans, *The Fabrication of Virtue: English Prison Architecture, 1750–1840* (Cambridge: Cambridge University Press, 1982).

32. *Rapport à M. le Comte de Montalivet . . . sur les pénitenciers des Etats-Unis* (Paris: Imprimerie Royale, 1837).

33. *Instruction et programme pour la construction des maisons d'arrêt et de justice* (Paris: Ministère de l'Intérieur, 1841).

34. Guillaume-Abel Blouet, *Projet de prison cellulaire pour 585 condamnés précédé d'observations sur le système pénitentiare* (Paris: Didot, 1843).

35. Mettray became perhaps the most famous of the reformed prisons of this time: Foucault, *Punir,* Part 4, Chapter 3; Henri Gail-

lac, *Les Maisons de correction* (Paris: Cujas, 1971), pp. 80–86. The anticlerical publicist Léo Taxil writes of his own stay in Mettray in his *Histoire d'une chute et d'une conversion* (Paris: Letouzey, n.d.).

36. The cellural system was discontinued by decree of August 17, 1853 (*JD*, August 20, 1853).

37. Brunot and Coquand, op. cit.; Antoine Picon, *Architectes et ingénieurs au siècle des lumières* (Marseilles: Parenthèse, 1988; translation: Cambridge University Press, 1992).

38. Alexandre de Laborde, *Projet d'organization des bâtiments civils dépendens du ministère de l'intérieur tendant à l'amélioration de l'architecture en France* (Paris: Baudouin, 1820). See Georges Teyssot, "Planning and Building in Towns: The System of the Bâtiments-Civils, 1795–1848," *The Beaux-Arts*, pp. 34–49.

39. "L'Architecture était pour tous une profession; pour beaucoup, sans doute, un art; mais pour aucun, ce n'était la fonction publique devenue aux yeux de celui qui en est vraiment digne: une sorte de Sacerdoce" (Georges Haussmann, *Mémoires*, III, p. 475).

40. "On ne peut assimiler les architectes à des fonctionnaires. Il n'y a pas de grade parmi les artistes, et le rang ne s'obtient que par des succès publics. Quel que soit le titre que le gouvernement donne à un architecte, il n'aura jamais d'autorité morale sur ses confrères, si des travaux éminents ne l'ont pas placé à un rang élève dans l'estime du public. Pour que des inspecteurs aient l'influence qu'ils doivent exercer, il faudra donc les choisir parmi les architectes qui ont acquis de la réputation. Mais, il est à peu près impossible d'en acquérir avant l'âge de 40 à 45 ans (car avant cet âge on n'a jamais de grands travaux à diriger). Or quel est l'architecte en réputation, âgé de 40 à 45 ans, qui renoncerait à une carrière brillante, à la gloire, peut-être à la fortune, pour une position précaire comme celle d'inspecteur? Où trouver un artiste qui renonce à des travaux considérables, à sa cliéntele particulière, pour une place assez modestement rétribuée qu'il ne peut exercer que pendant quelques années? Un fonctionnaire public sait qu'après 30 ans de bons services il aura une retraite. Mais quelle retraite est possible pour des hommes qui deviennent fonctionnaires à 45 ans? D'un autre côté, quels services utiles le gouvernement pourrait-il attendre d'inspecteurs vieillis dans le métier, affaiblis par l'âge, et que leur manque de pratique de l'art, met assez rapidement en dehors du progrès continuel?

"On de doit jamais perdre de vue ce qui est arrivé pour le Conseil des Bâtiments Civils. A son institution cette compagnie représentait admirablement l'élite des architectes. Eloignés de la pratique, ses membres ont perdu promptement toute leur autorité. Aujourd'hui, à la timidité de leurs jugements on peut deviner qu'eux-mêmes ont le sentiment de leur position arriérée et en dehors du mouvement de l'art." *Correspondence générale* (Louis Parturier, ed., Paris: le Divan, 1941–1964), 17 vols., VII, pp. 28–29 (AN F 19 4536). To A. A. de Contecin, directeur général de la Direction des Cultes.

41. Jean-Pierre Eperon and Maurice Culot, "Fontaine et les architectes," *Journal de P.-F.-L. Fontaine*, pp. xxxvii–lii, and a reference by Fontaine in that journal, August 19, 1804 (I, p. 84; also pp. 87, 93–99, 113–114, 686, 918, 1067). M.-C. B. de Montalivet, *Le Roi Louis-Philippe: liste civile* (Paris, Michel Levy, 1851). *Encyclopédie d'architecture*, I (1852), cols. 52–53. Cf. the final organization of the service of February 11, 1884: Bequet, op. cit., III, pp. 203–209.

42. Fontaine's *Journal* notes the smaller changes that accompanied each new intendant's or minister's appointment, for example, when Costaz took over in 1810 (I, p. 255).

43. P. 60. Cf. Fontaine's layout of the service in 1804: *Journal*, I, pp. 93–99, 113–114.

44. *Bulletin des lois*, no. 4016, vol. 139, pp. 1176–1178.

45. AN O5 40.

46. Fontaine, *Journal*, I, p. 257.

47. Berthault was employed by Rothschild, but his status as one of the king's architects must have recommended him. Pauline Prévost Marcilhacy is studying the Rothschild architectural patronage. See Olivier Poisson, "Foro e Palatino, 1809–1813: il progetto del giardino del Campidoglio," *Gli Orte farnesiana sul Palatino* (Rome:

Académie de France à Rome, 1990), pp. 587–603.

48. Famin, however, was not highly regarded. Fontaine won the Second Grand Prix in 1785, but was sent to Rome nonetheless.

49. Fontaine, *Journal*, pp. 976–977.

50. P.-F.-L. Fontaine and Charles Percier, *Journal des monuments de Paris, envoyé par Fontaine à l'Empereur de Russie, dans les années 1809, 1810, 1811, 1814 et 1815, complément avec un avertissement de Albert Vuaflart* (Paris: Rahir, 1892). Fontaine's original manuscript is in the Fontaine papers at the Art Institute of Chicago.

51. Jean-Marc Léri, "Les travaux parisiens sous le préfet Rambuteau," *Cahiers du centre de recherches de Paris et de l'Ile de France*, 18 (March 1987), pp. 203–213. Anne-Marie Châtelet, "La conception haussmannienne du rôle des ingénieurs et architectes municipaux," *Paris. Haussmann*, pp. 257–266.

52. *Almanach impérial*, 1804.

53. *Bulletin des lois*, no. 6454 (January 11, 1811) and no. 1782 (February 26, 1817). The exact nature of the powers seems vague: L. de Lanzac de Laborie, *Paris sous Napoléon* (Paris: Plon, 1905–1913), II; *Administration, Grands Travaux*, pp. 271ff; Navier, "Notice sur M. Bruyère," *Annales des ponts et chaussées*, 1S, no. 2 (1833), pp. 382–404; Bruyère, *Etudes relatives à l'art des constructions*, 2 vols. (Paris: Bance, 1823–1828). On Fontaine's rivalry: Eperon, op. cit. Cf. Fontaine, *Journal*, I, pp. 279–280.

54. *Bulletin de la société centrale des architectes*, 1871; *Recueil des actes administratifs*, III, p. 377; VI, pp. 35 ff. Anne-Marie Châtelet writes that the text of the November 30, 1840, reorganization is lost (*Paris. Haussmann*, p. 263). The Commune of 1871 also produced a reorganization: Paul Hippeau, *Les Fédérations artistiques sous la Commune* (Paris: Comptoir d'édition, 1890), pp. 17 ff.

55. *Almanach royal*, 1831, p. 739.

56. *Recueil des actes administratifs*, III, p. 377.

57. *Almanach royal*, 1830, p. 760.

58. See Mme. Charles Garnier, loc. cit.

59. The actual authority of the post is unclear and its salary – 2,000 francs per annum – is modest. It would be more important in latter transformations. (See Thérèse de Puy-laroque, "Pierre Baltard, peintre et dessinateur (1764–1846)," *Bulletin de la société de l'histoire de l'art français* (1976), pp. 331–339.

60. *Recueil des actes administratifs*, VI, p. 35. Before this date, projects arriving before the Conseil des Bâtiments Civils were accompanied by a letter from the prefect, after one from Baltard, and these were considerably more professional and critical.

61. Anthony Sutcliffe, *The Autumn of Central Paris* (Montreal: McGill University Press, 1971).

62. Dossiers du Musée d'Orsay, *L'architecture hospitalière au XIXe siècle: l'exemple parisien* (Paris, 1988). Further organic arrêtés followed April 24, 1849, and December 28, 1852: *RGA* XI (1853), cols. 404–406.

63. "L'Ecole impériale marche encore à la tête des générations artistiques, imprimant son cachet aux monuments achevés ou restaurés. Plus libre dans ses préférences, n'ayant pas comme la royauté et comme l'Etat des traditions à maintenir, des droits acquis à satisfaire, la ville de Paris agit dans la franchise de ses opinions et de ses goûts" (Pigeory, op. cit., p. 675).

64. "Enfin, les particuliers, plus indépendants encore que le conseil municipal, se montrent de moins en moins soucieux des règles académiques. De là, ces différences faciles à établir entre les oeuvres issues de la volonté royale, du vote des édiles, et de la fortune privée."

65. Horace Say, *Etudes sur l'administration de la ville de Paris et du département de la Seine* (Paris: Guillaumin, 1846), pp. 333–370. Say was the son of the economist Jean-Baptiste Say and father of the Third Republic minister of finance, Léon Say.

66. "A quels résultats plus grands que ceux qui ont été obtenus ne serait-on pas arrivé, si l'architecture avait su seulement être de son pays et de son siècle!" (ibid., p. 370).

67. *Mémoires*, III, pp. 474 ff.

68. Bequet, op. cit., "commune"; Bernard Lepetit, *Les villes dans la France moderne (1740–1840)* (Paris: Albin Michel, 1988), pp. 255–260; Georges Teyssot, "Citta-servizi: la produzione dei bâtiments-civils in Francia (1795–1848)," *Cassabella*, 424 (April 1977), pp. 56–64.

69. The 1852 law applied to departments (see *JD*, March 27, 1852); the 1861 law to communes (see *JD*, August 15, 1861).

70. Report by Persigny, published in *JD*, August 15, 1861.

71. Bauchal, op. cit., p. 616.

72. Gabet, op. cit., p. 522.

73. "examiner si les bâtiments répondent à leur destination, de signaler les améliorations dont ils lui paraîtront susceptibles et de préparer à la suite de cette inspection un projet général d'un lycée modèle." Bergdoll, *Leon Vaudoyer*, Ph.D. dissertation, Columbia University, 1989, p. 220. Cf. Bergdoll, *Les Vaudoyers, une dynastie d'architectes* (Paris: Réunion des Musées Nationaux, 1991).

74. Bequet, op. cit., XIX, p. 351; *Semaine des constructeurs*, V (October 9, 1880), pp. 176–177: The first commission included three fonctionnaires, four architects (Bouvard, Narjoux, Salleron, and Train), and a president, Gréart.

75. Dominique Varry, *Histoire des bibliothèques françaises*, vol. III *Les Bibliothèques de la révolution et du XIXe siècle* (Paris: Cercle de la Librairie, 1991), especially Jean Bleton, "Les Bâtiments," pp. 183–237.

76. Paul Léon, *La vie des monuments français* (Paris: Picard, 1951); Philippe Verdier, "Le service des monuments historiques," *Congrès archéologique* 2S, I (1934), pp. 53–261; Françoise Bercé, *Les premiers travaux de la Commission des Monuments Historiques, 1837–1848* (Paris: Picard, 1979); Jean-Michel Leniaud, *Jean-Baptiste Lassus (1805–1857) ou le temps retrouvé des cathédrales* (Geneva: Droz, 1980).

77. *MU*, October 29, 1830.

78. On the Comité and the *Bulletin archéologique*: Leniaud, op. cit., pp. 34–38.

79. Georg Germann, *The Gothic Revival in Europe and Britain* (Cambridge: MIT Press, 1972), pp. 81 ff, 151 ff.

80. Quoted in his necrology, *MU*, January 6, 1854, p. 23.

81. Perhaps this is too harsh. With the founding of the municipal commission in 1860, the establishment of the Musée Carnavalet (1865) under Charles Read, and the emergence of the Commission du Vieux Paris (1897) animated by Marcel Poëte, a distinct and important philosophy of urban form emerged, but very late in the period chronicled in this book. (See Anthony Sutcliffe, op. cit., Chapter 7; Léon, op. cit.; *Commission municipale du vieux Paris, procès verbal*, 1898–1932).

82. Léon, op. cit., pp. 244–252.

83. Leniaud, *Lassus*, p. 222, publishes an undated letter from Mérimée exploring how a professional track might be created in the Monuments Historiques.

84. Bergdoll, op. cit.; J.-M. Leniaud, "Viollet-le-Duc et le service des Edifices Diocésains," *Actes du colloque international Viollet-le-Duc* (Paris: Nouvelles Editions Latines, 1982), pp. 153–164, and "Les architectes diocésains," *Monuments historiques*, 113 (1981), pp. 3–33.

85. G. Massa-Gille, *Journal d'Hippolyte Fortoul* (Geneva: Droz, 1979); Paul Raphael and Maurice Gontard, *Hippolyte Fortoul, un ministre de l'Instruction Publique sous l'Empire autoritaire, 1851–1856* (Paris: PUF, 1975).

86. Léon, pp. 234–235; Leniaud, "Viollet-le-Duc et le service des Edifices Diocésains," loc. cit.

87. AN F19 7222.

88. Fortoul, *Journal*, March 15, 1855.

89. E.-E. Viollet-le-Duc, "Les mandarins à Paris," *Gazette des Beaux-Arts*, I (1859), pp. 90–97.

90. AN F19 7740.

91. I outline this in Chapter 2 of *Designing Paris*.

92. The sharp positivist critic Pierre Petroz devotes a chapter in his *L'art et la critique en France depuis 1822* (Paris: Germer Baillière, 1875) to architecture and asserts that the only substantial systems were those of Quatremère and Viollet-le-Duc.

93. AN F 19 7233 and F 19 8043.

94. AN F19 4571: letter of May 6, 1857, from Achille Fould requesting a list of major constructions carried out by the Edifices Diocésains since January 1, 1852. The list prepared in response by the administration ennumerates the restoration of the cathedrals at Angoulême (Abadie), Bayeux (Ruprich-Robert), Paris (Viollet-le-Duc), Périgueux (Abadie), and Troyes (Millet) as well as the seminaries at Beauvais (Verdier),

Coutances (Danjoy), Lyons (Desjardins), Nantes (Nau), and Rennes (Labrouste). These architects are all from the circles of either Labrouste or Viollet-le-Duc with the exception of two prominent local men, Desjardins in Lyons and Nau in Nantes.

95. General: Maurice Block, *Paris;* Jean Tulard, *Paris et son administration 1800–1890)* (Paris: Ville de Paris, 1976). More focused on *voirie*: Henri Davenne, *Législation et principes de la voirie urbaine* (Paris: Dupont, 1849); Pierre Pinon, "Les procédures et les services," *Paris. Haussmann,* pp. 94–101. Jeanne Pronteau, *Edme Verniquet, 1727–1804* (Paris: Ville de Paris, 1986). Haussmann, *Mémoires,* III, pp. 5–13. See also my "Visconti architecte-voyer" in *Visconti,* pp. 66–71.

96. Bequet, op. cit., XXI, p. 538: confirmed by successive decrees of May 1599; June 1604; February 1626; May 1635; April 10, 1783; October 27, 1808; March 26, 1852.

97. Davenne, op. cit., pp. 312–314.

98. Pronteau, *Verniquet,* pp. 315 ff.

99. Ibid., p 417.

100. Sylvie Buisson, "Le plan des artistes," *La Vie urbaine,* 55 (January–March, 1950), pp. 8–21; 57 (July–September, 1950), pp. 161–171; Hegemann, *Städtebau,* Figure 140.

101. Ville de Paris, *Recueil des clauses connues sous le nom de Réserves Dominales imposées aux acquéreurs des biens nationaux . . .* (Paris: Chaix, 1897).

102. Pronteau, op. cit., pp. 395–397.

103. Davenne, op. cit., pp. 420–424.

104. Pronteau, op. cit., p. 397.

105. Théodore Jacoubet, *Atlas général de la ville, des faubourgs et des monuments de Paris* (Paris: Hocq, 1836). See Jeanne Pronteau's introduction to *Petit atlas pittoresque des quarante-huit quartiers de la ville de Paris par A. M. Perrot, ingénieur* (Paris: Minuit, 1960).

106. Taxil, *Recueil.*

107. Lazare, *Dictionnaire,* 2nd ed. (1855), introduction; "Plan de Paris de 1830 à 1848," *Bibliothèque municipale,* I (1862), pp. 145–157; "Plan d'ensemble de Paris," *Courrier municipal,* II, no. 29 (1874), pp. 1–2.

108. Haussmann, *Mémoires,* III, pp. 1 ff.

109. Lavedan, *Déplacement;* Pierre Pinon, "Les conceptions urbaines au milieu du XIXe siècle," *Paris. Haussmann,* pp. 44–50. For example, T. Jacoubet, C. Grillon, and G. Callous, *Etudes d'un nouveau système d'alignemens et de percemens de voies publics faites en 1840 et 1841* (Paris: Chaillou, 1848); Perreymond, "Etudes sur la ville de Paris," *RGA* III (1842), cols. 540–554, 570–579, IV (1843), cols. 25–37, 72–87, 413–429, 449–469, 517–528; Hippolyte Meynadier, *Paris sous le point de vue pittoresque et monumental: ou élémens d'un plan général d'ensemble de ses travaux d'art et d'utilité publique* (Paris: Dauvin & Fontaine, 1843).

110. Lavedan, *Déplacement.* Françoise Paul-Levy, *La Ville en croix* (Paris: Librairie des Méridiens, 1984).

111. Horace Say, op. cit., p. 370; Lavedan, *Déplacement.*

112. Haussmann, *Mémoires,* II, p. 53; Merruau, *Souvenirs de l'Hôtel de Ville,* pp. 365–366; André Morizet, *Du vieux Paris à Paris moderne,* pp. 128–131; Hegemann, *Städtebau,* Figure 144; *Commission municipal du vieux Paris, procès verbal,* 1925, pp. 3–4.

113. Morizet, op. cit., pp. 117–122.

114. See Chapter 6.

115. Haussmann, *Mémoires,* I, p. 15. Napoleon III also had a huge plan of Paris on the wall of his office in the Tuileries that might have been similar (P. N. Sainte Fare Garnot and E. Jacquin, *Le château des Tuileries* (Paris: Herscher, 1988), p. 155.

116. Several versions of the plan are in the Salle des Cartes, Bibliothèque Nationale, dated variously 1864, 1865, and 1868. It is inscribed "Plan général de la ville de Paris indiquant les voies ouvertes et les édifices publiques construites depuis 1850 par M. le baron G. E. Haussmann . . . dressé par les géomètres du service du plan de Paris" and thus has been named after the chef de bureau of the Plan de Paris, Deschamps.

117. Davenne, op. cit. Also A. de Royau, *Traité pratique de la voirie à Paris* (Paris: Malateste, 1879); A. des Cilleuls, *Traité de la législation et de l'administration de la voirie urbaine* (Paris: Ducher, 1877). The resulting maps: AN F1a 2000.

118. The recent exhibition *Paris. Haussmann* displayed the expropiation plans surviving in the Service Technique de la Documentation Foncière and illustrated them in its catalog.

119. Regulation of September 28, 1826, reproduced in Davenne, op. cit., p. 421.

120. "... d'obtenir, autant qu'il est possible, par la régularité des lignes un moyen d'embellissement favorable au progrès des arts." De Royau, op. cit., p. 4.
121. 1818 budget: *Présentation des comptes et du règlement définitif du budget de 1818* (Paris: Imprimerie Royale, 1820).
122. Davenne, op. cit., pp. 420–424.
123. Van Zanten, "Visconti architecte-voyer," *Visconti*, pp. 66–71.
124. Undated letter to Rambuteau. Lazare, *Dictionnaire administratif et historique des rues de Paris et des ses monuments*, 1st ed. (1844), using the records of the bureau of Voirie of which he was an official, dates the *alignement* of these streets to 1826–1828.
125. Reproduced in Davenne, op. cit., pp. 505–514.
126. Loyer, op. cit., pp. 231 ff.
127. Ibid., 129 ff.
128. *Recueil des actes administratifs,* I, pp. 52–55.
129. Davenne, op. cit., pp. 140–141.
130. "Un maire ne peut par un arrêté déterminer, pour la construction des maisons, un mode particulier d'architecture, qui ne sera pas commandé par le nécessité de garantir la sûreté de la voie publique" (Ibid., p. 141). See des Cilleuls, op. cit., p. 299, who amplifies this point.
131. Taxil, op. cit., p. 16. Also *Recueil des actes administratifs,* I, pp. 126–128.
132. *Recueil des actes administratifs,* IX, pp. 88–91.
133. As a result of the concern that new construction be healthful. The quite slight remains of this very important archive are in the V. O. 11 series of the Archives de la Seine.
134. *Budget de la Ville de Paris* (Bibliothèque Administrative, Hôtel de Ville, Paris).
135. AS V. o. 11, avenue de l'Opéra.
136. "Monsieurs, jusqu'à ces derniers temps, l'administration de la voirie de Paris a laissé aux constructeurs de maisons la faculté de disposer à leur gré, dans la limite de la hauteur légale, les lignes des balcons, des corniches et des entablements.

"Il en est résulté un grave défaut d'harmonie entre les diverses constructions des mêmes groupes. La plupart des architectes privés, sans s'occuper, en effet, des lignes principales de façade des maisons contiguës, ont, sur beaucoup de points, créé au droit des mitoyennetés, des brisures, des

décrochements de ces lignes magistrales qui forment les effets les plus disgracieux, et ne déprécient pas moins, sous le point de vue du bon goût, chaque maison, que l'ensemble dont elle fait partie.

"L'Ordonnance générale de la ville souffre de ce défaut d'harmonie, et le devoir de l'édilité était d'y remédier.

"C'est pour arriver à ce but que j'ai prescrit, dans les contrats de vente des terrains qui appartiennent à la ville, l'insertion d'une clause qui oblige les acquéreurs à donner aux maisons de chaque îlot les mêmes lignes principales de façade, de manière que les balcons continus, les corniches et les toits soient *autant que possible* sur les mêmes plans.

"Cette disposition est tellement essentielle à l'effet architectonique, que je crois à propos de l'étendre à toute reconstruction de maison opérée, soit par suite d'un percement nouveau, soit par suite d'une simple mise à l'alignement. Le droit de l'administration est aussi incontestable dans ce dernier cas que dans le premier; car, aux termes des règlements, tout constructeurs doit soumettre à l'administration le plan et les coupes cotées de son bâtiment, et executer ses prescriptions. Il résulte de cette obligation règlementaire que l'action de la voirie peut exiger l'harmonie que j'ai en vue dans les lignes principales de l'architecture des maisons." (*Recueil des actes administratifs,* IV, pp. 167–169).
137. Preserved in the library of the Women's Christian Temperance Union, Evanston, Illinois. This citation was pointed out to me by Kathleen Wilson.
138. Davenne, op cit., pp. 443–448, the regulation of this service of January 31, 1830.

CHAPTER 3. THE FOREGROUND: THE FUNDAMENTALS OF REPRESENTATIONAL BUILDING

1. Louis-Pierre Baltard and Amaury Duval, *Paris et ses momumens*, 2 vols. (Paris: authors, 1803 and 1805), I, pp. 2–3. Diderot, *Encyclopédie; ou dictionnaire raisonné des Sciences, des arts et des métiers . . .*, 17 vols. (Paris: Briasson, 1751–1765). "palais," vol. XI (1765). Cf. Quatremère de Quincy, *Architecture,* vol. III (1825), "palais," p. 53.
2. "la résidence du Monarque dans la capitale

de son Royaume." J.-F. Blondel (completed by Pierre Patte), *Cours d'architecture*, 6 vols. (Paris: Desaint, 1771–1777), II, p. 233.

3. "Du reste aucune personne quelque qualifiée qu'elle soit ne peut faire mettre sur la porte de sa maison le titre *palais,* mais seulement celui de l'hôtel."

4. "Un palais est ainsi un édifice qui doit s'élever au dessus des maisons ordinaires et se distinguer au dessus d'elles par les divers moyens que l'architecture peut employer, pour affecter à chacun le degré de richesse et de magnificence qui lui convient."

5. Werner Szambien, "Durand and the Continuity of Tradition," *The Beaux-Arts,* 1982, pp. 18–33.

6. P.-F.-L. Fontaine, *Résidences de souverains,* pp. 12–13; *Journal,* I, pp. 262, 269, 281, 288, 289, 292, 323, 334, 351, 371, 376, 383, 415, 510, 545. Pierre Lavedan, "Projets de Napoléon pour l'ouest de Paris," *La Vie urbaine,* no. 59 (1951), pp. 1–10; "Projets d'aménagement de la rive gauche de la Seine entre les Invalides et le Champs de Mars," *Bulletin de la société de l'histoire de l'art français* (1951), pp. 83–85; Hans-Joachim Hassengier, *Das Palais du Roi de Rome auf dem Hügel von Chaillot* (Frankfurt: Lang, 1983). The drawings: AN N III Seine 1089–1090.

7. Philippe Boudon, *Richelieu, ville nouvelle* (Paris: Dunod, 1978); B. Jestaz, *Jules Hardouin Mansart: l'oeuvre personnel, les méthodes de travail et les collaborateurs,* thesis, Ecole des Chartes, 1962; P. Breillat, *Ville nouvelle, ville modèle: Versailles* (Versailles: Lys, 1985); Danielle Gallet-Guerne and Christian Baulez, *Versailles: dessins d'architecture de la Direction Générale des Bâtiments du Roi,* 2 vols. (Paris: Archives Nationales, 1983, 1989), II.

8. Norbert Elias, *Höfische Gesellschaft* (Darmstadt: Luchterhand, 1969), Chapters III and V. Cf. several seventeenth- and eighteenth-century books on royal power and its representation: Le Maitre, *Le métropole* (Amsterdam: van Gorp, 1682); Willebrand, *Grundriss einer schönen Stadt* (Hamburg and Leipzig: Bohn and Hirscher), 1776. The suggestions made already in the 1930s in Elias's work (focusing on France) have only

recently been extended: Marin, Apostolides, Burke, ops. cit., plus Marin, "Classical, Baroque: Versailles, or the Architecture of the Prince," *Yale French Studies* (1991), pp. 167–182. Also Stephen Greenblatt, *The Power of Forms in the English Renaissance* (Norman, OK: Pilgrim, 1982); Louis Marin, *Utopics: Spatial Play* (Atlantic Heights and London: Humanities Press, 1984), especially Chapters 10 and 11. Cf. Ballon, op. cit., Marie-Louise Biver, *Le Paris de Napoléon* (Paris: Plon, 1965).

9. Jean Bodin, *Six Books on Government* (Oxford: Blackwell, n. d.). Cf. Kantorowiscz, *The King's Two Bodies* (Princeton: Princeton University Press, 1957); Lynn Hunt, *The Family Romance of the French Revolution* (Berkeley: University of California Press, 1992).

10. Strangely enough this was the one great monument of nineteenth-century Paris not published by the government as a book (although the ministre d'état, Achille Fould, planned one – *JD,* February 19, 1856). Baldus's photographs were for this purpose and were published in book form. The progress of its construction was the subject of annual reports by Fould published in the *MU* (reports of February 28, 1855 and February 5, 1856). See F. de Clarac, *Musée de sculpture antique et moderne ou description historique et graphique du Louvre . . .,* 8 vols. (Paris: Imprimerie Royale, 1826–1853), especially I, pp. 237–669. Emmanuel Jacquin and David Van Zanten, *Visconti,* pp. 220–253. Also Fontaine, *Résidences de souverains,* pp. 53–60; Louis Hautecoeur, *Histoire du Louvre: le château – le palais – le musée* (Paris: Morance, 1924); Christine Aulanier, *Histoire du palais et du musée du Louvre,* 10 vols. (Paris: Editions des musées nationaux, 1947–1968); Jean-Pierre Babelon, "L.-T.-J. Visconti et le Louvre," *Etudes offertes à André Chastel* (Paris: Flammarion, 1987), pp. 617–632; Emmanuel Jacquin, "La Seconde République et l'achèvement du Louvre," *Bulletin de la société de l'histoire de Paris et de l'Ile de France* (1988), pp. 375–401; Jean-Claude Daufresne, *Le Louvre et les Tuileries: architectures de papier* (Liège: Mardaga, 1989); Robert Berger, *The*

Palace of the Sun: The Louvre of Louis XIV (University Park: Pennsylvania State University Press, 1993). Also Hubert Damisch, "La colonnade de Perrault et les fonctions de l'ordre classique," *L'Urbanisme de Paris et de l'Europe, 1600–1680*, Pierre Francastel, ed. (Paris: Klinksieck, 1969), pp. 85–94.

11. *MU*, July 26, 1852, p. 1137.

12. All published in Daufresne's volume except Duban's, which was lost.

13. "La décoration extérieure . . . sera conformé à ce qui est fait dans l'aile du Musée et dans l'aile neuve presque entièrement bâtie en face"; . . . "le plan et l'ordonnance sont indiqués par l'état et la décoration des constructions premières, et par la disposition du pavillon de l'Entrée du Musée" (Fontaine, *Résidences de souverains*, pp. 53–60).

14. "Ce passé [embodied in the palaces] n'a-t-il pas de frappantes analogies avec notre époque? Quoi! vous avez un magnifique parallélogramme, une place immense, telle qu'il n'en existe pas une pareille; et vous songez à la diminuer de moitié, à changer sa forme, quand rien ne vous y oblige!" (Pigeory, op. cit., pp. 192–193).

15. "Le caractère de la nouvelle architecture sera emprunté religieusement au vieux Louvre; tous les détails sont déjà moulés, et l'architecte fera abnégation de tout amour-propre pour conserver à ce monument le caractère que ses devanciers lui ont imprimé" (L.-T.-J. Visconti, *Description du modèle représentant l'achèvement du Louvre par M. Visconti, Architecte de l'Empereur* (Paris: Vinchon, 1853), reproduced in *Visconti*, p. 240).

16. In the family's hands.

17. "Ma mission désormais est toute tracée[:] finir le Louvre veut dire raccorder avec ce qui est fait[.] [J]e n'ai donc pas de grands frais d'imagination à faire[;] seulement du bon sens à avoir pour bien choisir" (Biblioteca apostolica Vaticana, Autografi Ferrajoli, Reccolta Visconti, no. 7392: letter of March 12, 1853, to Pietro Ercole Visconti). I owe this citation to Professor Daniela Gallo of the Scuola Normale Superiore, Pisa.

18. Vitet is mentioned warmly in Visconti's "Autobiography" of 1847, *Visconti*, p. 30.

19. "Il faut, selon nous, que le monument exprime quelque chose: pour que le Louvre fut achevé, il faudrait qu'il eut une destination sérieuse réelle: il n'y a pas lieu à construire un palais aujourd'hui; ce qui y a de mieux, ce qui y a de plus sincère, c'est donc que le Louvre reste interrompu: cette interruption sera un témoignage historique qui aura sa valeur et que, pour ma part, je préfère à une achèvement inutile et factice. Laissez donc le Louvre inachevé, arretez le là où il est. . . ." (*MU*, October 5, 1849, pp. 2968–2972; *JD*, same date)

20. L. Vitet, "Le Louvre," *Revue contemporaine*, September 15, 1852, pp. 363–446.

21. "On perdait avec lui [Visconti] non seulement son talent, son gôut, son experience, son culte respectueux de ce noble monument, son scrupuleux désir de le ménager avant tout; on perdait quelque chose de plus rare, une autorité suffisant pour tenir tête aux fantaisies, aux caprices qui assiègent tout architecte. . . ." L. Vitet, "Le nouveau Louvre et les nouvelles Tuileries," *Revue des Deux Mondes*, S2, 64 (July 1, 1866), pp. 57–93, specifically p. 62. Viollet-le-Duc, fils, answers Vitet interestingly: "Réponse à un article de M. Vitet sur le Nouveau Louvre et les Nouvelles Tuileries," *Gazette des architectes et du bâtiment*, IV (1866), pp. 161–165, VI (1868), pp. 98–102.

22. Its subject is given thus among the documents relating to decoration in the Archives Nationales, 64 Aj 63: "L'Empereur, fort de ses destinés, et l'appui qui lui donné la reconnaissance des français pour les bienfaits de Napoléon Ier, clôtère des révolutions et des discordes civiles, rappelle la concorde et l'union, invoque la paix, source des prospérités, fait fleurir la commerce, les arts et l'industrie, honore la religion et convie la France à l'exécution des vastes entreprises qui doivent illustrer son règne." "The Emperor, powerful in his sense of destiny and in the support the French give for the benefits of Napoleon I, suppresses revolutions and civil disorders, reestablishes harmony and union, invokes peace, the source of prosperity, makes flourish commerce and the arts and industry, honors religion and inspires France to the vast enterprises which will mark his reign."

23. *JD*, October 27 and 29, 1808; Fontaine, *Journal*, February 14, 1813.

24. Aulanier, op. cit., Vol. III, "Les trois Salles des Etats"; *JD*, February 15, 1851.

25. A. de Gisors, *Le palais du Luxembourg* (Paris: Plon, 1847).

26. "La plupart de ses événements sont déjà loin de nous; mais le palais de Marie, grand et majesteux comme à son origine, est là pour en perpétuer la mémoire." De Gisors, op. cit., p. 104.

27. Bauchal, op. cit., p. 715.

28. Victor Calliat, *Hôtel de ville de Paris, mesuré, dessiné, gravé et publié par Victor Calliat*, 2 vols. (Paris: author, 1844 and 1856) I, p. 25; Marius Vachon, *L'Ancien hôtel de ville de Paris* (Paris: Quantin, 1882); Caroline Steeves at Columbia University is finishing a doctoral dissertation on the subject of this building.

29. "Les lignes de l'architecture des bâtiments nouveaux correspondent avec une symétrie parfaite à celles des anciennes constructions; les détails de ces dernières ont mêmes étés reproduits dans quelques unes des parties neuves . . ." (Ibid., p. 25). Cf. *MU*, September 15, 1852.

30. "Les vieux édifices ne se transplantent pas plus que les vieux arbres; et, dans l'intérêt de l'art, il est heureux que l'Hôtel de ville soit terminé en restant aux lieux qu'il occupait jadis" (Pigeory, op. cit., p. 510).

31. Katherine Taylor, *The Palais de Justice of Paris: Modernization, Historical Consciousness and Their Pre-History in French Institutional Architecture, 1835–1869*, Ph.D. dissertation, Harvard University, 1989.

32. It is Huyot who thus states his intentions before the Conseil des Bâtiments Civils. The actual pavilion design does not seem eighteenth century, but rather sixteenth.

33. S., "Le Palais de Justice," *Revue des deux mondes* (1836), pp. 287–291.

34. "Le savoir et l'habileté de l'architecte sont parvenus à faire un ensemble de tant de parties distinctes. Son talent souple et fécond s'est prêté à tous les changemens, à satisfait à toutes les convenances, à toutes les demandes de la magistrature qu'on a judicieusement consultée sur toutes choses" (*JD*, August 25, 1836).

35. AN F215914: meeting of November 14, 1836.

36. Michael Driskel, *As Befits a Legend* (Kent, Ohio: Kent State Press, 1993). See his essays "By Competition or Administrative Decree? The Contest for the Tomb of Napoleon in 1841," *Art Journal*, 48, no. 1 (spring 1989), pp. 46–52; "Le Tombeau de Napoléon," *Visconti*, pp. 168–180.

37. Michael Marrinan, *Painting Politics for Louis-Philippe* (New Haven: Yale University Press, 1988), pp. 184–200.

38. "Se contentant de construire des calvaires et des chapelles expiatoires, il [the Restoration] laissa inachévé tous les monuments commencés sous l'Empire, et devait-il en être autrement, puisque, repoussant toute solidarité avec les faits accomplis dans cette période . . . les hommes d'Etat d'alors ne pouvaient consentir à contribuer à l'apothéose du souverain qu'ils nommaient l'usurpateur déchu, en complétant ou en achevant les monuments de son règne. . . .

"La révolution de Juillet, en supprimant une dynastie, fondait un principe. Elle renouait la chaîne interrompue des conquêtes sociales réalisées depuis le commencement du siècle; et, par cela même qu'elle adoptait toutes les illustrations, toutes les gloires du passé, sans répudier une seule des traditions conformes au voeu national, elle s'engageait à donner aux unes et aux autres une juste satisfaction. Dès ce moment, plus d'équivoque, plus d'incertitude. La réhabilitation de la mémoire de Napoléon est bientôt suivie de celle des hauts faits d'armes qui illustrèrent la République et l'Empire.

"Une ère nouvelle vient de s'ouvrir pour l'architecture, et lui rend la place qu'elle avait perdue. . . . Comme tous les mouvements populaires, celui de Juillet avait préludé, par la destruction, à sa tâche, qui était de réparer et de finir ce que les autres avaient commencé de beau ou d'utile." (Pigeory, op. cit., pp. 10–15)

39. AN F13 549. *MU*, May 25, 31, June 1, 1833; *JD*, May 8, 29, June 23, 1833; *RGA*, II (1841), cols. 350–352; III (1842), cols. 190–192.

40. We lack a systematic study of Thiers's intervention in the arts. See Henri Malo, "M. Thiers et les artistes de son temps," *Revue*

de Paris, 31 (Julÿ 1, 1924), pp. 140–159. Otherwise all we have is scattered but numerous references in, for example, Albert Boime's *Thomas Couture* (London-New Haven: Yale University Press, 1980), Michael Marrinan's *Painting Politics*, or Jacques de Caso's *David d'Angers* (Paris: Flammarion, 1988). The precise angle of Thiers's intervention changed with his position in the cabinet: October–December 1831: ministre de l'intérieur; December 1831–April 1834: ministre de commerce et des travaux publics; April 1834–February 1836: ministre de l'intérieur. During his first premiership he initiated the translation of the ashes of Napoleon although his ministre de l'intérieur, Rémusat, was directly in charge.

41. In the documents in AN F*13* 549 we see the following:

Arc de Triomphe: Blouet named architect, 1832. Sculptors proposed by Thiers, 1834: Cortot, Rude, Etex; projects for crowning solicited by Thiers from Pradier, Rude, and Bayre.

Madeleine: architect Huvé retained. Artists proposed by Thiers in 1834: pediment, Lamarre; altar group, Marichetti; doors, Triquetti; ceiling, Delaroche. (Ziegler given apse half-dome in 1835, Delaroche withdraws.)

Panthéon: architect Destouches retained; as pediment sculptor, David d'Angers.

Chamber of Deputies: architect de Joly retained. Pediment, Cortot; library ceiling, Delacroix.

Saint-Denis: architect Debret retained.

Colonne de Juillet: Duc, *inspecteur* under architect Alavoine, appointed architect upon the latter's death (1834). Sculptor Dumont retained.

"Palais d'Orsay": architect Lacornée retained; Léon Vaudoyer appointed his *inspecteur*.

Musée de l'Histoire Naturelle: architect Rohault de Fleury retained; Théodore Labrouste named his *inspecteur*.

Ecole des Beaux-Arts: Duban named architect, 1832, replacing Debret; Delaroche commissioned to paint hemicycle, 1836, apparently in compensation for Madeleine ceiling.

Collège de France: Letarouilly named architect, 1832.

42. The annual budget for this was usually 200,000 francs. AN F*13* 1021–1022. See Barry Bergdoll, "Metteur en scène des fêtes de juillet et de fastes du IIe Empire," *Visconti*, pp. 142–161.

43. In the narrower field of art policy, see Marrinan, op. cit.

44. De cette entrée qui aura tout le caractère de grandeur convenable, les regards, traversant la Place Dauphine, découvriront la statue équestre du Pont Neuf, le Louvre et les Tuileries" (*JD*, August 25, 1836).

45. Pigeory, op. cit., 201–206. The ceremony decorations are preserved in the plates of Percier and Fontaine, *Description des cérémonies et des fêtes qui ont eu lieu pour le mariage de Sa Majesté l'Empereur Napoléon à S. A. I. Madame l'Archiduchesse Marie-Louise d'Autriche* (Paris: Didot, 1810). Cf. *Fêtes à l'occasion du mariage de S. M. Napoléon, Empereur des Français, avec Marie-Louise, archiduchesse d'Autriche* (Paris: Soyer, 1810).

46. Cf. Rambuteau, *Compte-rendu de l'administration du départment de la Seine et de la ville de Paris pendant l'année 1836* (Paris: Préfecture de la Seine, 1837), pp. 124–126.

47. Ibid., pp. 125–127.

48. Baltard's assistant Max Vauthier was immediately in charge (Vachon, op. cit., pp. 54–55). This made permanent earlier temporary arrangements for formal ceremonies when the court was covered and sometimes decorated elaborately, for example on the occasion of the marriage of the Duc d'Orléans in 1837 when Visconti erected a space known from the drawing his draftsman Jules Bouchet executed and the family of Rambuteau kept (*Visconti*, p. 153; on exhibit at the Galerie Bayser et Turquin, March 1989).

49. *Ill*, XXVI (August 23, September 1, 1855), pp. 139–140, 145.

50. "Lorsque ces grands projets auront été entièrement réalisés, quelles seront les impressions d'un étranger qui, entrant pour la première fois dans Paris par la longue avenue de Vincennes, après avoir remarqué les hautes colonnes de la barrière du Trône,

verra à l'extremité d'une large rue, à la rencontre de deux boulevards magnifiques, la fontaine de la Bastille et le vaste canal dont elle paraît être la source? quelle sensation épouvera-t-il, lorsqu'après avoir traversé plusieurs places embellis par des monuments d'utilité publics, après avoir aperçu sur le cours de la Seine ses ponts, ses quais nouveaux, il arrivera par une large et belle rue à la colonnade du Louvre? lorsque, traversant ensuite la grande cour de ce palais et l'avant-cour plus grande encore, le vestibule et le portique de la place d'armes du Carrousel, passant sous l'arc du Carrousel, après avoir laissé de côté la fontaine à la rencontre de deux axes; lorsqu'en entrant dans la cour d'honneur du palais des Tuileries et de là dans le jardin, en suivant toujours la même direction à travers la place Louis XV et les Champs-Elysées jusqu'à la barrière de Chaillot, il s'arrêtera sous l'immense arc de triomphe élévé à la gloire des armées françaises, au sommet de la montagne des Champs-Elysées, quelles seront ses réflexions sur un aussi grand nombre de merveilles? Que pensera-t-il de la réunion des choses prodigieuses dont cette prompte traversée de la ville lui aura offert l'étonnant spectacle? Certes, malgré les préventions les plus contraires, il ne pourra s'empêcher de confesser qu'en aucun autre lieu du monde il n'existe rien de plus admirable; il félicitera les Français d'avoir été gouvernés successivement, depuis Henri IV, par plusieurs souverains, qui, malgré tant de revers et de désastres, auront su les faire jouir des bienfaits d'une civilisation brillante, et qui, par un sincère amour de la patrie, par les avantages d'une sage économie, ont su trouver les moyens de réparer les maux dont le sort les a tant de fois accablés." Op. cit., pp. 60–61. The same fragment is published with Fontaine's *Journal*, Vol. II, pp. 1131–1132.

51. "Debout, découvert, tenant la constitution à la main, j'ai passé en ligne droite sur les Champs-Elysées, les Tuileries, le Louvre, la rue du faubourg Saint-Antoine." Mona Ozouf, *La fête révolutionnaire, 1789–1799* (Paris: Gallimard, 1976), p. 217, quoting *Procès-verbal très intéressant du voyage aérien qui a eu lieu aux Champs-Elysées le 18 septembre 1791* . . . (Paris: Bailly, 1791). A century later Paul Léon was to lead readers down this same axis to convince them of the need to save monumental Paris: "La beauté de Paris," *Revue de Paris* (November 15, 1909), pp. 280–302, especially p. 293. To observe the importance of "scenographic" axes, however, is not to explain their power. Françoise Paul-Lévy (*La Ville en croix,* Paris: Dunod, 1984) analyzes Haussmann's axial reorganization of Paris diagramatically, taking off from Lévi-Strauss's analysis of the Bororo village in his *Tristes tropiques* (1955). See also her *Anthropologie de l'Espace* (Paris: Centre Pompidou, 1984). She thus emphasizes the symbolic quality of axes, like Mircea Eliade (*Forgerons et alchimistes,* Paris: Flammarion, 1956) and Joseph Rykwert (*The Idea of a Town,* Princeton: Princeton University Press, 1976) in other contexts. But this misses the active, ceremonial quality of such axes and the fact that they were created for the sovereign, confronting the city as he passes down them, and here they would seem to relate more to the structure of the royal entry ceremony (L. M. Bryant, *The King and the City in the Parisian Royal Entry Ceremony: Ritual and Art in the Renaissance,* Geneva: Droz, 1986) and to court ceremonial where everything and everyone was positioned to be legible before the eyes of the monarch. (See Antoine de Courtin, *Nouveau traité de la civilité,* 1671 with numerous later editions.) The experience of traversing a frontal, legible space is explored in David Le Roy's *Histoire de la disposition et des différtes formes que les chrétiens ont donnés à leurs temples* . . . (1674) and in Le Camus de Mézieres' *Génie de l'architecture* (1780). It has an analogy with the pictorial and the theatrical. I explored it tentatively in "Architectural Composition," *The Architecture of the Ecole des Beaux-Arts* (Arthur Drexler, ed.), pp. 142–185. See Louis Marin, *Le Portrait du Roi,* "Le Roi et son géomètre"; "Frontiers of Utopia: Past and Present," *Critical Inquiry,* 19, no. 3 (winter 1993), pp. 397–420. Cf. Foucault's *Surveiller et punir.* With Camillo Sitte's *Städtebau* of 1889 axiality dissolves.

52. *JD*, May 4, 1814; Ozouf, op. cit., Chapter VI; Françoise Waquet, *Les fêtes royales sous la Restauration ou l'ancien régime retrouvé* (Geneva: Droz, 1981); Lawrence Bryant, op. cit.
53. "Le Dieu de Saint Louis a revelé votre trône, vous raffermirez ses autels. *Dieu et le Roi,* telle est notre devise, . . ."
54. "Tous les corps de l'Etat et les grands du Royaume assistaient à la cérémonie."
55. I take the details of these events from the Orleanist *JD*. See G. de Bertier de Sauvigny, *La Restauration,* new edition (Paris: Flammarion, 1963), pp. 441 ff.
56. Bertier de Sauvigny, op. cit., pp. 441–456.
57. Bryant, op. cit., pp. 23–24. Claude Perrault was the architect: Antoine Picon, *Claude Perrault, 1613–1688, ou la curiosité d'un classique* (Paris: Picard, 1988), pp. 223–230; Christophe Frank, "Les artistes de l'entrée de Louis XIV en 1660," *Bulletin de la société de l'histoire de l'art français* (1989), pp. 53–74.
58. "Aucune troupe ne formait la haie, pas même la garde nationale; aussi le peuple se précipitait affamé, non pas de voir, mais de toucher le prince. Ce n'étaient pas que de serremens de main tout le long de la route. Les chevaux pouvaient à peine marcher. Des ouvriers les tenaient par la bride, et les princes avaient les deux mains mêlées à celles du peuple, qui se renouvelait avec une affluence prodigieuse" (*JD,* August 5, 1830).
59. "M. le duc d'Orléans s'inclina à plusieurs reprises devant la colonne . . . et les acclamations redoublèrent."
60. "Une chose remarquable: durant le long trajet, et au milieu d'un enthousiasme extraordinaire, les cris de *Vive la Charte! Vive le duc d'Orléans!* se firent seuls entendre. Le mot de république ne fut pas une seule fois prononcé, même dans le faubourg; et par un instinct merveilleux de légalité, le peuple, qui se retenait à peine de crier *Vive Louis-Philippe VII!*, semblaient ne pas vouloir devancer la décision des Chambres, auxquelles seules appartient de placer sur une autre tête, à la condition du maintien et du développement de nos libertés, cette couronne que la branche ainée des Bourbons a laissé tomber à terre, et que le peuple ne consentira jamais à lui rendre."
61. *JD*, August 10, 1830.
62. Marie-Louise Biver, *Le Paris de Napoléon,* pp. 187–188.
63. *JD,* May 30, 1837.
64. *JD,* June 5, 1837.
65. "La Ville de Paris connaît mon affection pour elle! Je suis heureux et fier de lui présenter ma fille d'adoption. Les Parisiens l'aimeront!"
66. "Je vous remercie de tout mon coeur, mes amis! Je suis bien sensible à votre accueil. . . ."
67. *JD,* December 2 and 3, 1852.
68. "Le nouveau règne que vous inaugurez aujourd'hui . . . est, vous venez de le déclarer, le résultat légal de la volonté de tout un peuple qui consolide au milieu du calme ce qu'il avait fondé au sien des agitations."
69. Erected by Baltard and Séchan.
70. This seems suggestive of the traditional royal "laying on of hands." Marc Block's *Les rois thaumaturges* (new edition, Paris: Gallimard, 1983) ends with the self-conscious efforts to resuscitate this for Charles X's *sacre* in 1826.
71. Barry Bergdoll analyzes the political theater of this *entrée* in his Ph.D. dissertation, *Léon Vaudoyer,* Columbia University Press, 1989.
72. *Ill,* XX (October 23, 1852), pp. 263–266.
73. "*Le Patrie* avait annoncé que ce bel triomphe était dû aux soins du Ministère d'Etat; mais le *Moniteur,* en rectifiant cette nouvelle, a declaré que toutes les manifestations de la Ville de Paris avaient été spontanées, et que le gouvernement n'avait rien fait pour les provoquer."
The Versailles government of 1871 never entered the city ceremonially. Until 1879 it planned to maintain the legislature at Versailles, the Senate in the eighteenth-century palace theater; the Chambre des Deputés in a specially constructed space (sketched by Jules de Joly fils, architect of the Chamber). Immediately after the suppression of the Commune a formal military review was held at the Longchamps racetrack in the far corner of the Bois de Boulogne, the government dignitaries coming directly from and returning directly to Versailles.
74. *JD,* May 24–26, May 30, June 2, 1885.

75. Todd Porterfield, op. cit.; Pigeory, op. cit., pp. 623–628. Fontaine (*Journal*, II, p. 895) was consulted about the memorial and on May 6, 1831, confided to his diary that he was "peu touché des honneurs qu'en différents temps j'ai vu les parties vainqueurs exiger des vaincus, peu certain de la durée de ces constructions que la passion élève, et qu'une autre passion détruit" – "Little affected by the honors that in another time I have seen the victors require of the vanquished, little convinced of the permanence of these constructions erected by emotion [and] which another emotion destroys," he suggested that the victims be commemorated at Père-Lachaise.

76. "Indépendamment des édifices destinés à l'habitation des têtes couronnées, il est des monuments qui annonce encore plus spécialement la gloire et la magnificence des Monarques, ainsi que la splendeur des cités où ces monuments se trouvent élevés" (J.-F. Blondel, *Cours*, II, p. 253).

77. Ballon, op. cit., pp. 199–207.

78. Bryant, op. cit., pp. 208–209; *L'entrée triomphante de leurs Majestés Louis XIV, roi de France et de Navarre, et de Marie Thérèse d'Autriche, son épouse, dans la ville de Paris* . . . (Paris: Lepetit, 1662).

79. Bausset, *Mémoires anecdotiques sur l'intérieur du Palais et sur quelques événements de l'Empire* (Paris: Baudoin, 1827); L. de Lanzac de Laborie, *Paris sous Napoléon* (Paris: Plon, 1905), II "Administration, Grands Travaux," Chapter IV; Biver, *Le Paris de Napoléon*. The Arc de Triomphe was projected by the Emperor at the place de la Bastille but Chalgrin convinced him that the Etoile site would be both more dramatic and more economical.

80. "S. M. l'Empereur revenant de la compagne d'Austerlitz, reçu par le Président de la Députation et suivi par les drapeaux qu'il destine au Corps Législatif, venant faire l'ouverture de la session de 1805."

81. There is an interesting editorial in the *JD*, January 18, 1816, about whether the symbolic traces of the Napoleonic regime (like N's carved into building decoration) should be expunged from Paris's monuments concluding that it was too dangerous to leave them.

82. Fontaine, *Journal*, II, p. 704.

83. Barry Bergdoll, "Le Panthéon/Sainte-Geneviève au XIXe siècle"; Isabelle Lemaistre, "De Sainte-Geneviève au Panthéon: les différentes programmes de sculpture"; Gerard Augier, "La coupole de Baron Gros," *Le Panthéon: symbole des révolutions* (Montreal: Centre canadien d'architecture), 1989.

84. Marrinan, op. cit., Chapter IV.

85. Albert Boime, "The Quasi-Open Competitions of the Quasi-Legitimate July Monarchy," *Arts Magazine,* 59 (April 1985), pp. 94–105.

86. Neil McWilliam, "David d'Angers and the Pantheon Commission: Politics and Public Works Under the July Monarchy," *Art History*, V, no. 4 (December 1982), pp. 426–446.

87. Michael Driskel, "By Competition or Administrative Decree."

88. Pigeory, op. cit., pp. 200–206. That statue was removed in 1848. Michael Driskel informs me it has found a home in front of the American Hospital in Neuilly. In the 1840s statues of Philippe-Auguste and Saint Louis were placed atop Ledoux's twin columns at the place du Trône and the elephant of the Bastille was to be reerected there (*RGA* II [1842] col. 473).

89. Bruno Foucart, Albert Boime, Michael Marrinan, Neil McWilliam, and Michael Driskel in numerous articles and several books have treated the artistic policy of the Monarchy of July as a unified whole.

90. The bibliography of Second Empire art policy is much larger and more various than that of the previous regimes, in part because of the emergence of a freer art market (the point of Patricia Mainardi's book cited earlier). There are studies of professional life (Harrison and Cynthia White, *Canvases and Careers,* New York: Wiley, 1965); of state art patronage (Mainardi, op. cit.; Pierre Angrand, "La commande des portraits officiels sous Napoléon III," *Gazette des Beaux-Arts,* 6S 70 (1967), p. 185, and "L'état mécène: période autoritaire du Second Empire (1851–1860), *Gazette des Beaux-Arts,* 6S 71 (1968), pp. 303–345); of state museum policy (Daniel Sherman, *Worthy Monuments: Art Museums and the Poli-*

tics of Culture in Nineteenth-Century France, Cambridge: Harvard University Press, 1989); of administrators (Philippe de Chennevières, "Souvenirs d'un directeur des beaux-arts," *L'Artiste,* 1883–1889 (shortly to be the subject of a book by Jane Roos); *Mémoires du comte Horace de Viel-Castel sur le règne de Napoléon III (1851–1864),* ed. Pierre Josserand (Paris: Le Prat, 1942); *Correspondance générale de Prosper Mérimée)* and of individual state artists, like Carpeaux (Anne Wagner, *Jean-Baptiste Carpeaux, Sculptor of the Second Empire* (New Haven and London: Yale University Press, 1986), Couture (Albert Boime, *Thomas Couture and the Eclectic Vision,* New Haven: Yale University Press, 1980), Lehmann (Marie-Madeleine Aubrun, *Henri Lehmann, 1814–1882, catalogue raisonné de l'oeuvre,* 2 vols. (Paris: Centre Nationale des Lettres, 1984), Mueller (Nancy Davenport, "Charles-Louis Mueller et ses décorations peintes au Louvre," *Bulletin de la société de l'histoire de l'art français,* 1986, pp. 145–163). See also the exhibition catalog *La sculpture française au XIXe siècle,* Grand Palais, 1986. We lack, however, a focused characterization of the regime of the sort that Foucart, Marrinan, McWilliam, and Driskel have formulated for the Monarchy of July. The short revolutionary moment in between is a different matter: T. J. Clark, *The Absolute Bourgeois: Artists and Politics in France, 1848–1851* (New York: Graphic Society, 1973).

Cf. H. N. Boon, *Rêve et réalité dans l'oeuvre économique et sociale de Napoléon III* (The Hague: Nijhoff, 1936); Georges Poisson, "La statuaire commémorative parisienne sous le Second Empire," *Gazette des Beaux-Arts,* 6S III (1988), pp. 93–102.

91. Victor Calliat, op. cit, vol. II. Lee Johnson, *The Paintings of Eugène Delacroix: A Critical Catalogue,* vol. 5 (Oxford: Clarendon, 1989), pp. 133–145.

92. *Henri Lehmann,* pp. 79–116.

93. Emile Le Senne, *Les projets de couronnement de l'Arc de Triomphe de l'Etoile* (Paris: Champion, 1911).

94. Bergdoll, *Panthéon,* p. 226. A cartoon of Amaury-Duval's painting was erected and lasted until the end of the Empire. One might expand this discussion to include the reconstruction of the monuments of Paris after the Commune. See, for example, Charles Garnier's series of articles in *Le Temps,* September 5, 7, and 9, 1871. (I owe this citation to Christopher Mead.)

95. Just how the iconography was determined here and in the cases of the other representational buildings of Paris is unclear. There usually was a committee of artists and functionaries in charge, as we know there was in the instance of Duban's contemporaneous restoration of the old Louvre (AN 64 Aj 18: Duban's letter of May 5, 1849, proposing the membership of that committee, Henri Labrouste, Viollet-le-Duc, Lassus, Lacornée). That committee would have overseen the attribution of the work to different artists and also approved the preliminary models they prepared. But just who constituted that committee in the case of the New Louvre and whether they (as opposed to the architect) established the iconographic system I cannot say beyond noting that the Bonapartist sculptor Lemaire appears in some documents as having an important advisory role. See Charles Millard, "Préault's Commissions for the New Louvre: Patronage and Politics in the Second Empire," *Burlington Magazine,* 131 (September 1989), pp. 625–630; D. Van Zanten, "Architectes, sculpteurs et peintres dans la décoration des bâtiments publics au milieu du XIXe siècle," *Milieux,* 32, pp. 66–73.

96. *JD,* 28, October 30, 1808. Clarac, op. cit., presents the Napoleonic iconography in great detail.

97. Glenn Benge, *Antoine Bayre: Sculptor of Romantic Realism* (University Park: Pennsylvania State University Press, 1984), pp. 56–59.

98. Boime, *Couture,* pp. 189–229, 283–291; Pierre Vaisse, "Couture et le Second Empire," *Revue de l'art* 37 (1977), pp. 43–68; Davenport, loc. cit.; Aulanier, op. cit., vol. 3, p. 49. A competing point might have been the court of the Old Louvre where Louis-Philippe had placed the commemorative equestrian statue of the dead crown prince but which Napoleon III left

void. Early in the 1850s Duban proposed moving the Fontaine des Innocents there. Again, August 10, 1856, the *JD* reports that a wooden mock-up of a statue of Henri IV has been erected there, but that is the last we hear of it.

99. *Revue des beaux-arts,* X (1859), pp. 62 ff.

100. "Les monuments, créations de l'homme dont s'embellit l'oeuvre de Dieu, sont de deux natures. Les uns ont étés conçus et exécutés suivant un plan unique, où le génie de l'artiste a pu se développer sans entraves et former un tout complet: là, si toutes les parties ne présentent pas entre elles l'accord des lignes et l'harmonie, la faute en est à l'auteur seul. Les autres résultent des travaux successifs, entreprises à différentes époques, sur des plans souvent modifiés; et ici, le talent de l'architecte qui vient y mettre la dernière main, ne peut prétendre qu'à la gloire de tirer le meilleur parti possible de l'oeuvre de ses devanciers. Il faut qu'il se soumette aux exigences des localités, aux vices des constructions, aux habitudes d'un autre temps, au conditions d'un autre emploi; il faut qu'il adopte des travaux et des plans les plus opposés peut-être à ceux que méditoit sa pensée, et qu'il les fasse entrer forcément dans l'achèvement de l'édifice: semblable à un poëte que l'on chargeroit de l'exécution d'une oeuvre tragique, à la condition d'y comprendre des actes déjà tracés et des scènes déjà faites. Peut-on nier que dans ce cas, sa tâche ne soit pénible, plus difficule, s'il étoît le maître de concevoir et d'exécuter le monument dans son ensemble et dans ses détails?" Jules de Joly, *Coups, élévations et détails de la restauration de la Chambre des Deputés* (Paris: Leclere, 1840). Cf. Violaine Lanselle, "Le Palais Bourbon et l'Hôtel de Lassay, *Monuments historiques,* 144 (April-May, 1986), pp. 109–132. Fontaine confided these same sentiments to his *Journal,* February 16, 1816, I, p. 510.

101. op. cit. II, p. 535. Again, Richelieu was claimed to be the architect of his chateau and ducal capital, Richelieu: Philippe Boudon, *Richelieu,* p. 161.

102. Vanvitelli, *Dichriarazione dei disegni del reale palazzo di Caserta* (Naples: Regia Stamperia, 1751). Cf. George Hersey, *Archi-tecture, Poetry and Number in the Royal Palace of Caserta* (Cambridge: MIT Press, 1983).

103. *Journal,* I, p. 472, August 19, 1815.

104. "Elle laisse les soins des autres édifices qui lui appartiennent à différénts tribunaux qui connaissent des réparations qu'il convient de faire pour les entretenir en bon état."

105. Bruno Pons, *De Paris à Versailles, 1699–1736: les sculpteurs ornemanistes parisiens et l'art décoratif des bâtiments du roi* (Strasbourg: University of Strasbourg, 1986), especially pp. 177 ff.

106. Gourlier et al., *Choix des edifices . . .,* gives costs.

107. AN F13 549.

108. Fontaine, *Journal,* I, pp. 106, 126, 150, 192, 220, 253, 321, 355, 495, 537, 557, etc.

109. AN F70 192.

110. AN O5 1.

111. Fontaine, *Résidences de souverains,* pp. 330–339.

112. Paris, Institut d'Art et Archéologie, Fondation Jacques Doucet, MS 15.

113. Jean-Marc Léri, "Le Palais du quai d'Orsay (1810–1871)," *Bulletin de la société de l'histoire de l'art français* (1976), pp. 387–393; A.-L. Lusson, *Notice nécrologique sur Jacques Lacornée, architecte* (Paris: Société Libre des Beaux-Arts, 1856).

114. "Je consulte aussi les monumens de France élevés sous Louis 14, car il faut vous dire cher cousin que cette époque a été admirable pour la France[.] [E]lle a produit des Monumens tels que Versailles[,] St Cloud[,] une grande partie du Louvre[,] la Monnaie [sic], les Tuileries, les Invalides, le Panthéon [sic] que sais-je des monumens qui seraient enviés par l'Italie . . . [L]a capitale du Monde n'a seulement que cette époque qui est un *grand cachet.*" (Visconti's emphasis) Biblioteca apostolica. Visconti wrongly attributes the Monnaie and the Panthéon to Louis XIV's reign.

115. Haussmann speaking before the Senate, June 6, 1861 (*JD,* June 8, 1861). I owe this to Professor David Jordan who sees it as a fundamental glimpse of Haussmann's ideal.

116. J.-M. Pérouse de Montclos, *Louis-Etienne Boullée, 1728–1799, de l'architecture clas-*

sique à l'architecture révolutionnaire (Paris: Arts et Métiers Graphiques, 1969); Wolfgang Herrmann, *Laugier and Eighteenth-Century French Theory* (London: Zwemmer, 1962); Joseph Rykwert, *On Adam's House in Paradise: The Idea of the Primitive Hut in Architecture* (New York: Museum of Modern Art, 1972); Allan Braham, *The Architecture of the French Enlightenment* (Berkeley: University of California Press, 1980). See Chapter 6 of my *Designing Paris*.

117. *Prozess der Civilization* (Basel: Haus zum Falken, 1939) (English: *The Civilizing Process*, New York: Urizen, 1978) and *Höfische Gesellschaft,* 1969. Focused architectural applications: Hubert Damisch, "Louvre"; Philippe Boudon, *Richelieu;* Louis Marin, *Portrait du Roi,* Apostolides, op. cit. Cf. Joseph Rykwert, *The First Moderns,* Cambridge: MIT Press, 1980; Alberto Perez-Gomez, *Architecture and the Crisis of Modern Science* (Cambridge: MIT Press, 1983). Cf. the parallel "New Historicist reformulation of English Renaissance culture: Stephen Greenblatt, op. cit. Also the classics, Kantorowicz, op. cit.; Marc Bloch, op. cit.

118. Foucault in *Les mots et les choses* (Paris: Gallimard, 1966) emphasizes the general mentality over concrete situations; Peter Burke's recent *Fabrication of Louis XIV* (London and New Haven: Yale University Press, 1992) attempts to balance the competing constructions.

119. Apostolides, op. cit., p. 31.

120. "Que si l'architecture a tant de part au travail, au péril & à la victoire, croyez, Messieurs, qu'elle n'en a pas moins à la magnificence du Triomphe. Elle érige d'abord des Trophées sur le champ de bataille, qu'elle enrichit des dépouilles des enemis. Elle rassemble les os des Citoyens qui sont morts en combattant pour la patrie, . . .

"Ensuite l'architecture prépare une entrée au Vainqueur. . . .

"Car c'est alors que l'architecture étale ce qu'elle a de plus grand & de plus magnifique: lorsque la fortune & la victoire ont mis entre les mains du vainqueur les richesses des nations soumises. C'est alors qu'elle n'épargne rien pour orner un pays de bâtiments somptueux, de Temples, de Basiliques, de Théâtres, de Cirques, de Portiques, de Bains, & de tous ces autres chefs d'oeuvres qui font le plaisir des Citoyens et l'admiration des étrangers." François Blondel, *Cours d'architecture enseigné dans l'academie d'architecture* (Paris: Lambert Roulland, 1675).

121. Pierre Clément, *Histoire de Colbert et de son administration* (Paris: Didier, 1874) and *Lettres, instructions et mémoires de Colbert,* 10 vols. (Paris: Imprimerie Impériale, 1861–1882); Jules Guiffrey, *Comptes des bâtiments du Roi sous le règne de Louis XIV* (Paris: Imprimérie Nationale, 1881); Nicole Felkay in *Colbert, 1619–1683* (Paris: Hôtel de la Monnaie, 1983).

122. Jestaz, op. cit.; Gallet-Guerne, op. cit.

123. Anthony Blunt, "The Hypnerotomachia in Seventeenth Century France," *Journal of the Warburg and Courtauld Institutes,* I, no. 2 (1937), pp. 117–137. Louis Savot (notes by François Blondel), *Architecture française* (Paris: Clouzier l'aîné, 1673); André Félibien, *Dissertation touchant sur l'architecture antique et l'architecture gothique* (Paris, 1699, p. 179).

124. "Car quelque idée avantageuse que Vitruve ait donnée de l'architecture antique, Poliphile semble encore la représenter avec plus de majesté et de grandeur: il l'a fait envisager comme la seule science qui régit tous les Arts & qui embrasse elle-mêmes les notions les plus sublimes. Il rapport à cette science non seulement l'ordonnance & la construction de toutes sortes d'édifices, mais encore l'intelligence parfaite de ce qui doit décorer & accompagner ces grandes ouvrages." Ibid.

125. Quatremère de Quincy, *Architecture,* I (1788), "Colonna"; J.-G. Legrand, *Songe de Poliphile* (Paris: Didot, 1805); Huyot, Bibliothèque Doucet MS 15; Alice Friedman, "Academic Theory and A.-L.-T. Vaudoyer's 'Dissertation sur l'architecture," *Art Bulletin,* 67 (1985), pp. 110–123; Hippolyte Fortoul, "L'Arc de Triomphe," *La France littéraire,* 26 (1836), pp. 67–82. Cf. Charles Nodier, *Franciscus Colonna* (Paris: Rechener, 1844); Gérard de Nerval, "Voyage à Cythèra," *L'Artiste,* S4, vol. 1 (June 30, 1844), pp. 129–131, 225–228.

126. On professionalism: Harold Perkin, *The Rise of Professional Society* (London: Routledge, 1989).

127. Aulanier, op. cit., vol. I.

128. Henri Delaborde, "M. Lefuel, architecte," *Encyclopédie d'architecture*, 3S 1 (1882), pp. 83–88.

129. *Ill*, June 12, 1869, p. 371; *JD*, July 8, 1869 (review by Adolphe Viollet-le-Duc).

130. The architectural sections of the *Grammaire* were first published in Blanc's *Gazette des Beaux-Arts* in 1861–1864. The critique: *Le Temps*, October 30, 1868. Katherine Taylor convincingly treats this as the central review of the series inspired by the structure.

131. "Les guichets du Louvre . . . sont . . . un des chefs d'oeuvre de l'architecture contemporaine, une des ces trouvailles définitives, un de ces entreprises absolument réussies, comme celles que nous ont valu, dans des ordres d'art et de besoins différents, la façade et le vestibule du nouveau Palais de Justice, les Halles Centrales, et le grand escalier de l'Opéra." Delaborde, "Lefuel," p. 87.

CHAPTER 4. THE BACKGROUND: THE FUNDAMENTALS OF PRIVATE AND INSTITUTIONAL BUILDING

1. Fontaine, *Journal*, I, pp. 38, 46, 52–55, 60, 63, 70–71, 74–76; the editors illustrate the evolution of the street in plans, pp. 48–49. Also Werner Szambien, *De la rue des Colonnes à la rue de Rivoli* (Paris: Délégation à l'Action Artistique, 1992).

2. Cf. Blondel, *Cours d'architecture,* vol. II (1771), Chapter VI, pp. 240 ff., on the correct articulation of such subordinate buildings, without orders. Also the instances of Karlsruhe and Mannheim: Helmut Friedmann, "Alt-Mannheim in Wandel seiner Physionomie, Struktur und Funktionen (1606–1965)," *Forschungen des deutschen Landeskunde*, Bad Godesburg, 1968; K. G. Fecht, *Geschichte der Haupt-und Residenzstadt Karlsruhe* (Karlsruhe; Macklot, 1887).

3. "Si le Roi juge à propos que l'on bâtisse aux environs de ses maisons ou châteaux, soit pour en rendre l'aspect plus agréable, ou pour la commodité publique, ce doit toujours être en conformité des plans qui sont agréés par sa Majesté, et sur les alignements donnés par la Surintendant des Bâtiments . . ." op. cit., I, p. 536.

4. Hilary Ballon is currently finishing a manuscript on the Collège and its urban situation.

5. That extension decreed May 3, 1848; the funds appropriated August 4, 1851; the expropriations declared of "utilité publique" December 23, 1852. See "La Grande Croisée de Paris," *Haussmann. Paris*, pp. 64–65.

6. Cf. Pierre Pinon, "Les conceptions urbaines au milieu du XIXe siècle," *Haussmann. Paris*, pp. 44–50.

7. This is a very large topic, two recent general studies of which are Paul Rabinow, *French Modern: Norms and Forms of the Social Environment* (Cambridge: MIT Press, 1989); Brian Ladd, *Urban Planning and Civic Order in Germany, 1860–1914* (Cambridge: Harvard University Press, 1990). See also Françoise Choaye, *La règle et le modèle: sur la théorie de l'urbanisme* (Paris: Seuil, 1980).

8. "Pour qu'une *ville* soit belle, il faut que les principales rues conduisent aux portes; qu'elles soient perpendiculaires les uns aux autres, autant qu'il est possible, afin que les encoignures des maisons soient à angles droits; qu'elles aient huit toises de large, & quatre pour les petites rues. Il faut encore que la distance d'une rue à celle qui lui est parallèle, soit telle qu'entre l'une et l'autre il y reste un espace pour deux maisons de bourgeois, dont l'une a la vue dans une rue, et l'autre celle qui lui est opposée. Chacune des ces maisons doit avoir environ cinq à six toises de larges, sur sept à huit d'enfoncement, avec une cour de pareille grandeur: ce qui donne la distance d'une rue à l'autre de trente-deux à trente-trois toises. Dans le concours des rues, on pratique des places dont la principale est celle où les grandes rues aboutissent, & on décore ces places en conservant une uniformité dans les façades des hôtels ou maisons qui les entourent, & avec des statues et des fontaines. Si avec cela les maisons sont bien bâtis, & leurs façades décorées, il y aura peu de choses à désirer." (J.-F. Blondel), "Ville," *Encyclopédie,* vol. XVII (1765), p. 277.

9. Gallet-Guerne, op. cit.

10. "Dans l'intérieur de Rhodes . . . on ne voyait point une petite maison à côté d'une grande; toutes les habitations étoient d'égale hauteur et offroient la même ordonnance d'architecture, de manière que la *ville* entière ne semble former qu'un seul édifice" (Quatremère's emphasis). Quatremère de Quincy, *Architecture: encyclopédie méthodique,* 3 vols. (Paris: Panckouke, 1788–1825), III, p. 592.

11. ". . . association politique avec son régime à part et sa magistrature municipale, sorte de république dans l'Etat, mais intimement rattaché à l'Etat, par les liens étroits de centralisation, les lois générales, les charges publiques et les grands intérêts nationaux, . . ." op. cit., II, p. 765).

12. Bruyère, op. cit., plates 1–4.

13. Bernard Lepetit, *Les villes dans la France moderne.*

14. Georges Teyssot, "Citta servizi, la produzione dei Bâtiments Civils in Francia (1795–1848)," *Casabella,* 324 (1977), pp. 56–64; "Planning and Building in Towns: The System of the Bâtiments-Civils in France, 1795–1848," *The Beaux-Arts and Nineteenth-Century French Architecture* (London: Thames and Hudson, 1982), pp. 34–49; Editor: *Le machine imperfette: architettura, programma, institutione nel 19. secolo* (Rome: Officina edizione, 1980).

15. Rabinow, op. cit.

16. Ann Lorenz Van Zanten, "The Palace and the Temple: Two Utopian Architectural Visions of the 1830s," *Art History,* II, no. 2 (June 1979), pp. 179–200; Paul Bénichou, *Le Temps des prophètes: doctrines de l'âge romantique* (Paris: Gallimard, 1977), pp. 301–304. Cf. the vision of the painter Gabriel Laviron, especially "Philosophie de l'art: coup d'oeil sur l'architecture, son passé et son avenir," *Revue indépendante* (September 1847), also published as a pamphlet.

17. Léonce Reynaud, *Traité d'architecture,* 2 vols. and atlas (Paris: Carlian-Goeury & Dalmont, 1850–1858), II, pp. 529–554.

18. "Les villes ainsi tracées sont ce qu'on appelle de belles villes, par suite des fausses idées qui ont cours en matière de beauté; mais qu'elles semblent tristes! comme l'ennui s'y gagne!" (p. 531).

19. "Telle partie de la ville, favorablement située, sera plus particulièrement habitée par la classe riche; telle autre attirera la majeure partie du mouvement commercial; ici se grouperont les établissements qui veulent éviter le tumulte, et recherchent les terrains dispendieux; là se parteront les usines et les nombreux ouvriers qu'elles emploient; en un mot, il se formera nécessairement plusieurs subdivisions distinctes dans l'intérieur de la cité, ayant chacune, leurs convenances spéciales en ce qui concerne le nombre, la largeur et la direction des rues; . . ." (p. 532).

20. "Qu'il voie dans sa ville un vaste monument, un et multiple à la fois, répondant pleinement aux exigences d'une vie collective et à toutes celles d'existences individuelles, présentant comme elles les aspects les plus divers, alliant en une juste mesure l'ordre et la liberté, et constituant une sorte de sublime concert par la savante réunion de toutes les formes variées et harmonieuses, expressions fidèles de la diversité des goûts, des positions et des besoins, des liens qui unissent et du sentiment d'art qui anime les habitants." (p. 550)

21. One of the earliest pieces of Marxist thinking, appropriately, is Friedrich Engel's analysis of the first capitalist metropolis, Manchester, in his *Condition of the Working-Class in England* (1845).

22. "Paris est vieux, mais ses maisons sont jeunes. La moitié d'entre elles ont vingt-cinq ans à peine – la vieillesse d'un cheval – il n'en est une sur quinze qui compte cent cinquante ans d'existence – l'âge où, dans la futaie, on tue les chênes: – Les logis s'etaient renouvelés jusqu'ici moins vite que les générations ne passaient; dans notre capitale actuelle c'est le contraire: la plupart des habitans sont nés depuis plus longtemps que les immeubles où ils demeurent." Georges d'Avenel, "Les mécanismes de la vie moderne: la maison parisienne," *Revue des Deux Mondes,* 4S 140 (April 14, 1897), pp. 279–309, 792–824) and 4S 141 (May 15, 1897), pp. 279–309; republished as a chapter in his *Mécanisme de la vie moderne,* 4 vols. (Paris: Colin, 1897–1900). Quote from vol. III, p. 2.

23. *JD,* September 26, 1854; January 27, 1855.

24. Daumard, op. cit.; C. Daly, *Architecture privée*; L.-M. Normand, op. cit.; V. Calliat, *Parallèle des maisons de Paris*; Barqui, op. cit.; Loyer, op. cit.; Jean Castex, op. cit.; Françoise Boudon, "immeubles."

25. On the economics rather than the architecture, David Harvey, *Consciousness and Urban Experience*. A model that might be folded back on Paris: Elizabeth Blackmar, *Manhattan for Rent, 1785–1850* (Ithaca: Cornell University Press, 1989). The end result was Chicago – cf. Paul Bourget, *Outre-mer* (Paris: Lemerre, 1895).

26. A subject needing much more study, as Loyer indicates, op. cit., p. 161.

27. "Le Louvre de Napoleon III vint de l'Aisne et de l'Oise; l'Hôtel de Ville vint de Bourgogne; il fut après la Commune, rebâti de pierres de Chatenay et de Courson (Yonne)." Op. cit., III, p. 22.

28. Avenel, op. cit., I, pp. 1–79 (department stores); Charles d'Ydewalle, *Au Bon Marché: de la boutique au grand magasin* (Paris: Plon, 1965); Michael Miller, *The Bon Marché* (Princeton: Princeton University Press, 1981); Bernard Marrey, *Les grands magasins: des origines à 1939* (Paris: Picard, 1979). The earliest department stores were on the ground floor only with rental space above: Au Tour Saint-Jacques by Rolland – Daly, *Architecture privée*, II (1869); the first Printemps by Jules Sédille – *L'Illustration*, November 4, 1865. Cf. Pevsner, *Building Types*, Chapter 16.

29. Clausen, op. cit.

30. Pevsner, *Building Types*, Chapters 12, 13. Zola in his *L'Argent* (1890) evokes two types of bank space, that established in a grand old hôtel (as were the Crédit Foncier and the Crédit Mobilier during the 1850s) and that creating a new palace around itself.

31. Charles Yriarte, *Les Cercles de Paris*.

32. Gustave Le Bon, *Psychologie des Foules* (Paris: Alcan, 1895). Karen Bowie develops the importance of Le Bon in her thèse du troisième cycle, *L'éclecticisme pittoresque et l'architecture des gares parisiennes au XIXe siècle* (Paris, 1985).

33. Anthony Vidler, *The Writing of the Walls: Architectural Theory in the Late Enlightenment* (Princeton: Princeton Architectural Press, 1987); B. Lepetit, op. cit.; Michel Foucault, *Surveiller et punir*.

34. Pierre Lavedan, *Histoire de l'urbanisme: époque contemporaine* (Paris: Hachette, 1952), pp. 32–34; Bruno Foucart and Veronique Noel-Bouton, "Les projets d'église pour Napoléonville (1802–1809)," *Bulletin de la société de l'histoire de l'art français* (1971), pp. 235–252; Georges Teyssot, "Pontivy-Napoléonville ou l'architecture des Ponts et Chaussées," *Monuments historiques de la France*, 109 (1980), pp. 17–20.

35. Biver, *Le Paris de Napoléon*; Fontaine, *Journal*, I, p. 371. Lepetit, to introduce this subject, cites the example of Dalbagio, architect of the new industrial city of Saint-Etienne, whose necrology lists him erecting a customs house, a bourse, a cemetery with chapel, public promenades and fountains, a grain market, law courts, a central police station, and a prison (op. cit., p. 255).

36. Adolphe Lance: *Abel Blouet: architecte, membre de l'Institut: sa vie et ses travaux* (Paris: Bance, 1854). Cf. Achille Hermant, *Abel Blouet* (Paris: Lacroix-Comon, 1857).

37. Michel Foucault, Bruno Fortier et al., *Machines à guérir*; Bruno Foucart, "Architecture carcérale et architectes fonctionalistes en France au XIXe siècle," *Revue de l'art*, 32 (1976), pp. 37–56; Robin Middleton and David Watkin, *Neoclassical and Nineteenth Century Architecture* (New York: Abrams, 1980), pp. 219–237.

38. "Le plan d'un hospice d'aliénés n'est point une chose indifférente et qu'on doive abandonner aux seuls architectes; le but d'un hôpital ordinaire est de rendre plus faciles et plus économiques les soins donnés aux indigènes malades. Un hôpital d'aliénés est un instrument de guérison." J.-E.-D. Esquirol, *Des Etablissements des aliénés en France* (Paris: Huzard, 1819), p. 30.

39. "Pour élever des prisons il faut avoir un système dont la programme devient la pensée, et le plan l'expression." F.-A. Demetz and Abel Blouet, op. cit., p. 4.

40. Abel Blouet, *Restoration des thermes d'Antonin Caracalla à Rome* (Paris: Didot, 1828).

41. Abel Blouet, *Expédition scientifique de Morée . . .*, 3 vols. (Paris: Didot, 1831–1838).

42. Foucault, *Surveiller et punir; Folie et déraison: histoire de la folie à l'âge classique;* "Politique de la santé au XVIIIe siècle," *Machines à guérir* (Liège: Mardaga, 1979), pp. 7–18.

43. David Van Zanten, "A French Architect in America in 1836," *Journal of the Society of Architectural Historians*, 29, no. 3 (October 1970), p. 255.

44. *Projet de prison cellulaire*, 1843.

45. Recently the subject of a careful study: Pierre Pinon, *L'hospice de Charenton* (Liège: Mardaga, 1989).

46. L. Cernesson, "Emile Gilbert: sa vie, ses oeuvres – notice biographique," *Annales de la société centrale des architectes*, IS 2 (1874).

47. Again Foucault gives the most vivid historical overview: *Histoire de la folie.*

48. We do not have the space to present all the details in which this was extended, for example, the use of ordinary doors between the wards and the service corridors which, however, had no handles on the side toward the wards.

49. Pinon explores this at particular length, op. cit., pp. 207 ff.

50. "La rectitude des lignes y est offerte comme un moyen propre à la rectitude des idées et du jugement. Les grandes surfaces unies des murs et les dispositions simples des toits permettent à l'oeil de s'y reposer à l'aise et d'en suivre tranquillement les contours. Les pierres trop saillantes, les moulures trop accusées, qui produisent parfois des effets de lumière et d'ombre plus ou moins bizarres, ont été évitées avec soin à fin de n'offrir aucun sujet de trouble ou d'effroi à des imaginations exhaltées. . . ."

51. César Daly, "Maison nationale de santé de Charenton," *RGA*, X (1852), cols. 384 ff., plates 28–34.

52. S. Girard, *Théodore Labrouste, architecte: sa vie, ses oeuvres, 1799–1885* (Paris: Chaix, 1886).

53. Fontaine, *Résidences de souverains*, plate 3; AN N III Seint 1089–1090; Pierre Lavedan, *La vie urbaine*, 1951; *Bulletin de la société de l'histoire de l'art français*, 1951.

54. "On se récria sur la place excessive que la municipalité avait ménagé dans son palais aux réunions solenelles et aux plaisirs d'une société privilégiée, et de la parcimonie avec laquelle on avait logé l'administration proprement dite" (op. cit., p. 38).

55. I treat this in *Designing Paris* (Chapters 2, 3, and 7 especially), working from Neil Levine's study of Labrouste, *Architectural Reasoning in the Age of Positivism: The Neo-Grec Idea of Labrouste's Bibliothèque Sainte-Geneviève*, Ph. D. dissertation, Yale University, 1975, partially published in several essays: "The Romantic Idea of Architectural Legibility: Henri Labrouste and the Neo-Grec," *The Architecture of the Ecole des Beaux-Arts*, pp. 325–416; "The Book and the Building: Hugo's Theory of Architecture and Labrouste's Bibliothèque Sainte-Geneviève," *The Beaux-Arts*, pp. 138–173. Cf. Hautecoeur, *Architecture classique*, VI, pp. 238–253.

56. "Le prison de Mazas n'est pas exclusivement une bâtisse bien étendue et un instrument administratif, c'est un oeuvre d'art" (op. cit., p. 223). We should note that some other architects involved in institutional building – Hippolyte Lebas of the prison of La Roquette and J.-J.-M. Huvé of the hospital administration, for example – were not so linked.

57. "Gilbert . . . n'était un esprit ni vaste, ni surtout libéral. Obstiné, exclusif, incapable de grâce ou d'élégance, il avait la droiture qui ne sait pas dévier, la conscience qui ne sait pas fléchir, la sincérité qui ne sait pas déguiser. . . ." Julien Guadet, *Eléments et théorie de l'architecture*, 4 vols. (Paris: Aulanier, 1901–1904), II, p. 509.

58. "J'ai horreur de cette architecture maniérée et grimaçante, généralement en honneur aujourd'hui et qui, ainsi que tout qui est mauvais, tend à se développer avec une exuberance désolante" (Musée d'Orsay, *Architecture hospitalière*, p. 54, citing a letter of January 9, 1861, in the library of Part Dieu, Lyons, MS PA 327). I am obliged to Pierre Guinard for finding and copying the original for me.

59. His lectures are reviewed in the *RGA*, VII (1847), cols. 431–441.

60. "La structure de cette époque, basée sur la raison, forme à elle seule l'édifice; et cet édifice est beau, parce que l'inutilé en est proscrite." Jean-Baptiste Rondelet, *Traité théorique et pratique de l'art de bâtir*, with supplement by Blouet (Paris: Firmin-Didot, 1847–1848), II, p. xxiv.

61. "Le principe, unique, éternel et fondamental de toute bonne architecture consiste . . . 1° à concevoir ce qu'il faut, rien de plus, et à le réaliser le plus simplement possible, ce qui ne peut être obtenu qu'en subordonnant d'abord ses conceptions qui doivent devenir des réalités aux moyens d'exécution et aux propriétés des matériaux dont on dispose; 2° à employer la décoration que pour compléter l'expression en ébauche dans la disposition et la construction, accentuer les parties en raison de leurs fonctions relatives et par suite avec plus de précision le caractère de l'édifice à l'aide des moyens que favorisent les matériaux auxquels ils sont appliqués, de moyens en un mot rendant sensibles à la fois la construction de l'édifice et sa destination." (Ibid., II, p. 227)

62. Jacquin, *Tuileries*, pp. 134–135.

63. Léon Labrouste, *La Bibliothèque Nationale: son début et ses accroissements, ses bâtiments et ses constructions* . . . (Paris: Lutier, 1885); Simone Balayé, *La Bibliothèque Nationale, des origines à 1800* (Geneva: Droz, 1988); Pevsner, *Building Types*, Chapter 7; H. M. Crass, *Bibliothekbauten des 19. Jahrhunderts in Deutschland* (Munich: Prestel, 1976). Cf. Dominique Varry (ed.), *Histoire des bibliothèques francaises*, vol. III: *De la Révolution et du XIXe siècle* (Paris: Promodis, 1992).

64. Levine's exhaustive dissertation gives the history of the building in detail.

65. Giedion, *Bauen im Frankreich*, pp. 22–25 and *Space, Time and Architecture*, 5th ed. (Cambridge: Harvard, 1941), pp. 220–228.

66. Bergdoll, *Panthéon*, especially pp. 71, 79. The shape of the *place* was sketched at the same time as the church.

67. *Recueil des actes administratifs*, I, pp. 126–128; Lazare, *Dictionnaire* (1844 edition), pp. 523–524; Taxil, *Recueil*, p. 16.

68. Rambuteau, *Compte rendu* . . . *1836*, p. 45: This involved a land exchange which, already in 1837, the prefect thought near completion. He specifies the repetition of Soufflot's facade on the *mairie*. Karl Hammer, *Jakob Ignaz Hittorf: ein Pariser Baumeister, 1792–1867* (Stuttgart: Hiersemann, 1968), pp. 196–197; Donald Schneider, *The Works and Doctrine of Jacques-Ignace Hittorff, 1792–1867*, Ph. D.

dissertation, Princeton University, 1970 (New York: Garland, 1977), pp. 548–549.

69. *Recueil des actes administratifs*, I, pp. 126–128; AS, VoII Place du Panthéon.

70. AN F21 1362, letter from the directeur des travaux publics of October 29, 1838. Cf. the prefect Rambuteau addressing the Chambre de Commerce, December 23, 1842: ". . . la construction de la bibliothèque Sainte-Geneviève et de la mairie du 12e arrondissement termineront dignement la place du Panthéon" (*RGA*, III [1842] col. 474). Jacoubet's atlas suggests that the *place* extended only up to the Panthéon's transepts.

71. I regret being unable to locate any correspondence between Labrouste and the Commissaire Voyer of the arrondissement in the 1840s, Van Cleemputte.

72. Simone Balayé, *La Bibliothèque Nationale*.

73. *Correspondance générale*, XVI, pp. 390–391: letter of February 1858. Labrouste's *inspecteur* André is said to have been made uncomfortable by Labrouste's treatment of the existing buildings.

74. *JD*, April 16, 1859. It had previously been an open paved square (and, before that, the Opéra).

75. Boullée's famous project for the Bibliothèque Nationale, however, would have filled the entire *cour d'honneur* with his dramatic reading room. For diagrammatic demonstration of these transformations see Bruno Fortier, *Métropole imaginaire*, pp. 121–134.

76. AN Versement d'Architecture, 5.

77. "Moralistes, philosophes, législateurs, flatteurs de la Civilisation! voici le plan de votre Paris mis en ordre, voici le plan perfectionné où toutes choses semblables sont réunies:

"Au centre et dans une première enceinte: Hôpitaux de toutes maladies, hospices de toutes misères, maisons de fous, prisons, bagnes d'hommes, de femmes et d'enfants.

"Autour de la première enceinte: casernes et tribunaux, hôtel de police, demeure des argousins, emplacement des échafauds, habitation du bourreau et de ses aides.

"Aux quatre coins: Chambre des députés, Chambre des pairs, Institut et Palais du Roi." Anonymous, "Bicetre," *La*

Phalange, August 10, 1836, cols. 112–115. Remember Victor Fournel's grim evocation of "Paris futur" in *Paris nouveau et Paris futur* (Paris: Lecoffre, 1865).

78. Levine's analysis of the Bibliothèque Sainte-Geneviève depicts it as a new, neutral construction to house the new industrially printed book. He sees Labrouste replacing the warm classical anthropomorphic vocabulary of architecture with the abstraction of printing where the shape set on the page has no direct relation to the idea it communicates. The building is a bookshelf; the names of authors inscribed between the facade arches is a catalog. The building was designed soon after formative contacts with Victor Hugo, Levine concludes, and was a response to Hugo's suggestion in *Notre-Dame de Paris* (1830–1832) that since printing had dethroned architecture as the "book" of humanity a new architecture must form itself on the model of the book.

79. "Etant donné un terrain de 84 mètres 75 centimètres en longeur, sur 21 mètres de large, et de plus un credit de 1,500,000 francs, élever une bibliothèque dont une seule salle puisse contenir, outre 95,000 volumes, quatre cents lecteurs commodément placés, avec toutes les conditions nécessaires de surveillance, de service, de clarté, de chauffage, pendant les heures du jour et les veillées de chaque soir. Voilà le programme. . . .

"A chaque édifice, un style, un caractère, des formes en rapport avec sa destination. Ainsi l'a très judicieusement compris M. Labrouste. . . .

"L'effet extérieure. . . ; un moment de réflexion l'explique. Puisque enfin on élevait une bibliothèque pour des livres, il fallait la faire à leur usage. Les livres ne se mettent point aux fenêtres, mais il s'appuient et se rangent commodément contre de longs murs. De là vient qu'il règne une assez large espace entre les fenêtres du rez-de-chaussée et les quarante croisées en cintre dont l'intérieur est éclairé. Qu'a t'on mis dans cet espace? Les noms des philosophes, des poëtes, des historiens, des savans de tous les siècles. Au dedans leurs oeuvres, au dehors leurs noms, comme on place le titre d'un bon ouvrage au dos du volume. Que l'architecte eût voulu placer son temple des muses

entre des allées d'arbres, près de studieux ombrages, loin du bruit de la voie publique, qui en doute? C'était son projet; mais l'intraitable voie publique ne lui a pas voulu céder un pied de plus. Ces ombrages existent, au moins, en peintures, sur le vestibule. . . ." (F. Barrière, "Embellissements de Paris," *JD,* December 31, 1850.)

80. This is presented by Foucart in his "Architecture carcérale."

81. De faire vivre de braves employés dans des cachots et tout cela pour donner aux façades ce que l'on est convenu d'appeler du caractère" (*RGA,* cols. 131–137).

82. Harou-Romain, *Projet de pénitencier* (Caen: Lesaulnier, 1840), p. 8. It is, in fact, the perfect application of Bentham's "panopticon" principle, although Harou-Romain does not admit it in his text and instead emphasizes the differences from the "Pennsylvania" type.

83. In 1839–1840 Labrouste won a competiton for a prison at Alessandria, Italy, but adopted the "Pennsylvania" type of Blouet. Pierre Saddy, *Henri Labrouste, architecte, 1801–1875* (Paris, Caisse Nationale des Monuments Historiques et des Sites, 1977), pp. 33–36.

84. Cf. the work of Frank Manuel (especially his synthetic *Utopian Thought in the Western World,* with Fritzie Manuel (Cambridge: Harvard University Press, 1979), Paul Bénichou, *Le Temps des prophètes, Le sacre des écrivains* (Paris: Corti, 1973).

CHAPTER 5. THE ARCHITECTS

1. This was established in the literature of the academic mainstream itself (Magne, Gromort, Hautecoeur) and in subsequent surveys, Hitchcock (1958), Egbert (1939, 1973, 1980), Middleton and Watkin (1980), Mignot (1983), and my own contribution to the *Architecture of the Ecole des Beaux-Arts* (1977).

2. The *procès verbal* of the Conseil des Bâtiments Civils shows him in fact performing this function already at the start of 1860.

3. To this one might add the permanent inspecteurs généraux functioning 1830–1870:
Rondelet, 1795–1839
Guy de Gisors, 1815–1835

Hubert Rohault de Fleury, 1819–1846
Caristie, 1835–1862
Biet, 1837–1857
Grillon, 1839–1854
Leclère, 1839–1853
Gourlier, 1831–1857
Debret, 1846–1850
Duban, 1854–1870
Alphonse de Gisors, 1857–1866
Questel, 1863–1888
Lefuel, 1866–1880
Extracted from Bauchal, *Dictionnaire*, and Gourlier, *Bâtiments Civils*, both, however, containing numerous inconsistencies.

4. The first among the professors and the author of the competition programs.

5. One must also note the members of the Académie des Beaux-Arts (1810–1870):
Fontaine, elected 1811
Huyot, 1822
A.-L.-T. Vaudoyer, 1823
Delespine, 1824
Lebas, 1825
Debret, 1825
Labarre, 1826
Molinos, 1829
Leclère, 1831
Guénepin, 1833
Huvé, 1838
Gauthier, 1842
Lesueur, 1846
Blouet, 1850
Hittorff, 1853
Gilbert, 1853
Visconti, 1853
Duban, 1854
de Gisors, 1854
Lefuel, 1855
Baltard, 1863
Duc, 1866
Labrouste, 1867
Léon Vaudoyer, 1868

6. For purposes of focus, I have so far discussed only the four most central individuals. Can this be extended to the wider array of leading architects outlined at the beginning of this chapter? A large number do fill the basic profile – successful study at the Ecole des Beaux-Arts (usually culminating in the Grand Prix de Rome), devoted duty in some architectural service (usually culminating in appointment to an oversight council), the commission for a major build-

ing in that service, election to Académie and/or a teaching post at the Ecole. Following Fontaine as architecte de l'empereur and architect of the Louvre was Visconti – Second Grand Prix, 1814; Prix Départmental, 1817; architect of the Tomb of Napoleon (in preference to Duban), 1841–1853; academician, 1853 – then Hector Lefuel – Grand Prix, 1839; architect of Fontainebleau, 1853; architect of the New Louvre, 1854; academician, 1855; vice president of the Conseil des Bâtiments Civils, 1870. Preceding Duban as vice president of the Conseil des Bâtiments Civils were Hubert Rohault de Fleury – architect of the hôpitaux et hospices, 1833 – then Auguste-Nicolas Caristie – Grand Prix, 1813; architect of the law courts at Rheims, 1841–1845; inspecteur général des Bâtiments Civils (1848–1862); conseiller municipal (1859–1860). In the Travaux d'Architecture of the city of Paris we find Jacques-Ignace Hittorff – architect of the Champs-Elysées, place de la Concorde, and the Bois de Boulogne, 1829 ff.; academician, 1853 – Théodore Ballu – Grand Prix, 1840; architect of the first section, 1860; architect of the new Hôtel de Ville, 1874: academician, 1872 – and Antoine-Nicolas Bailly – architect of the Tribunal de Commerce, 1858–1865; academician, 1875 – as well as Jean-Nicolas Huyot and Louis Duc – architects of the Palais de Justice; Grand Prix of 1807 and 1825; academicians 1822 and 1866. Blouet, inspecteur général des prisons, had won the Grand Prix in 1821, was named professor of theory at the Ecole in 1846, and an academician in 1850; his friend Gilbert of the "Mazas", Charenton, and the Hôtel Dieu had won the Grand Prix in 1822 and became an academician in 1853; Henri Labrouste had won the Grand Prix in 1824 and entered the Académie in 1867; Charles Garnier had won the Grand Prix in 1848 and entered the Académie in 1874.

What then becomes interesting, of course, are the exceptions. It seems to have been possible to rise by dint of hard work or good connections within the services themselves, but this usually did not lead to election to the Académie. Hippolyte Godde, after study with Lagardette (and a place *en loge* in the Grand Prix competition), entered the municipal service in 1805, was named chief of the second section of the Travaux de Paris (1813), then chief of the first section (1832), putting him in charge of Notre-Dame and of the Hôtel de Ville. But here, as we have noted, his luck ran out: In 1836 he was obliged to accept Lesueur (Grand Prix of 1819; professor of theory at the Ecole, 1854) as a design partner for the extension of the Hôtel de Ville; in 1843 he was pushed out of his post at Notre-Dame by Lassus and Viollet-le-Duc. Gabriel Davioud's later career ran somewhat parallel. After winning the Second Grand Prix (1849) and the Prix Départmental (1850), he entered the office of the Plan de Paris and from there was promoted by Haussmann to the architectural direction of the specially created Service des Promenades et Plantations (1856), designing in that capacity the theaters of the Châtelet, the Fontaine Saint-Michel, the (unbuilt) Orphaeum on the place de la République and the Trocadero. But he was treated roughly by critics and never elected to the Académie. Some figures accepted a modest life as architect of a single prominent building, like Jules de Joly at the Chambre des Députés (succeeded in that position by his son), Alphonse de Gisors at the Luxembourg (succeeded by his nephew, Scellier de Gisors), or Jacques Lacornée at the "Palais d'Orsay" and the Ministry of Foreign Affairs.

7. "J'ai résolu de ne pas entrer à l'Ecole parce que j'ai trop peur d'être emporté par le courant dans lequel elle vous entraîne. Si j'ai du talent, je percerai quand même et, si je n'en ai pas, l'Ecole ne m'en donnera pas, loin de là, car on en sort à l'état de moulage. M. Huyot a son moule, M. Percier a son moule, M. Lebas a son moule, de sorte qu'une fois sorti, je serai classé ou dans les Huyot, ou dans les Percier, ou dans les Lebas." *Lettres inédites de Viollet-le-Duc, recueillées et annotées par son fils* (Paris: Librairies-Impriméries Réunies, 1902), p. ii (December 3, 1831).

8. Geneviève Viollet le Duc, *Viollet-le-Duc: Lettres d'Italie, 1836–1837: addressées à sa famille* (Paris: Laget, 1971).

9. "Réponse aux considérations de l'Académie

. . .," *Annales archéologiques*, IV (1846), pp. 333–353.

10. Sumner Crosby, *The Royal Abbey of Saint-Denis* (New Haven-London: Yale University Press, 1987; Murphy, op. cit., Chapter 3.

11. AN *F19* 4544.; J.-M. Leniaud, "Viollet-le-Duc et le service des Edifices Diocésains."

12. *RGA*, X (1852), cols. 371–379.

13. "Cette mesure intéresse au plus haut point la bonne partie ouvrière de la population. Moi qui vois tout ce monde, je puis vous dire combien l'espoir d'une semblable direction a ranimé bien des esprits découragés" (Auzas, *Viollet-le-Duc,* p. 86). The correspondent is not identified.

14. "On peut encore . . . produire des oeuvres colossales comme les grands édifices romains, comme Versailles . . . mais supprimer la *dimension*, que reste-t-il de ces oeuvres? Des formules, pas autre chose" (Viollet-le-Duc's emphasis; col. 372).

15. "L'Architecte était . . . l'expression la plus vivante et la plus palpable des besoins de son temps; l'architecture, le livre dans lequel on lisait les goûts, les tendances, les passions d'une société. L'Architecte . . . résumait à lui seul tous les arts, profitant de tous les éléments qui lui formaient autour de lui: s'il ne sculptait pas ou ne peignait de sa main, il était l'âme du sculpteur et du peintre." (col. 375)

16. "Ce qu'il faut admettre toujours, c'est la vérité, la simplicité dans les moyens d'exécution; ce qu'il faut encourager, c'est l'étude consciencieuse et pratique; . . . Ce qu'il faut obtenir enfin, si nous voulons vivre, c'est l'agglomération morale des architectes, c'est une sorte de jury, de *chambre* composée d'hommes vieillis dans la pratique, honorables et instruits" (col. 378).

17. "Les spéculateurs à la bourse, les négociants enrichis, ne sont plus de la race des Jacques Coeur; les palais qu'ils élèvent, brillants, mais fragiles comme leurs fortune, sont bâtis au rabais par des entrepreneurs pour lesquels, comme pour leurs clients, *l'art* est le dernier des soucis" (Viollet-le-Duc's emphasis; col. 377).

18. "Les arts, en abandonnant les sommets où ils ne pouvaient plus vivre, se sont répondus en poussière dans les vallés; car en France ils sont vivants, ils circulent dans le sang de

la nation; ils sont partis de la foule, ils y retournent" (col. 377).

19. This is a large and important topic. See Albert Boime, "The Teaching Reforms of 1863 and the Origins of Modernism in France," *Art Quarterly*, NS, I (1977), pp. 1–39; Richard Chafee in *The Architecture of the Ecole des Beaux-Arts*, pp. 97–106. It produced a mass of published and unpublished pamphlets, especially those of Ingres (*Réponse au Rapport sur l'Ecole impériale des Beaux-Arts, addressée au Maréchal Vaillant . . . par M. Ingres*, Paris: Didier, 1863), Ernest Beulé ("L'Ecole de Rome au XIXe siècle," *Revue des deux mondes*, 2S vol. 48 [December 15, 1863], pp. 916–938), and Ludovic Vitet ("De l'enseignement des arts de dessin," *Revue des deux mondes*, 2S vol. 54 [November 1, 1864], pp. 74–107). Viollet-le-Duc had prepared his *coup* with his articles, "L'Enseignement des arts," *Gazette des Beaux-Arts*, XII (1862), pp. 393–402, 525–534; XIII, pp. 71–82, 249–255. Patricia Mainardi observes that the reform came on the heels of the Opéra competition (1860) and the Salon des Réfusés of May 1863): op. cit., Chapter 13.

20. *Ce que réclame au XIXe siècle l'enseignement de l'architecture* (Paris: Morel, 1869). Cf. his article, "L'Administration française," *La Philosophie positive*, XX (1878), pp. 371–384.

21. "Pour Louis XIV comme pour les démocrates de 1793, l'archéologie devait passer pour une sorte d'insurrection, d'opposition à l'ordre établi. L'archéologie conduit à l'indépendance dans les arts, il n'a pas d'art sans l'indépendance" (col. 371). . . .

"En quoi l'archéologie peut-elle favoriser l'indépendance dans les arts? . . . Parce qu'elle conduit à la collection des faits, indépendamment des influences du moment. Parce qu'elle fait voir que toutes les époques qui ont produit des oeuvres originales, logiques et belles en même temps, sont celles où l'art s'est développé sous l'influence puissante et fertile des artistes livrés à eux-mêmes, et non point sous la volonté ou le goût d'un souverain d'un ministre ou d'une académie (col. 372). . . .

"Qui de nous ne préfera ce siècle de saint Louis où l'on voyait s'élever des édi-

fices si faciles à classer par leur grande unité, mais si divers dans leurs ensemble et leurs détails, si pleins de poésie, tels que les cathédrales de Reims, de Laon . . . monuments issus de la même souche, membres de la même famille, mais où le génie de chaque architecte s'est développé en liberté, où chaque sculpteur produisait un chef d'oeuvre distinct, sorti sans contrainte de ses habiles mains!" (col. 372)

22. "[L]e jour où les communes verront les étrangers s'arrêtant devant leurs petits édifices, les examiner curieusement, les dessiner même parfois, elles comprendront que les imitations ridicules des grands monuments de la cité riche, exitent la rise, ne font pas leur affaire et que, chez eux, la simplicité vraie est une des qualités dont la charme ne s'altère jamais, parce qu'elle est la véritable marque de goût." Narjoux, *Architecture communale*, 3 vols. (Paris: Morel, 1870, 1880).

23. *Journal*, II, pp. 960, 973, 981.

24. Yet, as in the seventeenth century, there was a tendency for the premier architecte du roi to be promoted to lead the Conseil des Bâtiments Civils: When Fontaine resigned as architect of the Louvre in 1848 he became président honoraire of the Conseil; Duban was his successor in that post, albeit short lived; Lefuel, Duban's successor, followed Duban as vice president of the Conseil in 1870.

25. Beulé, "Eloge de Duban," *JD*, November 12, 1872; Charles Blanc, *Les Artistes de mon temps* (Paris: Firmin-Didot, 1876), pp. 1–22. César Daly had earlier made the same observation: "Le Palais de Justice à Paris," *RGA*, XXV (1867), cols. 9–10.

26. "Si le groupe auquel appartenait Duban a construit des monuments qu'on admire, cathédrales [Vaudoyer], bibliothèques [Labrouste], palais de justice [Duc], Duban n'a pas eu la même fortune: il n'a pu qu'achever des édifices déjà commencés."

27. "Ces échecs ne devaient point guérir un coeur déjà mélancholique. Duban s'assombrit; sa santé s'altera; il souffrit longtemps, victime de sa excessive sensibilité."

28. Jean-Louis Pascal, "M. Lefuel," *RGA*, XXXVIII (1881), col. 263.

29. Jacques de Caso, "Neuf lettres inédites de

Delacroix à Duban au sujet des travaux de la Galerie d'Apollon," "Duban et la restauration de la Galerie du bord de l'eau . . .", *Bulletin de la société de l'histoire de l'art français*, 1966, pp. 66–73, and 1973, pp. 332–245.

30. Jacquin (*Visconti*, p. 224) gives the date as December 1853, but the last letter signed by Duban in the *agence* letter book is dated March 21, 1854: AN 64 Aj 18.

31. "Au moment . . . l'Etat fait compléter et restaurer celles des parties du Vieux Louvre dont l'embellit principalement l'aspect de la cité je croix de mon devoir de vous signaler les parties sur lesquels le concours de la ville pourrait être invoqué, afin que grandes dépenses entreprises dans un noble but, ne puissent plus tard être objet d'aucun regret. . . .

"Peut-être aucun édifice des temps passé ne semble réclamer plus impérieusement que le Vieux Louvre cet isolement de toutes ses parties extérieures, isolement que dès la création successive de bâtiments qui le composent a été le point de départ de sa décoration architecturale." (AN 64 Aj 18)

32. *RGA*, XI (1855), col. 85; *JD*, April 29, 1954.

33. On April 12, 1855, Haussmann commissioned him to erect the *mairie* of the first arrondissement (before 1860 the fourth) as a part of a general scheme of shaping. On April 10, 1856, Hittorff's design, embodied in a model as well as drawings, was analyzed by the Conseil des Bâtiments Civils; in the following July contracts were being drawn up with builders to erect the houses at the north and south ends. By 1860 the composition was complete. Between 1853 and 1856 Duban's giant order had disappeared, the houses now flanking the central tableau merely continuing the design of the rue de Rivoli, and the *mairie* was made to repeat the mass and decoration of Saint-Germain-l'Auxerrois.

34. AN F21 1867.

35. "Seul en Europe peut-être de tous les monuments de cette nature le Théâtre Français est privé de cet espace nécessaire à son service et à sa dignité.

"L'élargissement donné sur le plan à la rue de Richelieu devant le péristyle du théâtre est une insuffissante concession faite à sa destination. Dégagée par une vaste espace, sa façade, oeuvre d'un célèbre architecte [Victor Louis], deviendrait un ornement de la cité.

"Il est incontestable que les combinaisons des bâtiments qui résultent d'intérêts divers qu'il faut ménager, ne pouvait que produire rien d'absoluement régulier. Mais, au moins, que dans ce quartier de luxe, voisin de plusieurs palais et du premier théâtre du monde, un centre de la population aisée, nos yeux ne soient pas affligés par la vue des défauts que l'on regrette de trouver dans les aboutissements de la nouvelle rue de Rivoli; qu'un aspect monumental, sinon régulier, résulte d'une savante répartition des pleins et vides. Tâchons, enfin, que le désordre sur une grande échelle ne remplace pas le désordre des quartiers qu'on veut régénérer avec tant de raison.

"Que si l'on objecte contre le projet d'une place, la proximité de celle du Palais Royal, on peut répondre que le rapprochement de ces espaces dans le voisinage du Palais du Souverain l'annonce en quelque sorte et ajoute à la commodité et à la dignité des abords; que ces deux places voisines n'offreront rien de semblable ni dans leurs aspect ni dans leurs destination; l'une monumentale, et servant de lien entre deux grands Palais; l'autre centre de riche commerce, et seul lieu de passage pour les voitures de la place de la Concorde au Pont Neuf." (AN F21 1867)

36. "On ne saurait trop regretter que la rue de la Paix qui doit son éclat aux Souverains de deux grands règnes, monumental en toutes par la variété même de ses aspects, reliée par les Tuileries au Palais du Souverain, n'ait pu obtenir par le grand remaniement de Paris, pour aboutissant et pour point de vue sur le boulevard que la coupe obliquement, qu'une face fuyante ou tout au plus un angle arrondi de propriétés particulières" (AN F21 1867, dated June 30, 1860).

37. AN F21 1868: reports of December 24, 1859, February 14, 1860 (Châtelet), June 30, 1860 (Opéra), September 11, 1861 (La Trinité). Cf. minutes of Conseil des Bâtiments Civils, F21 6395.

38. Institut de France, MS 1044–1045.

39. As we saw in Chapter 1, Duban had a long and complicated relationship to the project. As member of the Académie, he served on the jury of the Opéra competition in 1860–1861, as a member of the Conseil des Bâtiments Civils he analyzed the site plans before the competition and reported on the details of Garnier's design afterward, and finally as inspecteur général of the fourth circumscription of the Bâtiments Civils he regularly inspected the work as it progressed.

40. "Duban, qui avait pour moi une vraie affectation paternelle, était précisément l'inspecteur général chargé de surveiller mes travaux. . . . Il était tout disposé à causer avec moi, en confrère, comme il disait . . . et le rôle qu'il prenait était de m'encourager, de me soutenir dans les ennuis que j'approuvais . . . il me parlait comme s'il était mon admirateur et mon disciple.

"Une fois . . . il sortit de sa réserve, et ce fut au sujet de l'avant-foyer. Il me dit avec bien de réticences . . . qu'il lui semblait que le suppression des galeries du seconde et du troisième étage, du côté du foyer, permettant de faire la salle plus haute, plus noble, préparerait mieux à l'entrée de ce grand foyer, que ces petits couloirs écrasés. . . .

"[Duban] c'était une nature droite, élevée, animante, passionnée! Il plaçait l'art au-dessus de toutes les puissances humaines; il avait la foi, la conviction, et jamais, lui si doux et su bienvaillant pour les confrères jeunes ou vieux, il n'aurait cédé d'un pas devant les plus puissants, pour écouter une fantaisie qui eût, à ses yeux, constitué un crime artistique." (*Le nouvel Opéra de Paris*, Vol. I, pp. 282–284).

41. "Ces oeuvres-là ne s'analysent pas; il faut les admirer en bloc tout elles sont homogènes et *sui generis*.

"Vous devez être heureux et vous avez raison de vous complaire dans la contemplation de ce chef d'oeuvre, honneur de notre époque. Quant à moi; j'ai des raisons *que je sais* d'être heureux d'une telle réponse à des rancunes que vous savez." (Duban's emphasis) Bibliothèque de l'Opéra, Fonds Garnier, August 17, 1867. Published: *L'Architecture*, 1902; Mead, op. cit., p. 223.

42. ". . . persuader enfin à notre époque que ne s'en doute guère, que l'architecture dans ses conditions d'expression, de splendeur, et de magnificence, réglées par le goût, est le premier des arts."

43. Catherine Marmoz, "The Buildings of the Ecole des Beaux-Arts," *Designing Paris*, pp. 190–192.

44. *Designing Paris*, Chapter 2.

45. Fortoul, *De l'art en Allemagne*, 2 vols. (Paris: Labitte, 1842), I, p. 170.

46. Katherine Taylor, op. cit.; Van Zanten, *Designing Paris*, Chapter 6.

47. Jean-Marie Pérouse de Montclos, "Le Sixième Ordre d'Architecture ou la Pratique des Ordres Suivant les Nations," *Journal of the Society of Architectural Historians*, XXXVI, no. 4 (December 1977), pp. 223–240.

48. "Ces colonnes se trouvent engagées dans un pilier indiquent par là qu'elles font l'office des contreforts, c'est-à-dire que leurs entre-colonnements correspondent aux travées d'une voûte intérieure. . . . L'architecte ayant pris ce parti, a dû recouper son entablement, c'est-à-dire que, sur chaque demi-colonne, l'entablement fait retour en avant-corps" (*Le Temps*, October 30, 1868).

49. II (1872), p. 209, note.

50. Jean-Marie Pérouse de Montclos, *Architecture à la française* (Paris: Picard, 1982).

51. Paul Sédille, "Joseph-Louis Duc, architecte, 1802–1879"; Jean-Louis Pascal, "M. Duc et son influence sur le mouvement architectural contemporain," *Gazette des beaux-arts*, 2S. XIX (1879), pp. 430–443.

52. Starting in his first volume, "De l'Architecture domestique monumentale," I (1840), cols. 197–205.

53. "Il est évident que la spéculation particulière, protégée, encouragée par la paix, a contribué pour une bonne part aux magnificences du Paris actuel. . . .

"Les petits capitaux, agglomérés en millions, ont jetés des ponts sur la Seine, fondé de nombreux établissements, bâtis des embarcadères de chemins de fer, et ouvert des rues, des quartiers, des squares et des passages sur tous les points de la Babylone moderne. . . .

"Cette architecture civile, ou si on l'aime mieux ce style bourgeois succédant, par suite du progrès des moeurs et de l'infinie division de la propriété, aux grandes oeuvres de la renaissance, aux habitations fastueuses de Louis XIV et de Louis XV; ce style à cinq étages sur l'inexorable échelle de dix-sept mètres cinquante centimètres, est l'expression sans contredit la plus exacte de l'art de ce temps-ci; elle résume ses tendances, ses combinaisons, ses moyens." (Félix Pigeory, *Les monuments de Paris*, pp. 676–677).

54. Alexandre Dubois, *Biographie universelle des architectes*. Dubois's notes were used as the basis of Eli Brault's *Les Architectes par leurs oeuvres* published later in 1893, but by comparison with the much fuller text in Dubois's own first volume this is a sad shadow of what would have been possible.

55. Now the Académie d'Architecture. I am deeply indebted in the research that follows to the archivist Claudine de Vaulchier who made Lucas's notes available to me. See that institution's *Catalogue des collections*, I (1750–1900) (Paris: Académie d'Architecture, 1987).

56. Georges Duplessis, *Notice sur M. Alfred Armand, architecte* (Paris: Plon, 1888); *Notice sur M. Hippolyte Destailleur, architecte* (Paris: Morgand, 1895).

57. Bruyère was given a special retirement stipend of 5,000 francs per annum by the city of Paris in 1820. Other instances seem unique enough to be noted in the architectural journals.

58. See *The Second Empire: Art in France Under Napoleon III* (Philadelphia, Philadelphia Museum of Art, 1978), p. 258; Marius Vachon, *W. Bougereau* (Paris: Lahure, 1900), pp. 52–54.

59. *Biographie universelle des architectes*, p. 273, note 1:
Antoine, "dessinateur et inspecteur," Amiens station;
Crépinet, "chef de bureau des dessins et inspecteur des travaux," Grand Hôtel;
Crétin, "conducteur principal des travaux," Saint Germain and Versailles railroads;
Dablin, "dessinateur, inspecteur des travaux," Saint Quentin station;
Henri Dubois, "chef de bureau," Chemin de Fer du Nord and Hôtel du Louvre;
Layrix, "architecte-adjoint," Saint Germain station;
Mortier, "chef de bureau des dessins" and "inspecteur-en-chef des travaux," Gare Saint-Lazare.

60. He presented drawings as well as a book of photographs of his work to the Société Centrale des Architects: Académie d'Architecture, *Catalogue des collections*, I, pp. 68–73.

61. Receiving a detailed necrology in the *MU*, February 22, 1852.

62. *L'Architecture*, III (1890), pp. 576–577.

63. Maurice Parturier, *Morny et son temps* (Paris: Hachette, 1969), pp. 114–115; *RGA*, XXI (1863), cols. 141–142. See his illuminating personnel dossier in the Bâtiments Civils records, AN F 13 638a.

64. D'Avenel, op. cit.; *RGA*, XVI (1858), cols. 220–226; Charles Questel, *J.-M.-A. Lesoufaché: sa vie – ses oeuvres, 1804–1887* (Paris: Librairie Centrale des Chemins de Fer, 1887).

65. "il y a peu d'architectes qui aient construit des maisons aussi profitables à leurs propriétaires que M. Lesoufacher [sic], et un petit nombre des habitations privées bâties à Paris depuis vingt ans, reçu de leurs auteurs un aspect architectural aussi généralement approuvé par nos confrères et le public à travers les nombreuses variations de la mode et du goût." Ibid., col. 226.

66. This is now the Musée de l'Ile de France, and I am indebted to the kindness of the director, Gérard Rousset-Charny, for access to documents of the structure's history kept there.

67. Charles Lucas, "Louis Ponthieu – Théodore Belle," *RGA*, XXXVI (1879), cols. 136–137; J.-L. Bonillo, R. Borruey, J.-N. Espinas, Antoine Picon, *Marseilles: ville et port* (Paris: Parenthèse, 1992).

68. *RGA*, XVIII (1860), cols. 33–34, 66–68.

69. Marrey, *Grands Magasins*, pp. 97–109.

70. A famous collaboration. See Marrey, *Grands magasins*, pp. 69–83.

71. Bauchal, op.cit., pp. 644–645.

72. Séchan, *Souvenirs d'un homme de théâtre*, (Adolphe Bodin, ed.) (Paris: Levy, 1883); Jeanne Doin, "Charles Séchan et son atelier de décoration théâtrale," *Gazette des beaux-arts*, 5S. 11 (1925), pp. 344–360.

73. *Ill*, VIII (December 26, 1846), pp. 263–265,

(January 23, 1847), pp. 327–330; (January 30, 1847), pp. 340–341.

74. Gottfried Semper, *Das königliche Hoftheater zu Dresden* (Dresden, Brunswick: Vierweg, 1849).

75. Théophile Gautier, *MU*, July 29, 1857. Cf. the team employed by the Pereires to design and decorate the buildings at their seaside resort, Arcachon: Bernard Marrey et al., *La Ville d'hiver d'Arcachon* (Paris: Institut Français d'Architecture, 1983).

76. This is the subject of a study underway by Pauline Prévost Marcilhacy.

77. Olivier Poisson, loc. cit.

78. George F. Chadwick, *The Works of Joseph Paxton, 1803–1865* (London: Architectural Press, 1961), pp. 193–194.

79. Bernard Marrey and Paul Chemetov, *Architectures, Paris 1848–1914* (Paris: Caisse Nationale des Monuments Historiques et des Sites, 1972), pp. 31–32.

80. Charles Lucas, "M. Henri Blondel," *La Construction moderne*, September 18, 1897, p. 612; *L'Architecture*, September 25, 1897, p. 354; *American Architect and Building News*, LVIII, no. 1139 (October 23, 1897), p. 29; Bernard Marrey, *Familièrement inconnues* (Paris: Caisse national des Monuments Historiques et des Sites, 1976), p. 154.

81. Yriarte, *Les Cercles de Paris*; Marrey, *Architectures*, p. 154.

82. Strangely enough, this is in the one sympathetic necrology I have encountered, that in the *American Architect and Building News* cited earlier.

83. *Le Droit*, May 26, 1892.

84. Lucien Etienne, "La Vie et les oeuvres de Paul Sédille," *L'Architecture*, XIII, no. 34 (August 25, 1900), pp. 306–308; no. 35 (September 1, 1900), pp. 313–315.

85. "Architecture moderne en Angleterre," *Gazette des beaux-arts*, 2S. vol. 33, pp. 89–102, 194–208; vol. 34, pp. 89–106, 441–465; vol. 35, pp. 273–290.

86. "Ainsi delivrée de ses entraves présentes [of the restrictions of Voirie] notre architecture privée se revêt, dans un avenir prochain, une physionomie dont la caractère nouveau s'imposera au plus dédaigneux des effets de l'art moderne. . . . Comme au temps passé les moeurs nouvelles d'une génération nouvelle, ses besoins, ses aspirations bien définies, ses goûts impérieux, puis en même temps les modes de construction toujours transformés, influenceront si bien et quand même l'architecture privée qu'elle restera le témoin le plus sincère et le plus vrai des générations disparues." (Etienne, loc. cit., p. 308).

87. Edouard Charton, *Guide pour le choix d'un état* (Paris: author, 1842), pp. 16–27. (There were several later editions.) On the definition of the architecte see also A.-C. Quatremère de Quincy, *Architecture*, I (1788), pp. 108–109; *Dictionnaire de l'Académie française*; *Dictionnaire de l'Académie des Beaux-Arts*, II (1868), pp. 98 ff.

88. III, p. 473.

89. Op. cit., p. 30.

90. Jean Mallion, *Victor Hugo et l'art architectural* (Paris: PUF, 1962); Karl Scheffler, *Der Architekt* (Frankfurt: Ruetten & Loening, 1907). Cf. Philippe Hamon, *Expositions: littérature et architecture au XIXe siècle* (Paris: Corti, 1989).

91. Part II, Chapter X, with an illustration by Grandville.

92. "Campardon presents himself: 'J'ai été nommé architecte diocésain, oui à Evreux. Oh! une misère comme argent, en tout à peine deux mille francs par an. Mais il n'y a rien à faire, de temps à autre un voyage: pour le reste, je l'ai lá-bas un inspecteur. . . . Et voyez-vous, c'est beaucoup, quand on peut mettre sur ses cartes: architecte du gouvernement. Vous ne vous imaginez pas les travaux que cela me procure dans la haute société'" (Chapter 1). The Zola papers at the Bibliothèque Nationale include letters from J.-K. Huysmans (who was a *fonctionnaire* in the Ministry of the Interior) about the nature and status of architectes diocésains sent in response to Zola's request for information.

In 1841 Balzac wrote bemusedly in his *Physiologies* of this situation as it appears in the government bureaucracy.

"J'ai vu dans Paris des cartes ainsi conçues:

"Monsieur Tel, architecte du ministère de l'Intérieur, ou de la Chambre des députés, etc. . . .

"Cette place a sans doute été créée pour

montrer jusqu'à quel point un artiste peut devenir un employé ou jusqu'à quel point un employé peut devenir artiste.

"L'Architecte est comme la bibliothécaire, un employé dont le bonheur approche de la béatitude, il ne dépend que du ministre, et souvent le ministre dépend du lui" (*Les Employés*, Gallimard edition, 1970, pp. 322–323).

93. Meredith Clausen, *Frantz Jourdain and the Samaritaine* (Leiden: Brill, 1987).

94. "plus de murailles épaisses, plus d'axes obligatories, plus de pilastres inutiles, plus de proportions empiriques, . . . Chaque pièce posséderait son caractère, son ameublement personnels [sic] qui consacreraient l'harmonie du corps et l'esprit, en forçant le cerveau à subir l'influence du milieu." Frantz Jourdain, *L'Atelier Chantorel: moeurs d'artistes* (Paris: Charpentier and Fasquelle, 1893), pp. 283–285.

95. Ibid., p. 332.

96. For example, when the prefect Rambuteau visited the Bourse in 1836: *JD*, July 19, 1836.

97. The *MU* of December 16, 1852, specifies the uniform for the Corps des Ponts et Chaussées.

98. Cf. Ezra Suleiman, *Private Power and Centralization in France: the Notaries and the State* (Princeton: Princeton University Press, 1987).

99. Ollendorf, op. cit., p. 75.

100. Alexandre de Labrode, *Projet d'organisation des Bâtimens civils dépendans du ministère de l'intérieur, tendant à l'amélioration de l'architecture en France*; Georges Teyssot, "Planning and Building in Towns."

101. A document of June 22, 1841, surviving in the Visconti papers proposes that state work be restricted to architects with diplomas, that the examination for the diploma be each year "à issue des cours de l'Ecole Royale," that candidates must be twenty-years or older, that the jury consist of a member of the Académie des Beaux-Arts, a member of the Académie des Sciences, a member of the Conseil des Bâtiments Civils, an architecte-en-chef of the Bâtiments Civils and three professors at the Ecole. Gourlier discusses the 1856 proposition: "Observations sur la lettre de M. Viollet le-Duc . . . à propos du discours de M. le Ministre d'Etat," *Encyclopédie d'architecture,* VI (1856), cols. 28–36.

102. *RGA*, VI (1846–1847), cols. 256–265. Cf. Chafee, loc. cit., p. 105; Egbert, op. cit., p. 66; Richard Norman Shaw and T. G. Jackson, eds., *Architecture: A Profession or an Art* (London: Murray, 1892). Viollet-le-Duc in particular railed against this in the pages of the *Gazette des architectes et du bâtiment* because it reduced the architects' control of their own profession.

103. A.-C. Quatremère de Quincy, *Encyclopédie méthodique: architecture.* I (1978), "architecte."

104. Schmit was a more complex character, as we explore in Chapter 7. See Michael Driskel, "The Gothic Revival, the Revolution and the Abyss: J.-P. Schmit's Aesthetic of Authority," *Art History,* 13, no. 2 (June 1990), pp. 193–211.

105. *Arrêté* of November 9, 1866: *RGA*, XXIV (1866), col. 190. Another exception like Viollet-le-Duc's short period as *chef de bureau* is the case of Ernest Vinit, who was an architect trained in the atelier of Percier but who served as secretary of the Ecole des Beaux-Arts, 1832–1862.

106. Blanc was an engraver, de Mercey a painter, de Chennevières a critic and historian.

107. Cf. the pay records, AN o5 29.

108. Alfred-Pierre Blanche (1816–1893): trained in law; 1848, sous-directeur in Cultes, directeur of the short-lived Ecole d'Administration; 1851, secrétaire général in the Ministry of the Interior; 1858, secrétaire général of the Ministère d'Etat.

Marie-Louis-Anicet Blanc de Guizard (1797–1879): literatus; 1834–1839, directeur des Bâtiments Civils; 1839–1848, prefect of Aveyron Department; 1850–1852, chef de Division des Beaux-Arts.

Jean Vatout (1792–1848), literatus; 1822, librarian to the Duc d'Orléans; 1831, deputy; 1837, president of the Conseil des Bâtiments Civils; 1839–1848, directeur des Bâtiments Civils. He followed Louis-Philippe into exile at Claremont in 1848.

Jacques-Etienne comte de Cardaillac (1818–1879); 1839, enters administration of the Bâtiments Civils; 1853, chef de bureau des Bâtiments Civils; 1863, directeur des Bâtiments Civils, held to be remarkable for never leaving that administration from the age of twenty-one to retirement.

109. AN F21 2545 16, January 16, 1854.

110. "... l'administration qui vous consulte à impérieusement besoin de vos avis, elle n'a confiance qu'en vous, et c'est à vous qu'elle s'adresse."

111. "Mon grand-père était un artiste de grand talent et un honnête homme, dans la plus haute acceptation de ce mot. Mais il était quelque chose de plus rare que cela, parceque dans ce temps de physionomies éffacés, – il était un caractère. Il a vécu tout entier pour son art, l'aimant d'un amour exclusif, violent, passionné, dédaigneux de la fortune et du bruit, vivant dans son atelier au milieu de ses élèves ou seule chez lui, dans un grand cabinet où du matin au soir il dessinait. Ses confrères, avidement, se jetaient sur les affaires lucratives de l'architecture. Ils vivent à Paris au dix-neuvième siècle, au milieu des hôtels meublés et des gares de chemin de fer, il vivait à Rome, à Athènes, sous Auguste, sous Périclès. . . .

"Il avait près de 86 ans, mais jusqu'à plus de 80 ans il était resté jeune. Il a vécu heureux tant qu'il a pu aller tous les matins à son atelier, tous les mardis soirs à l'Ecole des Beaux-Arts et tous les samedis à l'Institut." Ludovic Halévy, *Carnets* (Paris: Calmann-Levy, 1935), I, pp. 171–172.

112. Adolphe Lance, "Architecte de départment," *Encyclopédie d'architecture*, NS 1 (1872), pp. 151–153; *RGA*, XXIX (1872), col. 41; XXX (1873), cols. 129–131; XXXII (1875), cols. 121–123.

113. John Hubbel Weiss, *The Making of Technological Man* (Cambridge: MIT Press, 1982).

114. For example, see the announcement for the examination for the post of architecte municipal for Nancy announced in the *Semaine des constructeurs*, V, no. 24 (December 11, 1881), p. 281.

115. *RGA*, XXXI (1874), col. 141; XXXII (1875), col. 127; XXXIII (1876), col. 178; XXXIV (1877), col. 179; XXXV (1878), col. 213; etc. *Bulletin de la société centrale des architectes* (1874), pp. 128, 170–172.

116. The record of the award survives at the Académie d'architecture, but lists only the recipients, not the buildings. Mme de Vaulchier was tremendously helpful in my work here.

117. Patricia Mainardi, op. cit.

CHAPTER 6. HAUSSMANN, BALTARD, AND MUNICIPAL ARCHITECTURE

1. Haussmann, *Mémoires*, II, pp. 303–304 on the meaning of this division.

2. Haussmann, *Mémoires*, II, Chapter 3.

3. "Une carte de Paris, sur laquelle on voyait tracées par Lui-Même, en bleu, en rouge, en jaune et en vert, suivant leur degré d'urgence, les différentes voies nouvelles qu'Il se proposait de faire exécuter." II, p. 53.

4. We have seen des Essarts's declaration that the sovereign is his own architect, extending the fiction of the king's "body politic" whereby the actions of the state are the personal actions of the sovereign. The topos appear elsewhere in history, for example, in the depiction of Pope Sixtus V laying out Rome: Mario Bevilacqua, ed., *Roma Sisto Quinto: arte, architettura e città fra rinascento e barocco* (Rome: Edizioni de Luca, 1992); Gianfranco Spagnesi et al., *La pianta di Roma al tempo di Sisto V (1585–1590)* (Rome: Multigrafica Editrice, 1992); Maria Piera Sette and Simona Benedetti, *Sisto V: architettura per la città* (Rome: Multigrafica Editrice, 1992).

5. Chapter 2: Saccard sneaks into the prefect's office and examines the map to find out where future expropriations will be. "Dans les rues, parfois, il regardait certaines maisons d'un air singulier, comme des connaissances, dont le sort, connu de lui seul, le touchait profondément."

6. Modern scholarship has been uncritical (e.g. *Paris. Haussmann*, pp. 51–55), even though the original does not exist. But the incident Haussmann records fits a topos too neatly to not be examined critically. In an important opposition address in the Corps Législatif in 1869 Adolphe Thiers denied that the transformation of Paris had been carefully coordinated (*JD*, February 24, 1869). However, there seems to be good evidence that the Second Network was settled upon between Haussmann and the emperor in the months after the prefect's appointment, both in the documents relating to the *Traité* of 1858 and in a remark of the prefect's in

1862 that he showed Napoleon III his first project for the network at Dieppe in September 1853 (*JD*, December 7, 1862). There is a reference at the meeting of the Conseil des Bâtiments Civils of February 20, 1854, to the single copy of the map marked in the emperor's hand (AN F21 2542 16: "Il n'en existe qu'un [plan of Paris] sur laquelle sa Majesté a tracé de sa main certaines directions, et qui n'a été que communiqué à l'administration préfectorale."

7. See Chapter 1, note 26.

8. AN, C 1058.

9. In the negotiations for the *Traité* certain parts, like the avenue de l'Opéra and the western section of the boulevard Saint-Germain, had to be put off. The "Deschamps" map is much more detailed than Merruau's and indicates these projected streets as well as the "Third Network."

10. The emperor's plans were sketched in several pamphlets: *Idées napoléoniennes* (Paris: Paulin, 1839); *Extinction du pauperisme* (Paris: Pagnerre, 1847). See H. N. Boon, *Rêve et réalité dans l'oeuvre économique et sociale de Napoléon III*, who tries to relate the emperor's early ideas and his later actions.

11. Lavedan, *Déplacement du centre de Paris*; Boudon, "Hôtel de Soissons"; André Chastel, Françoise Boudon, Françoise Hamon, *Système de l'architecture urbaine: le quartier des Halles à Paris*, 2 vols (Paris: CNRS, 1977). Also Victor Baltard and Ferdinand Callet, *Monographie des Halles centrales de Paris* (Paris: Morel, 1863).

12. Michel Clozier, *La Gare du Nord* (Paris: thèse de doctorat de la Faculté des Lettres, 1940).

13. Geneviève Massa-Gille, *Histoire des emprunts de la Ville de Paris 1814–1875* (Paris: Ville de Paris, 1973), pp. 175–196. The Conseil Municipal deliberations: *Conseil général de la Seine* (Paris: Ville de Paris, 1847).

14. Or so Persigny remembers in his *Mémoires du Duc de Persigny* (Paris: Plon, 1896), pp. 250–253.

15. Morizet depicts this moment well in his *Vieux Paris*. Cf. to the series of chapters Haussmann devotes to his first days in office in his *Mémoires*, II.

16. *Deliberations of the Conseil Général de la Seine*, 1853, 1854, 1855. The great burst of prosperity after the coup d'état of December 2, 1851, helped.

17. *Actes administratifs*, III, pp. 415–416; *JD*, June 21, 1854; Alphand, *Recueil des lettres patentes*, pp. 285–287. It was, of course, implicit in the line of the boulevard de Sébastopol decreed on March 10, 1852, and contracted on September 27 of that year.

18. Ibid., pp. 291–292. *MU*, August 11, 1855, p. 821.

19. Ibid., pp. 287–288; *MU*, June 26, 1852; Lazare, *Dictionnaire* (second edition), p. 710. Later, in 1859, the quarter around the Gare du Nord was rebuilt with the company and the city dividing the cost.

20. *JD*, April 25, 1856. David Pinkney states that by 1857 the city had received fifty-three million francs in state subsidies, op. cit., p. 183.

21. *MU*, July 3, 1861.

22. The mémoire: *JD*, April 9, 1858.

23. *Recueil des actes administratifs*, V, pp. 199–202; *Encyclopédie d'architecture*, VIII (1858) cols. 229–233. The bank was appropriated 10 million francs to begin with. On December 27, 1858, it issued bonds for a further 30 million and on January 6, 1859, bonds for 15 million more.

24. Haussmann's budget statement: *JD*, September 1, 2, 5, 1858.

25. *MU*, July 22, 1860, pp. 76–78.

26. Pinkney, op. cit., p. 188.

27. Massa-Gille, op. cit., Chapter 8.

28. Léon Say, "La Ville de Paris et le Crédit Foncier," *JD*, January and February 1865 (published in 1868 as a pamphlet); Jules Ferry, *Les comptes fantastiques d'Haussmann* (Paris: Le Cehvalier, 1868); J.-E. Horn, *Les finances de l'Hôtel de Ville* (Paris: Dentu, 1869). There was a feeble rebuttal: Jules Lan, *Parallèle entre le marquis de Pombal (1735–1777) et le baron Haussmann (1853–1869)* (Paris: Amyot, 1869).

29. *MU*, April 5–6, 1858, p. 429.

30. *Ill*, April 10, 1858 (vol. 32), pp. 225–226; *MU*, April 5, 1858, pp. 429, 431, 503; *JD*, April 3, 1858.

31. "Depuis quelques jours une foule immense

ne cesse de parcourir en tous sens, le boulevard de Sébastopol, dont l'ouverture définitive ne saurait tarder. Bientôt, dit-on, un vaste *vélum*, tombant à un moment donné, découvrira la perspective sans fin de cette voie grandiose auprès de laquelle eût pâlir le chemin sacré de l'ancien Rome.

. . .

"Une vive satisfaction se lit sur tout les visages à la vue de ces habitations sans nombre, spacieuses, élégantes, vivifiées déjà par le commerce, sorties de terre comme par enchantement, à la place qu'occupaient naguère ces inextricables lacis de rues et de ruelles qui n'avait jamais joui du bienfait de l'air et de lumière: la population parisienne témoigne aussi du haut prix qu'elle attache à la création de cette voie sans rivale dans le monde, oeuvre d'assainissement la plus gigantesque qui ait jamais été accompli dans la capitale d'un grand empire." (*MU*, March 30, 1858).

32. *Ill*, vol. 31, p. 226.

33. *MU*, April 7, 1858, p. 433.

34. "L'achèvement du Louvre, auquel je vous rend grâce d'avoir concouru avec tant de zèle et d'habilité, n'est pas le caprice d'un moment, c'est la réalisation d'un plan conçu pour la gloire et soutenu par l'instinct du pays pendant plus de trois cents ans" (*JD*, August 15, 1857).

35. "Nous sommes à une époque où la création des chemins de fer change toutes les conditions économiques d'un pays, car, non seulement pour leur création, ils absorbent la plupart des capitaux disponibles; mais quand ils sont créés ils favorisent l'agglomération dans les villes et modifient les rapports entre le producteur et le consommateur. Le conseil municipal avait donc une oeuvre multiple à accomplir: il fallait d'abord assurer les ressources financières du pays, favoriser les constructions nouvelles afin de pouvoir loger un exédant soudain de population, et, d'un autre côté, il était indispensable de démolir afin de créer des voies nouvelles qui faisaient pénétrer la lumierè et la salubrité dans les quartiers malsains, et formaient de grandes artères favorables au développement de la ville, en rapprochant le centre des extremités." (*JD*, April 7, 1858)

36. This is one of the most discussed aspects of Haussmann's work. See Jeanne Gaillard, *Paris*; T. J. Clark, *Painting of Modern Life*; Donald Olsen, *The City as a Work of Art: London, Paris, Vienna* (New Haven: Yale University Press, 1986), Chapter 9 (especially pp. 137 ff.).

37. *MU*, April 11, p. 422; June 4, p. 654; June 30, p. 771; July 16, p. 847; July 29, p. 906; August 10, p. 967; August 13, p. 979; August 15, p. 986; August 16, p. 987, 1860. Cf. *JD*, August 14, 1860.

38. Adolphe Lance, "La Fontaine Saint-Michel," *Encyclopédie d'architecture*, X, no. 11 (November 1860), cols. 162–168. Cf. Daniel Rabreau et al., *Gabriel Davioud, architecte de Paris* (Paris: Délégation à l'action artistique de la Ville de Paris, 1981), pp. 42–47.

39. *Ill*, August 24, 1861 (vol. 38, pp. 114–117); *MU*, 1861, pp. 1219, 1222; *JD*, August 14 and 15, 1861.

40. *Ill*, December 6, 1862 (vol. 40, pp. 376–378); *MU*, December 8, 1862, p. 1,683; *JD*, December 8 and 9, 1862.

41. "Lorsqu'on jette les yeux sur un plan de Paris, on est frappé de trouver, aux extrémités les plus éloignées de la Ville, sur les points où viennent aboutir ses deux plus magnifiques avenues, celles de Neuilly et de Vincennes, et d'où rayonnent des voies magistrales qui la pénètrent en tous sens, deux places à peu près symétriques qui se correspondent exactement à l'est et à l'ouest, et qui semblent préparées pour la même destination dans l'ordonnance générale de la cité. La pensée d'élever sur la place du Trône un monument à la gloire militaire du règne de Votre Majesté est de celles dont personne ne peut revendiquer l'initiative, parce qu'elle se présente naturellement à tous les esprits.

"Nous ne saurions prétendre avoir résolu, dans le travail improvisé d'une décoration temporaire, les questions d'art très complexes soulevées par une telle conception; mais nous sommes certains d'avoir été les interprètes fidèles du sentiment populaire lorsque nous avons songé à consacrer le lieu même où Votre Majesté, de retour d'Italie, est rentrée dans Paris, à la tête de ses troupes, par un arc triomphale dédié au vainqueur de Solferino et à ses vaillans soldats." *JD*, December 9, 1862)

42. In fact *Ill* says that the architects of the municipal service were all asked to submit designs in a closed competition.

43. Louis Lazare, *Les quartiers de l'est de Paris* (Paris: Bibliothèque Municipale, 1870), p. 88, attributes the design of the new *immeubles* on the *place* to Crépinet, the company's architect.

44. *JD*, December 24, 1862.

45. *Ill*, 1865 (vol. 46, pp. 115–116).

46. *JD*, October 29, 1868. The building was, however, opened for visits by the public and reviewed in many newspapers.

47. *JD*, July 29, 1870. This should be compared to the ceremonial departure down the boulevards of Paris for the North Italian War in 1859, *JD*, March 11, 1859.

48. Mead, op. cit., pp. 184–185.

49. *Paris. Haussmann*, pp. 120–125.

50. AS V. R. 1, meetings of November 15 and December 19, 1861.

51. *MU*, November 19, 1852.

52. Coincidentally with Napoleon III's 1860 free trade treaty with Britain: Arthur Louis Dunham, *The Anglo-French Treaty of Commerce of 1860* (Ann Arbor: University of Michigan, 1930).

53. Massa-Gille, op. cit., pp. 258–278.

54. *Mémoire présenté par le sénateur préfet de la Seine au conseil municipal de Paris au sujet d'une nouvelle émission d'obligations de la Ville, 15 juin 1860*, pp. 1–12 (Bibliothèque Administrative de la Ville de Paris).

55. *Mémoire du sénateur préfet de la Seine au conseil municipal – rapport du comité des finances, 21 avril 1865* (Bibliothèque Administrative de la Ville de Paris).

56. For example, *JD*, February 11, 1863; Adolphe Thiers, in remarks summarized in the *JD*, February 24, 1869; Louis Lazare, *Les quartiers de l'est de Paris*. Also Lucien Lambeau, *Histoire des communes annexées à Paris en 1859* (Paris: Leroux, 1916–1921).

57. *JD*, February 19, 1863.

58. François Loyer's and Donald Olsen's excellent books treat much of the material in this section from slightly different standpoints.

59. "A l'avenir, l'étude de tout plan d'alignement de rue devra nécessairement comprendre le nivellement; celui-ci sera soumis à toutes les formalités qui régissent l'alignement.

"Les façades des maisons seront constamment tenues en bon état de propreté. Elles seront grattées, repeintes ou badigeonnées au moins une fois des dix ans. . . ." (*Actes administratifs*, III, pp. 80–81).

60. Camus discusses the initiative in the *JD*, April 24, 1854. See also May 20, June 7, August 6, and September 12, 1854.

61. Haussmann, *Mémoires*, III, Chapter 5; Alphand, *Promenades de Paris*, plates "Profiles des voies publiques."

62. *Actes administratifs*, III, 365–367. Cf. *JD*, April 24, August 21, 1854.

63. *Actes administratifs*, VII, pp. 139–140.

64. *Actes administratifs*, III, pp. 384–385.

65. "sous la présidence du maire . . . à l'effet de s'entendre . . . sur le système d'ensemble à suivre pour mettre ses maisons en bon état de propreté."

66. *JD*, August 21, 1854; May 24–25, June 1, 1858.

67. *MU*, April 14, 1859; *JD*, April 16, 1858, August 2, 1859.

68. *Actes administratifs*, IV, pp. 149–150.

69. Haussmann, *Mémoires*; III, pp. 172–259; Alphand, *Les Promenades de Paris*, text, pp. 243–246; Rabreau, *Davioud*, p. 27.

70. *JD*, February 6, 1859.

71. Haussmann, *Mémoires*, III, Chapter 7; Alphand, *Promenades de Paris*; *JD*, July 4, 1858; February 6 and 17, March 23, June 7, September 10, 1859; Rabreau, *Davioud*, p. 53.

72. Macadam: *MU*, July 23, 1853; *JD*, March 14, 1854; May 15, 1858. Electricity: *JD*, October 29, 1856.

73. "Il . . . est interdit de louer aux bouchers, charcutiers, boulangers, marchands de vin ou débitants de liqueurs à comptoir, aux ouvriers à marteau ou à toute autre industrie incommode ou insalubre. . . ." Cf. Donald J. Olsen, *The City as a Work of Art: London, Paris, Vienna*, pp. 137–151.

74. On the transformation of the square Louvois: *JD*, August 2, 1859.

75. Alphand, *Promenades de Paris*, text, pp. 211–242.

76. *MU*, July 2, 1853; *JD*, April 1, September 6, 1853, April 27, 1854.

77. Chastel et al., *Système de l'architecture urbaine*, pp. 329–330. Illustrated: *Ill*,

August 21, 1852 (vol. 20, p. 121); *JD*, August 11 and 16, 1852. A violent storm damaged the roof and the *bal* only could be used two days later.

78. Paul Dufournet et al., *Hector Horeau*, pp. 89–95.

79. "Dans cette partie de Paris espacée et grandiose . . . sur ces larges boulevards plantés d'arbres, ces quais déserts, le brouillard planait immacule, en nappes nombreuses, avec des légèretés et des floconnements de ouate. C'était fermé, discret, presque luxueux, parce que le soleil derrière cette paresse de son lever commençait à répandre des teintes doucement pourprées, qui donnaient à la brume enveloppant jusqu'au faîte les hôtels alignés, l'aspect d'une mousseline blanche jetée sur des étoffes écarlates. On avait dit un grand rideau abritant le sommeil tardif et léger de la fortune, épais rideau où rien ne s'entendait que le battement discret d'une porte cochère, les mesures en fer-blanc des laitiers, les grelots d'un troupeau d'anesses passant au grand trot suivies du soufflot court et haletant de leur berger."

By the 1880s the German urbanists elaborated a theory of urban space (Hermann Maertens, *Der optische Massstab oder die Theorie und Parxis des ästhetischen Sehens in der bildenden Künsten* (Bonn: Cohen, 1877); Camillo Sitte, *Der Städte-bau nach seinen künstlerischen Grundsätzen* (Vienna: Graeser, 1889); and sometimes cited the impressionist painting of Paris as their inspiration: H. P. Berlage, "Bouwkunst en impressionisme," *Architectura*, II (1892), pp. 93–95, 98–100, 105–106, 109–110; August Endell, *Die Schönheit der grossen Stadt* (Stuttgart: Strecker & Schroder, 1908). Cf. Ladd, op. cit., Chapter 4; Christiane Crasemann Collins, *Camillo Sitte: The Birth of Modern City Planning* (New York: Rizzoli, 1986).

80. Haussmann, *Mémoires*, III, p. 480.

81. Christopher Mead is currently writing a monograph on Baltard and kindly has communicated this. See the catalog of the Halles material in the Bibliothèque Historique de la Ville de Paris: Patrice Broussel, *Victor Baltard: projets inédits pour les halles cen-*

trales (Paris: Bibliothèque Historique de la Ville de Paris, n. d.).

82. Decree of August 23, 1858: Alphand, *Recueil*, p. 308.

83. *Ill*, August 29, 1857 (vol. 30, pp. 136–137). Cf. *The Builder*, June 5, 1869.

84. Chapter 7.

85. E.-A.-J. Brame and E. Flachat, *Chemin de fer de jonction des halles centrales avec le chemin de fer de ceinture* (Paris: Dalmont, 1856). Line 4 of the Paris métro eventually accomplished this.

86. See *JD*, May 20, June 21, and October 21, 22, 27, 1854.

87. Lavedan, *La Question du déplacement de Paris*.

88. Alphand, *Recueil*, p. 238; *Actes administratifs*, II, p. 536; III, pp. 58, 310, 404; IV, p. 35; Baltard and Callet, *Monographie*, plate III. *MU*, February 17, 1853; *JD*, January 11, May 20, October 21, 22, 27, 1854.

89. *JD*, May 20, 1854.

90. Alphand, *Recueil*, p. 308.

91. Ibid., p. 319.

92. *RGA*, XX (1860), col. 258. The investors recorded in the VO11 series, Archives de la Seine, are Germain, Bailleux de Marisy (Germain's lieutenant later at the bank) Seydoux, and Darcy. I do not know the architect. I owe this information to Catherine Weese.

93. "Cette immense construction, toute simple, mais de bon goût, arbite déjà un monde de marchands et de revendeurs des Halles." *RGA* XX (1862) col. 285.

94. The Marville photographs at the Bibliothèque Historique de la Ville de Paris include thorough coverage of the quartier des Halles in the late 1860s and show no new construction beyond the "Massif des Innocents."

95. *JD*, October 21, 1854. *RGA*, 1860.

96. Alphand, *Recueil*, pp. 319, 453.

97. "Mais ce qui le surprenait, c'était, aux deux bords de la rue, de gigantesques pavillons, dont les toits superposés lui semblaient grandir, s'étendre, se perdre, au fond d'un poudroiement de lueurs. Il rêvait, l'esprit affaibli, à une suite de palais, énormes et réguliers, d'une légèreté de cristal, allumant sur leurs façades les milles raies de flamme de persiennes continues et sans fin. Entre les

arrêtes fines des piliers, ces minces barres jaunes mettaient des échelles de lumière, qui montaient jusqu'à la ligne sombre des premiers toits. . . .

"Quand il déboucha dans la grande rue du milieu, il songea à quelque ville étrange, avec ses quartiers distincts, ses faubourgs, ses villages, ses promenades et ses routes, ses places et ses carrefours, mise tout entière sous un hangar, un jour de pluie, par quelque caprice gigantesque. L'ombre, sommeillant dans les creux des toitures, multipliait la forêt des piliers, élargissait à l'infini les nervures délicates, les galeries découpées, les persiennes transparentes; et c'était au dessus de la ville, jusqu'au fond des ténèbres, toute une végétation, toute une floraison, monstrueux, épanouissement de métal, dont les tiges qui montaient en fusée, les branches qui se tordaient et se nouaient, couvraient un monde avec les légèretés de feuillage d'une futaie séculaire."

98. Leonard, op. cit.; Gardes, *Op. cit.*; Bruston, loc. cit.; also the writings of the Lyon architect Clair Tisseur, especially his *Lettres de Valère* (Lyon: Meton, 1881). Catherine Arland and Dominique Bertin, *De la rue Impériale à la rue de la République* (Lyon: Mun, 1992). On Bonnet: Brunot and Coquand, op. cit., pp. 217–218.

99. For example, *MU*, July 4 and 8, 1860.

100. Bailleux de Marisy, "La Transformation des grandes villes de France," *Revue des deux mondes,* May 15, 1865), pp. 357–386, especially p. 371. This was part of a series of articles later published under that title as a book. The Lyon tramway is noted in *JD*, October 24, 1859.

101. "Les affaires se concentrent dans un quartier peu étendu, limité au nord par la rue des Capucins, au sud par la place Bellecoeur, à l'est par le Rhône, à l'ouest par le Saône, et nous voyons se constituer sous nos yeux, pour me servir d'un mot qui n'a pas en France la signification précise qu'òn lui donne à Londres, une cité, c'est-à-dire une ville des affaires. C'est là que les banquiers, les négociants, les marchands, tous les hommes d'affaires, en un mot, seront obligés d'avoir leurs comptoirs et leurs magasins. Mais l'habitation proprement dite se reportera à Perrache et surtout aux Brot-

teaux, près du Parc, des grandes promenades publiques, des larges quais et des avenues, là où les terrains n'ayant pas acquis la valeur élevée que leur donne nécessairement une situation très centrale, recherchée par le commerce, on peut se loger convenablement à bon marché.

"Telle est la tendance de notre temps. . . ." (Archives Municipales de Lyon, 925 WP). I am indebted to the archivist, M. Maire.

102. "Il peut, dans une certaine limite, être utilisé pour le transport des voyageurs et notamment des ouvriers qui, par suite des transformations opérées dans les quartiers du centre, vont être obligés de se loger aux extremités de la ville" (Brame and Flachat, op. cit.).

103. Henri-Jules Borie, *Aérodomes: essai sur un nouveau mode de maisons d'habitation applicable aux quartiers les plus mouvementés des grandes villes* (Paris: Morris, 1865). Cf. Peter Wolf, "City Structuring and Social Sense in 19th and 20th Century Urbanism," *Perspecta 13 and 14* (New York: 1973, Wittenborn, pp. 222–233, where a comparison with the Halles quarter is suggested.

104. "Son aspect, quand on l'étudie plus en détail, révèle si peu de la trace de volontés individuelles, il y a si peu de caprice et de fantaisie dans ses monuments et dans ses rues qu'elles semblent l'oeuvre de quelque puissance impersonnelle, irrésistible, inconsciente comme une force de la nature, et au service de qui l'homme n'a été qu'un docile outil." Paul Bourget, *Outre Mer* (Paris: Lemerre, 1895), pp. 160–161.

105. Louis Normand, *Paris moderne,* IV, plates 21–24; Bercé, op. cit., pp. 209, 230, 241, 245; *RGA*, VIII (1848–1850), cols. 220–221; IX (1851), col. 43 – a project to restore the exterior to stand exposed by the construction of the Halles costing 200,000 francs. Boime, *Couture*, pp. 231–236; Fried, *Artforum*, 1970. *L'Artiste*, 6S, 2, pp. 231 ff.; *Revue des deux mondes*, 2S, 6, pp. 44 ff.; *MU* April 6, 1860, p. 406.

106. *RGA*, XX (1862), col. 236.

107. "Il tourna la tête, fâché d'ignorer où il était, inquiète par cette vision colossale et fragile; et, comme il levait les yeux, il aperçut le

cadran lumineux de Saint-Eustache, avec la masse grise de l'église. Cela l'étonne profondément. Il était à la pointe Saint-Eustache."

108. "C'est une curieuse rencontre, disait-il [Claude, a painter, to Florent], ce bout d'église encadré sous cette avenue de fonte. . . . Ceci tuera cela, le fer tuera la pierre, et les temps sont proches. . . . Voyez-vous, il y a là tout un manifeste: c'est l'art moderne, le réalisme, le naturalisme, comme vous voudrez l'appeler, qui a grandi en face de l'art ancien. . . . Les maçons du bon Dieu sont morts, la grande sagesse serait de ne plus construire ces laides carcasses de pierre, où nous n'avons personne à loger. . . . Depuis le commencement du siècle, on n'a bâti qu'un seul monument original, un monument qui ne soit copié nulle part, qui ait poussé naturellement dans le sol de l'époque; et ce sont les Halles centrales, entendez-vous, Florent, une oeuvre crâne, allez, et qui n'est encore qu'une révélation timide du vingtième siècle. . . ."

109. The principal critics of the period so spoke, some in Baltard's necrologies (Garnier, Sédille, Delaborde), others in specific reviews (Bouchet, *RGA*, XXVII (1869), cols. 84–88; Viollet-le-Duc *fils, Gazette des architectes et du bâtiment*, VI, no. 1 (1868), pp. 1–4).

110. "Il me semble qu'avant tout un caractère de méditation et de recueillement doit doucement dominer dans toutes les parties d'une église. Or, un des moyens de distinguer entre le caractère exceptionel du monument religieux et celui de tout autre monument c'est de réserver pour le premier des expressions caractéristiques ne se retrouvant dans aucun autre édifice où l'industrie joue un rôle quelconque" (col. 86).

111. "M. Baltard a su . . . réunir toutes les qualités reconnues nécessaires à notre art, et ce qui réclamait l'architecte d'Auguste [Vitruvius] a été donné bien amplement par l'architecte de M. Haussmann. . . . M. Baltard, en effet, était écrivain distingué, orateur abordant, dessinateur habile, administrateur judicieux et ingénieux constructeur. Il avait la netteté du jugement, la promptitude de la décision, la connaissance des hommes, la loyauté du soldat et la courtoisie du grand seigneur. . . ."

112. "Si les circonstances eussent amené M. Baltard à exercer une autre profession, . . . notre cher confrère eût pu être un docteur excellent ou un remarquable homme politique; il aurait pu devenir un savant ou un industriel, un poète ou un commerçant. . . .

"Malgré toutes ces qualités, ou plutôt à cause d'elles, M. Baltard aurait pu être condamné à ne pas dépasser dans les arts ce que l'on est convenu d'appeler une moyenne estimable; en effet, la pondération même de ses pensées et de ses tendances aurait pu devenir un obstacle à la production d'oeuvres hors ligne . . .

"Baltard aurait peut-être été englobé avec eux [the greatest artists], si, heureusement, il n'avait eu en lui une sorte de défaut qui l'a empêché d'être parfait. Il aimait un peu ce qui était compliqué; il se savait certain de vaincre les difficultés et se plaisait souvent à s'en créer de nouvelles, rien que pour avoir le plaisir et l'honneur de les vaincre."

113. "Grace aux halles centrales, le nom de M. Baltard ne devait jamais être oublié; et cependant on peut craindre que, par son excellence même, cet édifice soit impuissant à conserver, du moins pour la foule, la mémoire de celui qui l'a élevé. Je m'explique. Je viens de dire que les Halles ont déjà été bien souvent copiées; quelques artistes s'en sont seulement inspirés, mais plus d'un architecte a suivi presque point par point les idées de M. Baltard. Cette espèce de plagiat se répand de plus en plus, et il faut dire qu'il est presque nécessaire puisque, pour l'instant, c'est dans cette manière de comprendre un marché que se trouve réellement la solution pratique. Mais cet abondance d'édifices similaires, qui menacent de s'étendre encore, est destinée à englober le monument initial. La création d'un seul homme paraîtra un jour la création de tous, et lorsque, dans l'avenir, on admirera toutes ces grandes constructions, on ne saura peut-être pas distinguer le monument primitif, ni reconnaître alors le nom de l'éminent architecte qui a été le créateur du type original."

114. The construction of the building that would house it, the "Palais de l'Industrie," was decreed a year earlier, March 27, 1852: *MU*, March 30, 1852, p. 517.

115. Mark Demming, "Le mairie du 1er arrondissement," *Hittorff*, pp. 229–244; Leniaud, *Lassus*, pp. 114–115, 230 ff.; *JD,* April 15, November 29, 1856, May 11, 1859; *MU,* 1858, pp. 458, 890; *Ill,* 35 (January 7, 1860), pp. 31–32; *RGA* , XV (1857), cols. 108–109; *Builder,* December 4, 1858, p. 814. The *JD* of May 11, 1859, described the effect Hittorff sought interestingly: "Le résultat qu'on a encore voulu obtenir, c'est que les trois constructions ne présentent à l'oeil qu'une même facade légèrement courbée, comme l'offrirait une portion d'une vaste amphithéâtre dont les extremités s'étendraient bien au delà de la rue de Rivoli et du quai de l'Ecole."

116. "C'est à la suite de cet entretien que je cherchai, non sans peine, un agencement de la nouvelle Place dans lequel Saint-Germain-l'Auxerrois eût sa raison d'être. Je crus l'avoir trouvé dans l'élévation de la Mairie, suivant un alignement biais, en sens inverse de celui de l'Eglise et la construction d'une tour faisant face à la grande entrée du Louvre, qui leur servirait du lien et relèverait l'ensemble sous prétexte de clocher.

"Pour encadrer ce fond de place, deux massifs de maisons à toute hauteur, bâties, d'une part, à l'angle du quai de l'Ecole, d'autre part à l'angle de la rue de Rivoli, sur l'alignement de la rue du Louvre, parallèlement à la colonnade, vinrent rendre toute leur importance aux belles proportions de celle-ci, que cet immense vide semblait dévorer. . . .

"Pour justifier cette addition à Saint-Germain-l'Auxerrois, dont le clocher historique suffisait de reste à son service religieux, j'y fis installer un carillon modèle, avec le concours d'une commission composée de savants et d'artistes, et presidée par M. Dumas." (Haussmann, *Mémoires,* III, pp. 500–503).

117. Haussmann, *Mémoires*, III, pp. 47–64. Gabriel Davioud, *Les théâtres de la place du Châtelet.*

118. *Illustrated London News,* January 1854; the store Au Châtelet was advertising in the *JD,* December 3, 1853, as having been already open in April of that year.

119. *JD,* April 1, 1853.

120. Cf. Françoise Paul-Levy, op. cit.

121. Alphand, *Recueil,* p. 282; Cf. plans of the *place* in 1824 and 1858 in AS, VO11 639.

122. *JD,* April 25, 1854 (before the decree but while plans were on display for the *enquête*).

123. Haussmann, *Mémoires*, III, p. 531.

124. "La partie du Palais qui attire le plus l'attention est la coupole . . . inutile peut-être au monument en lui-même [il] sert à la décoration de l'ensemble général et forme un point saillant placé dans l'axe du boulevard de Sébastopol. . . . Le Tribunal de Commerce montre de loin un point décoratif qui se détache du milieu de l'ensemble des nouvelles voies reliant les quartiers de la rive droite à ceux de la rive gauche de la Seine. Il n'est pas écrasé par les immenses bâtiments du vieux Palais de Justice, dont il est si proche, et dont le voisinage était tout à redouter."

125. "Je n'ai jamais arrêté le tracé d'une voie quelconque, et à plus forte raison d'une artère principale de Paris, sans me préoccuper du point de vue qu'on pouvait lui donner. Or, l'examen du plan de Paris m'avait fait constater que M. Berger aurait pu donner une très faible déviation du tracé du boulevard de Strasbourg, déviation qui n'eût produit qu'un écart de quelques mètres à son arrivée sur la place du Châtelet. On aurait eu, de cette façon, le Dôme de la Sorbonne pour objectif. . . . Obligé d'y renoncer, je recommandai tout particulièrement à M. Bailly de ménager, dans son projet de Palais de la Justice commerciale, un motif principal, se détachant nettement de la masse de ses constructions, qu'il planterait en regard de la Gare de l'Est, dans l'axe du boulevard de Sébastopol." (*Mémoires,* III, p. 530)

126. Davioud, *Théâtres du place du Châtelet,* avant-propos.

127. Haussmann, *Mémoires,* II, p. 488.

128. Loviot, "Notice sur la vie et les oeuvres de M. Bailly," *Architecture* (1892), pp. 473–475; Charles Blanc, *Le temps,* December 16, 1867. Cf. Jules Lan, *Voyage de la bourse au palais de justice, ou Notice historique sur la translation du Tribunal de Commerce* (Paris: Guillaumin, 1864).

129. AN F21 6395, F21 1868, January 31, 1860, Duban reporting.

130. A practice passed on to his assistant Ernest Sanson, then by him to his assistant René

Sergent, by the turn of the century one of the most prestigious domestic practices in the world.

131. Cf. Duban's report for the Conseil des Bâtiments Civils: AN F21 6392, December 23, 1859.

132. Published with detailed plans: C. Daly, *Architecture privée*, vol. 2 (1864), 88, rue de Rivoli, by François Rolland.

133. *MU*, July 2, 1853, by N.-M. Troche.

134. "On suivrait ainsi le mode très pittoresque adapté depuis longtemps déjà pour l'ornementation des places et des carrefours."

135. Ezra Sulieman, *Private Power and Centralization in France: The Notaries and the State*; Theodore Zeldin, *The French, 1848–1945*, 5 vols. (New York: Pantheon, 1982), *Ambition and Law*, Chapter 3. The Chambre de Paris claims to host most important land sales in their space.

136. Alphand, *Recueil*, pp. 286–287, 291, 309; *Recueil des actes administratives*, IV, p. 169. The intersecting boulevard Saint-Germain was laid out by a law of June 19, 1857.

137. Van Zanten, *Designing Paris*, p. 108.

138. Davioud, *Théâtres du place du Châtelet*, avant-propos.

139. Rabreau, *Davioud*, p. 45.

140. "Au fond d'une vaste niche formant le centre de l'édifice, se trouvera la statue colossale de la France entourée de la Paix et de la Guerre figurées par deux Génies. A droite et à gauche de ce groupe, qui sera en bronze, s'élèveront quatre colonnes de marbre rouge avec chapitaux également en bronze, surmontés de statues en marbre blanc, représentant la Force, la Sagesse, etc., le tout recouvert d'un toit en ardoises dans le style de la Renaissance. Dans le bas, l'eau, s'échappant des mascarons, retombera dans des vasques et viendra se perdre dans bassins ornés de figures en bronze personnifiant le commerce, les beaux-arts, l'agriculture et l'industrie. Enfin le fronton sera orné d'une plaque de marbre sur laquelle se détachera l'inscription suivante écrite en lettres d'or:
"Sous le règne de Napoléon III
La Ville de Paris a élevé ce monument
pour pérpetuer le souvenir
de la glorieuse paix
signée par les plénipotentiaires au Congrès

de Paris le 30 mars 1856" (*JD*, April 21, 1858)

141. "Des circonstances particulières . . . ont dû amener un changement de programme dans l'édifice et modifier sensiblement le caractère général de son ornamentation première" (cited in *JD*, September 26, 1859).

142. Alfred Delvau et al., *Paris qui s'en va et Paris qui vient* (Paris: Cadart, 1860). The critique is Castagnary's.

143. *JD*, July 16, 1856.

144. "Du plus loin qu'arriverait le voyageur il apercevrait au même temps les deux monumens qui rappelleraient la grandeur et la gloire de deux générations et de deux Empires."

145. Paul Sédille, *Théodore Ballu, architecte . . .* (Paris: Chaix, 1886). I return to this in Chapter 7.

146. Rabreau, *Davioud*, p. 49.

147. Haussmann, *Mémoires*, III, pp. 89, 503.

148. Duban's report on the project for the Conseil des Bâtiments Civils: AN F21 6395 (2), June 12, 1860. Jane Hargrove, *Carrière-Belleuse*, pp. 165–166.

149. Clozier, op. cit.; Hammer, op. cit., pp. 206–216; Bowie, op. cit., pp. 95–116; *Hittorff*, pp. 266–277.

150. Jean Bouvier, *Les Rothschilds* (Paris: Fayard, 1967); Rondo Cameron, *France and the Economic Development of Europe, 1800–1914* (New York, Octagon, 1975), Chapter XI.

151. Library of the Women's Christian Temperance Union, Evanston, Ilinois: April 22, 1869.

152. AS V. O. 11.

153. Haussmann, *Mémoires*, III, p. 503.

154. Karen Bowie has found Rothschild's specifications for the subjects of these statues, which involved extra expense and were important to the financier.

155. J.-I. Hittorff, *Notice sur les ruines d'Agrigente* (Paris: Firmin-Didot, 1859).

156. J.-I. Hittorff, *Mémoire sur Pompéii et Pétra* (Paris: Imprimerie Impériale, 1866).

157. The *Gazette des architectes et du bâtiment* observed and criticized this juxtaposition in the same terms it had Baltard's Saint-Augustin.

CHAPTER 7. CHURCHES AND HISTORIC MONUMENTS

1. Françoise Choay *L'Allégorie de la patrimoine*, (Paris: Seuil, 1992); Kevin Murphy,

Memory and Modernity: Architectural Restoration in France, 1830–1848, Ph.D. dissertation, Northwestern University, 1992. A large and complex subject is interwoven in the essays of Pierre Nora's *Lieux de mémoire*. Anthony Vidler is devoting a forthcoming book to it. See also Daniel Hermant, "Destructions et vandalismes pendant la révolution française," *Annales*, 33, no. 4 (1878), pp. 703–719. For the classical conceptual foundation study see Alois Riegl, "Der moderne Denkmalkultus: sein Wesen und seine Entstehung" of 1903, *Gesammelte Aufsätze* (Augsburg-Vienna: Filser, 1929); in French with an introduction by Françoise Choay, *Le Culte moderne des monuments* (Paris: Seuil, 1984); in English, with analytical essays, *Oppositions*, 25 (fall 1982).

2. Sutcliffe, *Autumn*, Chapter 7.

3. On the definition of a monument: Frank Bowman, ed., *Abbé Grégoire, évêque des lumières* (Paris: France-Empire, 1988); Leniaud, *Lassus*, p. 222 ff.; Léon, op. cit.; Bercé, op. cit., pp. 14–17.

4. An important qualification to this is the Lyonnais treatment of the cathedral quarter as a quasi-cultural district under prefect Vaisse in the 1850s. See Bailleux de Marisy, loc. cit., p. 371. Cf. Paris legislation, Sutcliffe, op. cit., Chapter 7. In 1913 historic districts were legislated generally in France under the control of the Commission des Monuments Historiques: Léon, op. cit., pp. 351–357.

5. VIII (1866), pp. 14–34.

6. "Notre temps, et notre temps seulement depuis le commencement des siècles historiques, a pris en face du passé une attitude inusitée. Il a voulu l'analyser, le comparer, le classer et former sa véritable histoire, en suivant pas à pas la marche, les progrès, les transformations de l'humanité. . . . Notre temps n'aurait-t-il à transmettre aux siècles futurs que cette méthode nouvelle d'étudier les choses du passé, soit dans l'ordre matériél, soit dans l'ordre moral, qu'il aurait bien mérité de la postérité." (pp. 15, 16)

7. "Chaque édifice ou chaque partie d'un édifice doivent être restaurés dans le style qui leur appartient, non seulement comme apparence, mais comme structure" (p. 23).

8. "Si l'architecte chargé de la restauration d'un édifice doit connaître les formes, les styles appartenant à cet édifice et à l'école dont il est sorti, il doit mieux encore, s'il est possible, connaître sa structure, son anatomie, son tempérament, car avant tout il faut qu'il le fasse vivre" (p. 27).

9. "Dans les restaurations, il est une condition dominante qu'il faut toujours avoir présente à l'esprit. C'est de ne substituer à toute partie enlevée que des matériaux meilleurs et de moyens plus énergiques ou plus parfaits. Il faut que l'édifice restauré ait passé pour l'avenir, par suite de l'opération à laquelle on l'a soumis, un bail plus long que celui déjà écoulé" (p. 26).

10. "Notre temps ne se contente pas de jeter un regard scrutateur derrière lui: ce travail rétrospectif ne fait que développer les problèmes posés dans l'avenir et faciliter leur solution. C'est le synthèse qui suit l'analyse" (p. 16).

11. "Si le XIXe siècle possédait un style d'architecture qui lui fût propre, peut-être pourrait-on soutenir qu'il est bon d'en marquer le passage toutes les fois qu'une occasion se présente de compléter un vieux monument. Mais je ne crois pas que . . . on en soit arrivé à présenter ce style. . . . Notre temps possède, par contre, une qualité qui lui est particulière. . . . Il a su, par l'étude attentive du passé . . . en saisir l'esprit, la raison d'être et les formes déduites des conditions faites aux artistes de ces temps anciens. . . . Donc pour être de notre temps, il faut conserver les édifices dans leur forme primitive." Letter to Gustave Klotz, October 18, 1873: Auzas, op. cit., p. 174–175.

12. Cf. Leniaud, "Edifices Diocésains", pp. 156–157; Hubert Damisch, *Viollet-le-Duc: l'architecture raisonnée* (Paris: Hermann, 1964). Cf. Anatole Leroy-Beaulieu, "La restauration de nos monuments historiques devant l'art et devant le budget," *Revue des deux mondes*, 3S, no. 6 (December 1, 1874), pp. 606–625.

13. "Les monuments en général et ceux du Moyen âge en particulier ne sont pas faits pour être vus en géométral mais suivant certains angles et cela est tout naturel: le point géométral est unique, les autres sont infinis en nombre. Donc il faut faire les monuments non en prévision de ce point unique, mais bien en vue de ces points multiples"

(Auzas, op. cit., p. 82; cited in Leniaud, "Edifices diocésains," pp. 159–160).

14. The only truly urban scheme Viollet-le-Duc seems to have sketched was the unexecuted complex north of Notre-Dame on the Ile de la Cité to form a "cité épiscopal" but which seems compositionally conventional. At Clermont-Ferrand he squeezed a new two-towered facade into a space that left it invisible except as a distant silhouette.

15. Charles Nicholas, *Les budgets de la France depuis le commencement du XIXe siècle* (Paris: Lahure, 1882), pp. 290–291.

16. Alexandre L.-J. de Laborde, *Versailles ancien et moderne* (Paris: Everart, 1839). Cf. Marrinen, op. cit., pp. 164 ff.; Thomas Gaehtgens, *Versailles als Nationaldenkmal: die Galerie des Batailles im Musée Historique von Louis Philippe* (Berlin: Frolich & Kaufmann, 1988).

17. Decret sur les Biens Ecclésiastiques, November, 2–4, 1789: Commission de Recherche et de Publication des Documents Relatifs à la Vie Economique de la Révolution, *Recueil des textes législatifs et administratifs concernant les biens nationaux* (Paris: Imprimerie Nationale, 1926), I, pp. 1 ff.

18. Commission des Monuments Historiques, procès-verbaux, January 15, February 19, March 5, 1838: Bercé, op. cit., pp. 24, 29, 32.

19. Bruno Foucart, *La renouveau de la peinture religieuse en France (1800–1860)*, p. 56; Michael Driskel, "The 'Gothic', the Revolution and the Abyss: Jean-Philippe Schmit's Aesthetic Authority," *Art History*, 13, no. 2 (June 1990), pp. 195–211. Cf. Joseph Comblin, *Théologie de la ville* (Paris: Editions Universitaires, 1968), pp. 390–407.

20. "Franchissons donc ce seuil, pleins de l'émotion qui nous domine. O merveille! tout change subitement: au lieu de cet aspect solonnel et mélancolique de l'imposante façade, au lieu de cet image ménancante du Jugement, c'est un spectacle de gloire qui nous environne. . . . A contempler ce caractère d'immensité imprimé à l'oeuvre architectonique, on sent que son auteur était pénétré de celle du Dieu à qui elle est élevée; . . ." Jean-Philippe Schmit, *Les Eglises gothiques* (Paris: Angé, 1837, p. 55 ff).

21. "Les églises du moyen âge ne sont point faites pour être vues aussi à découvert: elles ne sont convenablement placées qu'au milieu du silence et de la retraite; elles aimait à se voir entourées de demeures modestes et paisibles, qui semblent venir se presser à leur pied; elles ont besoin surtout d'être environnées de ces cloîtres muets et solitaires, destinés à l'habitation des ministres et des serviteurs du temple, qui en formaient la garde, . . .

"Dès que l'église n'a plus été qu'un bâtiment accidentellement jeté sur la voie publique comme une salle de spectacle, comme un bazar, comme un café, on s'est dit naturellement: j'y entrerai en passant, comme on se dit: j'entrerai en passant au musée." Pp. 159,163

22. Leniaud, *Lassus*, pp. 34 ff.; E.-J. Delécluze, *Souvenirs de soixante années* (Paris: Lévy frères, 1862), pp. 494–502.

23. André Trannoy, *Le romantisme politique de Montalembert avant 1843* (Paris: Blond & Gay, 1942). Cf. Foucart, *Renouveau*, pp. 15–24.

24. Montalembert, *Du Vandalisme et du catholicisme dans l'art* (Paris: Debécourt, 1839, p. 160 ff).

25. F. de Guilhermy, *La Sainte-Chapelle* (Paris: "à la Sainte-Chapelle," 1867) and *La Sainte-Chapelle de Paris* (Paris: Bance, 1877). Cf. his *Iconographie de l'église impériale de Saint-Denis* (Paris, 1865).

26. Arthur Martin and Charles Cahier, *Monographie de la cathédrale de Bourges* (Paris: Pousielgue-Rusand, 1841–1844).

27. Villard de Honnecourt, ed., *Album* (Paris: Imprimerie Impériale, 1858); (with A. Duval) *Monographie de la cathédrale de Chartres* (Paris: Imprimerie Impériele, 1867).

28. Jean Maurain, *La politique ecclésiastique de la Second Empire* (Paris: Alcan, 1930).

29. Germann, *op. cit.*; Léon, *op. cit.*; Leniaud, *op. cit.*

30. *Annales archéologiques*, I (1844), pp. i–vii.

31. As we have noted, there was a bitter controversy about the project in general as well as in detail to which both Lassus and Viollet-le-Duc contributed pamphlets: Lassus, *Réaction de l'Académie des Beaux-Arts contre l'art gothique* (Paris: Didron, 1846); Viollet-le-Duc, "Réponse aux considérations de l'Académie des Beaux-Arts sur la

question de savoir s'il est convenable au XIXe siècle de bâtir des églises en style gothique," *Annales archeologiques,* IV (1846), pp. 333–353.

32. Leniaud, *Lassus,* pp. 146–148, 243–255.

33. In a very interesting paper delivered at the Architectural Association in London in 1978 Bruno Foucart suggested reasons why Burges might have been initially preferred to Lassus, specifically that the English project was more strictly correct liturgically.

34. Foucart, *Renouveau,* Chapters 4, 6.

35. Germann, op. cit., pp. 151–166.

36. On Rouen: Murphy, op. cit., Chapter 3.

37. *Annales archéologiques,* III (1845), pp. 175–184; *L'Univers,* October 1, 1842, March 11 and 16, April 21, 1843; AN F21 2537.

38. *Viollet-le-Duc,* 1981, pp. 178–181; Lucy McClintock, "Monumentality Versus Suitability: Viollet-le-Duc's Saint-Gimer at Carcassonne," *Journal of the Society of Architectural Historians,* XL, no. 3 (October 1981), pp. 218–235.

39. *Paul Abadie, architecte, 1812–1884,* Paris: Musée des Monuments Français, 1988), pp. 189 ff. Michael Driskel is finishing a study of the Sacré-Coeur. See David Harvey, "Monument and Myth: The Building of the Basilica of the Sacred Heart," *Consciousness and Urban Experience,* pp. 221–249.

40. Léon, op. cit., pp. 220–221; Bercé, op. cit., meetings of May 11, 1849; February 1, July 19, November 29, and December 6, 1850.

41. Foucart, *Renouveau,* especially pp. 53–60; Michael Driskel, "Painting Piety and Politics in 1848: Hippolyte Flandrin's Emblem of Equity at Nimes," *Art Bulletin,* LXVI, no. 2 (June,1984), pp. 270–285; *Representing Belief* (University Park: Pennsylvania State University, 1992). The movement was preceded by Hittorff's efforts to decorate the interior of his newly constructed church of Saint-Vincent-de-Paul (Claudine de Vaulchier, *Hittorff,* pp. 111–115). For an early anecdotal history of the development see Antoine Fillioux, "De la peinture monumentale," *L'Artiste,* 3S, 5, pp. 262–265.

42. *MU,* January 10, 1861; *RGA,* XX (1862), col. 236; Haussmann, *Mémoires,* III, p. 485.

43. *RGA,* XII (1854), col. 84.

44. AS M32 V32.

45. Narjoux, op. cit., vol. III; Haussmann, *Mémoires,* III, p. 484. Reviews: (Jules Bouchet) *RGA,* XXVII (1869), cols. 84–88; *Magasin pittoresque,* 1869, pp. 365–366; *Gazette des architectes et du bâtiment,* 1868, pp. 1–4.

46. Jules Bouchet in his review of the building in the *RGA* asks why the *alignements* were permitted to determine the design so completely.

47. Bruno Foucart, "Comment peut-on aimer une église du XIXe siècle ou la réhabilitation du pastiche," *Monuments historiques,* XX (1974), pp. 64–71.

48. Narjoux, *Paris,* III, Edifices Religieux; Bruno Foucart, "La 'cathédrale synthétique' de Louis-Auguste Boileau," *Revue de l'art,* 3 (1969), pp. 49–66.

49. *JD,* September 1, 2, and 5, 1858; expanded upon in his *mémoires* to the Conseil Municipal of June 15, 1860, and April 21, 1865.

50. "Un intérêt supérieur, celui du progrès des moeurs publiques, nous invite à seconder autant qu'il est en nous, les louables efforts du clergé."

51. All put before the Conseil des Bâtiments Civils simultaneously in early 1860: AN F21 6395, F21 1868.

52. "Exposé de la situation de l'Empire," *Encyclopédie d'architecture,* February 1861, col. 32; February 1862, cols. 29–30. Cf. letter from Napoleon III: *JD,* January 15, 1860. Also see Maurain, *La Politique ecclésiastique du Second Empire,* Chapter XVI.

53. All documented in Narjoux, op. cit., vol. III. See also *RGA,* XX (1862), cols. 232–240.

54. "Il suffit d'ériger aujourd'hui des églises suffisamment vastes, mais simplement conçues, commode pour le culte, mais remarquable par la convenance du dessin plus que par le nombre de rosaces et de statues." *JD,* September 5, 1858.

55. AS V I M31 1. Evidently Haussmann commissioned a model project from Boileau at that time. Cf. Leniaud, "Les Constructions d'églises sous le Second Empire: architecture et le prix revient," *Revue de l'histoire de l'église en France,* 65 (1979), pp. 268–278.

56. See de Baudot's analysis of Viollet-le-Duc's parish church of Notre-Dame-de-l'Estrée in Saint-Denis, *Gazette des architectes et du*

bâtiment, "L'Eglise paroissiale de Saint-Denis," IV, no. 8 (1866), pp. 113–114, 193–195.

57. "Que le but constant soit la recherche d'une économie conciliable avec la haute destination de ces édifices, suprême expression d'une époque. . . ."

58. Called Saint-Pierre-de-Chaillot: *Viollet-le-Duc* ,1980, pp.196–199.

59. "La Trinité est en effet un véritable église parisienne du XIXe siècle, suffisamment religieuse et sévère, en ce siècle de foi trop attiédie, convenablement luxueuse et confortable pour satisfaire aux habitudes mondaines de la bourgeoisie aisée qui fréquente cette église. Son large nef est un cadre somptueux et aimable qui invite aux riantes espérances des mariages heureux; et cependant nous nous souvenons que, voilée de deuil, cette nef unique prend aussi une grande solennité quand vous faites station dernière et douloureuse après d'une dépouille

amie." Paul Sédille, "Théodore Ballu, architecte, 1817–1885," *Bulletin de la société centrale des architectes,* 1886 (also published as pamphlet). Cf. C. Detain, *Monographie de l'église de Saint-Ambroise* (Paris: Ducher, 1874).

60. Théodore Ballu, *Monographie de l'église de la Sainte Trinité* (Paris: Dupuis, 1868); C. Detain, *Monographie de l'église Saint-Ambroise.*

61. His large parish church at Argenteuil, first sketched in 1852 and erected in 1862–1865, likewise played an important role in that community's self-imaging, although in a different sense, as is evident in the discussions of the Conseil Municipal and in a pamphlet written by the mayor, Touzelin, in 1852, all preserved at the Hôtel de Ville. I am obliged to the municipal archivist, M. Paretti, for showing these to me.

BIBLIOGRAPHY

NINETEENTH-CENTURY SERIALS
AND COLLECTIVITIES

Almanach national.
Annales archéologiques, 1844–1881.
Architecture, 1888 ff.
Le Bâtiment, 1864 ff.
Bibliothèque municipale, 1862–1868.
Budget de la Ville de Paris, 1818 ff.
Bulletin archéologique, 1843–1853.
Bulletin des lois.
Bulletin de la société centrale des architectes, 1842 ff.
Commission municipale du vieux Paris, procès-verbal, 1898–1932.
La Construction moderne, 1885 ff.
Courrier municipal, 1873–1879.
Encyclopédie d'architecture, 1851–1862, 1872–1892.
Gazette des architectes et du bâtiment, 1863–1871.
Gazette des beaux-arts, 1859 ff.
Illustrated London News, 1842 ff.
L'Illustration, 1843 ff.
Journal des chemins de fer, des mines et des travaux publics, 1842 ff.
Journal des débats, 1789 ff.
Le Monde illustré, 1857 ff.
Le Moniteur des architectes, 1847–1900.
Moniteur universel, 1789–1868.
Recueil des actes administratifs de la préfecture du département de la Seine, 9 vols. (Paris: Paul Dupont, 1876).
Recueil des clauses connues sous le nom de Réserves Dominales imposées aux acquéreurs des biens nationaux . . . (Paris: Chaix, 1897).
Revue générale de l'architecture et des travaux publics, 1840–1889.
Revue municipale, 1848–1862.
Semaine des constructeurs, 1876 ff.

EXHIBITION CATALOGS

Grand Palais, *La sculpture française au XIXe siècle,* 1986.
Hôtel de la Monnaie, *Colbert, 1619–1683,* 1983.
Musée Carnavelet, *Henri Lehmann, 1814–1882,* Paris, 1983.
Musée des Monuments Français, *Paul Abadie, architecte, 1812–1884,* 1988.
Pavillon de l'Arsenal, *Paris. Haussmann,* 1991.
Philadelphia Art Museum, *The Second Empire: Art in France Under Napoleon III,* 1978.
Réunion des Musées Nationaux, *Viollet-le-Duc,* 1980.

BOOKS AND ARTICLES

Académie d'Architecture, *Catalogue des Collections,* I (1750–1900) (Paris: Académie d'Architecture, 1987).
Jean-Pierre Allinne, *Banquiers et bâtisseurs* (Paris: CNRS, 1984).
Adolphe Alphand, *Recueil des lettres patantes, ordonnances royales, décrets et arrêtés préfectoraux concernant les voies publiques* (Paris: Imprimerie Nouvelle, 1886).

Adolphe Alphand, *Les promenades de Paris* (Paris: Rothschild, 1867–1873).

Pierre Angrand, "La commande des portraits officiels sous Napoléon III," *Gazette des Beaux-Arts,* 6S 70 (1967), p. 185.

Pierre Angrand, "L'état mécène: période autoritaire du Second Empire (1851–1860), *Gazette des Beaux-Arts,* 6S 71 (1968), pp. 303–345.

Catherine Arland and Dominique Bertin, *De la rue Impériale à la rue de la République* (Lyon: Mun, 1991).

Christine Aulanier, *Histoire du palais et du musée du Louvre,* 10 vols. (Paris: Editions des musées nationaux, 1947–1968).

Henri Duc d'Aumale, *Notice sur le comte de Cardaillac* (Paris: Firmin-Didot, 1880).

Jean Autin, *Les frères Pereire: le bonheur d'entreprendre* (Paris: Perrin, 1984).

Pierre Auzas, *Viollet-le-Duc 1814–1879,* 2nd ed. (Paris: Caisse Nationale des Monuments Historiques et des Sites, 1978).

Georges d'Avenel, "Les mécanismes de la vie moderne: La Maison parisienne," *Revue des Deux Mondes,* 4S 145 (April 15, 1897), pp. 792–824 and 4S146 (May 15, 1897), pp. 279–309, published as a book under that title, 4 vols. (Paris: Colin, 1897–1900).

Jean-Pierre Babelon, "L.-T.-J. Visconti et le Louvre," *Etudes offertes à André Chastel* (Paris: Flammarion, 1987), pp. 617–632.

Alexis Bailleux de Marisy, *La Transformation des grandes villes de France* (Paris: Hachette, 1867).

Simone Balayé, *La Bibliothèque nationale, des origines à 1800* (Geneva: Droz, 1988).

Hilary Ballon, *The Paris of Henri IV* (Cambridge, MIT Press, 1991).

Théodore Ballu, *Monographie de l'église de la Sainte-Trinité* (Paris: Dupuis, 1868).

Louis.-Pierre Baltard and Amaury Duval, *Paris et ses Monuments,* 2 vols. (Paris: authors, 1803 and 1805).

Victor Baltard and F.-E. Callet, *Monographie des Halles centrales de Paris* (Paris: Morel, 1863).

F. Barqui, *Architecture moderne en France* (Paris: Baudry, 1871).

Charles Bauchal, *Nouveau Dictionnaire biographique et critique des architectes français* (Paris: André Daly fils, 1887).

Anatole de Baudot, *Eglises de bourgs et villages,* 2 vols. (Paris: Morel, 1867).

Anatole de Baudot, *L'Architecture: le passé, le présent, l'avenir* (Paris: Laurens, 1916).

Reinhard Baumeister, *Stadt-Erweiterungen in technischer, baupolizeilicher und wirtschaftlicher Beziehung* (Berlin: Ernst & Korn, 1876).

Glenn Benge, *Antoine Bayre: Sculptor of Romantic Realism* (University Park: Pennsylvania State University, 1984).

Paul Bénichou, *Le Sacre de l'écrivain, 1750–1830* (Paris: Corti, 1973).

Paul Bénichou, *Le Temps des prophètes: doctrines de l'âge romantique* (Paris: Gallimard, 1977).

Walter Benjamin, *Charles Baudelaire: A Lyric Poetic in the Era of High Capitalism* (London: NLB, 1973).

Léon Bequet, *Répertoire du droit administratif,* 24 vols. (Paris: Dupont, 1882–1914).

Françoise Bercé, *Les premiers travaux de la Commission des Monuments Historiques, 1837–1848* (Paris: Picard, 1979).

Barry Bergdoll, *Léon Vaudoyer,* Ph.D. dissertation, Columbia University, 1989.

Barry Bergdoll, *Le Panthéon: symbole des révolutions* (Montreal, Centre canadien d'architecture, 1989).

Barry Bergdoll, *Les Vaudoyer, une dynastie d'architectes* (Paris: Musée d'Orsay, 1991).

Robert Berger, *The Palace of the Sun: the Louvre of Louis XIV* (University Park: Pennsylvania State University, 1993).

Marie Berhaut, *Gustave Caillebotte: sa vie et son oeuvre* (Paris: Bibliothèque des Arts, 1978).

Ernest Beulé, "L'Ecole de Rome au XIXe siècle," *Revue des deux mondes,* 2S vol. 48 (December 15, 1863), pp. 916–938.

L.-N.-D. Biet, Gourlier, Grillon, and Tardieu, *Choix des édifices publics projetés et construits en France depuis le commencement du XIXe siècle,* 3 vols. (Paris: Colas, 1825–1850).

Marie-Louise Biver, *Pierre Fontaine* (Paris: Plon, 1964).

Marie-Louise Biver, *Le Paris de Napoléon* (Paris: Plon, 1965).

Charles Blanc, *Les Artistes de mon temps* (Paris: Firmin-Didot, 1876).

Charles Blanc, *Grammaire des arts de dessin,* (Paris: Rounard, 1867).

Jean Bleton, "Les Bâtiments," in Dominique Varry, *Histoire des bibliothèques françaises,* vol. III. *Les Bibliothèques de la Révolution et du XIXe siècle* (Paris: Cercle de la Librairie, 1991), pp. 183–237.

Marc Bloch, *Les rois thaumaturges,* new ed. (Paris: Galimard, 1983).

Maurice Block, *Administration de la ville de Paris et du département de la Seine* (Paris: Guillaumin, 1884).

Maurice Block, *Dictionnaire de l'Administration française,* 3rd ed. (Paris: Berger-Levrault, 1891).

François Blondel, *Cours d'architecture enseigné dans l'académie royale d'architecture* (Paris: Lambert Roulland, 1675–1683).

J.-F. BLondel (completed by Pierre Patte), *Cours d'architecture,* 6 vols. (Paris: Desaint, 1771–1777).

Abel Blouet and F.-A. Desmetz, *Rapport à M. le Comte de Montalivet . . . sur les pénitenciers des Etats-Unis* (Paris: Imprimerie Royale, 1837).

Abel Blouet, Hector Horeau, Harou Romain, *Instruction et programme pour la construction des maisons d'arrêt et de justice* (Paris: Ministère de l'Intérieur, 1841).

Abel Blouet, *Projet de prison cellulaire pour 585 condamnés précédé d'observations sur le système pénitentiare* (Paris: Didot, 1843).

Anthony Blunt, "The Hypnerotomachia in Seventeenth-Century France," *Journal of the Warburg and Courtauld Institutes,* I, no. 2 (1937), pp. 117–137.

Albert Boime, "The Teaching Reforms of 1863 and the Origins of Modernism in France," *Art Quarterly,* NS, I (1977), pp. 1–39.

Albert Boime, *Thomas Couture and the Eclectic Vision* (London-New Haven: Yale University Press, 1980).

H. N. Boon, *Rêve et réalité dans l'oeuvre économique et sociale de Napoléon III* (The Hague: Nijhoff, 1936).

Adolphe Borie, *Aérodomes: essai sur un nouveau mode de maisons d'habitation applicable aux quartiers les plus mouvementés des grandes villes* (Paris: Morris, 1865).

Françoise Boudon, "L'Urbanisme et spéculation à Paris au XVIIIe siècle: le terrain de l'hôtel de Soissons," *Journal of the Society of Architectural Historians,* 32, no. 4 (December 1973), pp. 267–307.

Françoise Boudon, "La 'Maison à Loyer' de la ville haussmannienne," *Revue de l'art,* no. 79 (1988), pp. 63–72.

Philippe Boudon, *Richelieu, ville nouvelle* (Paris: Dunod, 1978).

Nicolas Boussu, *Etudes administratives: l'administration des beaux-arts* (Paris: Baltenweck, 1877).

Jean Bouvier, *Le Crédit Lyonnais de 1863 à 1881* Paris: SEVPEN, 1961).

Karen Bowie, *L'éclecticisme pittoresque et l'architecture des gares parisiennes au XIXe siècle* (Paris, thèse du troisième cycle, 1985).

Karen Bowie, *Les Gares parisiennes du XIXe siècle* (Paris: Délégation à l'Action Artistique de la Ville de Paris, 1987).

Frank Bowman, ed., *Abbé Grégoire, évêque des lumières* (Paris: France-Empire, 1988).

Allan Braham, *The Architecture of the French Enlightenment* (Berkeley: University of California Press, 1980).

Elie Brault, *Les Architectes par leurs oeuvres,* 3 vols. (Paris: Laurens, 1893).

P. Breillat, *Ville nouvelle, ville modèle: Versailles* (Versailles: Lys, 1985).

Patrice Broussel, *Victor Baltard: projets inédits pour les halles centrales* (Paris: BHVP, 1978).

André Brunot and Roger Coquand, *Le Corps des ponts et chaussées* (Paris: CNRS, 1982).

Louis Bruyère, *Etudes relatives à l'art des constructions,* 2 vols. (Paris: Bance, 1823–1828).

L. M. Bryant, *The King and the City in the Parisian Royal Entry Ceremony: Ritual and Art in the Renaissance* (Geneva: Droz, 1986).

Susan Buck-Morss, *The Dialectics of Seeing: Walter Benjamin and the Arcades Project* (Cambridge, MIT Press, 1989).

Sylvie Buisson, "Le plan des artistes," *La Vie urbaine,* 55 (January-March, 1950), pp. 8–21; 57 (July-September, 1950), pp. 161–171.

Victor Calliat, *Hôtel de Ville de Paris, mesuré, dessiné, gravé et publié par Victor Calliat,* 2 vols. (Paris: author, 1844 and 1856).

Jacques de Caso, "Neuf lettres inédites de Delacroix à Duban au sujet des travaux de la Galerie d'Apollon," *Bulletin de la société de l'histoire de l'art français* (1966), pp. 66–73.

Jacques de Caso, "Duban et la restauration de la Galerie du bord de l'eau . . .," *Bulletin de la société de l'histoire de l'art français* (1973), pp. 332–345.

Jean Castex, *Formes urbaines: de l'îlot à la barre* (Paris: Bordas, 1977).

Ildefonso Cerdà, *Teoría general de la urbanizacion*, 2 vols. (Madrid: Imprenta Espanola, 1867) (republished with introductory volume by Antonio Barrera de Irimo, Madrid: Instituto de Estudios fiscales, 1968).

Ildefonso Cerdà, *Teoría de la construccion de las ciudades*, 2 vols. (Madrid: Instituto de administración publica, 1991).

L. Cernesson, "Emile Gilbert: sa vie, ses oeuvres – notice biographique," *Annales de la société centrale des architectes*, IS 2 (1874).

J. M. Chapman and Brian Chapman, *The Life and Times of Baron Haussmann* (London: Weidenfeld, 1957).

Edouard Charton, *Guide pour le choix d'un état* (Paris: author, 1842).

André Chastel, Françoise Boudon, Hélène Couzy, Françoise Hamon, *Système de l'architecture urbaine: le quartier des Halles à Paris*, 2 vols. (Paris: CNRS, 1977).

Philippe de Chennevières, "Souvenirs d'un directeur des beaux-arts," *L'Artiste*, 1883–1889. Published as a book under that title (Paris: Arthéna, 1979).

Françoise Choay, *La règle et le modèle: sur la théorie de l'urbanisme* (Paris: Seuil, 1980).

Françoise Choay, *L'Allégorie de la patrimoine* (Paris: Seuil, 1992).

Alfred des Cilleuls, *Traité de la législation et de l'administration de la voirie urbaine* (Paris: Ducher, 1877).

Pierre Citron, *La poésie de Paris dans la littérature française de Rousseau à Baudelaire*, 2 vols. (Paris: Minuit, 1961).

Frédéric de Clarac, *Musée de sculpture antique et moderne ou Description historique et graphique du Louvre . . .* 8 vols. (Paris: Imprimerie Royale, 1826–1853).

T. J. Clark, *The Absolute Bourgeois: Artists and Politics in France, 1848–1851* (New York: New York Graphic Society, 1973).

T. J. Clark, *The Painting of Modern Life: Paris in the Art of Manet and his Followers* (New York: Knopf, 1985.).

Meredith Clausen, *Frantz Jourdain and the Samaritaine: Art Nouveau Theory and Criticism* (Leiden: Brill, 1987).

Gloria C. Clifton, *Professionalism, Patronage, and Public Service in Victorian London: The Staff of the Metropolitan Board of Works, 1856–1889* (London: Athlone, 1992).

Michel Clozier, *La Gare du Nord* (Paris: thèse de doctorat de la Faculté des Lettres, 1940).

Christiane Crasemann Collins, *Camillo Sitte and the Birth of Modern City Planning* (New York: Rizzoli, 1986).

Maurice Culot and Jean-Pierre Eperon, "Fontaine et les architectes," *Journal de P.-F.-L. Fontaine*, pp. xxxvii–lii.

Léon Daffrey de la Monnoye, *Théorie et pratique de l'expropriation pour cause d'utilité publique* (Paris: Pedone-Lauriel, 1879).

César Daly, *Architecture privée au XIXe siècle sous Napoléon III*, 6 vols. (Paris: Morel, 1864–1877).

Hubert Damisch ed., *Viollet-le-Duc: l'architecture raisonnée* (Paris: Hermann, 1964).

Hubert Damisch, "La colonnade de Perrault et les fonctions de l'ordre classique," *L'Urbanisme de Paris et de l'Europe, 1600–1680*, Pierre Francastel, ed. (Paris: Klinksieck, 1969), pp. 85–94.

Jean-Claude Daufresne, *Le Louvre et les Tuileries: architectures de papier*, (Liège: Mardaga, 1989).

Marie Daumard, *Maisons de Paris et propriétaires parisiennes au XIXe siècle* (Paris: Cujas, 1965).

Henri Davenne, *Législation et principes de la voirie urbaine* (Paris: Dupont, 1849).

Nancy Davenport, "Charles-Louis Mueller et ses décorations peintes au Louvre," *Bulletin de la société de l'histoire de l'art français* (1986), pp. 145–163.

Gabriel Davioud and César Daly, *Les théâtres de la place du Châtelet* (Paris: Ducher, 1865).

Pierre Debofle, *La Politique d'urbanisme de la ville de Paris sous la Restauration* (Paris: thèse d'état, 1992).

Eugène Delaire, *Architectes élèves de l'Ecole des Beaux-Arts* (Paris, Chaix, 1895; second expanded edition, 1907).

E.-J. Delécluze, *Souvenirs de soixante années* (Paris: Lévy frères, 1862).

Jean Des Cars, *Haussmann: la gloire du Second Empire* (Paris, 1978).

E. Deschamps, *Atlas des 20 arrondissements de la ville de Paris* (Paris: Ville de Paris, 1868).

C. Detain, *Monographie de l'église Saint-Ambroise* (Paris: Ducher, 1874).

Alfred Delvau et al., *Paris qui s'en va et Paris qui vient* (Paris: Cadart, 1860).

Pierre Deyon, *Le temps des prisons* (Lille: Université de Lille, 1975).

Jeanne Doin, "Charles Séchan et son atelier de décoration théâtrale pendant le romantisme," *Gazette des Beaux-Arts*, 5S II (1925), pp. 344–360.

Arthur Drexler ed., *The Architecture of the Ecole des Beaux-Arts* (New York: MOMA, 1977).

Michael Driskel, "The 'Gothic', the Revolution and the Abyss: Jean-Philippe Schmit's Aesthetic of Authority," *Art History*, 13, no. 2 (June 1990), pp. 193–211.

Michael Driskel, *Representing Belief* (University Park: Pennsylvania State University, 1992).

Michael Driskel, *As Befits a Legend: Building a Tomb for Napoleon, 1840–1861* (Kent, Ohio: Kent State University, 1993).

Alexandre Dubois and Charles Lucas, *Biographie universelle des architectes célèbres* (Paris: Lahure, 1868).

Paul Dufournet, ed., *Hector Horeau, 1801–1872* (Paris: Académie d'Architecture, 1979), pp. 93–95.

Georges Duplessis, *Notice sur M. Hippolyte Destailleur, architecte* (Paris: Morgand, 1895).

Georges Duplessis, *Notice sur M. Alfred Armand, architecte* (Paris: Plon, 1888).

Paul Dupré and Gustave Ollendorf, *Traité de l'administration des beaux-arts* (Paris: Dupont, 1885).

Donald Drew Egbert, *The Beaux-Arts Tradition in French Architecture* Princeton: Princeton University Press, 1980).

William Underwood Eiland, *Napoleon III and the Administration of the Fine Arts* Ph.D. dissertation, University of Virginia, 1978.

Norbert Elias, *Prozess der Civilization* (Basel: Haus zum Falken, 1939) (English: *The Civilizing Process,* New York: Urizen, 1978).

Norbert Elias, *Höfische Gesellschaft* (Darmstadt: Luchterhand, 1969) (English: *The Court Society,* New York: Pantheon, 1983).

Jean-Pierre Eperon, *Architecture: une anthologie,* 3 vols. (Liège: Mardaga, 1992–1993).

J.-E.-D. Esquirol, *Des Etablissements des aliénés en France* (Paris: Juzard, 1819).

N.-T. Le Moyne des Essarts, *Dictionnaire universel de police,* 8 vols. (Paris: Moutard, 1786–1790).

Lucien Etienne, "La Vie et les oeuvres de Paul Sédille," *L'Architecture,* XIII, no. 34 (August 25, 1900), pp. 306–308, no. 35 (September 1, 1900), pp. 313–315.

Robin Evans, *The Fabrication of Virtue: English Prison Architecture, 1750–1840* (Cambridge: Cambridge University Press, 1982).

André Félibien, *Dissertation touchant sur l'architecture antique et l'architecture gothique* (Paris, 1699).

Jules Ferry, *Les Comptes fantastiques d'Haussmann* (Paris: Le Chevalier, 1868).

P.-F.-L. Fontaine, *Journal, 1799–1853,* 2 vols. (Paris: IFA, 1987).

P.-F.-L. Fontaine and Charles Percier, *Résidences de souverains: parallèle entre plusieurs résidences de souverains de France, d'Allemagne, de Suède, de Russie, d'Espagne et d'Italie* (Paris: authors, 1833).

P.-F.-L. Fontaine and Charles Percier, *Journal des monuments de Paris, envoyé par Fontaine à l'Empereur de Russie, dans les années 1809, 1810, 1811, 1814 et 1815, complément avec un avertissement de Albert Vuaflart* (Paris: Rahir, 1892).

Bruno Fortier, ed., *Machines à guérir* (Liège: Mardaga, 1979).

Hippolyte Fortoul, *De l'art en Allemagne,* 2 vols. (Paris: Labitte, 1842).

Bruno Foucart, "La 'cathédrale synthétique' de Louis-Auguste Boileau," *Revue de l'art,* 3 (1969), pp. 46–66.

Bruno Foucart, "Comment peut-on aimer une église du XIXe siècle ou la réhabilitation du pastiche," *Monuments historiques,* XX (1974), pp. 64–71.

Bruno Foucart, "Architecture carcérale et architectes fonctionalistes en France au XIXe siècle," *Revue de l'art,* 32 (1976), pp. 37–56.

Bruno Foucart, *Le renouveau de la peinture religieuse en France (1800–1860)* (Paris: Arthéna, 1987).

Bruno Foucart and Véronique Noel-Bouton, "Les projets d'église pour Napoléonville (1802–1809)," *Bulletin de la société de l'histoire de l'art français* (1971), pp. 235–252.

Michel Foucault, *Folie et déraison: histoire de la folie à l'âge classique* (Paris: Plon, 1961).

Michel Foucault, *Surveiller et punir: naissance de la prison* (Paris: Gallimard, 1975).

Michel Foucault, "La politique de la santé au XVIIIe siècle," *Les machines à guerir* (Liège: Mardaga, 1979).

Victor Fournel, *Paris nouveau, Paris futur* (Paris: Lecoffre, 1865).

Alice Friedman, "Academic Theory and A.-L.-T. Vaudoyer's 'Dissertation sur l'architecture,'" *Art Bulletin*, 67 (1985), pp. 110–123.

Jane Fulcher, *The Nation's Image: French Grand Opera as Politics and Politicized Art* (Cambridge-New York: Cambridge University Press, 1987).

Charles Gabet, *Dictionnaire des artistes de l'école française* (Paris: Vergne, 1831).

Thomas Gaehtgens, *Versailles als National-aldenkmal: die Galerie des Batailles im Musée Historique von Louis Philippe* (Berlin: Frolich & Kaufmann, 1988).

Henri Gaillac, *Les Maisons de correction* Paris: (Cujas, 1971).

Jeanne Gaillard, *Paris, la ville, 1852–1870* (Paris: Champion, 1976).

Danielle Gallet-Guerne and Christian Baulez, *Versailles: dessins d'architecture de la Direction Générale des Bâtiments du Roi*, 2 vols. (Paris: Archives Nationales, 1983, 1989).

Charles Garnier, *Le Théâtre* (Paris: Hachette, 1871).

Charles Garnier, *Le nouvel Opéra de Paris*, 2 vols. and atlas (Paris: Ducher, 1878–1881).

"Charles Garnier par Mme. Garnier," *L'Architecture*, 38, no. 21, pp. 377–390.

Johann Friedrich Geist and Klaus Kürvers, *Das Berliner Mietshaus*, 3 vols. (Munich: Prestel, 1980–1989).

Georg Germann, *The Gothic Revival in Europe and Britain* (Cambridge, MIT Press, 1972).

Sigfried Giedion, *Bauen in Frankreich* (Berlin: Klinkhardt & Biermann, 1928).

Louis Girard, *La Politique des travaux publics du Second Empire* (Paris: Colin, 1952).

Simon Girard, *Théodore Labrouste, architecte: sa vie, ses oeuvres, 1799–1885* (Paris: Chaix, 1886).

Alphonse de Gisors, *Le palais du Luxembourg* (Paris: Plon, 1847).

Charles Gourlier, *Notice historique sur le service des travaux des bâtiments civils* (Paris: Colas, 1848).

Stephen Greenblatt, ed., *The Power of Forms in the English Renaissance* (Norman, OK: Pilgrim, 1982).

Georges Gromort, "Architecture," *Histoire générale de l'art français de la révolution à nos jours*, 3 vols. (Paris: Librairie de France, 1922).

Julien Guadet, *Eléments et théorie de l'architecture*, 4 vols. (Paris: Aulanier, 1901–1904).

Jules Guiffrey, *Comptes des bâtiments du Roi sous le règne de Louis XIV* (Paris: Imprimerie Nationale, 1881).

C.-P.-Marie Haas, *Administration de la France*, 2nd ed., 4 vols. (Paris: Cosse & Marchal, 1861).

Karl Hammer, *Jakob Ignaz Hittorf: ein Pariser Baumeister, 1792–1867* (Stuttgart: Hiersemann, 1968).

Françoise Hamon, Charles MacCallum, et al., *Louis Visconti, 1791–1853* (Paris: Délégation à l'Action Artistique de la Ville de Paris, 1991).

Philippe Hamon, *Expositions: littérature et architecture au XIXe siècle* (Paris: Corti, 1989). Translated as *Expositions: Literature and Architecture in Nineteenth-Century France* (Berkeley: University of California Press, 1992).

Jean-Louis Harouel, *L'Embellissement des villes: l'urbanisme français au XVIIIe siècle* (Paris: Picard, 1993).

Nicolas-Philippe Harou-Romain, *Projet de pénitencier* (Caen: Lesaulnier, 1840).

David Harvey, *Consciousness and the Urban Experience: Studies in the History and Theory of Capitalist Urbanization* (Baltimore: Johns Hopkins University Press, 1986).

Hans-Joachim Hassengier, *Das Palais du Roi de Rome auf dem Hugel von Chaillot* (Frankfurt: Lang, 1983).

Georges Haussmann, *Mémoires du baron Haussmann*, 3 vols. (Paris: Victor-Havard, 1890–1893).

Louis Hautecoeur, *Histoire du Louvre: le château – le palais – le musée* (Paris: Morance, 1924).

Louis Hautecoeur, *Histoire de l'architecture classique en France*, 7 vols. (Paris: Picard, 1943–1957).

Werner Hegemann, *Der Städtebau nach den*

Ergebnissen der Allgemeinen Städtebau-ausstellung in Berlin, 2 vols. (Berlin: Wasmuth, 1911–1913).

Robert Herbert, *Impressionism: Art, Leisure and Parisian Society* (New Haven: Yale University Press, 1988).

Wolfgang Herrmann, *Laugier and Eighteenth-Century French Theory* (London: Zwemmer, 1962).

George Hersey, *Architecture, Poetry and Number in the Royal Palace at Caserta* (Cambridge: MIT Press, 1983).

Paul Hippeau, *Les Féderations artistiques sous la Commune* (Paris: Comptoir d'édition, 1890).

Lynn Hunt, *The Family Romance of the French Revolution* (Berkeley: University of California Press, 1992).

J.-A.-D. Ingres, *Réponse au Rapport sur l'Ecole impériale des beaux-arts, addressée au Maréchal Vaillant . . . par M. Ingres* (Paris: Didier, 1863).

Annie Jacques, *La carrière de l'architecte au XIXe siècle* (Paris: Musée d'Orsay, 1986).

Théodore Jacoubet, *Atlas général de la ville de Paris, ses faubourgs et ses monuments* (Paris: Hocq, 1836).

T. Jacoubet, C. Grillon, and G. Callou, *Etudes d'un nouveau système d'alignemens et de percemens de voies publiques faites en 1840 et 1841* (Paris: Chaillou, 1848).

Emmanuel Jacquin, "La Seconde République et l'achèvement du Louvre," *Bulletin de la société de l'histoire de Paris et de l'Ile de France* (1988), pp. 375–401.

Emmanuel Jacquin and P.-N. Sainte Far Garnot, *Le Château des Tuileries* (Paris: Herscher, 1988).

B. Jestaz, *Jules Hardouin Mansart: l'oeuvre personnel, les méthodes de travail et les collaborateurs*, thesis, Ecole des Chartes, 1962.

Jules de Joly, *Coups, élévations et détails de la restauration de la Chambre des Députés* (Paris: Leclère, 1840).

Frantz Jourdain, *L'Atelier Chantorel: moeurs d'artistes* (Paris: Charpentier & Fasquelle, 1893).

Erust Kantorowiscz, *The King's Two Bodies* (Princeton: Princeton University Press, 1957).

Thierry Kozak, "L'agence centrale de la Société Générale à Paris (1908–1912)," *Histoire de l'art*, 1/2 (1988), pp. 51–60.

Alexandre de Laborde, *Projet d'organisation des bâtiments civils dépendens du ministère de l'Intérieur, tendant à l'amélioration de l'architecture en France* (Paris: Baudouin, 1820).

Léon Labrouste, *La Bibliothèque nationale: son début et ses accroissements, ses bâtiments et ses constructions* (Paris: Lutier, 1885).

Brian Ladd, *Urban Planning and Civic Order in Germany, 1860–1914* (Cambridge: Harvard University Press, 1990).

Charles de Lalleau (extended by Jousselin), *Traité de l'expropriation* (Paris: Cosse & Marchal, 1866).

Nicholas de Lamarre, *Traité de la police*, 4 vols. (Paris: Cot, 1704–1738).

Lucien Lambeau, *Histoire des communes annexées à Paris en 1859*, 5 vols. (Paris: Leroux, 1916–1921).

Jules Lan, *Parallèle entre le marquis de Pombal (1735–1777) et le baron Haussmann (1853–1869)* (Paris: Amyot, 1869).

Adolphe Lance, *Abel Blouet: architecte, membre de l'Institut: sa vie et ses travaux* (Paris: Bance, 1854).

Adolphe Lance, *Dictionnaire des architectes français au XIXe siècle*, 2 vols. (Paris: Morel, 1872).

L. de Lanzac de Laborie, *Paris sous Napoléon*, 8 vols. (Paris: Plon, 1905–1913).

Jean-Baptiste-Antoine Lassus, *Réaction de l'Académie des beaux-arts contre l'art gothique* (Paris: Didron, 1846).

Jean-Baptiste-Antoine Lassus, *Album de Villard de Honnecourt* (Paris: Imprimerie Impériale, 1858).

Jean-Baptiste-Antoine Lassus (completed by Amaury Duval), *Monographie de la cathédrale de Chartres* (Paris: Imprimerie Impériale, 1867).

Pierre Lavedan, "Projets d'aménagement de la rive gauche de la Seine entre les Invalides et le Champs de Mars," *Bulletin de la société de l'histoire de l'art français* (1951), pp. 83–85.

Pierre Lavedan, "Projets de Napoléon Ier pour l'ouest de Paris," *La Vie urbaine*, no. 59 (1951), pp. 1–10.

Pierre Lavedan, *Histoire de l'urbanisme: époque*

contemporaine (Paris: Hachette, 1952, pp. 32–34).

Pierre Lavedan, *La Question du déplacement du centre de Paris et du transfert des Halles* (Paris: Ville de Paris, 1969).

Pierre Lavedan, *Nouvelle histoire de Paris: histoire de l'urbanisme à cle:Paris* (Paris: Hachette, 1975).

F. Lazare and L. Lazare, *Dictionnaire administratif et historique des rues et des monuments de Paris* (Paris: Lazare, 1845, 2nd ed., 1855).

Louis Lazare, *Les Quartiers de l'est de Paris* (Paris: Bibliothèque Municipale, 1870).

J. Leauté, *Criminologie et science pénitentiaire* (Paris: PUF, 1972).

Gustave Le Bon, *Psychologie des foules* (Paris: Alcan, 1895).

Nicolas Le Camus de Mézières, *Le Génie de l'architecture* (Paris: author, 1780) (translated with introduction by Robin Middleton, Chicago: Chicago University Press, 1992).

James A. Leith, *Space and Revolution: Projects for Monuments, Squares and Public Buildings in Paris, 1789–1799* (Montreal-Kingston: McGill-Queen's, 1991).

Jean-Michel Leniaud, *Les cathédrales au XIXe siècle: Etude du Service des Edifices Diocésains* (Paris: Economica, 1993).

Jean-Michel Leniaud, "Les Constructions d'églises sous le Second Empire: architecture et le prix revient," *Revue de l'histoire de l'église en France,* 65 (1979), pp. 268–278.

Jean-Michel Leniaud, *Jean-Baptiste Lassus (1805–1857) ou le temps retrouvé des cathédrales* (Geneva: Droz, 1980).

Jean-Michel Leniaud, "Les architectes diocésains," *Monuments historiques,* 113 (1981), pp. 3–33.

Jean-Michel Leniaud, "Viollet-le-Duc et le service des Edifices Diocésains," *Actes du colloque international Viollet-le-Duc* (Paris: Nouvelles Editions Latines, 1982), pp. 153–164.

Paul Léon, *La vie des monuments français* (Paris: Picard, 1951).

Marie Leonard, *Lyon Transformed: The Public Works of the Second Empire, 1853–1864* (Berkeley: University of California Press, 1961).

Bernard Lepetit, *Les villes dans la France moderne (1740–1840)* (Paris: Albin Michel, 1988).

David Le Roy, *Histoire de la disposition et des formes différentes que les chrétiens ont données à leurs temples . . .* (Paris: Desaint, 1764).

M. Lescure, *Les Sociétés immobilières en France au XIXe siècle* (Paris: Sorbonne, 1980).

M. Lescure, *Les Banques, l'Etat et le marché immobilier en France à l'époque contemporaine, 1820–1940* (Paris: Ecole des Hautes Etudes, 1982).

Neil Levine, *Architectural Reasoning in the Age of Positivism: the Neo-Grec Idea of Labrouste's Bibliothèque Sainte-Geneviève,* Ph.D. dissertation, Yale University, 1975.

Neil Levine, "The Book and the Building: Hugo's Theory of Architecture and Labrouste's Bibliothèque Sainte-Geneviève," *The Beaux-Arts* (London: Thames & Hudson, 1982), Robin Middleton, ed., pp. 138–173.

Enrico Londei, *La Parigi di Haussmann: la trasformazione urbanistica di Parigi durante il Secondo Impero* (Rome: Kappa, 1982).

Edouard Loviot, "Notice sur la vie et les oeuvres de M. Bailly," *Architecture,* 5, no. 14, 1892, pp. 473–475.

François Loyer, *Paris XIXe siècle: l'immeuble et la rue* (Paris: Hazon, 1987). Translated as *Paris Nineteenth Century* (New York: Abbeville Press, 1988).

Neil McWilliam, "David d'Angers and the Panthéon Commission: Politics and Public Works Under the July Monarchy," *Art History,* V, no. 4 (December 1982), pp. 426–446.

Auguste-Joseph Magne, *Monographie du nouveau théâtre du Vaudeville . . .* (Paris: Ducher, 1873).

Lucien Magne, *L'Architecture française du siècle* (Paris: Firmin-Didot, 1889).

Patricia Mainardi, *Art and Politics of the Second Empire: The Universal Expositions of 1855 and 1867* (New Haven: Yale University Press, 1987).

Henri Malet, *Le baron Haussmann et la rénovation de Paris* (Paris: Editions Municipales, 1973).

Jean Mallion, *Victor Hugo et l'art architectural* (Paris: PUF, 1962).

Frank Manuel and Fritzie Manuel, *Utopian Thought in the Western World* (Cambridge: Harvard University Press, 1979).

Louis Marin, *Le Portrait du roi*, (Paris: Minuit, 1981). Translated as *Portrait of the King* (Minneapolis: University of Minnesota Press, 1988).

Louis Marin, *Utopiques: jeux d'espaces* (Paris: Minuit, 1975). Translated as *Utopics: Spatial Play* (Atlantic Heights and London: Humanities Press, 1984).

Louis Marin, "Classical, Baroque: Versailles, or the Architecture of the Prince," *Yale French Studies* (1991), pp. 167–182.

Louis Marin, "Frontiers of Utopia: Past and Present," *Critical Inquiry*, 19, no. 3 (winter 1993), pp. 397–420.

Catherine Marmoz, "The Buildings of the Ecole des Beaux-Arts," *The Beaux-Arts and Nineteenth-Century French Architecture,* Robin Middleton, ed., (London: Thames and Hudson, 1982), pp. 124–137.

Bernard Marrey and Paul Chemetov, *Architectures, Paris, 1848–1914* (Paris: Dunod, 1972).

Bernard Marrey, *Les Grands Magasins: des origines à 1939* (Paris: Picard, 1979).

Bernard Marrey et al., *La Ville d'hiver d'Arcachon* (Paris: IFA, 1983).

Michael Marrinan, *Painting Politics for Louis Philippe* (London-New Haven: Yale University Press, 1988.)

Arthur Martin and Charles Cahier, *Monographie de la cathédrale de Bourges* (Paris: Pousielgue-Rusand, 1841–1844).

Geneviève Massa-Gille, *Histoire des emprunts de la ville de Paris, 1814–1875* (Paris: Ville de Paris, 1973).

Geneviève Massa-Gille, *Journal d'Hippolyte Fortoul* (Geneva: Droz, 1979).

Jean Maurain, *La Politique ecclésiastique du Second Empire* (Paris: Alcan, 1930).

Elizabeth Anne McCauley, *Industrial Madness: Commercial Photography in Paris, 1848–1871* (New Haven and London: Yale, 1994).

Lucy McClintock, "Monumentality Versus Suitability: Viollet-le-Duc's Saint-Gimer at Carcassonne," *Journal of the Society of Architectural Historians,* XL, no. 3 (October 1981), pp. 218–235.

Christopher Mead, *Charles Garnier's Paris Opera* (New York: Architectural History Foundation, 1991).

Jean Merol, *Paris dans la littérature américaine* (Paris: CNRS, 1983).

Prosper Mérimée, *Correspondance générale*, Louis Parturier, ed., 17 vols. (Paris: le Divan, 1941–1964).

Charles Merruau, *Souvenirs de l'Hôtel de Ville de Paris, 1848–1852* (Paris: Plon, 1875).

Hippolyte Meynadier, *Paris sous le point de vue pittoresque et monumental: ou éléments d'un plan général d'ensemble de ses travaux d'art et d'utilité publique* (Paris: Dauvin & Fontaine, 1843).

Robin Middleton and David Watkin, *Neoclassical and Nineteenth-Century Architecture* (New York: Abrams, 1980).

Michael Miller, *The Bon Marché* (Princeton: Princeton University Press, 1981).

Charles-René-Forbes de Montalembert, *Du Vandalisme et du catholicisme dans l'art* (Paris: Debécourt, 1839).

Marthe-Camille Bachasson de Montalivet, *Le Roi Louis-Philippe: liste civile* (Paris, Michel Lévy, 1851).

Bernard de Montgolfier, *Les boulevards* (Paris: Musée Carnavelet, 1985).

Andre Morizet, *Du vieux Paris à Paris moderne: Haussmann et ses prédécesseurs* (Paris: Hachette, 1932).

Kevin Murphy, *Memory and Modernity: Architectural Restoration in France, 1830–1848*, Ph.D. dissertation, Northwestern University, 1992.

Félix Narjoux, *Architecture communale*, 3 vols. (Paris: Morel, 1870, 1880).

Félix Narjoux, *Paris: Monuments élevés par la ville, 1850–1880*, 4 vols. (Paris: Morel, 1880–1883).

Claude M.-L.-H. Navier, "Notice sur M. Bruyère," *Annales des ponts et chaussées*, 1S, no. 2 (1833), pp. 382–404.

Pierre Nora, ed., *Les Lieux de mémoire: II, la nation* (Paris: Gallimard, 1986).

Louis-Narie Normand, *Paris moderne*, 4 vols. (Paris: author, 1836–1857).

Patricia O'Brien, *The Promise of Punishment: Prisons in Nineteenth-Century France* (Princeton: Princeton University Press, 1982).

Lauren O'Connell, *Architecture and the French Revolution: Change and Continuity Under the Conseil des Bâtiments Civils*, Ph.D. dissertation, Cornell University, 1989.

Emile Ollivier, *Journal, 1846–1869*, Theodore Zeldin and Anne Troisier de Diaz, eds. (Paris: Juillard, 1961).

Donald Olsen, *The City as a Work of Art: London, Paris, Vienna* (London-New Haven: Yale University Press, 1986).

Jean d'Ormesson et al., *Grand Hôtel* (New York: Vendome, 1984).

Mona Ozouf, *La fête révolutionnaire, 1789–1799* (Paris: Gallimard, 1976). Translated as *Festivals and the French Revolution* (Cambridge: Harvard University Press, 1988).

Jean-Louis Pascal, "M. Duc et son influence sur le mouvement architectural contemporain," *Gazette des beaux-arts,* 2S XIX (1879), pp. 430–443.

Françoise Paul-Lévy, *La Ville en croix* (Paris: Méridiens, 1984).

Alberto Perez-Gomez, *Architecture and the Crisis of Modern Science* (Cambridge: MIT Press, 1983).

Harold Perkin, *The Rise of Professional Society* (London: Routledge, 1989).

J.-M. Pérouse de Montclos, *Louis-Etienne Boullée, 1728–1799, de l'architecture classique à l'architecture révolutionnaire* (Paris: Arts et Métiers Graphiques, 1969).

J.-M. Pérouse de Montclos, *Architecture à la française* (Paris: Picard, 1982).

J.-M. Pérouse de Montclos, *Histoire de l'architecture française: de la Renaissance à la Révolution* (Paris: Menges, 1989).

Perreymond, "Etudes sur la ville de Paris," *Revue générale de l'architecture* III (1842), cols. 540–554, 570–579, IV (1843), cols. 25–37, 72–87, 413–429, 449–469, 517–528.

Pierre Petroz, *L'art et la critique en France depuis 1822* (Paris: Germer Baillière, 1875).

Niklaus Pevsner, *A History of Building Types* (Princeton: Princeton University Press, 1976).

Antoine Picon, *Claude Perrault, 1613–1688, ou, la curiosité d'un classique* (Paris: Picard, 1988).

Antoine Picon, *Architectes et ingénieurs au siècle des lumières* (Marseilles: Parenthèse, 1988). Translated as *French Architects and Engineers in the Age of Enlightenment* (Cambridge University Press, 1992).

Félix Pigeory, *Les Monuments de Paris* (Paris: Hermitte, 1847).

David Pinkney, *Napoleon III and the Rebuilding of Paris* (Princeton: Princeton University Press, 1958).

Pierre Pinon, *L'Hospice de Charenton* (Liège: Mardaga, 1989).

Pierre Pinon, Jean des Cars, eds., *Paris . Haussmann* (Paris: Picard, 1991).

Olivier Poisson, "Foro e Palatino, 1809–1813: il progetto del giardino del Campidoglio," *Gli Orte farnesiana sul Palatino,* Rome: Académie française à Rome, 1990), pp. 587–603.

Bruno Pons, *De Paris à Versailles, 1699–1736: les sculpteurs ornamanistes parisiens et l'art décoratif des Bâtiments du roi* (Strasbourg: University of Strasbourg, 1986).

Todd Porterfield, *Art in the Service of French Imperialism in the Near East, 1798–1848: Four Case Studies,* Ph.D. dissertation, Boston University, 1991.

Jeanne Pronteau, *Edme Verniquet, 1727–1804* (Paris: Ville de Paris, 1986).

Jeanne Pronteau, ed., *Petit atlas pittoresque des quarante-huit quartiers de la ville de Paris par A. M. Perrot, ingénieur* (Paris: Minuit, 1960).

Thérèse de Puylaroque, "Pierre Baltard, peintre et dessinateur (1764-1846)," *Bulletin de la société de l'histoire de l'art français* (1976), pp. 331–339.

A.-C. Quatremère de Quincy, "Architecture," in *Encyclopédie méthodique,* 3 vols. (Paris: Panckouke, 1788-1825).

Charles Questel, *J.-M.-A. Le Soufaché: sa vie – ses oeuvres, 1804–1887* (Paris: Librairie Centrale des Chemins de Fer, 1887).

Paul Rabinow, *French Modern: Norms and Forms of the Social Environment* (Cambridge, MIT Press, 1989).

Daniel Rabreau, *Gabriel Davioud, architecte, 1824-1881* (Paris: Délégation à l'Action Artistique de la Ville de Paris, 1981).

Paul Raphael and Maurice Gontard, *Hippolyte Fortoul, 1851-1856, un ministre de l'Instruction Publique sous l'Empire autoritaire* (Paris: PUF, 1975).

Joseph-Antoine Ray, *Histoire du Jockey Club de Paris* (Paris: Marcel Rivière, 1958).

Léonce Reynaud, *Traité d'architecture,* 2 vols. and atlas (Paris: Goeury & Dalmont, 1850-1858).

Alois Riegl, "Der moderne Denkmalkultus: sein Wesen und seine Entstehung," *Entwurf einer gesetzlichen Organization der Denkmalpflege in Österreich* (1903). Reproduced in *Gesammelte Aufsätze* (Augsburg-Vienna: Filser, 1929).

Jean-Baptiste Rondelet, *Traité théorique et pratique de l'art de bâtir,* with supplement by Abel Blouet (Paris: Firmin-Didot, 1847–1848).

Bernard Rouleau, *Le Tracé des rues de Paris: formation, typologie, fonctions* (Paris: CNRS, 1967).

Gérard Rousset-Charny, *Les Palais parisiens de la belle époque* (Paris: Délégation à l'Action Artistique de la Ville de Paris, 1990).

A. de Royau, *Traité pratique de la voirie à Paris* (Paris: Malateste, 1879).

Joseph Rykwert, *On Adam's House in Paradise: The Idea of the Primitive Hut in Architectural History* (New York: Museum of Modern Art, 1972).

Joseph Rykwert, *The First Moderns* (Cambridge: MIT Press, 1980).

Marc Saboya, *Presse et architecture au XIXe siècle* (Paris: Picard, 1991).

Pierre Saddy, *Henri Labrouste, architecte, 1801–1875* (Paris: Caisse Nationale des Monuments Historiques et des Sites, 1977).

Nicolas Sainte Far Garnot, *L'architecture hospitalière au XIXe siècle: l'exemple parisien* (Paris, Musée d'Orsay, 1988).

Louis Savot (notes by François Blondel), *Architecture françoise* (Paris: Clouzier l'aîné, 1673).

Horace Say, *Etudes sur l'administration de la ville de Paris et du département de la Seine* (Paris: Guillaumin, 1846).

Aaron Scharf, *Art and Photography* (Baltimore: Penguin, 1974).

Jean-Philippe Schmit, *Les Eglises gothiques* (Paris: Ange, 1837).

Donald Schneider, *The Works and Doctrine of Jacques-Ignace Hittorff, 1792–1867,* Ph.D. dissertation, Princeton University, 1970. Published (New York: Garland, 1977).

Charles Séchan, *Souvenirs d'un homme de théâtre* (Paris: Lévy, 1883).

Paul Sédille, "Joseph-Louis Duc, architecte, 1802–1879," *Encyclopédie d'architecture,* 2S 8 (1879), pp. 65–74.

Paul Sédille, "Architecture moderne en Angleterre," *Gazette des Beaux-Arts,* 2S. vol. 33 (1886), pp. 89–102, 194–208; vol. 34 (1886), pp. 89–106, 441–465; vol. 35 (1887), pp. 273–290 (published as a book, Paris: Librairie des Bibliophiles, 1890).

Paul Sédille, *Théodore Ballu, architecte, (1817–1885)* (Paris: Chaix, 1886).

Emile Senne, *Les projets de couronnement de l'Arc de Triomphe de l'Etoile* (Paris: Champion, 1911).

Richard Norman Shaw and T. G. Jackson, *Architecture: A Profession or an Art?* (London: Murray, 1892).

Daniel Sherman, *Worthy Monuments: Art Museums and the Politics of Culture in Nineteenth-Century France* (Cambridge: Harvard, 1989).

Camillo Sitte, *Städtebau nach seinen künstlerischen Grundsätzen* (Vienna: Gaeser, 1889).

Monika Steinhauser, *Die Architektur der Pariser Oper* Munich: (Prestel, 1969).

Anthony Sutcliffe, *The Autumn of Central Paris* (Montreal: McGill University Press, 1971).

Anthony Sutcliffe, *Paris: An Architectural History* (New Haven and London: Yale, 1993).

Werner Szambien, *De la rue des Colonnes à la rue de Rivoli* (Paris: Délégation à l'Action Artistique de la Ville de Paris, 1992).

Katherine Taylor, *The Palais de Justice of Paris: Modernization, Historical Consciousness, and Their Pre-History in French Institutional Architecture, 1835–1869,* Ph.D. dissertation, Harvard University, 1989.

Katherine Taylor, *In the Theatre of Criminal Justice: The Palais de Justice in Second Empire Paris* (Princeton: Princeton University Press, 1993).

Henri Terson, *Origines et évolution du ministère de l'Intérieur,* Montpellier, 1913.

Georges Teyssot, "Citta-servizi: la produzione dei bâtiments-civils in Francia (1795–1848)," *Cassabella,* 424 (April 1977), pp. 56–64.

Georges Teyssot, "Pontivy-Napoléonville ou l'architecture des Ponts et Chaussées," *Monuments historiques,* 109 (1980), pp. 17–20.

Georges Teyssot, "Planning and Building in Towns: The System of the Bâtiments Civils in France, 1795–1848," *The Beaux-Arts* (London: Thames & Hudson, 1982), Robin Middleton, ed., pp. 34–49.

Georges Toudouze, *Gabriel Toudouze, architecte et graveur* (Paris: Le Musee, 1906).

Jean Tulard, *Paris et son administration (1800–1890)* (Paris: Ville de Paris, 1976.)

Geoffrey Tyack, *Sir James Pennethorne and the Making of Victorian London* (London: Cambridge University Press, 1992).

Marius Vachon, *L'Ancien Hôtel de ville de Paris* (Paris: Quantin, 1882).

Pierre Vaisse, *La Troisième République et les*

peintres: recherches sur le rapport du pouvoir et de la peinture en France de 1870 à 1914, thèse d'état, Paris IV, 1980.

Luigi Vanvitelli, *Dichriarazione dei disegni del reale palazzo di Caserta* (Naples: Regia Stamperia, 1751).

Claudine de Vaulchier, Thomas von Joest, eds., *Hittorff, 1792–1867* (Paris: Musée Carnavalet, 1986).

Ann Lorenz Van Zanten, "The Palace and the Temple: Two Utopian Architectural Visions of the 1830s," *Art History*, 2, no. 2 (June 1979), pp. 179–200.

David Van Zanten, *Designing Paris: The Architecture of Duban, Labrouste, Duc, and Vaudoyer* (Cambridge: MIT Press, 1987).

David Van Zanten, "The Nineteenth-Century French Government Architectural Services and the Design of the Monuments of Paris," *Art Journal*, 48 no. 1 (spring 1989), pp. 16–22.

Kirk T. Varnedoe, *Gustave Caillebotte* (New Haven: Yale University Press, 1987).

Kirk T. Varnedoe and Thomas P. Lee, *Gustave Caillebotte: A Retrospective Exhibition* (Houston: Museum of Fine Arts, 1976).

Philippe Verdier, "Le service des monuments historiques," *Congrès archéologique* 2S, I (1934), pp. 53–261.

Anthony Vidler, *The Writing of the Walls* (Princeton: Princeton Architectural Press, 1987).

Horace de Viel-Castel, *Mémoires du comte Horace de Viel-Castel sur le règne de Napoléon III (1851–1864),* Pierre Josserand, ed. (Paris: Le Prat, 1942).

E.-E. Viollet-le-Duc, "De la construction des édifices religieux en France depuis le commencement de Christianisme jusqu'au XVIe siècle," *Annales archéologiques*, I (1844), pp. 334–347; II (1845), pp. 78–85, 143–150, 336–349; III (1845), pp. 321–336; IV (1846), pp. 266–283; VI (1847), pp. 194–205, 247–255.

E.-E. Viollet-le-Duc, "Réponse aux considérations de l'Académie des Beaux-Arts sur la question de savoir s'il est convenable au XIXe siècle de bâtir des églises en style gothique," *Annales archéologiques*, IV (1846), pp. 333–353.

E.-E. Viollet-le-Duc, "Un mot sur l'architecture en 1852," *Revue générale de l'architecture*

et des travaux publics, X (1852), cols. 371–379.

E.-E. Viollet-le-Duc, *Dictionnaire raisonné de l'architecture française du XIe au XVIe siècle,* 9 vols. and index (Paris: Bance, 1854–1868).

E.-E. Viollet-le-Duc, "Les mandarins à Paris," *Gazette des Beaux-Arts*, I (1859), pp. 90–97.

E.-E. Viollet-le-Duc, "L'Enseignement des arts," *Gazette des Beaux-Arts*, XII (1862), pp. 393–402, 525–534; XIII, pp. 71–82, 249–255.

E.-E. Viollet-le-Duc, *Entretiens sur l'architecture,* 2 vols. and atlas (Paris: Morel, 1863, 1872).

E.-E. Viollet-le-Duc, *Ce que réclame au XIXe siècle l'enseignement de l'architecture* (Paris: Morel, 1869).

E.-E. Viollet-le-Duc and Félix Narjous, *Habitations modernes,* 2 vols. (Paris: Morel, 1875–1877).

E.-E. Viollet-le-Duc, "L'Administration française," *La Philosophie positive*, XX (1878), pp. 371–384.

Lettres inédites de Viollet-le-Duc, recueillées et annotées par son fils (Paris: Librairies-Imprimeries Réunies, 1902).

Geneviève Viollet le Duc, *Viollet-le-Duc: lettres d'Italie, 1836–1837, adressées à sa famille* (Paris: Laget, 1971).

Ludovic Vitet, "Le Louvre," *Revue contemporaine* (September 15, 1852), pp. 363–446.

Ludovic Vitet, "De l'enseignement des arts de dessin," *Revue des deux mondes*, 2S vol. 54 (November 1, 1864), pp. 74–107.

Ludovic Vitet, "Le nouveau Louvre et les nouvelles Tuileries," *Revue des deux Mondes*, 2S vol. 64 (July 1, 1866), pp. 57–93.

Françoise Waquet, *Les fêtes royales sous la Restauration, ou, l'Ancien Régime retrouvé* (Geneva: Droz, 1981).

Anne Wagner, *Jean-Baptiste Carpeaux: Sculptor of the Second Empire* (New Haven and London: Yale University Press, 1986).

John Hubbel Weiss, *The Making of Technological Man* (Cambridge: MIT Press, 1982).

Harrison White and Cynthia White, *Canvases and Careers* (New York: Wiley, 1965).

William H. White, *Architecture and Public Buildings* (London, P. S. King & Son, 1884).

Peter Wolf, "City Structuring and Social Sense in

19th and 20th Century Urbanism," *Perspecta 13 and 14,* (1973), pp. 222–233.

Charles d'Ydewalle, *Au Bon Marché: de la boutique au grand magasin* (Paris: Plon, 1965).

Charles-Emile Yriarte, *Les Cercles de Paris, 1828–1864* (Paris: Dupray de la Mahérie, 1864).

ILLUSTRATION CREDITS

All references are to figure numbers.

Académie d'Architecture: 26, 27, 30, 89
Adolphe Alphand, *Les Promenades de Paris*, 1867–1873: 106
Annales archéologiques: 136, 137
Archives historiques du diocèse de Lille: 141
Archives Nationales: 7, 8, 11, 34, 35, 36, 58, 69, 72, 79, 100, 109
Art Institute of Chicago: 12, 40
Atlas des XX arrondissements de Paris, 1868: 6, 9, 125, 129
Christine Aulanier, *Histoire du palais et du musée du Louvre*: 45
James Austin: 73, 75, 77, 81, 85, 86, 144
Author: 3, 15, 16, 17, 19, 20, 21, 22, 23, 25, 28, 44, 60, 66, 67, 70, 74, 80, 82, 83, 90, 93, 94, 95, 96, 112, 113, 116, 121, 122, 123, 126, 127, 130, 131, 132, 133, 134, 135, 140, 145, 146, 147, 148, 149, 150
Author's collection: 53, 54, 138, 139
Victor Baltard and F.-E. Callet, *Monographie des Halles centrales de Paris*, 1863: 108, 110
Anatole de Baudot, *Eglises de bourgs et villages*, 1867: 142
Bibliothèque Nationale: 1, 57
Bibliothèque de l'Opéra: 13, 14
Abel Blouet, *Projet de prison cellulaire pour 585 condamnés*, 1843: 68
Hector Brame-Jean Lorenceau: 4, 31
Louis Bruyère, *Art des constructions*, 1823–1828: 62, 63
Victor Calliat, *Hôtel de ville de Paris mesuré, dessiné, gravé et publié par Victor Calliat*, 1844–1856: 54
Musée Carnavalet: 55

Frédéric de Clarac, *Musée de sculpture antique et moderne ou description historique et graphique du Louvre*, 1826–1853: **41, 42**

César Daly, *Architecture privée au XIXe siècle sous Napoléon III*, 1864: **64, 65**

Deutsche Bauzeitung: **105**

Documents relatifs au palais de Justice de Paris, 1858: **56, 87, 118**

J.-N.-L. Durand, *Précis des leçons d'architecture données à l'Ecole Polytechnique*, 1802–1805: **32**

Ecole Nationale Supérieure des Beaux-Arts: **84**

Léon Feuchère, *L'Art industriel*, 1842–1844: **91**

P.-F.-L. Fontaine, *Résidences de souverains*, 1833: **33**

Giraudon: **2**

Alphonse de Gisors, *Le palais du Luxembourg*, 1847: **46, 47, 48, 49, 50**

Armand Guérinet, *Les grands prix de Rome d'architecture*: **119, 120**

Nicolas Harou-Romain, *Projet de pénitencier*, 1840: **78**

Werner Hegemann, *Der Stædtebau nach den Ergebnissen der Allgemeinen Stædtebauaustellung in Berlin*, 1911–1913: **98**

L'Illustration: **24, 29, 101, 103, 104, 111**

Théodore Jacoubet, *Atlas général de la ville de Paris, ses faubourgs et ses monuments*, 1836: **10, 71, 107, 124**

Charles Merruau, *Souvenirs de l'hôtel de ville de Paris*, 1875: **99**

Nelson Atkins Museum, Kansas City: **5**

Northwestern University, Department of Art History: **18, 43, 61, 88, 102, 114, 115**

Northwestern University Library, Special Collections: **38, 51, 76, 117**

Paul Prouté: **127**

Jean Reybaud, *Jérôme Paturot à la recherche d'une position sociale*, 1843: **97**

Cervin Robinson: **92**

Roger Viollet: **39, 59, 143**

L.-T.-J. Visconti, *Description du modèle du Louvre*: **37**

INDEX

Index

Index